Bakhtin and the Movies

Bakhtin and the Movies
New Ways of Understanding Hollywood Film

Martin Flanagan

© Martin Flanagan 2009

All rights reserved. No reproduction, copy or transmission of this publication may be made without written permission.

No portion of this publication may be reproduced, copied or transmitted save with written permission or in accordance with the provisions of the Copyright, Designs and Patents Act 1988, or under the terms of any licence permitting limited copying issued by the Copyright Licensing Agency, Saffron House, 6-10 Kirby Street, London EC1N 8TS.

Any person who does any unauthorized act in relation to this publication may be liable to criminal prosecution and civil claims for damages.

The author has asserted his right to be identified as the author of this work in accordance with the Copyright, Designs and Patents Act 1988.

First published 2009 by
PALGRAVE MACMILLAN

Palgrave Macmillan in the UK is an imprint of Macmillan Publishers Limited, registered in England, company number 785998, of Houndmills, Basingstoke, Hampshire RG21 6XS.

Palgrave Macmillan in the US is a division of St Martin's Press LLC, 175 Fifth Avenue, New York, NY 10010.

Palgrave Macmillan is the global academic imprint of the above companies and has companies and representatives throughout the world.

Palgrave® and Macmillan® are registered trademarks in the United States, the United Kingdom, Europe and other countries.

ISBN-13: 978–0–230–20296–2 hardback
ISBN-10: 0–230–20296–9 hardback

This book is printed on paper suitable for recycling and made from fully managed and sustained forest sources. Logging, pulping and manufacturing processes are expected to conform to the environmental regulations of the country of origin.

A catalogue record for this book is available from the British Library.
A catalog record for this book is available from the Library of Congress.

10 9 8 7 6 5 4 3 2 1
18 17 16 15 14 13 12 11 10 09

Printed and bound in Great Britain by

CPI Antony Rowe, Chippenham and Eastbourne

For Craig Stafford

Contents

Acknowledgments ix
Abbreviations of Bakhtin Circle works xi

Introduction 1
   Mikhail Bakhtin (1895–1975) 2
   Dialogism: spectator, text and context 6
   A note on two aspects of authorship 15

1 Dialogism and Film Studies: The Dialogic Spectator 17
   Introduction: Bakhtin and the novel 17
   Early Christian Metz and 'Cine-semiotics' 23
   Psychoanalytic and apparatus theories: the positioning of the spectator 31
   Making meaning, consuming meaning: Neo-formalist and Cultural Studies models 39
   Two-way textuality? 48

2 Chronotope I: Time, Space, Narrative – 'Get Ready for Rush Hour' 53
   Introduction: 'Big loud action movies' 53
   Forms of the chronotope 56
   Adventure time in ancient Greece and Hollywood 62
   Action heroes and their worlds 69
   Space and plot 74
   The movie as rollercoaster ride 79

3 Chronotope II: Time, Space and Genre in the Western Film 83
   Introduction 83
   Time and myth: 'generic memory' 90
   Spectacle and landscape: the star as monument 96
   Women and domestic space 101
   The horror of miscegenation 105
   Lone Star: crossing borders 110
   Space, masculinity, representation 113
   Re-presenting the past: challenging notions of cinematic time 118

	'Print the legend'	123
	Conclusion: the chronotope and genre	124
4	**Polyphony: Authorship and Power**	**127**
	Introduction	127
	The politics of representation	132
	Eyes wide shut	136
	The framer framed	141
	Noir motifs in *House of Games*	145
	Breaking the classical frame	148
	Conclusion: Mamet and polyphony	153
5	**Hollywood Calling: Cinema's Technological Address**	**155**
	Introduction	155
	Shiny happy 'people'? Questions of CGI aesthetics	160
	'Filmed entirely on location': the worlds of *Toy Story 2* and *The Incredibles*	164
	Remediating the address	173
	Conclusion	178

Conclusion: Making it Real 181

Notes 189

Filmography 216

Bibliography 217

Index 230

Acknowledgments

The completion of this book was made possible by a sabbatical which was supported through the Educational Development Unit of the University of Bolton. For the EDU, I thank Sue Burkinshaw and Denise Mercer, and for the School of Arts, Media and Education, I am grateful to Sam Johnson and Barbara Thomas. I thank my other Bolton colleagues, especially in the library, for their interest and support. The staff of the John Rylands library at University of Manchester were also most helpful.

The core of this material initially took form as a thesis undertaken at the University of Sheffield, and I shall always be indebted to Sue Vice for providing a supervisory environment that was as close to ideal as I can imagine. This period of doctoral research was supported by the Edgar Allen scholarship. Ian Mackillop and Bryan Burns inspired me in various ways during that time; both are extremely fondly remembered and missed. Invaluable commentary and various sorts of feedback on the content have been received over a long period from Martin Hall, Yvonne Tasker and Simon Beecroft. I am also grateful for the generous and incisive comments of the authors of anonymous reader reports. Contributions from the many delegates of two international Bakhtin conferences (in 1999 and 2008), and students and scholars in other venues, also left an impression on this work in various ways.

For Palgrave, Christabel Scaife's tolerance and guidance has been truly appreciated. When moral support was needed through a year that was difficult for reasons unrelated to this project, friends and family gave it freely, for which I am hugely grateful. Special thanks to Kieron Flanagan and John McAuley. I am also grateful to David Shepherd for an extended book loan, to Elsie Walker for a calming whiskey, and to Zam Salim, who held back his breakthrough project all these years just so that we could work in parallel and mither each other.

Much of Chapter 2 was originally published as 'Get Ready for Rush Hour: The Chronotope in Action' in Yvonne Tasker (ed.), *Action and Adventure Cinema* (2004), pp.103–18, and is republished by kind permission from Routledge. Chapter 3 was previously published in a different form in *Reconstruction* (www.reconstruction.eserver.org), volume 7, number 3 (2007). I am grateful to the editors of the journal and of the issue.

This book would not exist without the love and understanding of my wife, Ruth Hannan, and the commitment of my parents, Bridget and Gerald Flanagan.

M.F.
December 2008

Abbreviations of Bakhtin Circle works

B = 'The *Bildungsroman* and Its Significance in the History of Realism'
DIN = 'Discourse in the Novel'
FM = *The Formal Method in Literary Scholarship* [P. N. Medvedev]
FR = *Freudianism: A Marxist Critique* [V. N. Voloshinov]
FTC = 'Forms of Time and of the Chronotope in the Novel'
MHS = 'Towards a Methodology for the Human Sciences'
MPL = *Marxism and the Philosophy of Language* [V. N. Voloshinov]
N70 = 'From Notes Made in 1970–71'
NM = 'Response to a Question from the *Novy Mir* Editorial Staff'
PDP = *Problems of Dostoevsky's Poetics*
PSG = 'The Problem of Speech Genres'
PT = 'The Problem of the Text in Linguistics, Philology and the Human Sciences: An Experiment in Philosophical Analysis'
RW = *Rabelais and His World*

Introduction

It is the contention of this book that the theories of the Russian linguist, literary critic and philosopher Mikhail Bakhtin (1895–1975), though highly suggestive for helping to understand the processes and meanings of cinema, have yet to be fully articulated in relation to the key debates of film studies. It will be demonstrated that a richer engagement with the Bakhtinian matrix of ideas (incorporating the works of others in what has become known as the 'Bakhtin Circle') will enhance the field of film studies. This is the first full-length study to apply the major Bakhtinian categories to the formal strategies of Hollywood film, and also the first publication solely dedicated to Mikhail Bakhtin and the cinema in over 15 years.[1] Through providing detailed analytical case studies of key films, I hope to afford stimulating evidence that the Bakhtinian approach can provide new points of access into some of the key questions of cinema study.

'How do films work on us?' is one side of the equation underpinning this study. Its counterpart is 'what work do we perform in watching the film?'. Extrapolations of Bakhtinian theories and concepts will provide the framework to address both sides of the question. The notion of the chronotope, a concept for analysing the formal and ideological significance of space/time representations, is a core value in the distinctiveness of my approach. Two central chapters will employ the chronotope in order to explore how the structures of genre, as expressed in spatio-temporal configurations, sustain (and occasionally deconstruct) the institutional values of Hollywood, and apprise viewers of a particular sense of history. This discussion of narrative construction and its role in producing a 'reading' of the film text supports the approach to cinema 'textuality' that the book will develop in terms of its general theoretical procedure, via the integration of Bakhtinian thinking with some of the most important existing ideas in the field.

Hollywood cinema supplies the case studies in this work. This is, obviously, a deliberate choice and one that already conveys a position being taken. Hollywood stands at the crossroads of popular and academic discourse on film; it can be used to symbolize values of domination as well as entertainment, and thus as a field of communication it is richly multivalent, speaking with an often contradictory 'voice' that merits a sensitive hearing. Defining Hollywood in terms of a singular and uniform entity underestimates it (it contains within it a diverse artistic history and concept of 'American film'). Then again, for many viewers not as desirous of wrestling with terminology, it has a simple, axiomatic, perhaps even 'natural' status as the norm around which other cinema is defined and judged. It speaks of and in a language of power that the world has become inclined to listen to in reverence for its authority: 'Hollywood proposed to tell the story of other nations not only to Americans, but also for the other nations themselves, and always in English' (Shohat and Stam, 1985, p.36). Its lofty disposition towards spectators is often taken as read (see Stam, 1989, p.47), fuelling a certain reifying tendency that is not the perception subscribed to in the following work.

Mikhail Bakhtin (1895–1975)

Since his death in 1975, Mikhail Bakhtin has emerged as an important thinker within literary and cultural theory, a status made all the more ironic by the obscurity in which he lived whilst composing most of his key works.[2] Born on November 16, 1895 in Orel (south of Moscow), Bakhtin was raised in the polyglot and multicultural environments of Polish-inflected Vilnius and the Jewish enclave of Odessa, locales that would seem to have influenced his future attitudes to cultural and linguistic diversity. Enrolled into university at Petersburg (or Petrograd as it would become known) in 1914, he nurtured a long-standing leaning towards classical scholarship. After leaving university, in 1918, Bakhtin relocated to the country, living at Nevel, then Vitebsk. Around this time he became embroiled with a small group of intellectuals who would meet for debates centring on the finer points of German philosophy. Within this group, Bakhtin would not only initiate his own philosophical speculations, but also meet colleagues with whom he would later (controversially – see below) collaborate and on whom the title 'Bakhtin Circle' would later be conferred: Pavel Medvedev, Valentin Voloshinov and Matvei Kagan. From 1918 to 1924, this group continued their ruminations while Bakhtin honed his own philosophy within the prevailing Neo-Kantian paradigm

(Hirschkop, 1999, pp.141–4). In 1924, Bakhtin returned to Petrograd just before its identity changed once more to Leningrad. His intellectual life and friendships continued to flourish even though poor health and an unorthodox political reputation conspired to prevent his taking a good job, leaving the burden of subsistence on his wife Elena Alexandrovna. However, this financially impoverished period yielded a number of the works that would later build his reputation, even if the complex claims of authorship attached to them remain unresolved to this day. During the period 1924–1929, the works *The Formal Method in Literary Scholarship* (attributed to Medvedev), *Freudianism: A Critical Sketch* and *Marxism and the Philosophy of Language* (both attributed to Voloshinov), as well as *Problems of Dostoevsky's Poetics* (issued under Bakhtin's own name) were all written and published. Bakhtin's resistance to 'monologic' structures that sought to falsely lend authority to the 'givenness' of cultural arrangements[3] and stress on social and historical value in the analysis of speech and literature were all established in these works; scholars disagree on whether Bakhtin's shifting of focus from ethical philosophy (in the early 1920s) to a project in the literary critical mode (the move to 'a philosophy of discourse' – Hirschkop, 1999, p.173) is an organic one or not, yet as a concentrated source of ideas these works sustain a great degree of the subsequent reputation of the Bakhtin School.[4] However, any personal eminence resulting from these texts was truncated in 1929, when Bakhtin was arrested (likely as a consequence of participating in prohibited religious activities – Holquist, 2002, p.9) and exiled to the Siberia/Kazakhstan border (escaping confinement in a concentration camp on grounds of his poor health). In Kazakhstan, he taught book-keeping and worked on his own study of the origins of novelistic discourse, producing the classic texts 'Discourse in the Novel' (1934–5) and 'Forms of Time and of the Chronotope in the Novel' (1937–8). His exile officially ceasing in 1934, Bakhtin intermittently taught and wrote during the Second World War and submitted a postgraduate thesis on Rabelais (later the basis of the book which became, in English translation, *Rabelais and His World* [1984]) in 1946, although the conferral of the higher degree became mired in controversy (see Holquist, 2002, p.10; Hirschkop, 1999, pp.184–5). He carved out a successful post-war career as a teacher in Saransk, where he remained until his works were 'rediscovered' by a group of young scholars at the Gorky Institute in the early 1960s, who encouraged his relocation to the Moscow area (which was accomplished in the light of relaxed political circumstances and a degree of well-connected patronage – see Hirschkop, 1999, p.191). A comprehensive programme of publication (and later, translation) eventually resulted from this 'rehabilitation', including the revision of elements of his earliest moral philosophy. After his wife's death in 1971, Bakhtin continued to live in Moscow, working on new essays and revisions of earlier works, including the adding of an important clarifying section to the essay on the chronotope in 1973. Mikhail Mikhailovich died on March 7, 1975.

A few years after his death, Bakhtin's oeuvre could finally be contemplated in something like its entirety (and increasingly, in translation), and became widely disseminated and just as broadly applied (every discipline from music to geography to sculpture has benefited from the intervention of Bakhtinian thought).[5] However, the dynamics of this dissemination – particularly in the way that its sequencing was seen to disclose an agenda to cultivate 'versions' of Bakhtin (philosopher or literary critic; Marxist or Christian) – have hardly been unproblematic. These dynamics are discussed in several books (Morson and Emerson, 1990; Hirschkop, 1999); Holquist even uses the outlines of these debates to form a basis for distinguishing between types of *Bakhtinians* (2002, pp.183–95). The very fact that such distinctions are drawn indicates that the freedom with which Bakhtin Circle ideas have been 'applied' since their wider exposure has provided a source of disquiet (see Chapter 1).

In terms of methodology, the belief standing behind this work is that Bakhtinian concepts can be 're-accentuated' to bring out their sensitivity to the kind of medium that cinema is. Chapter 1, in particular, is designed to show that many aspects of film theory can be augmented, or opened out of rigidity, by bringing a Bakhtinian perspective to bear. Although that chapter engages most fully with classic film theories propounded by figures such as Christian Metz and Laura Mulvey, in terms of the disciplinary 'bigger picture', it will be recognized that interpretative models and text/spectator relations have continued to be proposed and reworked throughout what might be termed (after Bordwell and Carroll, 1996) the 'post-theory' era. During that period, influential moves have been made by scholars such as Martin Barker, Henry Jenkins and many others to reconsider the ways in which films are understood, consumed and absorbed into audiences' lives. Some of these moves bear the imprint of Bakhtin Circle thinking, as we shall see. Those scholars sought to adapt or go beyond cine-semiotics and other dimensions of 1970s orthodoxy by restoring to cinema study aspects of the socio-historical, the emotional or the political. In the same spirit, it will be shown here that Bakhtin's work not only builds upon but can also transcend some tenets of previous theoretical moments.

This work has been structured, for clarity but also to reflect my interests, around three major Bakhtinian concepts (dialogism, chronotope and polyphony), which are elaborated (and hopefully expanded) with respect to a range of film texts. Performing exegesis of Bakhtinian concepts in this textually focused way reflects a belief that it is in analytical practice that those categories can best emerge as multiple and complementary modes for reading Hollywood film texts. In this method I follow Bakhtin himself; terms such as dialogism are heavily rooted in material and constantly evolving textuality, as works like 'Discourse in the Novel' and 'Forms of Time and of the Chronotope in the Novel' demonstrate with their lengthy surveys of sometimes remarkably disparate texts (Dickens, Sterne, Turgenev, Pushkin, Fielding and Dostoevsky in the former; Petronius, Plutarch, Dante, Rabelais, Gogol, Flaubert and Tolstoy in the latter). Bakhtin's stance towards his own concepts is a profoundly exploratory one, sometimes unfolding through revisions that span decades as well as spilling out beyond the housing of a single essay or volume. His definitions always leave enough room for an unwarranted surprise that may change the direction of thought or at least uncover another aspect of his rich, multivalent critical devices. The rather loose, unsystematic quality of Bakhtin's exegetical style does not, however, preclude a sense of internal coherence to his project; his fixation with 'openendedness' (DIN, p.361) may not value the idea of discrete, linear phases, but the most vital areas, such as the relationship between form and content and the nature of artistic time, tend to keep returning and were still being demonstrably refined at the end of his life, as the *Speech Genres* collection (2006; first English publication 1986) indicates. The umbrella of 'the dialogic' provides the closest thing there is to a dominant metaphor in the Bakhtinian *oeuvre*, but even this term was being revised and imbued with new meanings in the final years of Bakhtin's life.

I hope to have emulated the sense that each Bakhtinian concept must be discovered anew in each encounter with the artistic utterance. What I hope to have avoided is the imposition of a theoretical regime from a monologic position high above the 'event' of the text. I also hope to have avoided a reductive, mechanical 'application' of Bakhtinian terms to a series of films preselected for their suitability; while I would not deny that I am in the business of application, I would contend that the concepts featured here have not been rendered sacred, complete and beyond criticism. Indeed, a reason for embarking on this work was a conviction that concepts such as the chronotope have been neglected enough in my own discipline of film studies to make it evident that their *own* semantic boundaries were ripe to be extended in new ways.

Dialogism: spectator, text and context

With dialogism, Bakhtin's motivation is to establish a philosophical basis for the understanding of how discourse in life relates to discourse in art, to deal with the 'life and behaviour of discourse in a contradictory and multi-languaged world' (DIN, p.275). Dialogism is characterized by a reciprocal, two-way relationship between semantic positions. In the case of spoken language, this takes the form of the orientation of every linguistic utterance to the anticipated response of an interlocutor. This response determines the semantic composition of the utterance. The dialogic mode of address is therefore one which takes into account the 'specific conceptual horizon' (DIN, p.282) pertaining to the world of the listener, while retaining consciousness of its own unique value and the importance of context in defining meaning ('*Who* speaks and under what conditions he speaks: this is what determines the word's actual meaning' [401]). The dialogic word is always made up of (at least) two positions, existing equally on the same semantic plane but, in content and intonation, often clashing and contradictory, embodying different ideological positions. Dialogism is not a way of rendering all statements into a cosy consensus, a way of levelling differences; it is rather the process that ensures that language relations are democratic and that two (or more) voices resound in each utterance: 'Within the arena of almost every utterance an intense interaction and struggle between one's own and another's word is being waged, a process in which they oppose or dialogically interanimate each other' (354). Each utterance embodies a 'specific point of view on the world' (291); speech exchange, then, becomes an ideologically charged process in every new configuration. The environment within which discourse lives is a volatile, constantly evolving one, where meaning is constantly in dispute.

Within concrete speech situations, then, dialogism throws a discursive bridge between expressive positions. The utterance is semantically inflected by both positions in speech exchange, the word of the speaker anticipating and building into its composition the response of the listener. All discursive activity is thus partially a jockeying for position, an ideological struggle between accents, intonations and meanings, but also, crucially, an interaction producing communication and understanding. The understanding – it does not have to be agreement – is crucial if there is to be a continuation to the exchange. We can extrapolate from the internal dialogic composition of the word a view of texts as existing within a dialogic network of meaning. The concept of intertextuality overlaps with dialogism somewhat here, although dialogism transcends mere quotation, as each text/utterance retains all of its previous meanings even when co-opted into a new or hostile environment (see Chapter 1). Thus, utterances are never completely cleansed of previous intonations, can never sound with singular meaning.

Bakhtin is concerned with literary forms, such as the novel, that place themselves firmly within social networks of experience, both in internal composition (heteroglossia) and in modes of transmission (dialogism). The high dialogic potential of the novel is linked to its easy incorporation of heteroglossia. Described as the 'social diversity of speech types' (DIN, p.263), the term enunciates the multi-voiced, decentralized notion of language that runs through the dialogic project. By way of 'dialogized heteroglossia' (272), dialects, intonations and social voices enter into the novel, creating the method by which theme is dispersed into living, concrete language usage, 'the rivulets and droplets of social heteroglossia' (263). Some of the forms this process may take include the 'parodic stylization' of official literary language found in the comic novels of Fielding and Sterne (301); or the 'hybrid constructions' (utterances that simultaneously project two 'belief systems' or contrasting voices) often used in Dickens to deflate or 'unmask' self-important figures like Mr Merdle of *Little Dorrit* (304–5).[6]

The novel is the ultimate dialogic artform for Bakhtin because it has otherness built into its structure, existing 'on the boundary between its own context and another, alien context' (284). As the following chapters will seek to demonstrate, a certain hybrid mode of construction can be identified in the way that film communication works, although this capacity to contain and project otherness is subject to variance in the range of cinematic forms. Speaking of the medium itself as inherently dialogic in the way that Bakhtin understood the novel requires a degree of equivocation, because this avenue leads us into areas that cut against justified views of Hollywood's 'monologic' address, as Chapter 5 explores. Monologism is the general 'situation wherein the matrix of values, signifying practices, and creative impulses that constitute the living reality of language and socio-cultural life are subordinated to the dictates of a single, unified consciousness or perspective' (Gardiner, 1998, p.65). It is associated with the forces that rationalize and unify 'ideological life', manifesting for Bakhtin in post-Enlightenment European prose traditions that prevail until different ways of ordering textuality appear (see PDP, pp.79–85). The state of language does not naturally tend towards monologism, but a pervasive cultural illusion is orchestrated in its name.[7] Any cultural force or expressive mode that does not admit another view, or seeks to artificially bond an official meaning to an utterance, would be considered monologic in Bakhtin's thinking.

Bakhtinian thought does not offer up dialogism as an instant formula for an empowered spectator, exploding monologism wherever she finds it. My purport in using it here is to illustrate its value as a flexible way of understanding filmic textuality that can bring into play critical sensitivities that certain disciplinary models have tended to adulterate (see Chapter 1). Dialogism presupposes communication, and argues that this takes place wherever understanding and response takes place, even in the face of monologic appearance or intention (DIN, p.315; 374). This makes it a good fit with Hollywood. In watching films, we commune with various speaking agents behind the textual utterance. Clearly, filmmakers constitute one such entity (aspects of this dynamic are considered in Chapter 4). Institutions also frame the textual message. The traces of power relations that dialogic reading renders adumbrate the weight of institutional accents, but dialogism does not conceive these as singularly determining; sensitivity to the way texts shape their address gives us a map of institutional contours, a snapshot of values. Construed as a reading strategy, the distinctiveness of dialogism is its sensitivity to context. Voloshinov's work, particularly, stresses the ideological layers that accrue to any unit of discourse as it travels through communicative channels (see Chapter 1). This is implicated in the joining of consciousnesses to each other in an ideological 'chain' of understanding; indeed, the existence of the chain predates that of the sign that is exchanged, reinforcing the concept that meaning cannot unfold in isolation – multiple points of view are required (MPL, pp.10–11).

Heteroglossia, which helps us to understand the co-ordination of languages, and the chronotope, which highlights the relation between time and space that lends form to a text, are devices that can be used to calibrate the values clustering around individuals understood as perceptual 'microcommunities' (Pechey, 2007, p.206); dialogism is the medium of transmission that forms these zones into the 'chain' proposed by Voloshinov. If this sounds disconcertingly abstract,[8] it can be grounded in a sense that film readings matter in real ways. Consumption of a filmic text, under any set of viewing conditions, gains us entrance into an interpretative community based around that text. Our 'take', or reading, on the text is projected outwards into a discourse sustained by the other members of that community. There are many outlets for such opinions with varying degrees of 'official' stamp – reviews in magazines and newspapers, polls on websites, academic seminars, fan clubs, informal discussion with friends and so on. Bakhtin would have it that once we have voiced our opinion on a text – once we have formulated our answer to it – that response becomes a part of the discourse associated with the text, becomes one of many framing voices, contending, conflicting, clamouring to be heard; there is a 'continual renewing of the work through the creative perception of listeners and readers' (FTC, p.254). The phrase 'creative perception' implies something more than passive consumption, something that creates, that changes, at the same time as it perceives, receives and watches. Some viewers will, of course, be stimulated to become filmmakers themselves (see Chapter 5), but the assumption of any spectatorial position involves us in these kinds of dialogical relations. We situate ourselves to receive the semantic message of the filmic text, but also to respond to it; to assemble a series of edits into a coherent narrative pattern; to process various patches of light and depth relations into a meaningful image; to organize what we see into an archive of cinematic experience. Our encounter with the film finds expression not only in external manifestations such as exchanging views with a friend or writing a review, but in the act of understanding itself. This act is unique because dialogism positions every spectator in a unique way based around the limitations and specificities of their own perceptual 'horizons'. It hardly needs illustrating that people react to films in radically different ways based on the influence of their cultural horizon; we are all familiar with 'against the grain' readings, and undoubtedly with the experience of hearing comments in the cinema foyer that make us feel that we must have watched a completely different film from some other patrons. The ebb and flow of critical estimation as recorded in canons (like the 'greatest film' poll organized by *Sight and Sound* magazine on a ten-year cycle, most recently in 2002[9]) and the attraction of cult valuation to certain films years after an initial indifferent release also attest to this. All of these phenomena occur in a diachronic way that engenders in film a fluidity that precludes its meaning becoming frozen at a given historical juncture. Texts are conceived as having 'lives', unfolding over time and within different incarnations of society. It is a contention of film criticism that our cinema viewing is a factor in how we construct ourselves socially; film studies has given this notion currency in various ways (see Chapter 1). The most radical of these ways form the crux of a conservative hostility that redraws boundaries between film and world in an atavistic fashion.[10] Bakhtin is more inclined to see these relations in terms of the discursive world modelling the knowledge that we must acquire to understand ourselves, through understanding our dependence on others: 'What is realized in the novel is the process of coming to know one's own language as it is perceived in someone else's language, coming to know one's own horizon within someone else's horizon' (DIN, p.365). This is not a mere process of mimetic repetition;

film is not life, any more than the novel is, and we will not experience life in any improved way by copying it. Exposure to the novel, for Bakhtin, opens doors on the world; or more accurately, on other worlds, other levels of being, enlightening not just material existence but the social networks that map and structure that existence: 'Languages of heteroglossia, like mirrors that face each other, each reflecting in its own way a piece, a tiny corner of the world, force us to guess at and grasp for a world behind their mutually reflecting aspects that is broader, more multi-levelled, containing more and varied horizons than would be available to a single language or a single mirror' (415). Note that the 'mirrors' of heteroglossia do not straightforwardly reveal things for our easy contemplation but spur us on to further activity, to guess and grasp, to remain active and eschew a passive role. Film, through its heteroglot system of effects (visual, audio, written and so on), points at such 'varied horizons', impelling us to engage with other aspects of social experience and other members of the interpretative community, generating a network of 'creative perception' and dialogic participation.

'Text' in this book denotes a concrete example of cinematic discourse or 'utterance', an artistic system constantly shaped by its exposure within spectatorial communities and multiple ideological horizons. This does not, however, draw impermeable boundaries separating the privileged 'main' narrative off from discourses that surround and give shape to it; in the course of this work, readings will often be enhanced and expanded by reference to the field of critical, promotional and various types of 'unofficial' discourse that make up the 'framing text' of the contemporary cinematic narrative (PT, p.104).

Dialogism can be thought of as a matrix surrounding and interpenetrating all discourses, maintaining in their current form the presence of all their previous speakings and usages and hosting their future renewal. Polyphony and chronotope, the two other major Bakhtinian concepts I address within this book, can be clarified more easily with respect to the styles of representation that foreground their activities. The chapter summaries that follow include a few explicatory comments to help give readers a handle on those concepts. A supplementary concept is used sparingly in Chapter 3, but its implications mesh nicely with the broader contours of dialogism that I am attempting to bring out, and so a brief description is justified. 'Outsideness', in Bakhtinian theory, refers to a prerequisite of *creative understanding* (i.e., the full assimilation of a foreign culture in dialogic exchange). Bakhtin remarks that 'In order to understand, it is immensely important for the person who understands to be *located outside* the object of his or her creative understanding – in time, in space, in culture' (NM, p.7). This stance of 'outsideness' enables the understanding person to partake of the specificities of the new culture while retaining the unique vantage-point, and crucial social values, of their own position within their own epoch or culture. This concept is used in Chapter 3 to address the problem of evaluating the cultural products of a past era within the ideological terms of the present day.

Chapter 1. Dialogism and film studies: the dialogic spectator

The chapter will explore Bakhtin's salience for film studies, asking: What can Bakhtin offer that other theorists cannot? Where can his work intervene in a way that resolves some of the contradictions and gaps of competing theoretical models? It will be important to establish major currents that have shaped the field today. The grounding of film studies in semiotic models will provide a starting point. Bakhtin's orientation towards dialogic discourse has tended to be seen as somewhat divergent from the semiotic repertoire that emerges strictly from Saussurean linguistics, but nevertheless a sign-based approach to communication is the general position taken by the Bakhtin Circle, particularly through the work of Voloshinov. Starting at this point enables 'classic' film studies perspectives on what constitutes the 'film text' to be placed in constructive tension with Bakhtinian ways of thinking about textuality.

To develop this difference and potential, the chapter will proceed to map a sequence of crucial stages in film theory, including Christian Metz on film language, Laura Mulvey on narrative film form and ideology, and David Bordwell on spectators as conscious 'meaning makers', culminating with the contributions of cultural studies initiatives that have rather different political imperatives in mind in approaching the ideological basis of popular culture. Mulvey and Bordwell have been deliberately selected for the paradigm-altering impact of their contributions, and the ubiquity of their work will be interrogated by the application of a Bakhtinian perspective. This chapter ends by opening up the notion of 'two-way textuality' as an attempt to locate dialogism in specific cinematic practices (which looks forward to the concerns of Chapter 5).

Chapter 2. Chronotope I: time, space, narrative – 'get ready for rush hour'

With this chapter, the focus shifts and narrows from broadly theoretical matters towards a close textual and aesthetic perspective. Bakhtin's crucial notion of the chronotope is introduced. The term delineates the fusion of time and space in the generation or material production of the substance that we think of as 'text', rendering narrative events visible. Yet its sense is not limited to describing blocks of narrative material; it also resonates on philosophical, generic and communicative planes. The three main, interconnected meanings attributed to the term in 'Forms of Time and of the Chronotope in the Novel' highlight the different (but related) levels of textuality on which the chronotope operates. The first sense is used to demarcate stable generic forms, such as the folkloric chronotope or chronotope of 'adventure-time', which are classified according to methods of representing time and space. Secondly, the term is used to signify localized renderings of time and space within the text, or chronotopic motifs, such as the castle, road or salon. The third sense involves a chronotopic element in the process of reading; here, the chronotope is drawn together with dialogism to describe how the worlds of real and represented appear to be linked by the mediations of chronotopes. The overlapping nature of these definitions is discussed in the chapter; for now, it will suffice to say that the chronotope is used to analyze the narrative formulas of the contemporary Hollywood action narrative. This is a form where mainstream film most vividly realizes cinema's kinetic capabilities (a process that is implicated in how film's illusion of presence draws spectatorial investment in the spaces onscreen). Pointing towards a way to dialogically amalgamate spectatorial issues with a consideration of the material existence of cinematic space and time, Bakhtin's work on Ancient Greek romances and 'novels of ordeal' (in the 1937–8 essay 'Forms of Time and of the Chronotope in the Novel') will be utilized. Bakhtin's study of these epic forms and their extraordinary, incident-packed dramatic logic yields the concept of 'adventure-time', a privileged zone of temporality wherein narrative spaces adapt to the demands of contingent, ever-changing action, coalescing into 'organizing centers for [...] fundamental narrative events' (FTC, p.250). A comparison will be drawn between the functions of adventure-time identified in the romances of Heliodorus and others, and the forms of space and time in which Hollywood action heroes like James Bond, Indiana Jones and the protagonists of the *Die Hard* films experience their adventures, with particular reference to the 'fusing' of space with plot (for instance, the level-by-level construction of *Die Hard*'s corporate tower rescue can be construed as a sequential mission in the style of a computer game). Also considered will be the elasticity of the time within which action heroes exist, and generic roots in the purely kinetic 'cinema of attractions', which thrilled early audiences with tropes of rides and journeys based around the promise of 'moving' the viewer in a spectacular fashion.

Chapter 3. Chronotope II: time, space and genre in the Western film

Having illustrated, in the previous chapter, the crucial role that the chronotope can play in expanding critical understanding of space and time in film narrative, attention will now shift to a different level of chronotopic activity. Bakhtin, who is philosophically predisposed to search for the social meanings underlying particular aesthetic effects, suggests that concentrated social and historical values and meanings can be read off the typical spatio-temporal locales of literary genres. Scholarship on the Western genre has linked its dominance during the classical period of Hollywood production to connotations of ideological imperialism and the warping of history. Filmmakers approaching the form after its demise in the 1970s have reacted to these implications in a number of ways, most commonly by adopting a stance of knowing pastiche or the displacement of ideological pressures onto a reverential sense of the genre's mythic 'timelessness'. John Sayles' 1996 film *Lone Star*, while not strictly a Western in form, attempts to restore 'timeliness' to the Western, by closely examining its ideological repercussions through one half century of American history. Bakhtin also reserves the chronotope for discussion of those privileged time-space sites where dramatic power is most condensed in texts, such as the various physical manifestations of the 'threshold' motif found in Dostoevsky (PDP, pp.169–76). As Chapter 2 will have established, chronotopes lace narrative structures with such moments of intensity, but in placing *Lone Star* alongside John Ford's canonical 1956 Western *The Searchers*, my analysis will prompt other questions about why certain combinations become wedded to generic vocabularies.

Through the application of two crucial ideas derived from Bakhtin – those of 'chronotope' and 'genre memory' – this chapter will propose an intriguing textual dialogue that can be traced between *Lone Star* and *The Searchers*, towards the ultimate end of assessing Sayles' achievement in challenging genre orthodoxy around the representation of time, memory and history.

Chapter 4. Polyphony: authorship and power

The films written and directed by celebrated American dramatist David Mamet explore how utterances, stories and verbal performances of all kinds drive the power games that characterize human interaction in a mercantile, late capitalist society. Mamet's films, particularly his *noir*-like debut *House of Games*, represent intriguing territory for an examination of Bakhtinian 'polyphony'. Like heteroglossia, polyphony can be construed as a manifestation of the dialogic principle in textual practice. The polyphonic text is one that rejects the rigidities of monologic structure – the traditional formula for author–hero relations, where the most powerful consciousness is that of the author, who allows information to trickle out to the audience, thus illuminating the motives and nuances of the subservient, puppet-like characters – and instead unfurls within a non-hierarchical realm of equal and interdependent consciousnesses. Relations are reconfigured onto a dialogically level playing-field, the author, characters and reader/spectators all partaking in a *'plurality of independent and unmerged voices and consciousnesses'* (PDP, 6, italics in the original) that refuses to objectify (and thus finalize) the discourse of a character, leaving their word (and by extension, their *world*) semantically open. For Bakhtin, Dostoevsky is the pre-eminent polyphonic novelist, the guarantor of *'equal rights'* to his characters (6), although this democratizing principle is informed by such carnivalesque predecessors and generic influences as the 'serio-comic' menippean satires of Varro, Seneca, Petronius and others. Although his films feature many colourful and clashing voices, and forge their narratives around spectacular verbal battles, misunderstandings and transactions, Mamet is renowned for high levels of textual control and problematic representations of women (particularly in *Oleanna* [1994], which explores the uses and abuses of political correctness). In this section, Bakhtin's generally positive and optimistic theories of discourse will be tested as we ask in what sense an author can be said to 'speak' a film text, which is an apposite question in an age of 'director's commentaries'. The chapter will reflect on what the answer to this might mean for our understanding of film as a depiction of acts of communication and, simultaneously, a communication *process* implying the circulation of knowledge and power.

Chapter 5. Hollywood calling: cinema's technological address

Unlike earlier chapters, Chapter 5 is not built around the explication of a specific Bakhtinian concept. Rather, it tries to bring into play various functions and facets of dialogism in a flexible way that responds to the manifold implications of digital forms as they impinge upon and 'remediate' the film experience. Key to Bakhtin's notion of the dialogic is the principle that textual communication is a two-way process, with spectator/consumers participating in a negotiation of meaning that can sometimes contradict or rework the desired ideological 'message' of a text. This attractively utopian idea may appear provocative in its application to Hollywood film, a form of text that has tended to be seen as 'monologic' in its construction of meaning. Do developments in contemporary Hollywood film promise to solicit an authentic viewer 'response'? What might this consist of? Hollywood's own technological history self-promotes a constant revision of modes of address that narrative films deploy to enhance the intensity of experience, yet in terms of privileged values, the status quo seems to remain intact.

Certainly, ways of accessing and using film change, as do their accompanying modes of temporality and the roles (such as consumer, fan or 'fan-producer') that they call into being. The technologies of DVD and the Internet, as they are called upon in marketing, delivering and contextualizing the film text, will be considered. Such issues lead us into the area of how representational 'screens' match up to 'real' spaces and experiences, with the move from celluloid to digital calling into question certain ontological precepts on which prior theories have depended. Looping back to some elements deployed in work on the chronotope in Chapter 2, the computer-generated aesthetics found in Pixar's successful animated films *Toy Story 2* and *The Incredibles* will be examined.

Conclusion: Making it real

In a Bakhtinian spirit of openness and 'unfinalizability', framing the end of a book as a traditional conclusion smacks of the monologic, but clearly some gathering up of ideas and reflections will be needed. The section will summarize and draw together the key strands of the book, reiterating how a Bakhtinian contribution, particularly focused on dialogism and chronotope, offers new conceptual tools and frameworks that can have a real effect on our film studies work.

A note on two aspects of authorship

As has already been indicated, a number of works of the 'Bakhtin Circle' became embroiled in a dispute over the attribution of authorship. Medvedev's *The Formal Method in Literary Scholarship* (originally published in 1928) and Voloshinov's *Freudianism* (1927) and *Marxism and the Philosophy of Language* (1929), among other texts (such as certain works of I. I. Kanaev), have been fairly widely attributed to Bakhtin in Russia and by Western scholars like Clark and Holquist (1984). Others contend that Bakhtin probably took a role in the generation and development of ideas contained within these books (the emergence of which seem to reflect a certain conceptual cross-fertilization during the group debates of the 1920s, or at least an orientation towards similar problems) but was not heavily involved in their writing (Morson and Emerson, 1990; Titunink, 1986). The championing of one position over another has so saturated the aura around these works – and depreciated the roles of Medvedev and Voloshinov, both of whom died in the 1930s – that it drives someone like Ken Hirschkop to settle a recent passage on the affair by suggesting that attempts to straighten out Bakhtin's publishing history, as his personal biography, almost inevitably 'sustain as many myths as [they] debunk' (1999, p.140). This will not be attempted here. The texts concerned are infrequently alluded to within the present work. I have included these texts within the parameters of abbreviated 'Bakhtin Circle' works not to take a position, but in the interest of the clarity, and light apparatus, that is my uppermost concern. The empirical degree to which Bakhtin may or may not have participated in their composition will not be at issue. Where these texts enter the discussion, they do so in the understanding that my attribution of them is to the authors whose names they were originally published under.

Almost as complex and fraught a methodological issue is the attribution of authorship within the institutional and creative structures of Hollywood film. While noting the often crucial influence of screenwriters, cinematographers, composers, production designers, producers, actors, editors and others on the artistic shape taken by the 'finished' product, we will adhere within this study to the broad position formulated by the *Cahiers du Cinéma* critics, and their American acolytes such as Andrew Sarris, that ascribes the controlling authorial consciousness and responsibility for artistic organization in film to the director. The status of 'author' comes into the thematic frame in Chapter 4, but not in this sense (i.e., with respect to industrial organization – unless one counts characters as co-workers; the polyphonic paradigm is arguably open enough to license such a conception).

1
Dialogism and Film Studies: The Dialogic Spectator

Introduction: Bakhtin and the novel

> [G]reat novelistic images continue to grow and develop even after the moment of their creation; they are capable of being creatively transformed in different eras, far distant from the day and hour of their original birth
>
> (DIN, p.422)

Bakhtin's valorization of the novel derives from his belief that the diverse, multi-languaged voices of heteroglossia (a term that refers to the situation by which an ever-changing multiplicity of social languages and speech types are artistically organized in the text) find their fullest expression in the novel, and can only be incompletely represented in 'monologic' forms such as poetry, epic and drama.[1] For Bakhtin, the novel is equipped to deal with heteroglossia because it is an open form, where the word is not bonded to a singular ideological meaning but contains enough ambiguity to encourage multiple readings. Furthermore, it is a form that is sensitive to social value ('[t]he novelistic word [...] registers with extreme subtlety the tiniest shifts and oscillations of the social atmosphere', DIN, p.300), and one that encourages active engagement and not passive consumption on the part of the reader (282). As a text, the novel is structured by the interaction and dialogical interanimation of voices, stratified by an infinite range of languages (social, generic, professional and national), dialects and accents, all of which possess a particular and unique 'world view' (299). Socially dynamic and 'historically concrete' (331), the living embodiment of an uninterrupted struggle for precedence among an infinite number of languages and meanings, the novel is important to Bakhtin precisely as a form of *discourse* – a series of meanings and ideas materialized through language – and not as an example of abstract, semantically fixed and dead 'language', with pretensions to singularity, sanctification or ultimate truth. Bakhtin spends much of the early part of 'Discourse in the Novel' railing against the tendency of 'traditional stylistics' to approach discourse not as a living entity in perpetual and self-recreating conflict but as a petrified linguistic 'specimen' of the powers of an individual creative consciousness (259). According to Bakhtin, the Russian Formalist approach (which, at the time of the composition of Bakhtin's essay, was itself going through a retooling process to regain official legitimacy) too often dismisses novelistic prose as 'artistically neutral'; consequently, its situation within a living speech event goes undervalued and under-theorized (260). Bakhtin's project in the essay is to expose prose stylistics to the more philosophical approach to discourse that he feels is missing from linguistics, which, with its emphasis on uniformity, advances the 'verbal-ideological centralization' of life (272).

The most important attribute of the novel form for Bakhtin is thus its heterogeneity – it is 'a phenomenon multiform in style and variform in voice' (261). The idea of interaction or combination of diverse elements is the key to Bakhtin's conception of the novel; he suggests that it cannot be reduced to any single 'stylistic unity' (262). The meaning of any one element changes when it is removed from the complex of dialogic relations, and therefore its true function can never be discerned in isolation from the novelistic whole. Form and content are inseparable (259), and the meaning of every element is related not only to its present function, but to all of its past usages also; the dialogical utterance finds its object

> [a]lready as it were overlaid with qualifications, open to dispute, charged with value [...] The living utterance, having taken meaning and shape at a particular historical moment in a socially specific environment, cannot fail to brush up against thousands of living dialogic threads woven by socio-ideological consciousness.
>
> (276)

Utterances form dialogic networks across time, linking texts and interpretative communities, together; clearly, dialogism has much in common with the literary notion of intertextuality.[2] However, dialogic reference between texts is not a mere matter of quotation; all of the associations of the original text are carried through into the new usage of the utterance, creating a chain of meaning that resounds in history and is saturated with socio-ideological value. No word or utterance is neutral; nobody comes to a word in complete innocence; and no word can ever sound in a vacuum. The meaning of a word is the sum of all of its previous meanings, and all of its previous speakers sound once more in the act of its reproduction. As Brandist points out, by housing their assembly, the novel lends a kind of unity to the multiple diachronic perspectives that can renew the meanings of utterances (2002, pp.168–9).

'Otherness' is at the heart of the novel; like the dialogic word as described by Bakhtin, the novel exists 'on the boundary between its own context and another, alien context' (284), that is, a perceptual horizon that is not a direct referent of the text but which can enrich novelistic interpretation if applied to a reading. The 'alien context' into which the properties of the novel (or 'novelness' – FTC, p.147) which so exercise and engage Bakhtin will be introduced here is a cinematic one. This chapter will endeavour to provide some answers that might obviate a question that might be on the minds of some readers: why attempt the transfer of Bakhtin's novelistic paradigm to film at all? Such an objection could be anticipated both from those within film studies who resent the squeezing of film criticism into parameters that are imported from the study of literature and from those in the – as it were – 'pure' Bakhtinian camp who, since not long after the end of the first wave of English translations in the late 1980s, have allowed a perception to build that the 'application' of Bakhtin had reached a point of saturation, and represented a less vital use of scholarly resources than work that placed him in context (particularly with regard to Russian cultural history).[3] I happen to agree with Robert Stam's conviction that Bakhtin's work is committed to 'breaking down [...] walls' (1989, p.19) at all sorts of levels within and *between* discourses (for instance, between the popular and the official). This iconoclastic tendency is fully grounded in the principles of interaction and cross-fertilization (whether that process be easy or conflictual in character) that are the intellectual foundations of dialogism. Yet, there are those who would point out that appealing to the Bakhtinian 'spirit' to justify another adventure in appropriation is to fail to recognize that such a spirit is itself a construction of the inflections on Bakhtin's legacy that accompanied his popularity and widespread usage from the 1970s onwards.[4]

Stam, such a valuable contributor to the encounter of Bakhtinian approaches with cinema, warns against blocking the momentum of the 'cross-discipinary drift' of method that seems written into the concepts themselves, as well as being a feature of the academic field of film studies (1989, pp.16–7). What counts is that Bakhtin's attitude to the infectious energy of the novel suggests an aestheticizing process that renders experiences into texts; these can be read via dialogics, which is what this book intends to do. Film texts are part of human culture and communication and take their place, and should be located within, the back and forth of anticipation, interpretation, reception and, inevitably, argument that makes up that sphere in all its complexity and vitality. It is clear that, although we cannot take the special properties that Bakhtin found in the novel as unproblematically and without qualification obtaining in films, Bakhtin's ideas as outlined in 'Discourse in the Novel' and amplified across his hugely varied career pertain to the novel *as a form of textual discourse* and thus, in a broader sense, potentially possess relevance for artistic forms beyond the remit of the purely novelistic. The film text is not a novel but it might incorporate many features of *romannost* (translated as 'novelness' by Holquist).[5] This 'form of knowledge' is no less than the 'hero' of Bakhtin's project, a force in art which animates 'orders of experience [...] into dialogue with each other' (Holquist, 2002, p.83, 87). Wayne Booth treats this power of the novel more as a sort of energy, a 'tendency or possibility' of representing 'the inescapably dialogical quality of human life' and its many voices (1997, p.xxii). For Tihanov, Bakhtin's heroic view of the novel endows it with the power to place literary and social values into a relation whereby they 'reshape' each other (2000, p.82); however, Booth and Holquist agree that the resultant energy or consciousness can exceed the confines of the novel as genre.

Michael Holquist's characterization of Bakhtin as interested in 'the necessary changes that textualization brings about in a message' (2002, p.194) is a generous reading but not a misrepresentation, and is highly congenial to my own way of understanding Bakhtin's project and critical principles. If part of Bakhtin's 'message' was to identify the animating power of 'novelness' as a medium for the distribution of cultural ideas and voices, then film can be seen as another mode of textualization that enacts its own changes, and produces its own type of semiotic energy. It is also readable through dialogics. In my view, the invitation that the theoretical corpus holds out transcends the certainly strange fact that Bakhtin did not turn his own critical acumen upon cinema (see Stam, 1989, p.16). This blind spot is particularly odd given the productivity within the Circle during the 1920s, a period when film in the Soviet Union was becoming politically recognized for its communicative potentialities, and theoretically codified for its artistic specificity (with Formalist critics at the forefront of this process). It is not hard to imagine that the official aura surrounding cinema and its great practitioners like Eisenstein and Pudovkin may actually have been the off-putting element for Bakhtin, even if, as with the treatment of Formalism, state endorsements could hardly be taken as permanent (Cook, 1996, pp.193–5).

We should not, of course, discount the version that Bakhtin simply underestimated the value of cinematic expression in the same way that the Formal method, in his opinion, 'dismissed' novelistic prose.

Not every element of dialogism is worked out with direct regard to voices captured within novelistic frames; Bakhtin is inspired by 'discourse in life' as much as 'discourse in art', to paraphrase from one of the disputed works.[6] The conversation between social beings, respecting and informed by social positions, is the key image at its most undiluted. The 'drift' of method that Stam notes makes any conception of 'text' derived from Bakhtin a risky business, multi-levelled and imbued with the potential for contradiction; suffice to say that what shall be understood here as the filmic text, that is, the artistically shaped series of meanings that comprise the 'movie', finds an approximate analogue in Bakhtin's 'utterance', that is, the verbal or artistic statement in its dialogically animated, living, open state. It is possible to speak of film as a kind of utterance because, as I will argue, it is not only the producer of meaning but also the site and recipient of meanings projected back onto it by its dialogic communicant and adversary, the spectator. For our purposes, film will be considered as a form of artistic discourse comparable to the novel in Bakhtin's conception (although the comparison will not be carried through to the level of form, where the considerable differences of the two media must be respected at all times). It is to be hoped that any changes enacted upon Bakhtinian ideas in their 're-accentuation' here shall only be positive ones.[7] A key imperative of the Bakhtinian project is surely the continuation of dialogue, which can never be constrained to a single context but must always seek out new fields in which to test the validity of its own discourse; thus, when Stam's 'drift' of Bakhtinian influence can be felt gathering pace again, it seems an unduly negative response to see it as an intrusion or dilution rather than a new opportunity.

The proper dialogic emphasis, as mentioned above, is on otherness, and it is the 'other' half of the cinematic equation, the dialogic spectatorial addressee of film as a mode of textual and social communication, whom I wish to place at the centre of things in this chapter. Although several of Bakhtin's key works were written in the 1920s, their genuine global circulation took another five decades to find its full reach; thus, advantages of time and dissemination have given film theory the chance to develop a well-defined, albeit heterogeneous, literature on the activity of spectators, while a concrete programme on the nature of the reader's input to the novel along Bakhtinian lines has emerged more tentatively, and has resisted being 'plucked ready-formed' from the legacy of Bakhtin (Shepherd, 2001, p.136). Still, just as a series of competing models of the spectator emerged from film theory, forcing us into an ordering process of appropriateness here (even if many more have claims to be included), several forms of the 'reader' have been teased out of work by Bakhtin, and not all critics can agree on their constitution.[8] In Bakhtin, much of what we can say about the reader – and there is much we *can* say – is worked up from the dialogic *implications* of Bakhtin's tenets, rather than from direct reference.[9] For, if the image of the reader is not fully 'fleshed out' in Bakhtin, then dialogism, the process through which that reader interacts with the text, is substantial enough for us to extrapolate from it something like a generalized 'Bakhtinian reader'; and from there, we can begin to think about what a Bakhtinian spectator might be like. Many of the following writers address questions such as whether cinema embodies a circuit of communication, what that process is like and what kinds of ideological trace this exchange leaves upon us. A dialogical analysis may help us to appreciate some of the complexities of those issues from a new perspective.

The development of film theory over the last four decades can be broadly traced back to two crucial intellectual strands, shades of which can be discerned in almost all of what follows: the semiotic and the psychoanalytic. Not only are these two strands interrelated, but each feeds, to some degree, into all of the subsequent academic discourse concerning the medium (even if only serving as an antagonistic stimulus, as in neo-formalism and some forms of cultural studies). To isolate representative theorists for key approaches is no doubt a methodologically risky procedure, but none could deny the massive impact that the respective works of Christian Metz, Laura Mulvey and David Bordwell have had within the field. Here, we will examine some central tenets of film theory as elucidated by the semiotic and psychoanalytic models, then go on to explore some of the challenges and revisions to them (such as Bordwell's opposition to the linguistic metaphor), while bringing to bear Bakhtinian theory in the places where it can enrich our understanding. A productive dialogic encounter between Bakhtin and the key thinkers of modern film theory is the intention; to this end, we will also refer in a more modest degree to some of the theorists who have extended or challenged the discursive parameters of the semiotic and psychoanalytic positions (Stephen Heath, Colin MacCabe, Martin Barker). Although the major moves in film theory that will be surveyed here represent one minaturized history of how questions of spectatorship have moved through the discipline's intellectual sequence, what follows is not intended to be even a partial recitation of several decades of film theory. Where critical voices have been separated out from the polyphonic background supplied by dozens of others who played their part, the intention has been to bring into focus certain key questions – concerning the nature of the cinematic sign, how it is transmitted to viewers, how and why we understand and assimilate the message, or the potential to mean something, contained within that sign – to which a Bakhtinian view seems able to contribute a useful response.

Early Christian Metz and 'Cine-semiotics'

Although the work on signs performed by Charles S. Pierce also received much attention in the development of the broad semiotic model, the form of semiotics that was adopted in cultural critique (and, crucially, in literary study) owes its greatest debt to the work of Ferdinand de Saussure. It was his rigorous systematization of the question of language and his notion that lingustic processes could be broken down into a set of observable 'rules' which provided the theoretical foundation for film scholars such as Christian Metz. The initial overriding interest in the application of semiotics to the cinema by scholars such as Metz was to determine to what extent film constituted a language, and what such a 'language' had in common with natural (spoken) language. As noted by Herbert Eagle, the 'language question' that anchored so much activity in film criticism from the late 1960s until the mid-1970s was a return to and elaboration of the engagement that Formalist film theory had pursued with regard to Saussure's model of language decades before (Eagle, 1981, pp.52–3). The Formalist semiotics undertaken in the work of Yury Tynyanov and Boris Eichenbaum (two critics openly praised by Bakhtin in later life, despite his long-standing divergence of opinion with the Formalist school on the very grounds of language[10]) migrates into Metz's cine-semiotics, where it encounters the similarly profound influence of the vanguard post-structuralist semiotics of Roland Barthes.[11] Barthes emulated pioneers like Claude Lèvi-Strauss in bringing Saussure's frameworks into general application to the diverse signs within culture, although other influences of a more directly filmo-linguistic nature were extant even as Barthes' work gained favour (as noted by Stam, 1989, pp.26–8).

The differences in the views of language that come out of Bakhtin and Saussure have been extensively discussed,[12] and are usefully summed up by Sue Vice. Drawing upon the criticism of what is referred to as 'traditional stylistics' in 'Discourse in the Novel', Vice points out that in that essay, Bakhtin attempts to venture decisively beyond Saussure's postulation of an essential 'unity of language' (Vice, 1997, p.11). Such a hypothetical unity tends to 'abstract the social' within itself (Heath, 1981, p.196).

Bakhtin explains the shortcomings of the Saussurean outlook (in relation to heteroglossia):

> Such a combining of languages and styles into a higher unity [as that achieved by the novel] is unknown to traditional stylistics; it has no method for approaching the distinctive social dialogue among languages that is present in the novel. Thus stylistic analysis is not oriented toward the novel as a whole, but only toward one or another of its subordinated stylistic unities.
>
> (DIN, p.263)

Saussure's model stands as a critical influence (Holquist, 2002, p.43) on the turn to a sociological linguistics that Voloshinov's work confidently announces, thereafter being developed into Bakhtin's 1930s presentation of novelistic discourse as the ultimate cultural crucible for the interpenetration of social languages and discourses.[13] Influential though it is, however, Saussure's approach rules out precisely what Voloshinov/Bakhtin deem essential: a flexible, ideologically aware accommodation between the commonality that is the basis of shared expression and the 'violation [and] reconstruction of norms' (Hirschkop, 1999, p.219) that powers the life of language as it flows through time and outgrows old contexts. Ken Hirschkop pithily suggests that it is in Saussure's *Course*[14] that it is 'written that politics and language don't mix' (1999, p.16); the Bakhtinian counter view to Saussure, much of the substance of which emerges in Voloshinov's book,[15] is grounded in a refutation of the assumption that in linguistic exchange, the participating subject is shielded from other forces and responsibilities which – for Saussure – do not encroach on language operations.[16] Hirschkop encapsulates much of this counter view in the following:

> Language does not articulate values or principles from a neutral perspective, making their acceptance or rejection a matter for individual initiative: its meanings are positions taken or refused, its forms opportunities for ethical relationships
>
> (1999, p.35)

Critiques of the linguistic roots of Saussurean semiology have tended to hew very closely to the charge of ahistoricalism put forward by Bakhtin/Voloshinov.[17] Even Bakhtin's style – in Michael Holquist's estimation, that of a 'baggy monster' to Saussure's cool systematician (1994, pp.xviii) – has tended to sharpen the contrast between the thinkers.

Bakhtin would undoubtedly find Metz's treatment of film in *Language and Cinema* (1974a), an argument worthy of full and unrestrained dialogical engagement, although Metz's link with Saussure was not at all an uncritical one. As Lapsley and Westlake point out, Metz refrained from the 'wholesale importation of Saussure's concepts' based on the recognition that Saussure's presentation of language as incorporating an underlying system (*langue*) within which all individual utterances (*parole*) were organized, diverged from the 'language' that was at work in the cinema, which, Metz argued, did not operate through a *langue* (Lapsley and Westlake, 1996, p.38). One of the core reasons for this rejection of *langue* embodies why Metz's theory must inevitably come under criticism from a position informed by dialogism: he believes that cinema does not constitute a form of inter-communication like spoken language, but instead embodies a one-way circuit that 'does not authorize the immediate play of bilateral exchange' (Metz, 1974a, p.288). Not being a form of inter-communication, cinema does not require a *langue* or system of rules to police the meaning transactions that go on within it. This point is not anti-Bakhtinian in itself (Bakhtin not being a proponent of the Saussurean 'take' on language systems anyway), but is symptomatic of a fundamental difference between Metz and Bakhtin. As evidenced even in the (sometimes implied) critiques of Saussurean linguistics in the Dostovesky book, in 'The Problem of Speech Genres' (pp.67–9), and more substantially in Voloshinov (MPL, pp.58–71), a Bakhtinian way of understanding meaning exchange places huge emphasis on the response of the 'other', which assumes a determining semantic role in constructing the utterance/event. Metz's proposal of a uni-directional textual system, his perspective on cinema as 'one-way communication' (Lapsley and Westlake, 1996, p.38), shuts off the film text to the dialogic participation of the spectator. This renders the film viewing as a 'closed discourse', something that can be witnessed and decoded but not shared (Metz, 1974a, p.17).

In laying the foundations for a model of cinematic meaning that hinged upon a passive spectator, Metz in the late 1960s (when the material translated as *Language and Cinema* was written) anticipated moves made later and elsewhere (predominantly in 'apparatus' and 'subject-position' debates, key moments in which are rehearsed below). Accounts of film's meaning flow as operating only in a single direction served a certain political imperative of theory at this time: that of revealing the ideological mechanisms of cinema. This imperative, for better or worse, enshrined the passive or uninvolved spectator as a virtual orthodoxy until this model was challenged by the work of 'cultural studies' theorists, a group with a quite different political frame of reference, in the later 1970s. What concerns us for now is another area of revealing divergence between the theoretical standpoint of Metz in the *Language and Cinema* period and a Bakhtinian approach, which is in the definition of the borders of the cinematic text itself (the object of study for those interested in the filmic equivalent of 'novelness'). Bakhtin emphasizes the crucial importance of historical and social elements in the analysis of a text, which in the study of film would suggest the incorporation of information about the cinematic apparatus in its socio-economic and institutional dimensions: aspects such as film's mode of address and reception in society, film as product within a network of promotion and commodification, the capacity of the cinema to reproduce ideology and shape social trends and so forth. Metz, however, sets out as one of his key methodological moves the establishment of a dichotomy between the terms 'cinema' and 'film', which effectively erases much of the productive complexity of this area. A large part of the discursive agenda of *Language and Cinema* is taken up with this problem, with Metz concluding that, although the study of what he terms the 'cinematic' elements (technical, economic factors; cinema as institution and social phenomenon) deserves attention *elsewhere*, such aspects are not a priority in his examination of how the individual signifying discourse, the 'film', organizes narrative through the manipulation of codes and subcodes. Indeed, in separating a rich array of contextual factors out under the category 'cinema', Metz goes so far as to suggest that these dimensions are *only* present in the act of analysis: '[...T]he cinema does not exist independently; [...it] consists only of what the analyst puts into it' (1974a, p.49).

This polarization of terms draws a rather unhelpfully arbitrary border around a complex of crucial factors in meaning formation, and is extremely challenging to a Bakhtinian point of view. First, film is a medium where factors of production such as economic and technical factors cannot be overlooked as their effect on the text at the level of signification is enormous: concepts such as the Star System, which is informed by the economic study of the relations maintained by studios with the star actor, are vital to any serious study of cinematic meaning and audience identification.[18] For instance, a big-budget, studio-backed production of *Hamlet*, such as Franco Zeffirelli's 1990 version starring Mel Gibson, will be globally understood in a very different fashion to a low-budget work with an unknown actor as protagonist; say, Aki Kaurismäki's casting of Pirkka-Pekka Petelius in the adaptation *Hamlet Liikemaailmassa/Hamlet Goes Business* (1987). Radically different interpretations of Hamlet's stature as 'hero' could easily be engendered via this contrast, quite apart from other changes wrought on the source material. Similarly, technical aspects should not be treated as if existing on a plane removed from the central business of meaning creation; numerous components of the diegetic material of a film – many of which are completely constructed in post-production – reside within this area, as the special effects or computer-generated battle sequences of *Lord of the Rings* (Peter Jackson, 2001–3) or *Matrix* (Wachowski Brothers, 1999–2003) trilogies will testify. Stanley Kubrick is cited as deferring production on the project that eventually became *AI Artificial Intelligence* (Steven Spielberg, 2001) until effects tools had reached the paradigm-altering standard evinced in *Jurassic Park* (Steven Spielberg, 1993), believing that the story could not be told according to his vision until this stage of technological development had been attained (Rose, 2000). Visual and audio effects and imagery contribute to the cumulative narrative sense and impact of the film just as influentially as any other element such as dialogue, music or editing, and thus it seems perverse to withdraw them from analysis alongside those other codes. Metz's treatment of the 'technical' is almost an unfortunate anticipation of film studies' tendency to arrange codes or layers of textual meaning within value-laden hierarchies, particularly around those elements which are said to serve 'narrative' purposes as opposed to those which serve 'spectacle' (an imbalance which has recently been redressed in works by Warren Buckland and Scott Bukatman amongst others).[19] In fact, the migration of cinema as an experience into the digital world means that such elements can radically alter the way in which the film is watched; the dialogic implications of special effects, and Computer Generated Imagery in particular, will be assessed in greater detail in Chapter 5.

Secondly, Metz's approach to the filmic text drastically underestimates the dialogic role of the viewer in constructing the film as a meaningful discourse. It is true that Metz places a certain amount of emphasis on the position of the 'analyst' in identifying and constructing the codes of the cinema ('[W]e can say that [...] the analysis "creates" the codes of the cinema; it should elucidate them, make them explicit, *establish them as objects*, while in nature they remain buried in films, which alone are objects which exist prior to the analysis', italics in original; 1974a, p.49). However, the general spectator tends to remain at a certain distance from the cinematic meaning event in this early Metzian account. The 'one-way' model prevents Metz from acknowledging the influence of the viewer as multiply present – both addressee *and* participant in the textual process. For Bakhtin, conversely, the utterance, in art as in social speech exchange, is constructed around a dialogic relationship with the anticipated response of the other.[20] The nature of his theoretical project is to disprove the view that the artistic work is a 'self-sufficient and closed authorial monologue, one that presumes only passive listeners beyond its own boundaries' and redefine it as 'a rejoinder in a given dialogue, whose style is determined by its interrelationship with other rejoinders [other texts, the interpretations of other spectators] in the same dialogue' (DIN, p.274). This dialogue does not only occur between the multiple voices that sound within narrative (in the sense of heteroglossia) but beyond the level of the text in the relationship between utterance and addressee (reader/spectator), and further, between that addressee and all the other addressees of the same text, generating a linked interpretative community. Because Bakhtin conceives of these relations in diachronic, continually evolving terms, a response to a filmic utterance does not have to be immediate to take its place in the overall communication (Stam et al, 1992, p.35), ensuring that the text continues to 'live' through semantic re-accentuations long after its first enunciation or the moment of its widest circulation (we might think of the different meaning profiles that an enduring text like *The Wizard of Oz* [Victor Fleming, 1939] goes through; for instance, its journey from children's literature adaptation to a cult participatory event for grown-ups with a considerable gay audience). A wide network of understanding, radiating outward from the text and encompassing all strands of debate that help to foster its emerging interpretation, is thus produced. This network of 'framing' (PT, p.104) commentary and thought around the original text is central to the dialogic concept; codes and their operations in the text remain open so that style and meaning may continue to be determined 'by the interrelationship with other rejoinders in the same dialogue'.

Metz's separation of the 'textual system' from the wider socio-economic presence and circulation of cinema is consistent with the Saussurean paradigm that motivates *Language and Cinema*. Metz privileges the 'code' – that which links all films formally to each other – in his filmic model, serving the same homogenizing function as Saussure's conception of language as a 'system of normatively identical forms' (MPL, p.60). This is a philosophy that a Bakhtinian approach could not endorse; Bakhtin is much more interested in what sets utterances in dialogic relation, and often conflict, with each other, than in which formal features can be identified as stable and fixed in every utterance. His priority is the 'unrepeatable' quality of the utterance or text (PT, p.108), a condition of immediacy which is difficult to square with Metz's schema and its vocabulary of messages and codes which roll out in distinct stages of meaning separated by time and governed by agents (the cinéaste and the semiotician) who do not appear to communicate directly. The pursuit of a level of scientific rigour that risks erasing the uniqueness of the film as social event echoes in Metz's most elaborate theoretical construct, the 'Grande Syntagmatique', his attempt to classify the structuration of cinematic narrative into a hierarchical system starting from the humble shot and rising to the sequence.[21]

Ultimately, it seems that the Metzian notion of 'film' (the individual signifying discourse) relies too heavily on the homogeneity of codes to satisfy the vital social and historical parameters set by Bakhtin Circle thinking. On the other hand, what Metz, at this stage of his thinking, categorizes as 'cinema'– reducible to institutional, technical, economic and social aspects – fails to supply the basic textual material for Bakhtinian analysis: the utterance. In the first instance, text is robbed of context; in the second, context divorced from text. A terminological opposition addressed by Bakhtin in a fragmentary note encapsulates the fundamental difference between the two approaches:

> Context and code. A context is potentially unfinalized; a code must be finalized. A code is only a technical means of transmitting information; it does not have cognitive, creative significance. A code is a deliberately established, killed context.
>
> (N70, p.147)

A systematic analysis along Metzian lines would render an efficient account of the way that narrative codes are arranged in the text but, through failing to appreciate rich contextual factors such as the film's capacity to dialogically refer to and communicate with other texts, would inevitably bypass many important resonances on the narrative level. For example, the narrative understanding of a genre horror movie such as Wes Craven's *Scream* (1996) is greatly enhanced by examining it against its 'dialogizing background' (DIN, p.340), in this case, its generic context (a process that is explicitly encouraged by the film's constant allusion to the horror canon). To this we might add further elements that do not fall into Metz's purview, but whose influence is weighted equally between the diegetic and the extra-diegetic (the citation of social debates about screen violence, pop culture references and so on). These may include thoughts on the casting of Courtney Cox, star of sitcom *Friends* (1994–2004), as a famous television newscaster, or that of Neve Campbell, well-known from hit teen show *Party of Five* (1994–2000), as the vulnerable but resourceful heroine Sidney. The producers of the film obviously calculated that cheaper-to-hire television stars would bring their own cultural frame of reference, fit into the self-conscious, media-savvy ethos of the script, and enable the fresh, sexy ensemble dynamic needed to market the film to its target teen demographic (seen most explicitly in the central ensemble image used to promote the film and its sequels, *Scream 2* [Craven, 1998] and *Scream 3* [Craven, 2000]). *Scream* illustrates the commercial exploitation of a dialogical relationship stretching across forms of discourse (movies and television). Such considerations undoubtedly contributed greatly to the film's success, and the method was reprised in the first sequel, where Sarah Michelle Gellar, star of TV's cult hit *Buffy the Vampire Slayer* (1997–2003), is used in a similar fashion. Campbell's character Sidney also signals an allusion to, or revamp of, the figure that Carol J. Clover discerns in the 'Final Girl' syndrome of classic slasher films (Clover, 1989, pp.106–9). This archetype, embodied by Jamie Lee Curtis' Laurie in *Halloween* (John Carpenter, 1978), is constituted by a heroine, often on the cusp of sexual maturity, who displays sufficient mental and emotional strength to evade the sexualized male threat and survive to the final credits. A point is made here in terms of the overturning of earlier, reactionary horror constructions of the passive female, reflecting modified 1990s attitudes.[22] One could go on; the point is that social and economic factors such as star casting, genre-inflected cross-media marketing and appeal (however calculated) to gender discourse have a huge impact on the way that the story is told and understood.

Film is a 'closed text' for Metz (1974a, p.18); the meaning event is apparently suspended between the moment that work on the production side finishes and the moment when the analyst starts to pick apart the (finalized, pre-formed) codes of the narrative. Furthermore, his over-reliance on the linguistic metaphor leads to an extremely narrow conceptualization of what constitutes a 'film'. This is displayed throughout *Language and Cinema*; for example, in discussing the competitive nature of sub-codes as opposed to the peaceful relations that obtain between codes, Metz states that '[t]he film must be lighted *and* must be edited' (1974a, p.142), suggesting that both functions are irreplaceable and thus do not enter into competition with each other. Yet *Blue* (Derek Jarman, 1993), theatrically released and thus, in the eyes of the industry, a film, featured no film editing but rather a single, static image. Aleksandr Sokurov's *Russkiy Kovcheg/Russian Ark* (2002) famously features no internal film editing, but unfolds in one remarkably choreographed shot/take. Entirely computer-generated films, from *Toy Story* (John Lasseter, 1995) to *Beowulf* (Robert Zemeckis, 2007) – not to mention traditional 'drawn' animated features – do not literally employ conventional lighting methods, yet could hardly be excluded from classification as 'films' on this basis.[23] Any understanding of film must approach its signifying codes as engaged in a process of dialogical interaction and competition; only in this way can the diversity and productive internal contradiction of cinematic representation be accounted for. For instance, sound and image are often at odds with each other, as Ella Shohat and Robert Stam (1985) have explored from a Bakhtinian position. Along these lines, *What's Up Tiger Lily?* (Senkichi Taniguchi/Woody Allen, 1966) exploits the unstable relationship of sound and image to comic ends, Allen taking an obscure Japanese thriller and redubbing it. This process not only inevitably changes the narrative course of the film, but also generates comedy from an ironic celebration of the often shoddy process of dubbing foreign films for English-speaking markets. This availability of the sound/image relation for parodic retooling lives on as the core conceit of British comedy series like *Director's Commentary* (2004) and *Badly Dubbed Porn* (2005–).

The spaces that exist between layers of signification in the film text, and the complex meaning processes that they accommodate, can sometimes be manipulated to support institutional authority in a way that delimits potential readings. Thomas Elsaesser discusses the re-editing of John Huston's *Red Badge of Courage* (1951), wherein a more linear application of musical cues was appended to assuage MGM's concern that the narrative drive typical of a war film was absent (Elsaesser, 1990, p.50). In this case, directorial intention is subverted by studio manipulation of one signifying mechanism over another, demonstrating the complex relationship that obtains between cinematic codes, and how shifting the internal dialogic stresses of codes can be used to enforce a monologic homogeneity. It is in areas like these where Metz's premise disappoints: simultaneously too narrow in that it omits broad categories of films, and too broad in its focus on what is regular and uniform in film 'language' while failing to supply analytical tools to help appraise the individual text within its own unique socio-ideological context.

Psychoanalytic and apparatus theories: the positioning of the spectator

To stress Metz's debt to Saussure is no doubt to run the risk of simplifying his overall contribution; his later explicitly psychoanalytical work on the 'Imaginary Signifier' introduces a much more fluid vision of how signifying processes characterize cinema as a form of 'institutionalised social activity' (1994, p.49). But the persistence of a Saussurean unity of language in the singularity of the textual filmic system envisioned by Metz emerges as a defining problem when related to Bakhtin's 'more relativistic and pluralistic' take on language operations (Stam, 1989, p.53). Stephen Heath's wise observation that the parameters of the 1970s film theory debate were insufficiently aware of history is worth looking at, for it equally alludes to the pitfalls of over-schematicism that hamper attempts to counter that ahistoricality:

> Debate around film often [...] deadlocks on either 'the text itself', its meaning 'in it', or else the text as non-existent other than 'outside itself', in the particular responses it happens to engage from any individual or individual audience – the text 'closed' or 'open'. The reading (viewing, reception, understanding, reaction) of a film, however, must be seen as neither constrained absolutely nor free absolutely but historical
>
> (1981, p.243)

Film theory's 'discourse of positionality' (Stam, 1989, p.53), perhaps peaking in the mid-1970s but bearing an active influence on developments in the field for at least a decade after this,[24] was strongly imprinted with a specific political slant (inspired by the revolutionary moment of France during 1968 and intellectually in thrall to Marxism of the Althusserian stripe). The result was the widespread circulation of a model of film viewing as predicated on the positioning, fixing or force-feeding of desirable images to a passive consumer by the dominant cultural order. In this paradigm, staked out in influential theories such as those around the 'apparatus' proposed in 1968 by Jean-Louis Baudry (Baudry, 1999) or, a few years later, Laura Mulvey's feminist work on the gaze (Mulvey, 1999), mainstream narrative film, in particular, is represented as a vehicle for social conditioning through the reproduction of certain ideological myths. Laudable though it is to deploy an ideological study of cinema in the service of social critique, an obvious limitation that arises from the methods employed by the subject-position tradition is that the spectator, both as an individual and as part of an amorphous, easily duped 'mass audience', is too readily seen as a mindless, passive vessel for the filtering through of cultural myths. The spectator is here denied any degree of control or choice over his or her part in the cinematic process, which is figured as unidirectional, a linear passage of meaning from text to consumer. Fixed in a culturally desirable position, any trace of social dissatisfaction in the viewer is 'entertained' away, and what is more, s/he apparently enters into this contract fully aware of the nature of its constraints; even armed with the psychoanalytic concept of disavowal,[25] no cultural theorist has yet been able to explain how a megabudgeted 'surefire hit' such as *Hudson Hawk* (Michael Lehmann, 1991) or *Speed Racer* (Larry and Andy Wachowski, 2008) can fail at the box office even with an apparently 'naive' mass audience to exploit. In the version of spectatorship put forward by apparatus theory, the spectator has no response, no reply, no real work to do in the construction of the film as signifying discourse; his or her role is 'just' to watch. Such theories presented themselves as revealing the interpellatory promise of film entertainment, wherein techniques like suture persuade the subject into assuming a self-image as the 'ground of intelligibility' (Heath, 1981, p.239), as all the while the system functions to remove all major interpretive decisions from their hands.

Admittedly, this is an extreme characterization of the rigidity of spectator/text relations in such theory. However, reverberations of apparatus/subject-position models and their psychoanalytic/Marxist underpinnings continued to be felt in many strands of film theory, justified by such (necessary) contentions as Mulvey's call, in her 1975 article 'Visual Pleasure and Narrative Cinema', for the dismantling of the masculinized system of identification operating in mainstream cinema. Clearly, Hollywood does have a role to play in the maintenance of the social structure, as do all forms of artistic expression, and its construction of a politically conservative, homogeneous formula clearly exercises a strong influence on the tastes and expectations of a global audience (in parallel with its marketing and distribution operation, which dictates availability and access to film on a global basis). Systems such as genre, in one sense, teach us to accept what we are given by Hollywood, and even to ask for more. This fact is adumbrated in Metz's formulation of the two 'machines' operating within cinema as institution: the primary commercial one of publicity and production, and secondarily, the mental conditioning of the psyche to experience the text as pleasurable and thus guarantee the wish for more of the same (Metz, 1994, p.7). However, the problem remains that a conception of mainstream cinematic practice as entailing an intellectual 'petrification of the spectator' (MacCabe, 1985, p.54) robs him or her of the dialogic discursive involvement that, according to Bakhtin, characterizes our orientation to any form of utterance. Bakhtin would have it that any meaning is constructed through the gates of dialogue, and that discursive forms that claim the status of the 'authoritative word' (DIN, 342), that seek to suppress the response of the addressee, will ultimately fail and wither in a social context because they cannot evolve, are semantically 'static and dead' (343). However, the field of film studies took significant notice of models that posited a spectator confined within the ideological strictures of popular film's address. Ideas underlying such accounts were permitted to mature into orthodoxies that, inevitably, invited opposition and alternative models of reception that looked elsewhere than semiotics and psychoanalysis for their bases. We will first revisit a foundational case of the former, then go on to look at approaches that embody the latter.

Laura Mulvey's 'Visual Pleasure and Narrative Cinema', published 34 years ago but still, deservedly, widely taught as a starting-point for debates around visuality and gender representation, draws heavily on the classical Freudian tropes of identification, voyeurism and fetishism. Mulvey considers that mainstream narrative film operates as an illusion of plenitude and sexual mastery, empowering the male spectator through heroic identification and masking the castration anxiety evoked by the presence of the female (as signifier of sexual difference by the lack of the penis) through a complex structure of looks. Three looks predominate in the cinema: 'that of the camera as it records the pro-filmic event, that of the audience as it watches the final product, and that of the characters at each other within the screen illusion' (Mulvey, 1999, p.33).[26] By subordinating the first two looks to the third, narrative cinema removes from the field of contemplation both the material fact of the operations of recording and projection and the viewing of the spectator as a critical, stand-alone process. For the narrative film to succeed, the spectator must be suspended in a fantasy world, unaware of the workings of technology and ideology, blind to both the constructed nature of his 'own' vantage point and to the existence of other, more critically detached perspectives. In the interests of maintaining the smooth, illusory flow of the diegesis, woman is reduced to an abstract signifier of voyeuristic contemplation and pleasure, devoid of depth and reality, bearing the 'flatness, the quality of a cut-out or icon' (Mulvey, 1999, p.27). In this way, the invocation of the crisis of castration in the male viewer threatened by the represented female is controlled and annulled.

Mulvey's archetypal cinematic figure for the spectator, bound into position and oblivious to the enforced character of his passivity, is L.B. Jeffries (James Stewart), the wheelchair-bound protagonist of Alfred Hitchcock's *Rear Window* (1954). Mulvey intentionally loads the example with certain assumptions by selecting Hitchcock, perhaps the major cinematic theorist-practitioner of voyeurism and erotic identity games, for analysis. Jeffries, for Mulvey, metaphorically doubles the cinematic spectator:

> Jeffries is the audience, the events in the apartment block opposite correspond to the screen. As he watches, an erotic dimension is added to his look, a central image to the drama. His girlfriend Lisa had been of little interest to him, more or less a drag, so long as she remained on the spectator side. When she crosses the barrier between his room and the block opposite, their relationship is reborn erotically [...] [H]is enforced inactivity, binding him to the seat as a spectator, puts him squarely in the fantasy position of the cinema audience
>
> (Mulvey, 1999, p.31)

Mulvey's reading of Jeffries' scopophilic tendencies, and the erotic charge he feels from seeing Lisa (Grace Kelly) in danger, is persuasive. However, Mulvey overlooks the fact that the text depicts more than one spectator fascinated by the goings-on in the apartment block; another 'look' is active, that of Lisa herself, who is denied any agency in the narrative by Mulvey. She actually initiates the plan to investigate the murderer Thorwald's apartment while he is out, to Jeffries' initial protests. Moreover, Lisa is encouraged and aided in her exploits by another formidable female, the insurance company nurse, Stella (Thelma Ritter). A reading of Hitchcock as empowering, rather than victimizing, his female characters still seems rather problematic despite the reassessments of recent critical views,[27] and is rather difficult to sustain given the necessary brevity of the present analysis. But what cannot be denied about *Rear Window* is that it is Lisa who negotiates her own entrance into the masculinized game of cat-and-mouse between Thorwald and Jeffries; who decides for herself that the fixed position of watching is unsatisfactory; and who takes it upon herself to transcend the static role of love interest and impel the narrative forward. It may be true that Jeffries uses Lisa's plight for some kind of erotic stimulation that finds its parallel with the fetishistic gaze of the cinema spectator, and indeed that her motivation for going through with the whole business is to maintain Jeffries' attention. But the power of Lisa's look and her ability to translate contemplation into action (and to turn Jeffries, who has accused her of leading a frivolous life, into a powerless watcher) should not be simply discounted for the convenience of Mulvey's reading.

At the risk of sounding pedantic for taking Mulvey to task over her neglect of the character Lisa in *Rear Window*, there is nevertheless an important point to be drawn out here about the deficiencies in Mulvey's analysis. By limiting the possibility of viewer identification to Jeffries, Mulvey shuts off other options for the spectator, precluding the possibility that spectators of either gender might instead choose to identify with Lisa. Mulvey contends that strategies such as the 'skilful use of identification processes and liberal use of subjective camera from the point of view of the male protagonist' (31) are used by Hitchcock to draw the spectator into sharing his 'uneasy gaze'. However, voyeuristic associations are layered onto the film in such an overdetermined fashion – Jeffries is a news photographer by trade, Lisa works in the fashion industry and is seen modelling her own stock, thus doubly establishing her as a site of male erotic contemplation[28] – that it is possible to imagine Hitchcock inviting us to read against the grain of the text's ostensible gender values in order to decipher a dialogic undercurrent beneath the smooth monologic surface. After all, Jeffries can *only* look; his gaze is one of impotence rather than mastery, as he needs Lisa's physical intervention to progress with bringing Thorwald to justice (and thus legitimize his own voyeuristic instincts). She is the one who moves freely throughout the textual spaces, the agent of much of the action, and the one who precipitates narrative resolution, a pro-active presence rather than merely a 'passive image of visual perfection' (31). Could Lisa embody an alternative, more dynamic representative of the spectator? At one point she actually refers to herself as a guest at the 'opening night' of the final week of Jeffries' confinement in a leg cast, commenting that she has 'bought out the house' of tickets. Hitchcock took care to cast the popular Grace Kelly, who had memorably led a battered Gary Cooper into the sunset at the end of *High Noon* (Fred Zinneman, 1952), in a role that could easily have been filled by a less appealing actress who would have exhibited more deference to the star power of James Stewart, suggesting that the character was always intended to hold her own opposite the male star.[29]

The case for the 'gaze' put forward so influentially by Mulvey in 'Visual Pleasure' – building on but also reacting to apparatus theory's psychoanalytic reading of the production of an exclusively 'masculine cine-subject whose desire is activated' by the address of mainstream film (Stam et al, 1992, p.174) – establishes a conception of subject positions in cinema as fixed and pre-formed. Despite the motivation of her paper to reveal the 'psychical obsessions' (Mulvey, 1999, p.23) of the socially produced mainstream cinema so that alternative cinema may structure itself in counterpoint, a concomitant effect is the negation of any possibility of individual choice or ideological resistance on the part of the spectator of mainstream movies. This latter factor, it must be said, was promptly and numerously challenged (see Bordwell and Carroll, 1996, p.8), a reaction that prompted Mulvey's own revisitation of the original paper in 1981 (Mulvey, 1989). Mulvey's conception of the artistic strategies of narrative cinema as dedicated to maintaining the sexual status quo was provocative but also limiting, a reading that perhaps presumes too much on the side of the spectator without ever really considering their individual response to the text in detail. The assumption that the female spectator can engage with the text on its own terms only tells half of the story. As certain approaches that followed hard on apparatus theory's 1970s peak strived to show, the pleasure one takes from the text is sometimes at odds with the pleasure calculated and allotted for us by the controlling artistic presence; ideas of 'resistant readers' replace those of subversive texts (Bordwell and Carroll, 1996, p.10). An example: a number of untrustworthy, deceitful, even murderous female characters in the *film noir* genre, explicitly demonized and punished by their male directors, have embodied some of the most enduring identifications available to women viewers and critics in the history of cinema. These include Barbara Stanwyck as Phyllis Dietrichson in *Double Indemnity* (Billy Wilder, 1944), Joan Crawford as Mildred Pierce in Michael Curtiz' 1945 film of the same name, and Rita Hayworth as the titular protagonist of *Gilda* (Charles Vidor, 1946). Subsequent generations have found layers to these characters that put their representation at odds with the masculinized logic controlling questions of morality and criminality in the films (see Gledhill, 2000, and Chapter 4 of this book). It is precisely the willingness of spectators to identify with these 'undesirable' characters – in new, dialogically charged contexts and against the grain of a given text's historically situated ideological stance (such as that shaped by the films' initial, Hays Code-era viewing conditions) – that makes such new readings possible. As Bakhtin points out in 'Discourse in the Novel', the fictional image that appears single-voiced can eventually yield up another double-voiced meaning, long undetected, through the careful application of a contextual analysis that reflects the preoccupations of the present era of reading as well as past ones (DIN, p.374).

By bringing new dialogical assumptions and inflections to the film, we contribute to the ongoing life and relevance of the text, achieving this by – sometimes – 'positioning' ourselves at an angle contrary to the vantage point deemed desirable by the film and its prevailing ideology, by stepping into the shoes of another dialogical perspective. In this we are fulfilling Stella's rather Bakhtinian edict in *Rear Window* when she, remonstrating with Jeffries for his unhealthy interest in the neighbourhood's business, complains, 'We've become a race of peeping toms. What people oughta do is get outside their own home and look in for a change.' Mulvey's approach in 'Visual Pleasure and Narrative Cinema' is dependent on a fixed, inert and singular conception of the spectator that misses a crucial distinction elaborated by fellow *Screen* writer Colin MacCabe:

> Applied to the film this is the distinction between the spectator as viewer, the comforting 'I', the fixed point, and the spectator as he or she is caught up in the play of events on the screen, as he or she 'utters', 'enounces' the film. Hollywood cinema is largely concerned to make these two coincide so that we can ignore what is at risk. But this coincidence can never be perfect because it is exactly in the divorce between the two that the film's existence is possible
> (1985, p.68).

Rather than dismantling this structure of coincidence, much of 1970s film theory perhaps unwittingly strengthens it; by overlooking what Stam calls the distinct 'dialogical angle' (1992, p.43) brought by a specific viewing community to a film, such theory fails to acknowledge that '[t]he textually constructed reader/spectator does not necessarily coincide with the sociohistorical reader/spectator' (43). Thinking through such roles outside of a politically specific 'discourse of positionality' (one that, ironically, can be seen to channel power away from the already disempowered spectator) was a challenge to film studies after 1975. This challenge created an opening for lines of thought that offered ways of circumventing the familiar oppositions functioning to diminish the position of popular film (see Jancovich, 1995, pp.144–5). As we explore these, what must be avoided, as ever, is an opportunistic promotion of dialogism as a corrective for all the ideological inadequacies of Hollywood film. Lynne Pearce is mindful of the need for us to check the heady feelings of readerly power that emerge when contemplating a text through the liberating prism of dialogism. She advocates the keeping in mind of all of the complexities of text/reader relations, suggesting that critical rehabilitation must be tempered with the recognition that the text, in its polyphonic multiple address, is liable to promise us a 'special relationship' while all the time entertaining, even preferring, other interpretative positions. As Pearce describes her experience, 'the text I pretended was mine was all the time in dialogue with someone else' (Pearce, 1995, p.89). The figure of the passive spectator tricked into singular, enforced interpretation by the controlling text may be a rigid and inadequate paradigm, but, as strong as the impulse to rewrite the terms of textual engagement can be, wrenching texts from the conditions of their historical production must not be allowed to pass for a dialogical reading strategy. If we do allow this, we are practising our own, subtle form of monologization. As Pearce puts it:

> While I, the reader, exist in dialogic relationship with the text (any text), I am nevertheless *positioned* by it, and the challenge and excitement of the reading process depends on my not knowing, in advance, if it will embrace or reject me: position me as an ally or an antagonist [...] Even as the text positions me, so may I (re)position my relationship to it.
>
> (1995, p.92)

Making meaning, consuming meaning: Neo-formalist and Cultural Studies models

The routes pursued in the 1970s by *Screen* critics like Laura Mulvey, Colin MacCabe and others (which came to be collectively known as 'screen theory'[30]) were in some significant respects more flexible than those propounded by the Christian Metz of *Language and Cinema*; as we have commented, Mulvey went on to theorize the female spectator's problematic identificatory 'transvestism' more deeply in a later paper, while MacCabe (1985) recognized the potential of certain films, like those of Roberto Rossellini, to invite the participation of the spectator without predetermining the conditions of their interpretation. Yet in one crucial area – the understanding of film as a one-way linear flow of information – things moved on little from Metz. For Mulvey, the 'gaze' locked the male cinema spectator into a mute, unquestioning economy of vision that hinged on the propensity of the erotic female to 'freeze' the action; for female viewers, pleasure as inscribed in the conformist text depended on taking up the same, unsatisfactory series of identifications. In MacCabe's case, mainstream cinema peddled a realist practice that was reactionary at heart, the spectator assuming a position of pseudo-dominance into which s/he is manipulated by the controlling discourse or metalanguage, placing them 'outside the realm of contradiction and of action – outside of production' (MacCabe, 1985, p.54). In these two versions of spectatorship, the subject is paralysed, or to use MacCabe's term, 'petrified' by the apparatus of the cinema. Their responses go unsolicited by the text and play no part in the construction of meaning, except on the perfunctory level of a Pavlovian recognition of certain conventions and their bearing on narrative. The spectator is blind to ideology, indeed the real conditions of their lives are not engaged with at all, but repressed in an illusion of plenitude and omnipotence. The unwillingness of other scholars to accept this condition of blindness as intrinsic to the act of viewing drew reactions that were based in both aesthetic and political objections; these responses would strive for alternative, *active* models of film comprehension and interpretation. The challenging of apparatus/screen theory at this time was perhaps stoked by a feeling that intricate theory had a tendency to neglect the human centre of film viewing. A similar back-to-basics feeling was expressed more recently by Patrick Fuery, who notes that, notwithstanding postmodern and post-structuralist arguments which place the film viewer in various social and textual networks that make the apprehension of meaning a matter of shifting contingency, accounts of reception must not eliminate the 'point where what the spectator sees, and how he/she reacts, is derived from the unique position of their subjectivity' (2000, p.113). One of the most important critical proposals for restoring a sense of agency, control and rationality to film viewing can nevertheless be questioned on the basis of how it can account for that subjectivity in an adequately complex way.

David Bordwell (1985) critiqued MacCabe by deploying the Bakhtinian principle of dialogism and its 'montage of voices' (p.17) as a corrective to MacCabe's postulation of a single metalanguage, ideologically ruling the aesthetic operations of mainstream realist cinema, undisturbed by other voices. Bordwell tracks such incorrect moves to the assimilation of an impoverished theoretical base undergirding the models of language that were introduced into film studies during the semiotic phase (1985, pp.21–5).[31] The varied phases of Bordwell's own career have had a huge impact upon the field, encompassing a call for a model of narrative theory that does not have to conceptually depend on signs and the linguistic-film equation (Bordwell, 1985); a metacritical dissection of the rhetorical protocols of interpretive film criticism (Bordwell, 1996); and a polemical statement of the 'end' of the interpretive film theory project (1996, with Noël Carroll). What Bordwell has clearly tried to do in his interventions is interrogate and (to an extent) expose the role of critics in (to borrow Carroll's term) 'mystifying movies'[32] beyond the point where the strategies and competences needed to comprehend them can remain useful; that is, where the business of 'reading' films is moved into a codified realm, beyond a pragmatic, common-sense view of their functions and motivations in engaging a viewer in narrative. This is not the place to rehearse Bordwell's acknowledged debt to Russian Formalism (see Bordwell, 1985), nor to connect the Formalist thread that runs through projects such as *The Classical Hollywood Cinema* (1985, with Janet Staiger and Kristin Thompson) in light of Bordwell's more ambitious stated aim to consolidate a tradition of 'historical poetics' for application to cinema study.[33] However, Bordwell's work is worth dwelling on here both because its investment in the connection between narrative technique and active spectatorship mirrors aspects of a Bakhtinian approach, and also because in disciplinary terms, it emerges as perhaps the most significant challenge to the core psychoanalytic, semiotic and political underpinnings of screen theory. With this work, Bordwell, along with frequent collaborators Noël Carroll and Kristin Thompson plus a few other fellow travellers, has established a clear position in contradistinction to most of the axioms, methods and foci of the tradition(s) he has variously described as 'Interpretation, Inc' (1996, p.21), 'Grand Theory' (Bordwell and Carroll, 1996, p.3) and 'SLAB theory'.[34]

Bordwell distils the spirit of the Russian Formalist tradition that animates his work in a positive contrast of that school's 'vigorous, if variegated and incomplete, approach to studying the work in multiple contexts' with the less adequately contextualized 'brands of continental structuralism' that drive the 'SLAB' agenda (1985, p.xii). Despite this protest, the work in narratology, cognitivism and 'historical poetics' that has clustered around Bordwell has been challenged regularly enough on the grounds of sacrificing historical value to micro-aesthetic matters (see Bhaskar, 2003) that a mild defence was warranted. Slightly unexpectedly, one was provided by a distinguished voice of cultural studies, Henry Jenkins (1995). Simply grouping Bakhtin together with the orthodox Russian Formalist names of Viktor Shklovsky and Boris Eichenbaum is a contentious move considering the history, already mentioned, of attempts to move beyond and vigorously critique the premises of Formalism from within the Circle (notably, with regard to what Bakhtin conceived as an exaggerated inclination to separate art from the realm of life and ethics).[35] However, Jenkins does it, going on to argue that for Bordwell as for the original proponents of the Formal Method, 'historical explanations must start with the work itself and move gradually towards its most immediate contexts' (1995, p.100). This focus on the 'work itself' is the essence of how the range of methods used within the 'neo-formalist' approach to narrative film study are calibrated and given purpose, for all the headline value of 'multiple contexts'.

Narrative is seen as organizing filmic expression, yet the idea of a narrative 'discourse' orchestrated and enunciated by an ideological agency behind the text is resisted (Bordwell, 1985, p.21). The resulting image is not one of a victim being stitched into an imaginary – and unwittingly ideological – attitude of filmic pleasure but rather of a conscious and rational agent embracing the ambiguity of story and resolving to master it, much as we would negotiate any perceptual or epistemological challenge. Narratives can be composed in order to 'defeat the perceiver's search for coherence' as well as facilitate and ultimately reward it (Bordwell, 1985, p.38), but the problems and puzzles in fiction are surmountable through the application and honing of the same sorts of perceptual skills that guide us through everyday life. Film comprehension is what narratologist Edward Branigan calls *'a perceptual activity that organizes data into a special pattern which represents and explains experience'* (italics in original; 1998, p.3), that is, a knowledge-based activity entered into willingly, with defined goals on the part of the perceiver. To the extent that competence in any field will develop with experience and repeated exposure – a point Bordwell reiterates in his discussion of the artisanal routines of film criticism in *Making Meaning* (1996, p.250) – the perceiver remains in control of and responsible for their own experience, arguably retaining more agency than the 'petrified' spectator of some apparatus/subject-positioning accounts. Within cognitive approaches, the tools and prisms through which narrative comprehension can be observed and understood become crucial, manifesting in a language of 'perceivers', 'cues', 'hypotheses' and 'schema' (Bordwell 1985, Branigan 1998 *passim*), alongside originary Formalist terms like *fabula* and *sjuzhet*.[36] The concept of aesthetic 'norms' is developed by Bordwell from the work of the Formalist Jan Mukarovsky, assuming a specific application in *The Classical Hollywood Cinema* (norms are marshalled by the commercial classical Hollywood institution into a system that guarantees intelligibility and regulates stylistic and financial excess), as well as more generally running through the proposed methodology of historical poetics (Jenkins, 1995, p.102–4). Terms like these replace the familiar conceptual resources of sign and identification associated with 'grand' film theory; indeed, the main feature distinguishing Bordwell's critical enterprise from the dominant language of semiotic/psychoanalytic theory (and the same could be said of certain representation-based currents of cultural studies) is that it has proceeded without any recourse to the concept of signification.[37] As Robert Stam has noted, the 'cognitive theory' produced on this basis – which is arguably associated with the Bordwell of *Narration in the Fiction Film* more than any other figure or volume – lacks a general capacity to deal with politics because it treats the concept of ideology as an auxiliary to the signifier/signified relation and thus as unnecessary. Thus, '[i]n cognitive theory, a raceless, genderless, classless understander/interpreter encounters abstract schemata' (Stam, 2000, p.241); film viewing in this account takes on the properties of a problem-solving process where the intellect is stimulated, but the work that the film undertakes in line with or against the values of the human engaging with it at a certain juncture in history is absent.

Bordwell throws out the apparatus of signification because it is the fulcrum of a tradition of implicit and symptomatic reading of texts that he finds unsatisfactory. In place of this he promotes an approach based on the retrieval of referential and explicit meanings (comprehension rather than interpretation), which defines his work and that of others working in neo-formalism and cognitivism (Bhaskar, 2003). As we have seen, Bakhtin expressed antipathy to the inflexible and abstract elements of Saussure's attitude to language, but this did not stop him from pronouncing that 'only signs [...] have meaning' (PT, p.113). That the step from language to discourse that makes Bakhtinian analysis possible requires the sign can be clearly seen in Voloshinov's remark that '[t]he domain of ideology coincides with the domain of signs. They equate with one another. Wherever a sign is present, ideology is present, too. *Everything ideological possesses semiotic value*' (MPL, p.10, italics in original). The neo-formalist/cognitive 'take' on film comprehension engenders a somewhat ideologically neutral process that neither produces social identities nor engages viewers in questioning the 'given' status of such identities, or any other features or fictions of our social lives. This would be as true if the film was intended as 'just' entertainment or something else, and is a problem, for even if we accept the proposal that films are stable, comprehensible entities (which is more of a Metzian view than a Bakhtinian one), spectators are different and produce a variety of readings which splinter and proliferate into different ideological, value-laden responses. Bordwellian cognitivism is ill-equipped to deal with differentiation of this kind because, even in its more subtle manifestations, it depends upon a certain universality of response where a competent perceiver either 'gets' each inferential move the film invites or does not. What happens when the viewer, desirous of coherence, is defeated by the narrative obstacles presented by an abstruse text? In dialogism, a revision and recuperation of a monologic meaning is possible because the sign relation allows for the activation of counter-readings; however, the cognitive scheme seems to assume that the viewer will simply walk away from the film text, perhaps returning when their competence has sharpened (or their tastes have changed). Meaning as an evolving event is suspended because polysemy demands a social frame (and vice versa). The existence of the sign, for Voloshinov, is the materialization of 'the conditions [...] of social communication' (MPL, p.13), a tight relationship that Bordwell dismembers with the predictable result that, in the 'bigger picture' of film reception, the significance of such conditions is radically reduced.

Despite his aversion to the approaches and methods underlying them, Bordwell does find space within the generally antagonistic *Making Meaning* to acknowledge that the major accomplishments of the 1970s' cine-semiotic and subject-positioning traditions (he appears to have in mind essays or monographs by Baudry, Mulvey, Metz, and perhaps Heath) represent 'last gasp' exemplars of their kind of criticism, followed by a deluge of more 'ordinary' variations and slight refinements on those breakthroughs (1996, p.261). In the book, Bordwell itemizes many of the attractions of interpretive film criticism and theory both to readers (whose emotions are said to 'crystallize' around roles offered by the critic via rhetorical techniques) and to the institutional machine of academe, which keeps the whole ball rolling by training new generations of film scholars in the orthodoxies and conceptual tools of the trade that, for Bordwell, continue to govern the field (1996, pp.22–3).[38] With these concerns at its centre, *Making Meaning* itself cannot be described as a text that deals with questions of film reception; rather, it takes as its object the spread and unjustified domination of one powerful school of thought and associated methods on film studies. As the author of such a detailed discussion of the rhetorical address of film theory to its consumer, Bordwell is clearly aware that all studies of reception sooner or later attract criticism for picturing one ideal recipient for a given message. The approaches that have appeared under the neo-formalist banner seem to produce the outlines of a cinema viewer associated with a certain *type* of film, those bearing the traits of complex narrative and lack of obviousness. Although the wider principles associated with historical poetics are seen by Jenkins as having the potential to 'liberate [...] the study of popular cinema' through the evaluative neutrality of the concept of norms (1995, p.106), the reliance of cognitive film theory on a certain kind of narrative appears to Martin Barker as an elitist move, coding the 'difficult' art film as valid (Barker with Austin, 2000, p.37; p.13). This might be unsurprising given Stam's description of the original Formalist outlook as privileging 'deviations from aesthetic and technical norms of the kind proffered by avant-garde movements' in literature (2000, p.51). Barker pinpoints this problem in the reliance on *defamiliarization*, a concept that is handed down through the

Russian Formalist legacy. Barker views defamiliarization as over-stating art's 'capacity to undo routinism' (Barker with Austin, 2000, p.33). This leads off into the presumption that each experience of an artwork must surprise and shock the consumer into a more critically aware state of perception, an idea which does not help to combat the charge of elitism: the different pleasures associated with more simply constructed popular films are again relegated to the sidelines. Ray Carney has also criticized this stress on the centrality of defamiliarization because it 'trivializes' the meaningfulness of aspects of film that are not immediately related to the spectator's appreciation of formal play, such as emotional, moral or educational values (quoted in Bhaskar, 2003).

The disposal of the semiotic concept and the reluctance to understand the place of metaphor in accounts of filmic communication leave a deficit in terms of the suitability of Bordwell's approach for handling questions pertaining to ideology (Stam, 2000, pp.238–9). By contrast, dialogism regards the accrual of differentiated, clashing interpretations that can arise because of the polysemic nature of artistic communication as an indicator of the health and relevance of a text. This is a commitment to polysemic meaning – 'the dialogizing influence [words] have on each other' and their semantic 'unfinishedness' (DIN, p.346) – that Bordwell explicitly rules out, on the grounds that, if multiple meanings are encouraged around a text (as critical readings and re-readings mushroom around films in his example of the scholarly debate upon *Psycho*, Alfred Hitchcock, 1960), an uncontrollable escalation will result and 'no meaning will ever be difficult enough' (1996, p.246). A comment like this upholds the concern of Robert Stam that cognitivism and other strands of the neo-formalist project perhaps retreat too far in their withdrawal from the 'high-flying' speculation of Grand Theory and end up reducing the film experience to mere 'physiological response and cognitive processing' (2000, p.244).

Although Bordwell's critique of cultural studies, at least in its academic doctrinal form, focuses on its continuities with, and failure to produce a genuinely alternative set of premises and tools to, screen theory (Bordwell and Carroll, 1996, pp.12–26), many of the shaping concerns of cultural studies are actually built on convictions that are rather alien to apparatus/subject-positioning approaches. These underpinnings have a lot in common with key impulses in the Bakhtinian project, such as the social grounding of communication exchange, the relativity and impermanence of semantic boundaries and discursive positions, and an attitude to textual consumption that stresses choice and agency. Theorists like Pierre Bourdieu reveal how discourses acquire class accents, and the

Bakhtin Circle indicates a way of reading to accompany this knowledge, through which we can 'expose' discourses and prepare them for the best use our own interpretation and interests can make of them.[39] Cultural studies perspectives have generally been more comfortable with locating the consumption of texts and the derivation of meaning from them as activities (or sometimes rituals) that take their place within the realm of everyday life. Modern cultural studies tends to withhold value-laden preconceptions of 'quality' (bringing into question influential binaries in culture categorization that have come down from mass culture theory and the Frankfurt School[40]); however, the emphasis on the everyday does more than just render popular, mass-mediated texts as valid objects of study, it crucially activates the notion that experiences and sensations gleaned from texts are integrated into a continuum of experience making up the consumer's life.[41] This integration can happen with effects that may be socially determining (on how we dress, behave, or signify our existence in myriad ways), but such effects are only a few of a complex of factors involved in identity formation, which draws upon the subject's whole history, not just their time spent viewing films. There is room in cultural studies for those who feel that most of these factors are imposed, and for those who feel that the most important ones are chosen. A major influence in this area, Bourdieu provides an ideological impetus for questioning ideas of learned competences that appear in cognitivism, noting that 'the ideal of "pure" perception of a work of art qua work of art is the product of the enunciation and systematization of the principles of specifically aesthetic legitimacy which accompany the constituting of a relatively autonomous artistic field' (2003, p.30); these principles have the effect of drawing up fields (ones of academic study for instance) that may function to remove the work performed in interpreting film from the ambient power relations structuring everyday life. Bourdieu tells us that '[A]rt and cultural consumption are predisposed, consciously and deliberately or not, to fulfil a social function of legitimating social differences' (2003, p.7). Through class and other 'principles of division' (468), the valuation of culture is set up to keep great art in its own category, thus preserving the meanings and distinctions that are needed to legitimate the status quo. As Strinati points out, Bourdieu's discussion reveals how the stratification of tastes that organizes culture into 'high' and 'low' or 'elite' and 'mass' sectors truly reflects 'the social positions of particular groups [and] not universal values' (2000, p.76).

Here, the problems that exercise the Bakhtin Circle around language bear fruit in ways that directly galvanize cultural studies. Taste 'stands guard over the boundaries of a language', according to Craig Brandist in his elucidation of the work of the linguist Karl Vossler;[42] such an image of the forces that stabilize culture tallies readily with the Bakhtin–Voloshinov view of language as value-laden battleground, one that is shared by the Italian Marxist Antonio Gramsci (Ives, 2008, p.162), an essential thinker for the formation of cultural studies (as we shall see). Bakhtin makes clear that words – by extension, texts – have an internal force and momentum that can shape 'their own stylistic profile and tone' (DIN, p.277), but this can only happen in a context of heteroglossia, that is, against an 'environment full of alien words and variously evaluating accents' (277). Both consensus and conflict will result as the word bounces off other discursive surfaces. Studies of language as a vessel for meaning that is made up of some other material (rather than the substance being in the event of the exchange itself) fail to construe what Voloshinov sees as essential: that language has not just a political character that can be stamped onto it, but a political *life*. Ideological value is generated by every activity that goes on within the domain of signs; every ideological sign partakes of the reality it represents rather than simply standing for it (MPL, pp.10–11). It takes a special effort to try to curb this energy, to reify language and make the word into a thing (DIN, p.352); thus, Bakhtin alerts us to the guises that monologism takes. We sense it behind the official, authoritative word that brooks no reply (DIN, p.343), in the 'mythic and magical' attitude that posits a final bonding of a single ideological meaning to language (369); noting once again the kinship with Gramsci, its conformist logic underlies the hegemonic presentation of cultural preferences as universal and 'exemplary' (Brandist, 1996, p.63). Such reifying discourses may attract an aura of authority, but they also stimulate culture into producing dialogic responses that will refresh the heteroglottic proliferation of voices and attempt to 'overcome the official line' (DIN, p.345).

It is his contribution to recognizing and understanding such dynamics of opposition and resistance that cements Voloshinov's place in a triad of influences – alongside Bourdieu and Gramsci – that provides the platform for the important work produced by the Centre for Contemporary Cultural Studies at Birmingham University in the 1970s (as noted by Willis, 1995, pp.178–9; Ives, 2008, p.53). In order to resolve some political inadequacies of earlier British culturalist work (the tendency to see 'Americanized' mass culture as inauthentic; the passivity engendered by Althusserian structuralism's take on subjectivity), cultural studies essentially swapped brands of Marxism (to Gramsci and away from Althusser). For this new direction, Voloshinov's work on the multi-accented sign proved the most pertinent of all the material generated by the Bakhtin Circle.

Cultural studies utilizes Gramsci in the argument that the decisions that stratify culture are subject to the consent of the subordinate classes, and thus not permanent. Hegemony describes what is achieved when this consent is granted: the imposition of official ideas without the necessity for the implementation of force. But hegemony is inherently unstable, thus the dominant class occasionally has to remake itself and its messages to take a more popular form (Willis, 1995, pp.179–80). Hegemony's shaping of linguistic environments under a posited 'exemplary' mode of cultural speech tempers the optimistic conviction, in some cultural studies quarters, that the working class can use popular culture for radical purposes with an awareness that, although the textual sign is an 'arena of the class struggle' (MPL, p.23), sometimes victory does not go the way of the masses. In concepts like Stuart Hall's negotiated, preferred and oppositional readings (Hall, 1999), cultural studies recognizes that compromise is a feature of culture; as Staiger puts it, 'communication systems may function so well for the dominant class that hegemony often exists' (2002, p.60). When norms are absorbed into the bloodstream of communication structures, popular culture will find it harder to play its relativizing role, yet can still deploy its subjugated status with strategic 'irony and [...] sarcasm' (Brandist, 1996, p.63) in order to deflate the distance and pomposity of ruling culture, opening up a potential moment of subversive 'double-voicing'. More pertinently for our account of cultural studies, what the Bakhtin–Voloshinov notion of 'structured polysemy' (Staiger, 2002, p.62) palpably unlocks is a conception of differential readings that goes far beyond a simple pluralism that sees all significations and interpretations as equal, instead recognizing the ideologically soaked, transformative effects of communication and representation upon reality (Willis, 1995, p.183). In this vein, Martin Barker (1994) employs Voloshinov's work on the materiality of the sign as an approach to utterances of many kinds, from 'pub talk' to the artistically framed speech of broadcasts and comic books. Voloshinov's work helps Barker to raise the idea of a 'contract' that obtains between text and reader and which must reflect the interests of both, within a sphere of varying ideological forces. This approach contains a flavour of Gramscian hegemony allied to the influence of Voloshinov (Strinati, 2000, pp.253–4).

Two-way textuality?

Although many of the tenets and outcomes of 'screen theory' were interrogated and revised by cultural studies and attacked by the Bordwellian camp (see Staiger, 2002, pp.60–2), noteworthy work on spectatorship maintained a use for select psychoanalytic findings as well as the general tools of semiotics. In this, feminist inflections remained key in discussions of the gendering of cinema as address and institution (albeit more regularly considered alongside, and as interlaced with, other socio-historical identity factors like sexuality and race).[43] Feminist film theory became infused with methods and ideas from cultural studies, moving, as Jane Arthurs contends, fairly decisively on from Laura Mulvey's account of spectator positioning to an approach marked by 'more emphasis on the ways in which narrative offers a variety of points of identification which differentially position spectators' (1995, p.96). In this way, Hollywood and its genres were able to be partially rehabilitated as forms operating within patriarchal orthodoxy that could nevertheless be seen to invite subversion of their own ideological principles (Arthurs makes this point in a discussion of the 'feminist road movie' *Thelma and Louise* [Ridley Scott, 1991]; the earlier mentioned example of *film noir* would also serve in this context).

Less rigid than some of his *Screen* colleagues, Stephen Heath (1981) proposed a dynamic conception of spectator and text within a constant process of interaction that approaches more closely the principles of dialogism. Rather than being bound into position and bombarded with images, Heath's spectator is stitched into the very fabric of cinematic discourse itself through techniques such as 'suture' (the use of the shot/reverse shot figure to paper over the crack in spatial coherence resulting from a cut to the viewpoint of a different character).[44] 'Movement' becomes the crucial term in Heath's more narrative-based analysis; the fluid subject both constitutes and is constituted by filmic discourse, held, for sure, within an apparatus of looks and identifications, but nonetheless representing an integral site of power within the textual economy. Heath's subject – defined as the 'play between [the film's] multiple elements, including the social formation in which it finds its existence, and the spectator' (Heath, 1981, p.109) – is a *product* of the conjunction of spectator and text. The movement of the spectator in a dynamic of relations between symbolic and imaginary, text and social context 'makes' the film for Heath:

> [M]eaning is not just constructed 'in' the particular film, meanings circulate between social formation, spectator and film; a film is a series of acts of meaning, the spectator is there in a multiplicity of times.
> (Heath, 1981, p.107)

The desiring spectator 'solicits the image as much as it does him or her'; Heath is mindful of the criticism of previous versions of spectatorship using similar ingredients (1981, p.100). Although it would later draw criticism from some quarters (such as Noël Carroll [1996] and, in a fashion far more nuanced to Heath's original theoretical terms, Dana Polan [1985]), Heath's conception is in the order of a dialectic from which subject and meaning 'come into being together' (Lapsley and Westlake, 1996, p.143), and as such seems to anticipate certain elements of a dialogic model of spectatorship.[45] Indeed, the inclination of Heath's argument matched the general swing of contemporary film theory in the direction of multiple and contextual, rather than binary, models of identification, taking a lead from the integral polysemic principle that had come into the orbit of cultural studies with its taking up of Bakhtin and Voloshinov.

But, outside theory, what evidence is there that cinema represents a two-way system of communication, a dialogue with the viewer, rather than a form of unitary discourse, an utterance cast into a semantic vacuum that demands no response? My stance is that dialogical qualities inhere in reading strategies; in the sense that we adapt these to the institutional/textual address, there is a level at which they can be treated as residing within Hollywood discourse, but I will argue that without activation by the spectator, these tones stay silent. I revisit these issues in Chapter 5 and in the conclusion to this book (the *diversity* of stylistic voices that Hollywood contains is a matter for the case studies, all of which interrogate their texts for the power shifts and loopholes that betray a dialogical presence, even where a surface of monologism seems to prevail). There are commercial practices in Hollywood that solicit the empirical response of the spectator in a way that plays out in narrative construction; one is the test screening. Before their final cut and release, films are screened before audiences who are then asked to evaluate the movie, usually by the method of filling out response cards. Primarily a marketing tactic, to help determine audience demographics and advertising strategies for high budget, wide release films, many texts have nevertheless seen substantial changes at the narrative level as a result of unpopular preview screenings. One example is Ridley Scott's *Blade Runner* (1982), which lost its original downbeat ending and was saddled with a clumsy expository voice-over after studio changes implemented following disappointing previews.[46] Undoubtedly, such a process helps alter power relations between creative and financing interests when it comes to the shape of the filmic narrative in its final release (only the most commercially or critically consistent directors are awarded the power of 'final cut', which involves contractual provisos designed to preclude narrative interference). Certainly, alterations made after test screenings can substantially alter narratives; in the case of *Blade Runner*, the crucial implication that the protagonist Rick Deckard (Harrison Ford) is himself one of the persecuted 'replicants' was erased from the studio cut, and the audience-pleasing suggestion that he escapes to a better life beyond the city, accompanied by his romantic interest, added. The whole sense of Scott's intended original ending – that escape is impossible and that the romance will be shadowed by unknowable replicant 'expiry dates' – was changed to a more positive, less alienating one (in the studio's eyes, at least).

Clearly, although a fraction of the mass audience procures the opportunity to have input into the narrative process by means of the test screening, this practice can be called dialogic in only a limited sense. Changes implemented often displease certain portions of the wider audience, and as the whole process was developed as an aid to marketing (commonly being used to validate the instincts of studio executives on matters such as running time), it could be construed as working against artists, and reinforcing an aesthetic of the lowest common denominator.

However, phenomena such as the 'Director's Cut'; the 'Special Edition' released theatrically (*Star Wars Trilogy*, George Lucas, 1997) or on DVD (*Kingdom of Heaven*, Ridley Scott, 2005); sequels (*Mission: Impossible 3*, J. J. Abrams, 2006) and remakes (*The Day the Earth Stood Still*, Scott Derrickson, 2008) all attest to the nature of film as an 'open' text, at least where narrative content is concerned. Film narratives are never semantically closed, whether their continuation is undertaken by 'authors', studios or fans. Although many of the above strategies are dedicated to repackaging and thus extending the profitability of a film, some of them nevertheless arise from an acute awareness of the desires of audiences to see a narrative continued or developed. Paramount successfully spun off a long-running cinema franchise from a television show, *Star Trek* (1966–9), that was cancelled in its original run after attracting poor ratings. The most ingenious way to keep the franchise fresh was to import characters and storylines from the 1980s revamp of the show (*Star Trek: The Next Generation*, 1987–94) into the film series, while on television, spin-offs of the 'original' spin-off, such as *Star Trek: Voyager* (1995–2001) and *Enterprise* (2001–5) proliferated. The notoriously dedicated *Star Trek* fan base, the ranks of which swelled in the post-cancellation years as syndication helped the series to achieve cult status, made the reformatting of the narrative as a film possible in the first place (*Star Trek – The Motion Picture*, Robert Wise, 1979), and despite the commercial failure of *Star Trek: Nemesis* (Stuart Baird, 2002), a fresh cinematic instalment – expected to be a 'reboot' – has been produced for release in 2009.[47] Similarly, the loyalty shown by fans to the *Alien* product line (comic books, videogames and so on) after the film series was apparently terminated with the death of main character Ripley (in

Alien 3, David Fincher, 1992) led backers Twentieth Century Fox to pay actress Sigourney Weaver a reported $11 million to reprise the role in *Alien Resurrection* (Jean Pierre Jeunet, 1997). A series built around ongoing discourses concerning reproduction, hybridity and parasitism, the *Alien* saga has proved uncommonly amenable to reiteration in new forms; the most recent chapter to be released, *AVPR: Aliens vs. Predator – Requiem* (Colin and Greg Strause, 2007) is a sequel to a spin-off that was itself 'mated' with another franchise. A celebrated, fan-made pastiche also emphasized the series' signature hybrid quality by pitting the aliens against superhero Batman (*Batman: Dead End*, Sandy Collora, 2003).

In the science-fiction/fantasy genres, it is now virtually axiomatic that fans do not wait passively for films to hit the screen, but seek to have their opinions reflected in the creative process: readers of the 'Spider-Man' comic book were invited by magazines such as *Empire* to vote for the actor whom they believed should don the hero's costume in the film adaptation,[48] while many fans boycotted *Judge Dredd* (Danny Cannon, 1995) in protest at the casting of Sylvester Stallone (and his controversial rejection of the helmet traditionally worn by the character). Trailers for Peter Jackson's *The Lord of the Rings* cycle (2001–3), released on the Internet in June 2000, produced the biggest ever demand for downloads (beating the record previously held by *Star Wars Episode I: The Phantom Menace*, George Lucas, 1999). The recent popularity of the 'MySpace' social networking tool has allowed filmmakers to solicit opinions on aspects like casting, but arguably also to control the flow of information to fans (which can be presented not as official, institutional 'hard sell' to buoy up interest while the film is in production, but rather as the releasing of secrets, framed as it is within the interpersonal idiom of MySpace).[49]

As work on fandom such as Jenkins (2005) has shown, connections facilitated by interactive computer technology are empowering interpretative communities to renegotiate their relations with texts, and the consequences for cinema as it is brought into the orbit of other screen media and *their* 'user' dynamics are manifold. We will return to the issue of how cinema has exploited an increasingly synergistic relationship with digital technology in Chapter 5, where notions of the 'dialogic spectator' suggested earlier in this chapter will be tied in to developments in the new media landcape that increasingly overlaps with (even includes) cinema. Before this, however, we will see Bakhtin's dialogical project 'in action' over the next few chapters, where key concepts such as the chronotope and polyphony will be evaluated in terms of their usefulness to the analysis of individual filmic texts and 'utterances', and in a more general sense, to the discipline of film studies as a whole.

2
Chronotope I: Time, Space, Narrative – 'Get Ready for Rush Hour'

Introduction: 'Big loud action movies'

> It is because cinema as the art of space and time is the contrary of painting that it has something to add to it
> – André Bazin (1972, p.142)

> In literature and art itself, temporal and spatial determinations are inseparable from one another, and always colored by emotions and values.
> – Mikhail Bakhtin (FTC, p.243)

The action narrative has been a staple of film-making practice since Louis and Auguste Lumière's 1895 presentation of *L'Arrivée d'un Train en Gare de la Ciotat*, a single scene epic that is said to have caused cinematically naive spectators to run from the auditorium, believing that the titular train would crash through the screen. This fabled reaction perhaps marks out the Lumières as the Wachowski or Scott brothers of their era, progenitors of the cinema of spectacle that those modern-day directors have so successfully exploited. In Hollywood, forms of action picture have dominated production for the better part of a century, from the chase scenes of Edwin S. Porter's *Great Train Robbery* (1903) through the epic battles of Cecil B. De Mille and D. W. Griffith, hundreds of Westerns, gangster pictures, films noir, police thrillers and so on. All of these kinds of film depend on 'action' scenes to some extent, as do countless other genres in varying degrees. However, the major elements of the contemporary generic specimen known to audiences and industry as the 'action movie' can be seen to coalesce during the era of the aggressively marketed, high-octane blockbusters *Jaws* (Steven Spielberg, 1975), *Star Wars* (George Lucas, 1977) and

Close Encounters of the Third Kind (Steven Spielberg, 1977). As Larry Gross has pointed out, the 'Big Loud Action Movie' has been 'a central economic fact, structuring all life, thought and practice in Hollywood' since the late 1970s, when Spielberg and Lucas steered their comic-book and B-movie-inspired visions to record-breaking box-office success (Gross, 1995, p.7). The unprecedented commercial achievements of the above triumvirate of films revolutionized the way in which films were budgeted, scripted, shot and sold in Hollywood, restoring to cinema the principles of scale and visual spectacle that informed its earliest experiments. The downside of this revolution was that such filmmakers were accused of promoting a juvenilization of the artform, targeting the same (predominantly male, teenage) merchandise-hungry audience again and again, and sacrificing psychological insight and moral and social complexity for car chases, explosions and ever more elaborate fight scenes.[1] Certainly, apologists for the action movie today have to admit that psychological depth and social commentary are not the forte of the genre, although most would contend that these are not the concerns of the action narrative anyway. Some would argue, as does Larry Gross, that directors of 'prestige' pictures such as David Lean (*Lawrence of Arabia*, 1962), Stanley Kubrick (*Spartacus*, 1960) or Akira Kurosawa (*Seven Samurai*, 1954) were masters of action and spectacle as well as skilful handlers of serious themes (1995, p.7).

The cultural standing of action films is improving, at least by the measure of academic debate;[2] the Academy Awards, with some recent literary-derived exceptions such as the *Lord of the Rings* and *Bourne* films, tend to remain largely oblivious to the merits of genre films.[3] Such texts are still often dismissed as Saturday night multiplex fodder, 'popcorn movies', but it is unlikely that terms such as these would cause any offence to the audiences who queue around the block to see the latest mega-budget offerings. Whether these films do damage to international cinematic culture by limiting the distribution opportunities of non-Hollywood productions, or whether their often simplistic narratives work to the detriment of the wider culture by satisfying lowest-common-denominator audience expectations, is not at issue in this chapter. It is not my aim to determine whether the 'Big Loud Action Movie' is worthy of serious critical study, as scholars have already answered this question by increasingly bringing the genre into their focus in recent years. Neither is it my intention to rehabilitate the critical reputation of such films, for it is not the critical community that these movies are addressed to, any more than it is the response of critics that I am specifically interested in. From a Bakhtinian perspective, the communicative feat by which action texts reach and connect with the mass audience to which they typically play – cutting across the barriers of age, class, sex, ethnicity and nationality that many other genres fail to negotiate – is certainly deserving of critical attention.[4] Bakhtin, who prizes social and historical value over all else, seems fascinated by the novel at least partly because it is the dominant literary form in his historical era (although engaged at the time of much of Bakhtin's writing with film in a struggle for dominance within the wider cultural sphere, a struggle that goes ironically unrepresented in his work). He realizes that there is something intrinsic in the novel form that sustains this ability to connect with a huge, popular audience (as writers like Rabelais and Dostoevsky certainly did). Bakhtin identifies this quality as 'novelness'; as we saw in Chapter 1, this term is used to characterize 'any cultural activity that has treated language as dialogic' (Holquist 2002, p.68) and thus can extend beyond the boundaries of that form. However, there are other vital elements in novelistic discourse, elements that provide the very grounds for dialogic representation in art, and Bakhtin turns his attention to two of these crucial aspects in 'Forms of Time and of the Chronotope in the Novel'.[5] In this essay, the academically overlooked form of the Greek adventure narrative provides the platform for examining modes of temporal and spatial construction in the novel. Bakhtin utilizes the building-brick simplicity of the genre, which, with apologies to Larry Gross, we might term the 'Big Loud Action Novel', to lay out terms for the wider-ranging discussion to follow. Although Bakhtin could be accused of inflexibility in terms of his purview, the fact that he considers this now obscure but once hugely popular genre worthy of critical insight suggests the breadth of his analytical scope.

The chronotope is a device not only for analysing methods of narrative construction but also for measuring the relationship between text and reader; how the world of the reader '*creates* the text' and how the text completes the dialogical circuit by feeding back into the world of the reader (FTC, pp.253–7). These areas of concern constitute the agenda of this chapter, following on from the exploration of paradigms of spectatorship in the previous one. It will be argued that the action film can be approached as a crucible for scrutinizing the relationships that obtain between text and viewer at the commercial heart of the Hollywood cinema, and for studying the process by which these relationships become embedded over time in narrative formulas. Why do we flock in droves to variants of the action movie, making it the most commercially potent of all Hollywood forms? And what does the textual representation of time and space have to do with this success? Each of the films that have been chosen to illustrate my argument is centrally placed within the popular 'action' tradition. John McTiernan's *Die Hard* (1988) and Jan de Bont's

Speed (1994) exemplify Larry Gross' definition of the post-1977 blockbuster. Both are narratively lean, structurally simplistic adventures, with the emphasis on action rather than dialogue, characterization or emotion. Len Wiseman's 2007 third sequel *Live Free or Die Hard* (*Die Hard 4.0* in British release; hereafter, *Die Hard 4.0*) provides an up-to-the-minute specimen. Wiseman's film shows signs of conscious adaptation to a viewing climate that has moved on during the two decades since the original *Die Hard* (mainly in the curbing of bad language and modulation of violence to attract a lower US rating),[6] but largely stays true to the progenitor in terms of structural tendencies and the deployment of proven genre methods. The three films are formulaic, visually exciting, conceptually and politically shallow entertainment machines, each definitively representing a moment in the state of Hollywood's art at the time of their historical production.

Forms of the chronotope

Bakhtin's term 'chronotope' translates as 'time-space', and taking the concept at this literal level, it may be suggested that film is the artform which most thoroughly expresses chronotopic activity. The processes of transmission and reception of film are centred on the manipulation of time and space; at a particular place and a specific time, a visual representation of spatial reality unfolds at around 24 frames per second, projected onto a screen with definite spatial parameters. It is in its ability to show spatial changes through time, the capacity to represent motion figuratively, that film is set apart from other forms of expression, such as the novel or painting (as the André Bazin quotation at the beginning of this chapter implies). However, as Christian Metz has influentially argued, film's 'impression of reality' has an ambiguous basis. The cinema is no closer to an expression of direct, unmediated reality than any other artform. In fact, in a material sense, film is considerably less 'substantial' than, for instance, theatrical presentation, in that the content of the frame is never really present. The medium, however, turns this insubstantiality to its advantage. The illusion of proximity that film creates is more suggestive of life precisely because it expresses a lack, which the diegesis fills. Hence, according to Metz, the cinema spectator invests onscreen elements with diegetic value to a greater degree than he or she would the actors in stage drama, whose reality is all too apparent to sustain the same illusion: 'it is the total unreality of the filmic means [...] which allows the diegesis to assume reality' (Metz 1974b, p.13). Metz postulates movement, which is purely visual and therefore is as authentic in cinematic reproduction as in the original moment of inscription, as the crucial factor in this process. The great illusion of the apparatus is founded on the 'real presence of motion' (1974b, p.9). This is the principle on which the Lumière brothers startled their audiences. Time and space coalesce in the filmic presentation of motion, enabling the medium to appear animated and thus more lifelike than other visually static means of expression (still photography, painting and sculpture). The most innovative practitioners of film art, however, have derived powerful effects from a deformation of this verisimilitude, developing a range of techniques (slow-motion, freeze-frame and time-lapse photography) that self-consciously acknowledge the artificiality of filmic time and space; for instance, the device of the jump cut so prevalent in the early work of the French 'Nouvelle Vague'.[7]

Time and space, then, are the main constituents of film form, elevating the chronotope to an essential factor in any study of how cinematic texts create narrative effects. The chronotope is possibly the Bakhtinian concept most oriented towards filmic application, yet inevitably there are difficulties involved in giving a straightforward definition of the term. As Barry Rutland has commented, the chronotope is possibly the 'least developed' but the 'most suggestive' of Bakhtin's key concepts (Rutland, 1990, p.133) and this ambiguity stems from the essay in which Bakhtin establishes the term. In 'Forms of Time and of the Chronotope in the Novel', the term is prone to mutation between three apparently distinct categories of meaning. The first sense in which 'chronotope' is used is to demarcate stable generic forms which are classified according to methods of representing time and space, such as the 'folkloric chronotope' (FTC, p.146). Secondly, the term can signify a more localized rendering of time and space within the diegesis. Bakhtin refers to elements that fall into this second category as 'chronotopic motifs'; for example, the motifs of 'meeting' or 'the road' (FTC, p.98). A third level of meaning is added by Bakhtin in 1973 in the 'Concluding Remarks', where the chronotope is drawn together with dialogism in postulating a chronotopic element in reading.[8] Here, Bakhtin contends that the representational elements of the text emerge '[o]ut of the actual chronotopes of our world' (FTC, p.253). It would thus seem possible to theorize a chronotope of reception, or at least a way in which real and represented time/space configurations are linked via the operations of chronotopes.

In the 'Concluding Remarks' Bakhtin seems to realize that the theoretical basis of his device requires further clarification, and here he 'fleshes out' his idea, defining chronotopes as 'the organizing centers for the fundamental narrative events of the novel [...] the place where the knots of the narrative are tied and untied' (FTC, p.250). In this expansion of the original formulation, the integral role played by the chronotope within all levels of the text is underlined: chronotopes not only link disparate parts of narrative material together and play a part in the way in which we experience the text, but provide the very 'ground essential for the showing-forth, the representability of events' (FTC, p.250). Without chronotopes there would presumably be no narrative; for they make possible the combination of temporal and spatial co-ordinates that make narrative events 'visible ... [and] concrete, makes them take on flesh, causes blood to flow in their veins' (FTC, p.250). The anatomical metaphor, it should be noted, seems especially relevant to the medium which is said to bring fictional characters to 'life', and echoes the assertion of Christian Metz that an aspect of physical embodiment, albeit an illusory one, is intrinsic to the medium: 'the cinema is a body' (Metz, 1994, p.57).[9]

These are the main ways in which Bakhtin seems to intend the chronotope to be defined. However, complex interrelations can exist *between* chronotopes, and Bakhtin characterizes these relationships as 'dialogical'. As if to emphasize the different orders and functions of the chronotope, Bakhtin stresses that the 'relationships [...] that exist *among* chronotopes cannot enter into any of the relationships contained *within* chronotopes' (FTC, p.252, italics in original). This statement is never properly clarified, conveying some of the confusion that is an inevitable by-product of such a potentially all-encompassing term. Bakhtin's apparent resolution that the chronotope should be fully explicated in the 'Concluding Remarks' is not realized entirely successfully, forcing anyone foolhardy enough to attempt to define the term to fill in certain blanks around its uncertain edges and multiple definitions. The major problem engendered by the concept is determining the point where the classification of textual material as 'chronotopic' should stop. Sue Vice notes that the chronotope 'seems omnipresent to the point either of invisibility or of extreme obviousness' (Vice, 1997, p.201). At the outset of 'Forms of Time and of the Chronotope', Bakhtin cites Kant's claim that space and time are prerequisite categories of all forms of perception (FTC, p.85). The same criteria apply to the literary text, and accordingly all textual events must take place within time and space, even if these parameters are immaterial (for instance, in a character's memory or in the verbal account of a narrator). Although Bakhtin claims that 'any and every literary image is chronotopic', it does not necessarily follow that everything in the text is a chronotope; rather, that textual time and space is made concrete through the agency of chronotopes (FTC, p.251).

Chronotopic value is not defined merely by the presence of spatial and temporal indicators in the work – other devices have evolved in textual systems for this kind of purely formal designation. The borders of the 'scene' (in the sense of a block of dramatic narrative with pre-determined markers) may often coincide with those of the chronotope, but we must take care not to confuse the two. Similarly, the chronotope can be manifested as a physical motif and locus of action within the text – Bakhtin offers examples such as 'the road' (243) and the 'castle' (245) – but not every concrete object in the work should be considered a discrete, self-contained chronotope.[10] If we take a scene from the early stages of *Die Hard*, where the central character John McClane (Bruce Willis) is conveyed through Los Angeles in a limousine, it might seem fair to speak of the vehicle as a chronotope, in the sense that the physical properties of the car determine the spatial parameters of the sequence and the brevity of the scene. However, the limousine is not narratively central to *Die Hard*, despite the fact that it performs the necessary time-space manoeuvre that results in McClane arriving at the Nakatomi Plaza, where his adventures will begin. It would be more proper to talk of the car as contributing to a minor chronotope of *travel* or *arrival* in the film, one that underlines McClane's status as an 'outsider' in Los Angeles. The passenger bus featured in *Speed* plays a more significant role in that text; it is the major location, and can be referred to as a dominant chronotope because it is involved with the spatio-temporal organization of the film on a level other than the purely mechanical. The *narrative* properties of that vehicle lend it its chronotopic character, not its physical ones – although the physical nature of the vehicle does have implications for its significance within both time and space patterns. The nearest equivalent to this category of chronotope in *Die Hard* is the Nakatomi Tower, which provides a major locus for the action and shapes the way in which events are presented, necessitating a narrow timescheme (McClane cannot evade capture in a building forever) and a compressed spatial context (related to the physical dimensions of a real building). The most recent *Die Hard* release reworks the convention of a limited spatial context circumscribing the adventure with McClane visiting New Jersey, Washington D.C., and various sites in Maryland. Furthermore, the space hosting the physical action is 'doubled' by the alternative, virtual realm of cyberspace where the transgressions of villain Thomas Gabriel (Timothy Olyphant) occur. It is in cyberspace that McClane's new sidekick, computer hacker Matt Farrell (Justin Long), can effect his own heroic contribution. The wider spatial parameters enable different types of action to be presented (such as a freeway chase involving fighter planes), and facilitate the inevitable addition of CGI as production value, but perhaps lead to a less satisfying and far less suspenseful narrative overall.

Chronotopes seem to be arranged hierarchically in a given text, their relative importance determined by the role they play in narrative construction and by their function within the three main chronotopic categories. Bakhtin stresses that '[a]rt and literature are shot through with *chronotopic values* of varying degree and scope. Each motif, each separate aspect of artistic work bears value' (FTC, p.243, italics in original). Reference to Bakhtin's own textual examples may help to clarify the issue. He discusses the chronotope of the 'threshold' in the novels of Dostoevsky, arguing that stairways, foyers and landings all contribute to this central signifier. The chronotopic value of these motifs is derived from a combination of their *physical* functions and characteristics – their enabling of meetings, encounters and so on; and their *symbolic* associations – they represent the point where '*crisis*, radical change, an unexpected turn of fate takes place' (PDP, p.169). A third reason why thresholds are loaded with chronotopic value is because they facilitate a certain type of formal spatio-temporal construction. Narratives are formed from the combination of different varieties of these spatio-temporal modalities. Bakhtin demonstrates this by surveying many different types of narrative. He discovers that, for instance, the pre-novelistic 'adventure' text relies heavily on a certain pattern encompassing motifs such as long journeys, shipwrecks and so on, while the 'idyllic' text utilizes very different configurations (valleys, rivers, cyclical rhythms of time). The centrality of chronotopes to generic classification is hinted at here, but our main concern for the time being is the emphasis on the structural importance of chronotopes. Bakhtin argues that thresholds are the 'fundamental "points" of action' in Dostoevsky (PDP, p.170), in the same way that the bus is the fundamental point of action in *Speed*, or the highway takes narrative precedence in the road movie genre.

Another source of ambiguity in the application of the chronotope springs from the polysemic nature of its compositional elements. We can talk about 'time' in the text in multiple ways – the time we spend experiencing the text and its actual duration or running time, which are not necessarily the same (in the case of video or DVD, viewings of parts of a text may be staggered over a period of days, or the text condensed in line with the viewer's interests); the timescale of the story (*fabula*), the plot distortions executed upon the blueprint of the story (*sjuzhet*) and so on. For each of these modalities there appears to be a chronotopic equivalent.[11] Similarly, the concept of 'space' can signify much beyond the contents of the cinematic frame. How do we manage all of these implications within the forum of textual analysis? Bakhtin's assertion that chronotopes provide 'the ground essential for the showing forth, the representability of events' (FTC, p.250) also requires unpacking. If this is the case, and chronotopes are present in the text from the earliest moment of its genesis, can we ascribe a degree of intentionality to authors? Is the chronotope a structure that enters into the very process of textual construction or a device that helps us to look at existing patterns in a new light and as such, is projected onto the text by the critic? Since Bakhtin draws the chronotope together with dialogism in the new directions suggested, tantalizingly, in the 'Concluding Remarks', it becomes implicated in the complex network a text enacts 'with all its others: author, intertext, real and imagined addressees, and the communicative context' (Falkowska, 1996, p.25). Work in the area of chronotopic analysis must take note of such conceptual conundrums as these and avoid deploying the chronotope solely as a device to illustrate how textual specificity relates to generic tradition, a mere 'answer to a narratologist's prayers' (Shepherd, 1996, p.133). What can be stated unambiguously is that the chronotope has great value as a means of expanding the vocabulary with which we can think and speak about textual space and time.

This chapter will employ the three main senses of 'chronotope' in an interconnected way. The 'action' genre is delineated by a certain method of representing time, much as the Greek adventure narrative in Bakhtin's analysis. Within this mode of representation there are various chronotopic motifs of interest, corresponding with important time/space locales (the tower in *Die Hard*, the bus in *Speed*, a series of 'hubs' for the action scenes in *Die Hard 4.0*) or recurrent textual signifiers (e.g., the iconic male hero, the technological hardware prized in the action genre, or one of Bakhtin's own examples, 'the road'). Having constructed itself along these lines, the cinematic text *'faces outward away from itself'* (FTC, p.257, italics in original) and engages with the temporal and spatial environment of the spectator, invoking Bakhtin's formulation of the relationship between the worlds of the real and the represented. Thus, we will find that our contemplation of the chronotope will eventually return us to the fundamental dialogic equation of utterance (film text) and response (viewer), and prepare us for a different chronotopic journey in the next chapter (which deals with the appeal that historical value, expressed in the time-space of popular genres, makes to spectatorial understanding). Bakhtin stresses that time is the dominant element in the chronotope because 'literature's primary mode of representation *is* temporal' (FTC, p.146), and that dominance will be seen to cross over to our discussion of the action genre as well. However, analysis of the spatial coding of such texts will figure prominently, for the two components are 'inseparable' in narrative construction (FTC, p.243). Indeed, discourse on film is obligated to refer to spatial determinations and values as absolutely integral components of cinematic textuality.

Adventure time in ancient Greece and Hollywood

In 'Forms of Time and of the Chronotope in the Novel', Bakhtin analyses several genres, from pre-novelistic antiquity to the works of Tolstoy and Flaubert, in order to determine the chronotopic patterns therein. For the purpose of the present analysis of action films, the most pertinent of the genres that Bakhtin discusses is the Greek Romance or 'Adventure Novel of Ordeal'. Bakhtin identifies in this genre a special kind of temporal construction that influences every aspect of the text, from character to plot, which he calls 'Adventure-time' (FTC, p.87).[12] The main characteristics of this mode of temporality include a 'broad and varied geographical background' (FTC, p.88) against which the adventures take place; a lack of everyday cyclical, biographically or historically bound time, which is replaced by an elastic, 'extratemporal' order which has no 'internal limits' and therefore 'leaves no *trace*' in the personalities of the heroes (FTC, p.94; p.90, italics in original); and the heroes themselves, who are not realized in a psychologically complex way, or connected to real social or historical patterns, but have a purely physical, schematic function of 'enforced movement through space' (FTC, p.105). Adventure-time does not adhere to principles of realism, but rather 'possesses its own peculiar consistency and unity [...] its own ineluctable logic' (FTC, p.102). The world of the adventure chronotope is thus ruled by chance and coincidence, structured around wild detours from reality that despite their infeasibility are perfectly acceptable within the self-determined logic of the genre.

There are many correspondences between the kind of narrative that Bakhtin identifies in the works of Heliodorus, Achilles Tatius and others, and the Hollywood action tradition. These parallels are especially noticeable in a sub-category that we might call 'action-adventure' or 'action-fantasy'. The latter classification includes the (British-made but Hollywood-funded and distributed) James Bond series, the Indiana Jones and *Star Wars* sagas, and many serial superhero narratives in the 1990s and 2000s, including films based around the Batman, X-Men and Spider-Man characters. To deal with the first principle of adventure-time, many texts in this category employ a 'broad and varied geographical background'. The Bond films have a tradition of using exotic locations, and have even come to market themselves on this premise; a 'teaser' advertisement for *Tomorrow Never Dies* (Roger Spottiswoode, 1997), designed to whet the appetites of fans while the film was still in production, carried the legend 'Now shooting around the world'. Similarly, the Indiana Jones films reflect the mysterious foreign environments of the Saturday morning serials so beloved of co-creator George Lucas: Sri Lanka, Petra, Venice, Peru, remade by studio hands to look every inch the paradigmatic Middle Eastern casbah or European city of intrigue. However, in achieving archetypicality, the locations often lose touch with geographical verisimilitude, as is demonstrated in *Indiana Jones and the Last Crusade* (Steven Spielberg, 1989) where Almeria, Spain, stands in for Jordan (Baxter, 1997, p.343). Sue Vice points out a similar geographical distortion in a film from a different genre that nevertheless adheres to some of the conventions of the action film, Ridley Scott's *Thelma and Louise* (1991). The ultimate destination of the road journey undertaken by the female protagonists should, empirically speaking, be New Mexico and not Arizona, where the Grand Canyon (cited in the film's climax) is located (Vice, 1997, p.217). Yet the final scenes were actually filmed in New Mexico. This unstable relation of what we might term 'adventure-space' to its real geographical equivalent denotes a trend that, usually sanctioned by political or economic factors, has become embedded in film production, and as such has important implications for chronotopic studies. Vice suggests that the primary role of the chronotope is 'its mediation between real historical events and their appearance in the text' (1997, p.218). If this formulation were to be extrapolated to encompass spatial concerns, the role of the chronotope in the relationship between 'actual' space and its textual equivalent could also be explored. The central issue would be whether such distortions as those outlined above undermine the capacity of the chronotope to act as a 'bridge [...] between the two worlds' of real and represented (Clark and Holquist, 1984, p.279). Although this aspect of chronotopic function is not a major concern in this chapter, we will return to this issue of geographical accuracy in the chronotope later. For the time being, it should be noted that the 'action' movie of the *Die Hard* or *Speed* lineage, while taking its 'blockbuster' scale from the Indiana Jones/*Star Wars* template, and many narrative elements from the Bond series, does not necessarily adhere to the same premise of geographical variety. The 'spanner-in-the-works' sub-genre that those two films exemplify is actually predicated upon a rather more limited spatial axis.[13] However, those texts do follow many of the other structural and characterological principles of adventure-time, as I hope to demonstrate.

The kind of time in which the action hero exists represents a variant of the 'extratemporal hiatus between two moments of biographical time' that Bakhtin identifies in the Greek adventure narrative (FTC, p.90). The action hero is invariably a blue-collar, 'everyman' figure, exemplified by plain-talking East Coast cop John McClane in *Die Hard*. This archetype often displays a distrust of authority figures and/or 'maverick' tendencies (the latter trope is most clearly demonstrated by Mel Gibson's attractively psychotic Martin Riggs in the *Lethal Weapon* series [1987–98]). At the outset of the narrative, the protagonist is wrenched from normality and inserted into a chain of events over which he has little control.[14] *Die Hard* sees John McClane visiting his estranged family in Los Angeles when he becomes embroiled in a siege of the Nakatomi Corporation headquarters discharged by a group claiming at first to be terrorists but whose motive is subsequently revealed to be mere robbery. Jack Traven (Keanu Reeves) in *Speed* has no sooner received a commendation for his part in foiling psychopathic bomber Howard Payne (Dennis Hopper) than, next morning, he finds that Payne has engineered another plan to hold the city to ransom, in which he must play a central part. A slight departure is evident in *Die Hard 4.0*, where for the first time McClane is actually assigned to the case that becomes the main mission (albeit only because he is – by chance – the nearest senior officer to Matt Farrell's locality when the FBI call comes in to pick up the hacker, who has become a target for Gabriel's operation). Very little running time, in any of these films, is devoted to showing the heroes doing 'normal' things, bar the arrival at LAX airport of McClane and a quick visit to a coffee shop for Traven; on Traven's exit from the shop, a bus immediately explodes on the street outside. In *Die Hard 4.0*, an uncomfortable domestic row with his daughter Lucy (Mary Elizabeth Winstead) is the only preamble leading in to McClane's entrance into the main 'firesale'[15] storyline (this appearance is necessary in structural, as much as character, terms as Lucy – who will become a 'bargaining chip' later on in the narrative – needs to be introduced). Such fleeting moments of everyday life underline that the only routine known to the action hero is that of random contingency and wild plot deviation; the unpredictable can always be relied upon. Individual texts often play on this unwritten rule of the genre, as in *Lethal Weapon 3* (Richard Donner, 1992), where Riggs' peaceful enjoyment of a cigarette is disturbed so often by the exigencies of the plot that it becomes a running joke, or in *Die Hard 2* (Renny Harlin, 1990), where McClane, involved in another terrorist situation, exclaims, 'How can the same shit happen to the same guy *twice?*'.

Like the archetypal hero of the Greek romance, the action protagonist does not undergo any real biographical or maturational adjustment over the course of their adventures; in other words, adventure-time 'is not registered in the slightest way in the age of the heroes' (FTC, p.90). The most accurate analogy for this characteristic of the novel of ordeal can be found in James Bond (perhaps the single most influential character in the action genre), who has hardly aged over the course of four decades and 22 official releases.[16] This phenomenon is due, of course, to the smooth turnover of lead actors, a process that we as spectators endorse under the terms of the narrative consensus into which we enter with the filmmakers. In fact, Bond seems to be regressing, with the Daniel Craig of *Casino Royale* (Martin Campbell, 2006) several years younger in appearance than was Pierce Brosnan, who bowed out of the role in *Die Another Day* (Lee Tamahori, 2002); although, here, a 'reboot' is applicable which complicates the issue slightly.[17]

Heroes arrive fully formed and change little in the action film, thus precluding any real sense of spiritual or ideological 'becoming' (FTC, p.140). Despite the pretensions of McClane and Traven to normality, we are in no doubt as to their heroic credentials as soon as we are introduced to them. The first appearances of the heroes in their respective texts confirm this supposition. McClane startles a fellow air traveller who notices his firearm and receives a seductive glance from an air hostess, accentuating his toughness and sexual appeal. In *Speed*, Traven's maverick streak is revealed from the outset when he volunteers for the most dangerous assignment in the opening rescue sequence. They do not become heroes as a result of their exploits in the course of the narrative, they are *already* heroes, the only ones who could measure up to the requirements of the situation. Their adventures do not alter their personalities, they merely facilitate changes in their romantic status. Traven ends *Speed* linked to bus passenger Annie (Sandra Bullock), and McClane is reunited with his wife Holly (Bonnie Bedelia) at the conclusion of *Die Hard*; moreover, it is suggested that both women are won over precisely because of the brave exploits of the heroes (in fact, such feats are inevitable as their characterological status as 'heroes' would not allow for any other response). This rather one-dimensional treatment of gender, along with the tendency to attach hatred of American values to certain ethnicities, religions or nationally specific ideologies at certain times, has been one of the focal points in attracting evaluations of inherent political conservatism to the form.[18]

The Bond films' evasion of the issue of the character's age through recasting or the more drastic 'rebooting' tactic can be interpreted as part of a wider policy within the series to avoid, as far as possible, the incorporation of external historical or political developments. When such references do come, as in the storyline of *Goldeneye* (Martin Campbell, 1995) which draws upon the dissolution of the Soviet Union, they invariably represent a shallow co-opting of historical signifiers designed to give audiences a ready-made reference point that can be quickly assimilated and forgotten, enabling them to return to the basic business of attending to the action.[19] Similarly, the Nazis faced by Indiana Jones in *Raiders of the Lost Ark* (Steven Spielberg, 1981) or communists of *Indiana Jones and the Kingdom of the Crystal Skull* (Spielberg, 2008) afford a rather blank, conventionalized source of evil carefully detached from reality.[20] As with the limited specificity that Bakhtin finds in the adventure world of the Greek romance (FTC, p.100), films in the action blockbuster tradition rarely engage with a 'real' historical register, instead supplementing or conjoining historical allusion with self-conscious cinematic reference (the 'stormtroopers' of *Star Wars* can be read as a conflation of SS forces and the imperial ranks of Ming the Merciless, arch-villain in the 1930s *Flash Gordon* serials, an acknowledged inspiration of George Lucas). The blockbuster film incorporates historical reality in a mechanical fashion, in much the same way as the ancient biography as described by Bakhtin. In the characteristic chronotope of that form, historical reality serves as 'an arena for the disclosing and unfolding of human characters – nothing more' (FTC, p.141). In cinematic terms, this process of de-historicization can be identified in, for instance, the manner in which the Vietnam War was used as a sort of cinematic shorthand signifying 'troubled male psyche' in productions like *Rambo: First Blood Part II* (George Pan Cosmatos, 1985) and *Lethal Weapon* (see Pfeil, 1998, pp.148–9). The first Gulf War has recently performed a similar function in *The Rock* (Michael Bay 1996).

To digress briefly on this problem, a dialogic perspective holds that the time/space relations embodied in chronotopes always reflect 'the text's groundedness in a social and historical context' (Holquist, 2002, p.141). Yet texts such as those mentioned above continually enact a process of historical *displacement* (which is not quite the same as the 'historical inversion' discussed by Bakhtin in reference to the folkloric chronotope, whereby the past is enriched at the expense of the future [FTC, pp.146–8]). Complex events like the Vietnam or Gulf wars are wrenched from their moorings in socio-political reality, and a 'second history' engendered (Jeffords, 2006, p.288).[21] How then can we reconcile Bakhtin's insistence on the relationship between text and history, made concrete through the agency of chronotopes? Perhaps our conception of the relationship between history and chronotope is restrictively unidirectional. Chronotopes always reflect historical value, Bakhtin tells us. Could it be that the historically charged contexts used even in this arbitrary way say more about the time in which their parent narrative is produced than about the era which they are intended to evoke? Film is an extremely self-reflexive medium, and in its century of existence, chronotopic contexts have been revisited and recycled countless times. The need for certain narrative forms at certain times is undoubtedly a process governed by historical relations. To take a classic cinematic example, the Western enjoyed its heyday in the 1940s and 50s, reflecting a time when the American public had faith in its country as an honourable and protecting world force. The decent, upstanding cowboy archetype of films like *Shane* (George Stevens, 1953) provided America with a positive self-image. However, a number of factors (the Vietnam War chief among them) shattered this complacency in the 1960s, resulting in the 'revisionist' Westerns of Sam Peckinpah and others towards the end of that decade. *The Wild Bunch* (Sam Peckinpah, 1969) reconceives the Wild West as a domain of mercenaries, while Robert Aldrich's *Ulzana's Raid* (1972) uses the time and space of the 1880s Southwest allegorically to examine the moral issues surrounding America's involvement in Vietnam. These films self-consciously constructed themselves in opposition to earlier Westerns, as if to criticize the way that those narratives ignored or inflected ideological overtones in their unbalanced depiction of history. They emphasized this point by casting stars like Henry Fonda (*Once Upon a Time in the West*, Sergio Leone, 1968) or William Holden (*The Wild Bunch*), familiar as 'good guys' in conventional Westerns, as bloodthirsty killers. Perhaps certain genres of film, as of language, are intrinsically 'double-voiced' – that is, they serve two (historical) intonations and ideological meanings simultaneously. Bakhtin describes double-voiced discourse in terms of reflecting both the intention of the speaking character and the contrary intention of the author: 'In such discourse there are two voices, two meanings and two expressions. And all the while these two voices are dialogically interrelated, they – as it were – know about each other (just as two exchanges in a dialogue know of each other and are structured in this mutual knowledge of each other); it is as if they actually hold a conversation with each other' (DIN, p.324).

As an extension of the potential suggested by Bakhtin's term, this process is neither easy to grasp nor explain; the 'distortions' that fiction enacts on chronotopic patterns cannot be unwrapped from our reading of them, which naturally never occupies a fixed temporal point either

(Michael Holquist illustrates this point using the apposite example of Superman [2002, pp.119–21]). The chronotope, at once metaphysical manifestation of 'pure time' (141) and structural ground for the very possibility of fictive representation, uniquely hosts a kind of 'conversation' between historical and narrative energies. Inside the chronotope of a given text, and *through* the chronotopic motifs associated with its genre, displaced or alienated Vietnam veterans like Rambo may become popular culture's repudiated, 'broken idol' heroes (Schubart, 2001, p.194), or conversely find themselves so poorly rewarded as to develop the motivation to turn on the state as villain (*Die Hard 2, The Rock*). The repertoire of male anxieties fuelling Pfeil's 'male rampage films' is thus kept well-stocked until another crisis comes along and knocks history into another set of symbolic shapes.[22] No alibi is meant to be provided here for historical or political distortion; the films themselves are aware that they set themselves up as 'hostages to fortune' for the judgement of future reading communities.[23] Yet, even adventure fantasies like *Superman Returns* (Bryan Singer, 2006) are calibrated enough to real-world calendars to note that when Superman goes away for five years, his disappointed and vulnerable public experience the time as five *actual years*, and thus their feelings of abandonment are amplified.[24]

These kinds of events in the life of a genre are precisely what preoccupies Bakhtin in much of 'Forms of Time and of the Chronotope in the Novel'. Historically informed changes in the artistic representation of time and space constitute the dynamics of literature; it is the chronotope that 'defines genre and genre distinctions' (FTC, p.84). In the next chapter, we will examine more closely the impact of historical determinations on generic forms. For now, we note that the historical substance of the chronotope, although ambiguous in the sense of the purely mechanical relation of the text to the era it represents (e.g., in the case of Vietnam), manifests itself in a more complex and concrete fashion at other levels in the textual process. As with the problem of geographical precision raised earlier, the apparent contradiction of historical value in the chronotope forces us to shift our focus slightly, adhering to Michael Holquist's prescription of the 'bifocal' nature of the term: 'invoking [the chronotope] in any particular case, one must be careful to discriminate between its use as a lens for close-up work and its ability to serve as an optic for seeing at a distance' (Holquist, 2002, p.113). The implications of Holquist's visual terminology (the chronotope as a *way of seeing* or *making visible*) for the encounter between the chronotope and Film Studies should not be ignored. Holquist here follows Bakhtin himself, who constantly emphasizes the visual aspect of the chronotope ('Time becomes, in effect, palpable and *visible* [...] It is precisely the chronotope that provides the ground essential for the *showing forth*, the representability of events' (FTC, p.250, italics added). This tendency is most marked when Bakhtin is discussing the artistic methods of Balzac and Goethe; the former displayed an 'extraordinary' capacity to '*"see"* time in space' (FTC, p.247, italics in original), while the work of Goethe is enriched by the skill of 'chronotopic visualizing of locality and landscape' (B, p.36).

Action heroes and their worlds

Having dealt with the temporal aspect, we must now determine the nature of the 'space' in which action films take place. As with time, abstraction is the dominant tone. These are static, 'finished' worlds, broadly drawn, non-specific backdrops constructed according to the purely physical requirements of the action (FTC, p.110). This is not to say that action films take place in completely unfamiliar settings. In *Speed*, the iconography of 'actual' Los Angeles (Grauman's Chinese Theater, Hollywood Boulevard) is certainly intended to imbue the film with a degree of geographical credibility. However, the city does not become a major character in the text as it does in *Chinatown* (Roman Polanski, 1974) or *LA Confidential* (Curtis Hanson, 1997), both of which draw deeply on civic history for their themes of corruption. In de Bont's film, the signifiers of 'Los Angeles' merely embellish the 'everycity' model with a little local colour. Here is a less extreme version of the geographical distortion mentioned earlier in reference to *Indiana Jones and the Last Crusade* and *Thelma and Louise*; in a sense, it does not matter where or when the road in *Speed* is located, as its function is purely structural. That function is to enable the movement of the bus, and by extension the progression of the narrative, to continue unabated. To answer John McClane's rhetorical question, the same shit can happen to the same guy twice because the world of the action film, as expressed in time and space, is essentially *always the same*. The action world is a state of spatial organization, a certain configuration of things, rather than a concrete place; in this it more resembles a temporal modality (a state of being) than a spatial one. The Los Angeles depicted in *Speed* and *Die Hard* is not a place where people work and live their lives, but an action movie simulation lifted from the template of the real city (literally, in the case of *Die Hard 4.0*, where director Wiseman uses the DVD commentary track to point out scenes shot in the streets of Los Angeles that had Washington monuments digitally grafted onto them). The nature of cities in these films as sites of cinematic spectacle rather than quotidian existence is adumbrated in the identity of the building used to represent Nakatomi Plaza in *Die Hard*: the Century City headquarters of the studio that funded and distributed the movie, Twentieth Century Fox. Meanwhile, scenes in *Speed* set at LAX airport clearly show mountains in the background, exposing the ersatz geography of the sequence. Furthermore, John McClane in *Die Hard* is constantly characterized as an outsider, bemused by the bizarre behaviour of LA denizens, reinforcing the suggestion that Los Angeles, and by extension its most famous neighbourhood Hollywood, is a place at once familiar yet somehow unreal.

Action movies display the same '*interchangeability* in space' (FTC, p.100, italics in original) that Bakhtin notes with reference to the Greek Romance. In those texts, the abstract quality of space and time has a specific narrative motivation as catalyst for the work of chance: 'any concretization [...] would fetter the freedom and flexibility of the adventures and limit the absolute power of chance' (100). The description holds well for the action film; unlikely things *always* happen in these places which are at once strange and strangely familiar, and as such mimic the Metzian formulation of the primal space in which film unfolds, 'that simultaneously very close and definitively inaccessible "elsewhere"' (Metz, 1994, p.64). Thus, a combination of abstract time and space provides the crucial foundation for the type of plot construction preferred in both the Greek novel of ordeal and the modern action film.

The logic of chance and contingency in the action film closely shadows the way those elements are deployed in the texts described by Bakhtin. We will illustrate this point using a scene from *Speed*. In the Greek novel of adventure, the textual cues for the intervention of fate or chance are phrases such as 'suddenly' or 'at just that moment' (FTC, p.95). The equivalent in cinematic grammar of these intrusions of irrational forces occurs in de Bont's film when the bus (rigged by villain Payne to explode if its speed drops below 50 miles-per-hour) hurtles into the path of a woman crossing the road with a child's pram. The sequence is primed by two cuts from the speeding bus to establishing shots of the woman with the pram saying farewell to a friend and starting to cross the road. Our knowledge of the genre tells us that the bus is soon going to enter the same spatial context as the woman. However, we instinctively anticipate the disaster to be narrowly averted, as children do not often come to harm in mainstream Hollywood movies. De Bont then completely undercuts our pre-emptive reading of the situation by having the bus smash into the pram, sending it flying into the air and away from the horrified woman. This moment is extremely shocking on a first viewing. However, the pram turns out to be filled with aluminium cans collected for recycling, and our initial reaction of horror turns first to relief and then to embarrassment that such contrivance could catch us out. The set-piece uses our generic expectations to create a shock effect by reversing them, and is structured around two instances of chance. The first coincidence is that the woman should be crossing the road 'at just that moment' when the bus intersects her path; the second, irrational, coincidence is that the pram should be conveying cans rather than a child. Yet in the 'ineluctable logic' (FTC, p.102) of the action film, the wildly unlikely occurrence fits perfectly, and is in tune with a certain sense of ironic playfulness that pervades these films.

The nature of the hero in action texts, and their interaction with temporal and spatial elements, is also characterized by abstraction and limited specificity. In reference to the novel of ordeal, Bakhtin writes of the purely physical properties of adventure heroes. They must be as 'abstract' as the space in which they exist; details of individual psychology could expose a complex of historical and social relations and tie the narrative down to a certain temporal moment that could have 'really' happened. Character traits are given at the start of the narrative, from which there is no evolution; individuals are 'completely *passive*, completely *unchanging*' (FTC, p.105). This model is refined in the description of the Rabelaisian hero as 'completely external [...] All that a man is finds expression in actions and in dialogue' (FTC, p.239). The hero of the action film is traditionally constructed along similar lines, a 'sensory body but not a sensitive body', as Rikke Schubart maintains, citing Jean Baudrillard (Schubart, 2001, p.201). Physique supersedes psychology, and broad sentimentality replaces emotional complexity or depth. A prime example of the cinematic hero with no discernible interior life is James Bond who, especially in Sean Connery's incarnation, is almost cruelly physical and emotionally sterile. John Wayne, a figure whose connotations of masculinity seem 'absolutely fixed' (Tasker, 1995, p.234), is an iconic precursor of the action star (see Chapter 3), while the craggy-faced, borderline fascist heroes played by Clint Eastwood in *Dirty Harry* and Charles Bronson in *Death Wish* (Michael Winner, 1974) can also be included in this series. The method of constructing the hero as a combat machine, purely defined by their physical feats and characteristics, reaches its apotheosis in the cyborg protagonists of *Robocop* (Paul Verhoeven, 1987), *Terminator 2: Judgement Day* (James Cameron, 1991) and *Universal Soldier* (Roland Emmerich, 1992).[25]

The 'Rambo' archetype that held sway in the 1980s is now unfashionably associated with the hard-line Reaganite policies of that decade, but despite efforts to update action heroes for more caring times, the kind of purely physical narrative tasks assigned to the protagonist continue to define him (despite much progress in this area, the hero of the major blockbuster still tends to be male[26]) in terms of body rather than mind or personality. The stereotypical image of the muscles-for-brains protagonist, best embodied by Stallone's Rambo (1982–88, revived in *Rambo*, Sylvester Stallone, 2008) or the heroes played by Arnold Schwarzenegger in *Commando* (Mark L. Lester, 1985) and *Raw Deal* (John Irvin, 1986) is fading, but continues to inflect perceptions of the genre. The image of the body in the 1980s work of stars like Stallone and Schwarzenegger became another abstract space, a pumped-up, finely tuned locus of spectacle detached from most people's experience of a 'real' masculine body. Yvonne Tasker notes that in the action movie the presentation of the body is absorbed into the landscape of the film as a whole, the hero operating as a 'key aspect of the more general visual excess that this particular form of Hollywood production offers to its audience' (Tasker, 1995, p.233), or as Bakhtin puts it (in reference to the chivalric romance): 'the hero and the miraculous world in which he acts are of a piece, there is no separation between the two' (FTC, p.153). The aestheticized male body is so central to the economy of image in the action film that it may be possible to speak of a chronotope of the body, and one can certainly extract temporal data – including that relating to narrative duration – from the spatial codes of the physique (Purse, 2007, p.7). One way of measuring progress in an action film is to monitor the state of dress of the male lead – as in *Die Hard* and *Speed*, they will invariably start the film fully clothed and end it in a grubby vest or blood-soaked t-shirt. In the case of Arnold Schwarzenegger, one can interpret a whole career in bodily terms, as the bulk of *Pumping Iron* (George Butler/Robert Fiore, 1976) gradually softens and diminishes into the less freakish, more conventionally attractive (and electable) shape displayed in *Collateral Damage* (Andrew Davis, 2002). Perhaps the area of the action body is one where two key Bakhtinian concepts might be productively combined: the chronotope and carnival, the latter of which is much concerned with the materiality of bodies, as in the 'grotesque realism' evinced in Rabelais (RW, p.18). Before the 1990s, the male body that tended to anchor the action movie was signally not the protruding, multiple and excessive body of Rabelaisian grotesque realism, which celebrates many of the material aspects of life (eating, copulation, death, defecation) and becomes a textual site for the celebration of carnivalesque disorder. It is true that blood and dirt often adorn the body of the action hero – Steve Neale in his classic account notes the frequency with which this body is subject to beatings apparently designed to obviate worrying feelings of attraction on the part of male spectators (1995, p.14) – but in iconic series such as those involving Indiana Jones, James Bond and various Stallone and Eastwood characters, the central body is akin to the finished, hard body of classical art, a physical manifestation of the unimpeachable integrity of the hero, allowing nothing to pass beyond or across its margins. The body of Sean Connery's Bond is that required by an international agent of order and discipline; as with Stallone as Rambo, it seems to invite reading only as an 'impenetrable façade' (RW, p.320), with other, more subversive meanings bouncing off its smooth surfaces.[27] Carnivalesque inversion is unthinkable for this type of body, which has been erased of 'all signs of duality' and seems capable of reflecting only a single meaning (RW, p.321). Only when the emphasis moves away from the body to the voice, intellect and personality does the image become more open to interpretation, as Yvonne Tasker has noted in citing Bruce Willis's success as John McClane (1995, p.239). For Tasker, *Die Hard* is innovative in representing a movement away from the model of the cruel, intractable hero, shaping McClane along the lines of Willis' wisecracking television persona and shifting the emphasis from body to voice. Self-conscious on bodily issues by 1988 standards, the film ironically plays with the loaded associations of the action hero by alternately linking McClane with John Wayne (as he is labelled by arch-villain Hans Gruber) and the distinctly less masculine Roy Rogers (as McClane refers to himself). There is further meta-textual reference to Willis' own personality in the remark of a police official that the unidentified scourge of Gruber's terrorist outfit 'could be a fucking bartender' for all they know, with tending bar being one of Willis' many occupations before he achieved fame in the television series *Moonlighting* (1985–9). This remark has a double function, imbuing McClane with the 'regular guy' status attached to Willis as a result of his sudden rise to fame. The film positions McClane as nothing particularly special – indeed, something of a failure – in his personal life, yet incredibly capable when a threat emerges. The tradition of showing McClane pull himself out of a personal slump with a heroic performance against overwhelming odds in one of his 'wrong place, wrong time' episodes continues through to the 2007 instalment.

In time, even the Schwarzenegger body was able to sustain a brief, reversible carnivalesque holiday in the high concept comedy *Junior* (Ivan Reitman, 1994); the leading character's pregnancy played on the previous fixed connotations of Schwarzenegger's body. Nevertheless, the film falls outside the canon of the star's defining roles which are almost exclusively action ones. Nowadays, it seems that certain changes in the action body *are* possible without alienating audiences; the rise of Keanu Reeves in action roles could be cited here, alongside a recognition of the work of Will Smith, Nicolas Cage, Denzel Washington and Johnny Depp, who bring certain codings of 'otherness' to their action performances.[28] In terms of more radical trends of male body inscription at the heart of recent action narratives, Lisa Purse offers a reading that unites shifts in representational technologies with the type of action heroes demanded by contemporary audiences, noting that, despite the market expressing a taste for physics-defying superheroes, virtual CGI bodies seem to lack the 'visual integrity' of the profilmic body (2007, pp.15–6). More contentiously, in a piece that seems to rehearse the received narrative/spectacle binary, Schubart argues that the utopian masculinity contained within action bodies has become increasingly immaterial, with the result that audiences locate their point of identification with the pleasures of movement and special effects *around* the bodies (2001, p.205). Still, in 2009, it can be argued that many elements that fans would recognize from 1980s iterations of the genre remain intact. Those actors who can provide broadly physical profilmic[29] performances still tend to prosper, with the types of athletically demanding roles once dubbed 'hardbodies' by Susan Jeffords (1994) now often filled by former WWF wrestler Dwayne Johnson, aka 'The Rock', while both Johnson and the famously ethnically uncategorizable Vin Diesel have assumed righteous vigilante roles that were once the province of Stallone, Bronson or Eastwood.[30] The non-physical acting burden still frequently falls on the more technically gifted performers, often with theatrical associations, who are cast as villains – Alan Rickman in *Die Hard*, Jeremy Irons in *Die Hard With a Vengeance* (John McTiernan, 1995), Ian McDiarmid in various *Star Wars* films, Ian McKellen in the *X-Men* trilogy, Hugo Weaving in *The Matrix* and sequels, Willem Dafoe in *Speed 2* and *Spider-Man*, Timothy Olyphant in *Die Hard 4.0*, Cate Blanchett in *Indiana Jones and the Kingdom of the Crystal Skull*, Kevin Spacey in *Superman Returns*.

Space and plot

Although the action hero bears the outward signs of strength and self-control, he is characteristically powerless in the face of the irrational forces that dictate plot. In another correspondence between action films and the Greek novels of ordeal, Bakhtin characterizes the generic hero as 'a person to whom something happens' (FTC, p.95) rather than the driving force of narrative progression: 'He himself is deprived of any initiative. He is merely the physical subject of the action. And it follows that his actions will be by and large of an elementary-spatial sort. In essence, all the character's actions in Greek romance are reduced to *enforced movement through space* (escape, persecution, quests)' (FTC, p.105, italics in original). These spatial manoeuvres tend to be epic in scale in Greek adventure narratives, encompassing whole countries and expansive timelines. The progress of the modern action movie hero also takes the form of movement through abstract time and space, which can be similarly epic in geographical scope (Bond, Indiana Jones) but in the 'spanner-in-the-works' subgenre commonly occurs within drastically compressed markers. The events in *Die Hard* take place within a single night, *Die Hard 4.0* unfolds over a period of roughly 36 hours, while *Speed* is structured around just two days separated by an elided period of a few weeks.[31] In spatial terms, the original *Die Hard* and *Speed* opt for simplicity and compression; McClane spends mere minutes of the running time of *Die Hard* outside the environs of the Nakatomi Tower, while Traven is most often depicted on the speeding bus. There is further compression within these already narrow parameters; at one point, John McClane is forced to crawl through a tiny air vent to evade capture. A static camera witnesses his inexorable progress, as he quips, 'Now I know what a TV dinner feels like.' This is a quintessential example of 'enforced movement through space'; for Steve Neale, such tactics are highly characteristic of action-adventure: '[W]here locations are restricted [...] space, the control of space, and the ability to move freely through space or from one space to another are always important' (2004, p.74). Action plots compel the hero through a minimal spatial context, robbing them of any degree of initiative and forcing them to survive on wit alone. As noted earlier, *Die Hard 4.0* departs from routine for the series by forcing McClane into an unusual amount of travelling between geographically detached spaces, so much so that in the course of the DVD commentary track, the director, editor and star actually resituate the film in various subgenres (alluding to its 'buddy' and 'road movie' elements due to the amount of in-car bonding that takes place between McClane and Farrell). One of the challenges for the film, in making the project 'feel' like a traditional *Die Hard* movie, is imprinting a chase structure onto a story where the spatial object of the threat – cyberspace – has no physical centre. That the film succeeds can be measured by the fact that several of its most effective scenes are those where McClane has to protect himself and Farrell while negotiating tiny spaces (Farrell's apartment; an underground tunnel where the antagonists have directed the traffic flow from both directions to kill McClane; an SUV hanging down an elevator shaft; the cooling system of a government computer server facility).

In the 'Concluding Remarks', Bakhtin describes how time interacts with space to make 'narrative events concrete' (FTC, p.250). Another way of putting this is to say that in the text, space is time waiting to happen. This principle informs the entire visual style and spatial presentation of *Die Hard*. The typical spaces in that film – office areas on the deserted, unfinished floors of the Nakatomi building, lift-shafts, basements – all have the necessary physical attributes to make interesting settings for combat. These spaces seem to wait for the inevitable burst of action which will activate their potential; they resemble the characteristic spaces of the Greek romance, 'congealed "suddenlys", adventures turned into things', events waiting to be released into motion (FTC, p.102). Space is designed, in both set construction and shot composition, in a way that complements the action. The interaction of the hero with the spaces and objects around him drives the narrative, although it must be stressed that this is a very mechanical, physical relationship, and not one that affords any change in the broader, abstract world of the narrative. McClane evades capture by achieving an instinctive, intimate understanding of the layout of the building, using its secondary structures (access tunnels, air vents) to move around in.[32] Surfaces and objects become potential allies; McClane uses a table to protect himself from a hail of bullets while he positions himself to return fire. Another scene sees the hero defeat an opponent by exploiting the space of an empty office area (creating a noise that draws the terrorist into his sights). In terms of design within the frame, cinematographer Jan de Bont (later director of *Speed*) frequently elects to let the camera focus on empty spaces, generating the impression that the building is a major character; it is as if the hi-tech Nakatomi building has a consciousness of its own, entwined with that of the wilful, wandering camera. Occasionally, these empty spaces will be transgressed by the entrance of a character into the frame, for instance when the camera is positioned at the top of a flight of stairs where McClane will eventually enter into focus. This technique plays with the assumptions surrounding space that is traditionally offscreen, exploiting Noël Burch's observation that 'offscreen space has only an intermittent or, rather, *fluctuating* existence during any film, and structuring this fluctuation can become a powerful tool in the filmmaker's hands' (Burch, 1973, p.21, italics in original).[33] In accordance with Burch's classical prescription, the empty frame in *Die Hard* is used to define spatial areas as three-dimensional, making us more aware of offscreen space as we wait for something to fill the frame.

The spatial organization of *Die Hard* also exploits the widescreen format to great effect, notably when Al Powell (Reginald Veljohnson), the police officer who bonds with McClane through their radio communication, enters the Nakatomi building to ascertain whether the hero's frantic emergency call is authentic. As Gruber's henchman, posing as a security guard, invites Powell to look around, we can see his gun-toting colleague concealed from the policeman's sight behind a corner. Later, a similar effect singles out Hans Gruber's hidden firearm when he is confronted unexpectedly by McClane, the camera ironically focusing on the weapon that Gruber cannot quite reach. Audience tension is greatly heightened by this process of using the space within the widescreen frame to give us information that is unavailable to the protagonists.

Bakhtin is very fond of using spatial metaphors to talk about time ('the horizontal axis of time', FTC, p.148), and if we transpose this stratagem to examine the progression of narrative in *Die Hard* we can see that the construction of plot mirrors the vertical gradient of the Nakatomi building. Apart from short, external disruptions necessary to channel tension and support the story (the police and FBI reacting to the hostage situation, an unscrupulous television reporter chasing his exclusive), events are confined to the Nakatomi tower, and roughly proceed in an upwards direction culminating in the nailbiting scene where McClane and Gruber dangle out of an upper storey window and the villain falls to his death. Plot and space can be seen here to dialogically interact, the story dictating the nature of location but the organization of space within that setting shaping the particularities of smaller narrative segments (Gruber's death scene would be considerably disadvantaged if he plunged from a second-storey window). By contrast, *Speed* follows a more horizontal pattern, using a slightly less constricting time frame and unfurling within broader external parameters (although narrative time is overwhelmingly devoted to events aboard the bus).

The organization of the action plot as a series of narrative hurdles which the hero must overcome parallels the trope of 'testing' identified by Bakhtin in the Greek romance. This is a category devoid of any experiential value; '[n]o changes of any consequence occur, internal or external, as a result of the events recounted' (FTC, p.106). The tests are purely 'external and formal' in character (106), a method of plot structuration rather than anything with deeper social or psychological resonances. *Speed* and the *Die Hard* films are constructed around a string of set-piece sequences, each of which must trump the last for intensity, rising to a climactic crescendo. This type of structure resembles nothing so much as the linear, level-to-level construction of the computer 'platform' game.

Die Hard is explicitly modelled on this kind of physical arrangement, as its promotional tag line suggests: 'Suspense. Excitement. Adventure on every level!'. As in the computer game, the obstacles placed in the path of the hero become more challenging as time goes on. *Speed* also exhibits this simplistic structure, and can be broken down into three distinct segments. These are the opening rescue mission (which establishes Traven as hero and Payne as villain); the middle section detailing Traven's attempts to get the passengers off the bus without detonating Payne's explosive charge; and the climactic pursuit of Payne and hostage Annie on the subway train. Within these segments there are smaller interim climaxes, designed to keep the viewer at a desirable level of tension. These episodes include the explosion of the decoy bus, the death of a passenger as she makes a panicked attempt to disembark, and the spectacular collision of the exploding bus with a grounded plane at LA airport.

The structural motif of the 'game' appears so frequently in action texts that here we may have a strong contender for a characteristic internal chronotope of the genre. Payne, the villain in *Speed*, explicitly refers to his blackmail campaign as a game, quipping that his manipulation of Traven is like 'interactive TV' (a remark that comes back to haunt Payne when Traven foils his scheme using a looped video clip to give Payne the impression that everything is going to plan).[34] The manipulation of McClane by unseen opponents in *Die Hard With a Vengeance* and *Die Hard 4.0* is very similar, while *Dirty Harry*, *Die Hard With A Vengeance*, *The Running Man* (Paul Michael Glaser, 1987) and *Hard Target* (John Woo, 1993), all incorporate the same formal device of the 'deadly game'. The flow continues, with a seemingly 'straight' action remake of Paul Bartel's blackly comic, countercultural *Death Race 2000* arriving in 2008 from director Paul W.S. Anderson, and the bloody Japanese *Batoru Rowaiaru/Battle Royale* (Kinji Fukasaku, 2000) reportedly lined up for an American makeover (see Ito, 2006). With this preponderance of the game motif, it is perhaps unsurprising that *Die Hard*, its sequels, and *Speed* have all been successfully adapted to the computer game format.[35]

Bakhtin's description of basic adventure-time as breaking down into 'a sequence of adventure-fragments' more than adequately conveys the mechanical division of plot in the action film also (FTC, p.151). Filmmakers clearly believe that audiences want to see (and feel) intense action that builds in a predictable and linear way, with the greatest thrill always deferred until late in the day. Schubart, in a rather value-laden reading, notes that this assumption is so strong in contemporary filmmaking that the development of recent Hollywood action can be read in terms of a shift from an originary thematic structure premised on 'passion' (for instance, in the sacrifice and suffering of heroes like Rambo) to a more 'sadistic' action cinema that requires constant 'acceleration' to maintain audience interest (2001, p.199). Yet Schubart does capture the feeling expressed by Bakhtin when the latter states that 'the hammer of events shatters [...] and forges nothing' (FTC, p.107) in the Greek romance; ultimately, the constant, escalating movement and intense action effect little change in the circular, abstract adventure world, always resulting 'in stasis and inertia: the movement never moves anything' (Schubart, 2001, p.199). Nothing ever really moves except, it could be said, the viewer.

The movie as rollercoaster ride

The promotion of the action film as an 'interactive' experience in ancillary offshoots such as computer games reflects a broader textual strategy to involve the viewer in the events on the screen. As was suggested at the beginning of this chapter, the blockbuster action movie represents the legacy of film's first experiments in scale and spectacle. Other genres may have less formulaic plots and less predictable characters, but the action film defines itself by offering up new and incredible visual treats. Studios accentuate this aspect of the action film by selling them as thrilling, visceral experiences that physically grip the viewer. This has long been the case. Kitsch experiments such as 3D or William Castle's *The Tingler* (1959) (a horror movie where cinema seats were wired to electrical buzzers) attempted to capitalize on this idea of film as all-embracing physical experience. Recent technological developments have bolstered the aspirations of the film industry in this respect and, as we have seen with computer games, the action film is, alongside its sometime hybrid partner science-fiction, the genre most accommodating to other media: attractions based on characters and scenarios from *Robocop*, *Terminator*, *Aliens*, *Back to the Future* (1985–90), *Jurassic Park* and *Spider-Man* film series' have been available in theme parks since the 1990s.

We can trace the roots of this aspect of pseudo-interactivity even further back in American cinema history. The very origins of the cinema, as enunciated in the experiments of the Lumière brothers, are based on the principle that temporal and spatial organization can draw the viewer into a physical relationship with the text, thus producing the illusion that there is a correlation between the time and space in which they experience the film and that expressed within the frame. At the beginning of this chapter, we mentioned the Lumières' classic *L'Arrivée d'un Train en Gare de la Ciotat*, the 'realism' of which is said to have caused panic-stricken spectators to run for the exits.[36] Charles Musser describes how the earliest film shows utilized motifs such as railway travel, creating a 'railway subgenre' where the spectator's perception was framed in the role of 'passenger' (Musser, 1991, p.260). Railroad scenarios were ideally suited to promote a medium whose main selling point was the impression of movement through time and space, and a company called Hale's Tours took this analogous relationship to its logical conclusion, 'using a simulated railway carriage as a movie theater, with the audience sitting in the passenger seats and the screen replacing the view from the front or rear window' (264). Here, we can see an obvious precursor of the movie experience as defined by the modern blockbuster and its commercial spin-offs such as the theme park ride, and a literalization of film's chronotopic capacity to 'move' the viewer.

The 'Cinema of Attractions' that these early film shows constituted (often combining film with live music, vaudeville routines and so on) represented the first flowering of a philosophy of action, spectacle and audience participation from which Hollywood cinema has rarely deviated. The latest blockbuster impresarios may employ 'virtual' technologies and CGI manipulation, but the impulse to give the audience a thrilling 'ride' remains as central now as in 1903, when pioneers like Edwin S. Porter would integrate railway plots into films like *The Great Train Robbery* to meet audience expectations that associated the perception of kinesis with physical travel. Exemplifying this enduring notion, the fundamentally chronotopic tag line of *Speed* – 'Get Ready For Rush Hour!' – fuses the temporal ('rush hour') with the spatio-physical (we are told to 'get ready', because something is going to happen to us). That the film successfully translates this impression is conveyed by one of its reviewers, Marshall Julius:

> The story is uncomplicated because what matters is the action [...] the movie delivers in full: imaginative, exhilarating and brilliantly executed, it tears along faster than a speeding bullet and passes two hours in what seems like a couple of minutes [...] The edge of your seat doesn't have a chance (1996, pp.192–3)

The comments demand scrutiny because of what they reveal about habitual reception modes for action viewing. Julius is caught up in the confluence of time and plot that emerges in the metaphor of speed: 'It tears along faster than a speeding bullet and passes two hours in what seems like a couple of minutes.' The pace of the narrative and the nature of its contents (speeding buses and subway trains) combine to give the impression that the experience of the text *itself* is fast. In an interpretation such as this, boundaries between chronotopic categories – motifs, genres, modes of reception – are dissolved. The bus *is* the film and vice versa. And what is more, we are part of the process, physically incarnated in the action ('The edge of your seat doesn't have a chance'). The association between the chronotopic motifs within the text and the act of reception evokes Bakhtin's conception of the relationship between real and represented. We are beckoned into the text, invited to exploit the function of the chronotope as a 'bridge [...] between the two worlds' (Clark and Holquist, 1984, p.279). Vivian Sobchack, in the context of calling for a theory of carnal response to cinema, notes that the same kinds of impressions and metaphors of tactility and immersion as employed by Julius are actually common in reviews of a variety of film genres (2004, pp.53–4).

The narrative of *Speed* incorporates into its climax a moment where Bakhtin's 'bridge' is symbolically crossed. When Traven ploughs the runaway subway train through the end of the line and onto Hollywood Boulevard, the vehicle comes to rest with a gentle bump against a tour-bus offering views of Hollywood landmarks (almost a ghostly echo of 'Hale's Tours'). Its passengers disembark and immediately commence taking photographs of Annie and Jack as they clinch romantically. The starstruck tourists represent us, the audience, our desire for spectacle satiated and the conventional happy ending firmly in place. It cannot be a coincidence that the train emerges right outside Hollywood's famous Chinese Theater, where the marquee informs us that *2001: A Space Odyssey* (Stanley Kubrick, 1968) is playing. Kubrick's film is another 'journey' narrative, albeit one where the trip to the stars is a metaphor for an interior exploration of humanity. The gleefully unpretentious *Speed* cites these metaphysical concerns ironically.

Speed was enormously successful, effortlessly passing the golden figure of $100 million at the American box office alone. *Speed 2: Cruise Control*, also directed by de Bont (1997), was widely acknowledged as a flop, a fact that was largely credited to the absence of star Reeves. However, its basic premise – the spanner-in-the-works scenario dusted off once again, only this time on a cruise ship – seemed ill-judged, the tightness and fluidity that the first film derived from its limited spatial context dissipated (the concept of 'speed' is difficult to attach to a lumbering cruise liner). In desperation, the trailer for the film not only played up its illustrious heritage, but also the idea of the physical experience: 'This summer, if you didn't catch the bus, you won't want to miss the boat'. Contemporary practitioners of the action movie have continued to produce unofficial remakes of *Die Hard*, even while the official sequels, as we have seen, have shown some development away from the original in the handling of time and space. A notable aspect of the promotional activity for *Die Hard 4.0* were representations about the film's 'return' to practical (non-digital) effects and profilmic stunts: 'the only film you'll see this summer with real, live performed stunts' (Yamato, 2007).[37] The film contained impressive stunt work based on the physical activity of 'Parkour', yet followed the lead of the much older James Bond franchise in including this (*Casino Royale*). Such promotional and textual strategies sought to distinguish *Die Hard 4.0* from more fantastical action-adventure texts that had embraced CGI, and were perhaps also designed to mitigate, in the eyes of certain fans, its controversial PG-13 rating in American theatres. Bearing out Purse's ideas, this discourse of 'old school' values seems to show a worried industry addressing fan concerns around immaterial, inauthentic virtual signifiers, both of the action body and of the obstacles that challenge it; it is not usual to see a film studio wilfully introducing a concept of history to a form that inarguably thrives on its distancing from all signs of the historical. Generally, rules dictate that the action film dwells in a permanent, technologically aided now. Bakhtin discusses the lack of 'internal limits' in the Greek romance which allows adventures to be extended 'as long as one likes' (FTC, p.94), and the action film is spun from the same fabric. Series such as the Bond films or *Die Hard* can endlessly propagate themselves because their form, the very time and space of which they are constituted and within which their adventures unfold, is so adaptable, elastic, abstract.

3
Chronotope II: Time, Space and Genre in the Western Film

Introduction

Die Hard is fairly brazen when it comes to displaying its influences. Many elements of the narrative are straightforwardly imported from the Western, most prominent among these being the premise of the outsider hero who must battle his way through the ranks of the enemy until he faces a stand-off with the villain, whom he resembles in many ways and with whom he has formed a special bond of respect. The film constructs an amusing discourse foregrounding its own parasitical relationship to the classic Western. McClane's code name for himself is 'Roy' after the cowboy star Roy Rogers; Gruber refers to McClane as 'Mr Cowboy'; and the race-against-time structure recalls *High Noon* (Fred Zinneman, 1952), a film that is specifically referred to in dialogue between hero and villain. These and several other references[1] acknowledge the massive influence of the Western form on the action genre, and it can be argued that across all genres, Hollywood's defining principles of action, spectacle, tempo, drama and emotion have all developed in the wake of pioneering Westerns like Porter's *Great Train Robbery* (1903) and *Life of a Cowboy* (1905). Perhaps no other genre can be as readily identified as 'American' as the Western, despite the notable efforts of Sergio Leone, Akira Kurosawa and others to wrest such nationalistic associations from the form.[2] The critic Tag Gallagher contends that the influence of the Western does not stop in Hollywood, but deserves to be recognized on an even broader scale. Gallagher credits many innovations of the cinematic medium to the genre, arguing that, so integral was the popularity of the Western to the success of early cinema, 'rather than the cinema having invented the Western, it was the Western, already long existent in popular culture, that invented the cinema' (Gallagher, 1986, p.204).

Nevertheless, in spite of its appeal and adaptability across cultures, in production and narrative terms the genre is an American phenomenon, 'the American film par excellence' according to André Bazin (1972, p.140). Indeed, the term 'Western' itself ties the genre to a specific geographical location (and also implies fixed, albeit relative, temporal co-ordinates, infusing the term with significant chronotopic value).

Despite its status as one of the most exhaustively researched and documented genres in the history of film criticism, the Western has been the subject of some disagreement concerning the matter of generic constitution. Despite the fact that the Western is, arguably, more stable, in terms of iconography and narrative situation than many genres, the exact shape and historical trajectory of the canon remain a contentious area. In one of the most famous stand-alone studies of the genre, *Sixguns and Society* (1977), Will Wright draws sample materials for his structuralist analysis from the period 1931–72, which he regards as the most fertile spell in the genre's history. Within these temporal parameters, Wright identifies four major narrative tendencies in the Western: the 'Classical Plot', typified in films like *Shane* (George Stevens, 1953); the 'Vengeance Variation', into which Wright places *The Searchers* (John Ford, 1956) and also Ford's earlier *Stagecoach* (1939); the 'Transition Theme', exemplified by *High Noon*; and, finally, the 'Professional Plot', into which can be slotted Richard Brooks' *The Professionals* (1966) and Peckinpah's *The Wild Bunch* (1969). Corresponding, roughly, to overlapping historical periods, the four stages demonstrate, for Wright, a thematic development reflecting socio-political realities; the 'Classical' plot, for instance, in its common scenario of the 'outsider' coming to town and despatching the villain, a marginal figure who threatens society and the process of civilization, reflects the quandary of the Keynesian shift from a market economy to a centrally planned economic framework in postwar America. According to Wright's formula, by the time the genre has mutated into the 'Professional' period (1960s), narrative structures have broken down to the anarchy of *The Wild Bunch*, aping the erosion of social structures by a fully corporate economy. The 'heroes' are divested of any allegiance to an irrelevant, outdated notion of 'community', relying only on the other members of their own small group of 'skilled technicians', their talents available to the highest bidder (Wright, 1977, p. 187). Narrative methods become gradually more self-aware in a parallel transition, from the clean, clear-cut dynamics of the 'Classical' period to the self-conscious stylistics and ambiguous protagonists of the 'Professional' era.

Wright's approach has been criticized by many, including Tag Gallagher, who takes issue with the historical starting point of the survey

(Wright 'excludes the first thirty-five years of Western cinema' according to Gallagher), as well as Wright's dubious decision to include only 'top-grossing' (i.e., those that earn more than four million dollars) movies in his investigation, arguing that blockbusters may well be 'unrepresentative of the genre' (Gallagher, 1986, p.203). Furthermore, Wright's conceptualization of the Western as 'myth', enabling him to employ a combination of the structural criteria used in Lévi-Strauss' anthropology and Vladimir Propp's work on Russian folk tales, is criticized by Christopher Frayling, who suggests that such a position displaces interest in the Western as an expression of an 'entrepreneurial culture' and re-situates the genre, falsely, in the realms of 'folk culture' (Frayling, 1981, p.136). A more obvious drawback to Wright's approach is that, in his structuralist search for binary oppositions and resonances with historical moments, he concentrates almost exclusively on structures of plot and typology, barely glancing at the iconographic, expressive, technical and industrial properties of the genre. Wright's organization of his sample films into four dominant categories of narrative structure reflects a wider mania for the erection of boundaries between stable-seeming groupings of texts in the genre's body of criticism; not without reason is Gallagher's account entitled 'Shoot-Out at the Genre Corral'.

A dispute over historical terms centring on the Western is nothing new; genre and subject matter alike share an ability to incite controversy in this respect. A brief acquaintance with the literature is enough to convince one of the tremendous critical stakes of establishing a generic lineage of the Western, if not to persuade one of the plain impossibility of the task. To introduce Bakhtin to the furore surrounding a genre that is 'at root [...] a *social* phenomenon' (Frayling, 1981, p.139) is not only tempting but, as I hope to demonstrate, necessary; however, in order to derive fresh meaning from the genre (without making any monologic pretensions to a definitive word) we will need to look at an area conspicuously underdeveloped in many of the aforementioned studies. Having examined narrative organization through the prism of the chronotope in the previous chapter, we will now shift chronotopic focus towards the expressive, iconographic layer: the composition and mise-en-scène of the Western frame, so often posited as the quintessential experience of film viewing. As Bazin puts it, the 'secret' of the Western is one that identifies it with 'the essence of cinema' (1972, p.141). Westerns seem to represent some kind of master-genre irresistible to critics, reflected by the industrial dominance of the genre through several decades of Hollywood history and its infiltration into so many other kinds of cinematic narrative. One of the pitfalls of previous genre criticism that we hope to avoid is what Gallagher terms the tendency to 'ignore the evidence', to deal with the abstraction of narrative rather than engage with 'the phenomenon of cinema art' (1986, pp.202; 212). So, while plot and theme are important to our discussion of *The Searchers*, it is how these abstractions are expressed and their problems worked out *in the image* that is paramount here; and this is why, for a companion text, we will examine John Sayles' *Lone Star* (1996), a generic outsider that nevertheless constructs a critique of the Western through its expressive style.

The two narratives take place in roughly the same geographical locale; however, the Texas of *The Searchers* is separated from the modern day Texas of *Lone Star* by nearly 130 years. Sayles hints that the Western film has taken on the status of national myth in the intervening years, representing to America the legend of its own origin. However, this process has not been without its harmful repercussions, resulting in indentations on the national psyche that leave a heavy burden of authority on emotionally incapable men and all but exclude the feminine and racial other from the picture.[3] In *Lone Star* 'the West' is no longer a frontier but a porous, tension-ridden partition between the United States and Latin America, a geographical fissure reflecting the fragility of gender, racial and national identities. The same concerns can be seen to thread through Ford's film as well, although they are obviously less explicit and tempered by some of the casual racism and sexism that many critics, perhaps letting the filmmakers off the hook too easily, have labelled as almost prerequisites of the genre (Pye, 1996, p.235). The really fascinating link between the two movies is a temporal one. *Lone Star*'s narrative hinges on a sub-plot buried, metaphorically and literally, in 1957 – a year after the release of *The Searchers* – concerning the death of a corrupt racist sheriff, Charley Wade (Kris Kristofferson). Wade is an archetypal 'bad guy' hypocritically wearing the clothes of authority; the manner of his death, and the implication in it of the legendary Sheriff Buddy Deeds (Matthew McConaughey), leads to an unravelling of a history that an entire town has come to depend upon. Seeming to meditate, intertextually, on the famous line from Ford's 1962 Western *The Man Who Shot Liberty Valance* ('When the legend becomes fact, print the legend'), *Lone Star* searches for the roots of modern social tensions in a past at least partly determined and coloured by cinematic culture, and examines an ambiguity in the concept of heroism that mines the same unstable territory as *The Searchers*. The complex time frame (1868, 1956, 1957, 1996) evoked by the two films adumbrates a problem of identity that finds its expression in the movie frame. The ownership and composition of that quasi-sacred space is thus the main focus of this chapter.

A quotation from Bakhtin may suffice to reassure the reader that critical liberties are not being taken with the comparison between two films that, beyond a certain metafictional affinity, have little outwardly in common with one another, and whose respective releases are separated by four decades. Bakhtin warns us against isolating our critical responses to a given work within the value-laden logic of the epoch in which the work was produced:

> If it is impossible to study literature apart from an epoch's entire culture, it is even more fatal to encapsulate a literary phenomenon in the single epoch of its creation, in its own contemporaneity, so to speak [...] Enclosure within the epoch also makes it impossible to understand the work's future life in subsequent centuries [...] Works break through the boundaries of their own time, they live in centuries, that is, in *great time* and frequently (with great works, always) their lives there are more intense and fuller than are their lives within their own time
>
> (NM, pp.3–4).[4]

A certain degree of immersion within the 'contemporaneity' of the work is necessary, of course, to situate our understanding of it within the proper dialogic network; however, we must never underestimate the power of the text to mean in new ways and eras. Related to the gap between the periods in which the two films were released is their vastly different orientation in terms of production and economics. *The Searchers* is, in many ways, a picture that embodies the classical Hollywood cinema at its peak, and had the full weight of the studio system behind its production and promotion. *Lone Star*, at least spiritually (the mercurial context of 1990s independent cinema invites tentativeness),[5] comes from the 'independent' sector of modern American cinema, its 'outsider' credentials boosted by the reputation of its director as one of the most talented filmmakers working outside of the mainstream. It could be argued that the films are thus oriented towards markedly different audiences. However, this contention could be countered by the fact that, today, *The Searchers*, like much of Ford's work, finds favour with exactly the same kind of film-literate audience who would be interested in the work of a figure like John Sayles (without for a moment wishing to suggest that either film is unequipped for broader mass appeal; *The Searchers* was a hit on release in 1956, and *Lone Star* found success with an Academy Award nomination for Sayles' screenplay in 1997).[6] Again, time leaves its indelible trace on the way in which we view the text, and *The Searchers* becomes a film for in-depth critical study rather than a 'mere' genre picture.[7] The title of Peter Lehman's article on the 'repressed' discourse of black/white relations in Ford's film, 'Texas 1868/America 1956', hints at the matrix of temporal co-ordinates that demand to be included in the discussion, but omits the crucial appendage 1990, the time of Lehman's own viewing and interpretation.[8] Lehman's study thus fails to include what Bakhtin would call the 'decisive significance' of his own temporal position (NM, p.5).

Film genre criticism affirms that a central function of genre is to render social myths into digestible narratives. As the 'organizing center' (FTC, p.250) through which generic construction is realized, the chronotope becomes implicated in film's materialization of social value. Through the notion of 'generic memory', introduced in the Dostoevsky book, Bakhtin emphasizes the transformative potential of new contexts upon established chronotopic patterns: 'A genre lives in the present, but always *remembers* its past, its beginning' (PDP, p.106). Lucidly glossed by Janet Walker as 'the continuing existence of an earlier generic paradigm in the narrative sediment of a later one' (2001, p.222), generic memory regulates the way in which a genre interacts with the social experiences and expectations of an audience. It follows, then, that formal conventions can be re-accentuated and given fresh relevance through the adoption of a new context within the framework of generic memory; time and space patterns caught in images can alter the emotions and values with which they are initially coloured. Here, we see the connection emerge between Bakhtin's conviction that genres experience a life of 'constant renewal' (PDP, p.106), anchored by a core remembrance of the genre's archaic past, and another notion that peppers the late works and fragments that were collected together in translation as *Speech Genres and Other Late Essays*. 'Outsideness' [*vnenakhodimost*], a concept that Bakhtin typically expresses spatially, suggests a contemplating position that allows a given object or event to be fixed in space and completed in time (Holquist, 2002, p.31). Through it, the object is given definition within a larger order: 'It is only in the eyes of *another* culture that foreign culture reveals itself fully and profoundly' (NM, p.7). Outsideness in *temporal* terms signifies the ability to contemplate the reverberation of our actions in the future that is a special property of novelistic art (Hirschkop, 1999, pp.96–7); it opens up a window on 'great time' and liberates us from a single, limited point of view (thus conforming to the wider Bakhtinian conviction that truth cannot be apprehended by mere reference to one's immediate horizon).[9] Two layers or points in time – at least – will be involved in any event that interacts with a prior cultural 'speaking'; interpretation exists 'in my own context, in a contemporary context, and in a future one' (MHS, p.161). It is as if a text, genre or form must both multiply its *reserves* of time and expand its *awareness* of time to grow to true significance – to 'become', as, for Bakhtin, did the novel in the development of a modern culture. One could say that what heteroglossia achieves for the presence of language stratification and diversity in the novel, the chronotope accomplishes for time: that is, it expands and intensifies the representation of diverse registers of time, from the narrowly mythical (what Bakhtin calls the 'historically inverted' – FTC, pp.146–51) to the historically alive, fleshed out and future-oriented.[10] The characteristic chronotopes of genres are the shapes in which these various orders of time appear to us.

Lone Star will thus be used here to crystallize an outside perspective on the Western. The value of an interpretation that comes from outside reveals itself when we turn to the historicizing imperatives of genre study. Asif Agha talks about historical revisionism as a matter of overlapping chronotopes:

> [...H]istorical accounts themselves occur as events in particular times and places, and, as events, belong to certain chronotopes just as they model others. The outlines of the chronotope to which a representation *belongs* may appear far less clear to the historian than the one which it explicitly *denotes* until revisionist history appears on the scene and corrects 'the historical record' (the second chronotope) by locating prior views of it as the mistakes of 'an earlier age' (the first chronotope). History always turns out to be a relationship between chronotopes
>
> (Agha, 2007, p.324)

What exactly is it that is mediated by the chronotope? In the present context, 'fact and legend' would undoubtedly be a pat answer. Yet what transpires between the parts of that equation demands scrutiny. The idea that chronotopicity endures as a *sediment* (Walker, 2001, p.222; Pechey, 2007, p.101) brings into view a metaphor of layering and, indeed, unearthing; the archaeological reference, as we will see, leads right into the opening scene of *Lone Star*. It may be 'fatal' – or at least, unadvisable – to try to erect boundaries that the flow of great time will eventually rearrange (NM, p.3), yet Bakhtin, fascinated by thresholds and their rendering of crisis time, particularly in Dostoevsky, recognizes that borders can also be rich in meaning (creating a relation that sharpens up the meaning lying on either side).

Time and myth: 'generic memory'

Despite being ostensibly 'rooted in an objective thing which is the history of the United States' (Wagner, quoted in Frayling, 1981, p.137), pinning down time in the Western is not the most straightforward of critical tasks. On the one hand, temporality in the genre is bounded by strict, empirical parameters (very few Westerns are situated outside of the nineteenth century). *The Searchers*, like many Westerns, could not be more definite about the historical starting-point upon which its fiction is built, its setting in the aftermath of the Civil War established by the opening caption ('Texas 1868') and alluded to throughout. The idea that such a reference point confers any real historical specificity would be met with suspicion by the critical tendency that speaks of the Western as incorporating 'the structure [...] of myth' (Wright, 1977, p.14); far from being valued as historical representation, the genre is instead read for its 'timelessness' (Maltby, 1996a, 126). The durability of the genre's essential narrative conventions, which find renewal in disparate generic contexts even in disguised form, is often stated,[11] an attitude expressed memorably and succinctly by André Bazin: '[t]he Western does not age' (Bazin, 1972, p.141). Bazin supports this theory by outlining how the various myths that constitute the Western narrative are themselves expressions of an even simpler 'essential principle', that of 'the great epic Manicheism which sets the forces of evil over against the knights of the true cause' (145). Bazin's willingness to take the Western at face value apparently extends to its ideological undercurrents; he expresses no qualms about the genre's construction of a Manichean dichotomy between the 'pagan savagery' of the Indians and the 'strong, rough and courageous' white Christian settlers (145). The critic goes on to conflate the mythical with the epic, suggesting that 'cinema is the specifically epic art' and identifying the Western as symbolic of the epic dimensions of the artform, before comparing the Civil War as rendered in the Western to the Trojan War as envisioned in Homer (148).

Ultimately, Bazin's portentous analogies fail to shed any real critical light on the Western, even if his main point, the universality of Western themes and motifs, certainly has considerable substance.[12] Yet, the approach to the genre as a form for the expression of myths has an unhelpful effect of suggesting that the concerns engendered in narratives, and consequently the forms employed for this expression, remain the same over large expanses of historical time. Such an atavistic conception of cultural forms is questionable from a Bakhtinian perspective, threatening to erase the influences of social and historical context and reduce the 'life of the genre' to a static formal exercise (PDP, p.106). In this conception of a range of 'mythical' images, predetermined and available to the artist, there are echoes of the Formalist doctrine as espoused by Victor Shklovsky in 'Art as Technique' (originally published 1917). Shklovsky contends that 'images change little; from century to century, from nation to nation, from poet to poet, they flow on without changing [...] poets are much more concerned with arranging images than with creating them' (Shklovsky, 1965, p.7). Medvedev criticizes the Formalist conception of literary evolution in *The Formal Method in Literary Scholarship*, contending that Shklovsky's formulation precipitates a divorce of literature from 'the other ideological series and [...] socio-economic development' (FM, p.159). Literature is contemplated within a false realm of 'eternal contemporaneity' that erases the vital category of historical time (171). Literary criticism becomes 'the organ of the writer', originator of artistic trends, and is consequently deprived of its 'basic role of mediator between the social and general ideological demands of the epoch, on the one hand, and literature, on the other' (173). The fate of genre in such an interpretation is to be dehistoricized, reduced to a moribund reshuffling of perennially relevant but creatively dead components.

The mythical approach to the Western constrains spectators into a position that depicts them as only responsive to that mythical quotient with which they are familiar, their tastes untouched by social, historical or ideological currents from generation to generation. The conception of the Western as a store of given, 'mythical' images whose relevance depends only on some incontrovertible 'original' meaning, and not on the inflection cast upon them by each new usage, appears to be at odds with Bakhtin's emphasis on unfinalizability and the new meanings brought about by changes in dialogic context. 'Timelessness' begins to signify stasis rather than universality, and myth engenders a frozen, sanitized world of given meanings and gestures. Historical and political overtones become victims of the mythical impulse; according to Roland Barthes, myth is a form of 'depoliticized speech' that robs things of complexity, rendering them instead as politically and historically neutral 'essences' (Barthes, 1981, pp.142–3). Political value, as Barthes sees it, is not necessarily precluded by mythical structure, but exists in a state of fluctuation according to the 'strength' with which the myth resonates within the social constellation (becoming abruptly diluted in the 'strong' myth but fading 'like a colour', though not beyond resurrection under the right conditions, in the 'weak' myth – 1981, p.144). For Barthes, myth is an 'inflexion', distortion or purification of an image or signifier, not the outright denial of its 'true' meaning (129). For Bakhtin, myth is a more direct threat to the political value inherent in an image, and is often used to reinforce the claims of certain enshrined languages to ultimate authority. Bakhtin envisages myth in an oppositional relationship to the decentering forces of heteroglossia, serving to bolster the unitary identity of canonical languages (DIN, pp.369–70). However, Barthes and Bakhtin share an emphasis on myth as stripping language of its flexibility, expressiveness and democratic orientation.

In the light of these readings one can understand the tension between the mythical elements which might be desirable to the vested interests of classical Hollywood, and the critics who would argue that they impoverish the Western as a profoundly social form. Historical value is the first, and most grave, casualty of the process of mythicization, according to Barthes. It is a 'conjuring trick' whereby reality is inverted, emptied of history and naturalized, with the consequence that complex human acts are given 'the simplicity of essences' and resituated in a 'world which is without contradictions' (Barthes, 1981, pp.142–3). Even aside from the unwitting but excellent gloss of monologism captured in Barthes' 'world without contradictions', there are obvious correspondences with Bakhtin's conception of the golden age in this picture of a world cut off from history. For Bakhtin, an aura of 'ancient truth' and an externally imposed 'natural state' denote the 'mythological and literary relationship to the future' characteristic of the ancient novel, a failing that would eventually be remedied in Rabelais' historically sensitive re-accentuation of folkloric forms (FTC, pp.147–8). The world evoked in the Hollywood Western is all too often imbued with the same neutrality; in Barthes' terms it is an 'immobilized' world (1981, p.155), a landscape designed to host drama and spectacle but carefully expunged of living historical traces that might foreground the unpalatable realities of racial conflict. As shall be demonstrated in the analysis of *The Searchers* to follow, narrative strategies such as the fetishization of the hero and his close visual association with landscape serve the same naturalizing agency that Barthes speaks of in his critique of mythology. Our attention is directed towards the ordered beauty within the frame in an effort to deflect our contemplation of the untidiness beyond it; Barthes could be speaking of the Western when he writes, 'all that is left for one to do is to enjoy this beautiful object [the hero, the landscape] without wondering where it comes from' (1981, p.151).[13] Reinforcing this point, numerous Westerns feature heroes who ride into town fully formed, accompanied by a history only faintly alluded to: Ethan Edwards (John Wayne), in *The Searchers*, and the eponymous hero of *Shane* are prominent examples.

Will Wright's study attempts to circumvent such criticism by stressing the flexibility within mythical organization, using the fact that narrative structures change and develop through the classic era of Hollywood Westerns to prove that the meaning of the Western myth cannot be 'universal, biological and therefore static' but is in actuality responsive to developments in social history (1977, p.8). The tone of his discourse ringing vaguely Bakhtinian, Wright asserts that 'within each period the structure of the myth corresponds to the conceptual needs of social and self understanding required by the dominant social institutions of that period' (14). Wright's attention to the structure of myth, and how it is determined by cultural conditions, would seem to have implications for our study of genre, raising the issue of its relationship with myth. In the context of Yeats' 'mythical method', T.S. Eliot writes of myth that it imparts 'order and form' to art (quoted in Righter, 1975, p.34). Michael Gardiner remarks that, for Lévi-Strauss, myths represented one form of the 'universal human impulse to categorize and classify "reality" into cognitively manageable units' (Gardiner, 1992, p.144). If we substitute 'reality' in that sentence for 'narrative', we arrive at a workable, if unsophisticated, definition of the function of genre. According to Will Wright, myths 'use the past to tell us how to act out the present' (1977, p.187); that is, they arrange experience into a form that is made visible in the order of a spectacle ('acting out'). This function is comparable, to some extent, to that of genre in film.

Bakhtin's remarks on generic memory help to introduce a new dimension to the discussion about myth and genre:

> A literary genre, by its very nature, reflects the most stable, 'eternal' tendencies in literature's development. Always preserved in a genre are underlying elements of the *archaic*. True, these archaic elements are preserved in it only thanks to their constant *renewal*, which is to say, their contemporization. A genre is always the same and yet not the same, always old and new simultaneously. Genre is reborn and renewed at every new stage in the development of literature and in every individual work of a given genre. This constitutes the life of the genre [...] A genre lives in the present, but always *remembers* its past, its beginning. Genre is representative of creative memory in the process of literary development. Precisely for this reason genre is capable of guaranteeing the *unity* and *uninterrupted continuity* of this development.
>
> (PDP, p.106, italics in original)

This is a crucial (and much quoted) passage, not only for the present discussion, but for the entire Bakhtinian project. Bakhtin's understanding of literary progress sees it as an 'uninterrupted' and continuous event, a line of development characterized by subtle changes that nevertheless provoke new directions. For Boris Eichenbaum, literary succession enacts a 'destruction of old values' in a sequence of dramatic purges that is deemed necessary for the construction of new values (Eichenbaum, 1965, p.134); yet, as Medvedev observes, '[C]ontinuity can be far from peaceful and still be continuity' (FM, p.165). Genre, as perceived by Bakhtin, is an organic process, the shape of which is determined by interaction with the sphere of the social. It is also subject to the work of time, revised (albeit subtly) in every individual text and possessing a 'memory' that ensures that the integrity of the genre remains intact. The old and the new interacting in perfect degree, not necessarily harmoniously: this is the essence of dialogism (and also an indication of how different times can co-exist in the chronotope, something that is pertinent to the visual presentation of *Lone Star*, as we shall see shortly). Literary creation as conceived by Shklovsky, an unending flow of unchanging images, sees the past as totally structuring the present of creation. Bakhtin, conversely, sees in the novel (and its capacity to tap into generic memory) a past that 'provides limits' for the forging of new creative acts but, crucially, 'also allows for multiple options' (Morson, 1991, p.1083). Formal frameworks (genres) can be understood as 'congealed world view[s]' (MHS, p.165), as valuable resources that can be 'partially reconstructed under the pressure of new experiences' (Morson, 1991, p.1087) and used as foundations for new (textual) utterances. Perhaps it would be illuminating to think of 'myths' in a similar way, as expressions of 'world views' that have become 'congealed' or crystallized (but not fossilized or entombed) through generations of usage. The 'mythical' content of the Western film could thus be reassessed as 'congealed' but value-laden material that can be reactivated through the addition of a new social and cultural context and the crucial operations of genre (which are 'central to how change actually happens' – Morson, 1991, p. 1087). The generic forms that are passed down in literary creation are 'already heavily laden with meaning, filled with it' (NM, p.5); however, Bakhtin does not see this fact as stifling the process by which new utterances are generated, but as stimulating it and ensuring that the unbreakable chain of meanings attached to the text is solidified.

The idea of generic memory can perhaps help us to understand ambiguous attitudes to myth in critical work on the Western. It is a genre that has become acutely conscious of the operations of history despite widespread liberties taken with historical fact; such concerns can be identified in the often misguided attempts to redress the balance of Western ideology from a Native American point of view, such as John Ford's *Cheyenne Autumn* (1964), which, as Richard Maltby points out, limits its revisionism to a mechanical insertion of Indian values into the same paradigm of community that characterizes the approach to settlers or cavalry in other Ford films (1996b, p.40). *Lone Star*, as we shall see, dramatizes this theme of revisionism in its palpable sense of how cultural reparation and the establishment of truth haunts the development of American society. Yet, at the level of narrative, the Western is condemned by its empirical basis to exist within a closed historical circuit. The value and purpose of historical progression is diminished when closure is imposed upon its flow, and as Barthes asserts, myth, often equated with 'timelessness', is implicated in this process. Not only can mythical elements signify the romantic ideal of a period lost to time (the 'golden age' tendency of which Bakhtin is so suspicious) but, if used insensitively, they can also be exploited as an alibi for historical inaccuracy or bias, threatening to 'close' time and thus render narrative as a monologization. As Gary Saul Morson says in a very different context (a discussion of Bakhtin's resistance to 'theoretism' and its implied reduction of creativity to 'mere *discovery*'), '[t]hus do timeless laws close down time' (Morson, 1991, pp.1074–5).

Myth, as Jon Tuska points out, is too often used by apologists to denote 'that part of [a Western] which they know to be a lie, but which, for whatever reason, they still wish to embrace' (quoted in Maltby, 1996b, p.36). However, the Western genre ingeniously finds a way of turning this epistemological problem to its advantage. The tension between two registers of temporality – the mythical/'timeless' and the historical/everyday – becomes the creative fulcrum in many superior Westerns, which often meditate, to some degree, on their own cinematic processes for representing history: *High Noon, Liberty Valance, The Wild Bunch, Unforgiven* (Clint Eastwood, 1992), *The Assassination of Jesse James by the Coward Robert Ford* (Andrew Dominik, 2007). The gap between these two apparently antithetical registers of time reverberates with the gap between the time depicted in the narrative and that of the story's articulation. As Peter Lehman suggests in his analysis of *The Searchers*, 'America 1956' is just as important as 'Texas 1868' in the complex life the film conducts in history, even if the classical Hollywood conventions employed by Ford do function to 'repress' this fact (Lehman, 1990, p.402).

It can be stated with certainty, then, that Westerns express fundamental social and psychological obsessions, the stuff of myth; however, the real interest, and the genius of the genre, lies in the development of visual means for codifying and dramatizing these abstractions. The Western formulates its own distinctive apparatus for the figurative rendering of philosophical and ideological meanings that is the central capacity of cinema. It is this aspect of *The Searchers* to which we now turn, bearing in mind that what is left *out* of the frame in the ideological schema of the classical Western is often as revealing as what is present. To this end, we will consider significant absences and misrepresentations within the text, namely those involving gender and race. Here, also, we will re-introduce the chronotope. Bakhtin's device can offer much to the debate around genre, for genres are determined by particular configurations of narrative, the organization of the narrative world into coherent and recognizable shapes; and these configurations are determined by chronotopes.

Spectacle and landscape: the star as monument

The Searchers opens with Ethan Edwards (John Wayne), absent for several years, returning to the Texas homestead where his brother Aaron (Walter Coy) and sister-in-law Martha (Dorothy Jordan) have raised a family. It is the aftermath of the Civil War; however, the immediate threat to the fragile band of settlers comes from a marauding Comanche war party led by chief Scar (Henry Brandon). The day after Ethan's return he volunteers to assist in an investigation concerning stolen cattle, accompanied by Martin Pawley (Jeffrey Hunter), a foundling of Cherokee extraction, who has been adopted into Aaron's family. While they are gone, the Comanche attack the Edwards' homestead, killing Aaron, Martha and their son, and kidnapping their small daughter Debbie (Lana Wood) and teenager Lucy (Pippa Scott). An enraged Ethan sets out to find the girls and exact revenge upon Scar (along the way, we learn that Ethan had a romantic attachment to Martha apparently predating her marriage to Aaron). Martin insists on joining him, the necessity of his involvement becoming more urgent after Ethan finds Lucy dead and the pair learn that Debbie has been taken as Scar's wife, whereupon Martin begins to suspect Ethan of intending to kill Debbie rather than let her live as a Comanche squaw. The search continues for several years, during which time a misinterpretation of tribal protocol leads Martin to find himself betrothed to an Indian squaw, whom Ethan christens 'Look' (Beulah Archuletta). Various clues fail to lead to Debbie. Rejected by Martin, Look is later killed in a cavalry raid on the camp of her tribe. Eventually, the trail having cooled, Ethan learns that Scar is camped nearby, and the settlers, aided by the cavalry, launch a successful raid on the Comanche. Ethan catches up with a terrified Debbie (played as an adult by Natalie Wood), whom he does not kill but tenderly embraces before returning her to white civilization. Martin and his sweetheart Laurie (Vera Miles) are reunited, but Ethan apparently rejects the invitation to rejoin society.

'Who controls the frame?' is not a difficult question to answer in regard to *The Searchers*; like the great majority of Westerns, the male director/male star axis is firmly in place.[14] Throughout the film, the camera is transfixed by Wayne, even as his racist, misanthropic character Ethan Edwards is repelling the sensibilities of the spectator. Wayne's redoubtable visual charisma establishes an antithetical relation with the negative aspects of his character's personality; we are *directed* to look at him, even though he offends us. There is no doubt that the film encourages us to find the attitudes of the protagonist abhorrent; his attitudes are unambiguously framed as racism from an early point in the film (his first interactions with Martin). Yet Ford still capitalizes on the magic of Wayne's presence, and relies on our faith in the star to fabricate an uneasy rapport with the character. In this respect, the spectator finds herself occupying a very similar position to that of the junior partner of the titular searchers, Martin Pawley. Despite his obvious admiration for Ethan, Martin, being of uncertain parentage – 'an eighth Cherokee and the rest [...] Welsh and English' – becomes the first target of Edwards' latent racism ('Fella could mistake you for a half-breed'), immediately engaging our sympathy. Martin's admiration of Ethan's abilities is thus tempered with the same horror at his bigotry that we feel; yet Martin is clearly also a version of Ethan, possessing the same determination and energy but without the cynicism. As several commentators have pointed out, clues in the text also suggest that Martin is another *biological* version of Ethan, the son he refuses to recognize.[15]

This is not the only instance of Ethan being bound up with an apparently antithetical character in the text; his avowed enemy Scar is the most obvious candidate, a link that mise-en-scène and editing stress time and again with cross-cutting and similar framing techniques (leading us to infer a greater degree of likeness between the two than Ethan would admit). Captain Clayton (Ward Bond), similarly incorrigible but choosing to practice on the right side of moral and governmental law, and the marginalized 'holy fool' figure Mose Harper (Hank Worden) are also included in this series, as is the minor character Lieutenant Greenhill, played by Wayne's own son Patrick in a telling piece of casting. The naive Greenhill is sent to aid Clayton by his 'pa', a cavalry supremo; as this is an archetype essayed by Wayne in Ford's 'cavalry trilogy' (*Fort Apache*,

1948; *She Wore A Yellow Ribbon*, 1949; *Rio Grande*, 1950[16]), we can infer that Wayne's status as controlling patriarch and monolithic male presence is being reaffirmed here. In the system of power relations that governs the film, Wayne's only rival to ultimate power is the 'father' figure who has given him celluloid 'life' and immortality – John Ford. Just as, according to Richard Maltby (1996b, p.40), most of Wayne's screen roles can be seen to reflect elements of one another and of the star's image (if not his 'true' personality which, as with any star, is rendered onscreen with a greater complexity), the supporting characters planted around Wayne also reflect and refract his colossal presence. This is symptomatic of the film's fetishization of Wayne/Edwards: even when we are watching somebody else (in the rare intervals between Wayne's appearances) we are still, to some degree, watching John Wayne.

So rooted in the popular cinematic imagination has his likeness become, Wayne's dimensions suggest those of the frame itself. His body is a screen onto which various signifiers of masculinity, morality and political conservatism, the constituent values of 'John Wayne', are projected, creating a powerful bodily chronotope that dominates his films. A very precise tailoring of space is required to frame and aggrandize Wayne's loaded physical presence to maximum effect, and more often than not the chosen backdrop is the Western landscape. Consequently, his characters in town-situated, domestic Westerns that make less use of landscape are arguably less memorable (John T. Chance in Howard Hawks' *Rio Bravo*, 1959, Tom Doniphon in *Liberty Valance*), and he would have been a poor choice for the role of Wyatt Earp in Ford's *My Darling Clementine* (1946). In that film the morally ambiguous town of Tombstone is rendered in a chiaroscuro, quasi-*noir* lighting scheme to which Henry Fonda's pragmatic Wyatt Earp is charged to bring the light of justice; Wayne, conversely, must always be in full view, celebrating the 'clarity of [the hero's] physical image against his bare landscape' (Warshow, 1999, p.656). Iconographically, he can be more readily equated with the church that the citizens of Tombstone erect against the Monument Valley backdrop, Ford's 'most cherished image of civilization-being-born' (Dowell, 1995, p.8) – and Wayne is meant to be worshipped accordingly. This rule pertains in *The Searchers* even when the hero's moral credentials are in some doubt; the number of close-ups and isolated frames of Wayne does not decrease when his true, terrifying motivation for finding Debbie is revealed. In fact, the film reverses this pattern to great effect. When Ethan and Martin visit an army camp and are shown a number of white female captives recovered from a raid on a group of Comanche, Edwards fails to suppress his disgust at the state of the women, about whom he spits, 'They ain't white anymore, they're Comanche'. The camera zooms in on Wayne, who looms menacingly into the frame, in grim close-up, moments after Edwards' darkest exclamation. The spectacle of John Wayne thus overrides even the moral reprehensibility of such appalling racism, and Ford draws on his star's power to attract the audience even as Edwards repels them.

The plot, dialogue, camerawork, lighting, locations, music and even credits of *The Searchers* are all marshalled in support of Wayne's centrality. The opening titles are projected onto an image of a stone wall which refers not only to Edwards' exclusion from civilized society and the realm of the domestic but also, surely, to the physical stature of the actor. The process, remarked upon by Deborah Thomas (1996, p.76), by which Wayne is analogized with durable natural materials such as stone is compounded in the film by yet another visual and thematic coupling involving Wayne/Edwards, whereby the star is often photographed within or against the backdrop of Monument Valley. Situated within the Navajo reservation that straddles Utah and Arizona, the dramatic geological formations of Monument Valley, redolent, for Philip French, of 'cathedrals [...] rising out of the flat red desert', provide the visual manifestation of the Fordian 'moral universe' in eight of the director's major Westerns (French, 1973, p.104). Using Bakhtinian terminology, we can go further than this, and identify Monument Valley as a major chronotope within the Fordian imaginary, a locale saturated with the emotional power of displaced frontier existence. Wayne/Edwards can be seen riding into view from within the valley in the opening moments of *The Searchers*, and much of the procedure of tracking Debbie, as well as the major chases and Indian attacks, is enacted within the area. The desert becomes indelibly associated with Ethan, his ease and familiarity within its harsh environs underscoring his alienation from frontier society. Wayne is photographed in a very specific fashion in Monument Valley, framed in such a way that he appears to sprout from the ground, encouraging us to consider him not as distinct from the buttes and mesas that rise grandly from the earth but as a companion to them, a natural monolith at home in such exaggeratedly imposing surroundings. Wayne's quintessential screen moment, his initial appearance in *Stagecoach*, frames him in the same manner, emphasizing his statuesque physique as comparable to the Monument Valley landscape.[17]

A central chronotopic motif within the textual economy of *The Searchers*, Monument Valley is laden with concrete but contradictory values. For all his apparent comfort within its environs and his obvious bond of empathy with the land, the wilderness also delineates a series of potentially devastating fractures in Edwards' psyche. As McBride and Wilmington argue, the 'demons which drive [Edwards] onward, almost against his will, seem to emanate from the "devilish and grinning" land around him', taunting him with his desire to return to civilization and the realization of his feelings for Martha while exploiting an almost 'supernatural' hold over him that pre-empts any potential exchange of wilderness for domesticity (McBride and Wilmington, 1974, pp.147–8). Furthermore, Edwards' extensive and intuitive knowledge of the territory and its potential hazards, especially up among the rocks where he often ventures alone,[18] raises the spectre of what would presumably be his most keenly repressed fear: that he is just like the Indians he despises. McBride and Wilmington observe that generic convention usually has the Indians, and not the white man, moving freely among the rocks and crevices that represent the untamed unconscious of Ford's psychological landscape (147). That the landscape can convey so much profound and disparate information confirms the status of Monument Valley as a major chronotope, a place where the 'knots of the narrative' (Edwards' psychological alienation, resulting in his hostility to structures of family and society; his uncomfortable affinity with the Indians, which accounts for his twisted view of interaction between the races) are 'tied and untied' (FTC, p.250). The motif is also vital in generic terms, conveying in a single frame the fact that this is a Western and, more than that, that it is a John Ford Western.[19] Finally, as the textual site where '[t]ime, as it were, fuses together with space and flows in it' (as Bakhtin says of a related motif, the 'road' – FTC, p.243), the depiction of Monument Valley also has implications for the discourse of time and history enunciated by the film. The time spent by Ethan and Marty in the wilderness in their search for Debbie operates along radically different temporal principles to the more regimented time experienced by the settlers. As Philippe Haudiquet observes, Ford often structures the central actions of his films 'according to the secret and mysterious rules of an ideal time' that is 'outside real time':

> In *Stagecoach*, the attack on the coach by the Apaches seems to last an eternity, when in fact it takes no more than five minutes. Inversely, in *The Searchers*, the lengthy, circuitous trek of Ethan Edwards and Martin Pawley does not appear to last more than a few weeks, when in actuality it takes several years. The significance of this is that time has a different meaning for Ethan and Martin, who live a nomadic existence, and for the Jourgensons (particularly Laurie), who live a fixed life on the land.
>
> (quoted in McBride and Wilmington, 1974, pp.155–6)

Time may 'fuse together with space and flow in it' within the chronotope, but here (inverting the formulation that we observed in regard to the action film in the previous chapter), spatial factors are undoubtedly dominant. The configurations of Monument Valley compress and seal off time, perhaps serving Ford's intention of 'abolishing time' as Haudiquet states (quoted in McBride and Wilmington, 1974, p.155). Whether the 'abolition' of time is a necessary adjunct of historical representation, or even an end in itself, is uncertain; however, the effect here is that time, its linear flow blocked off, instead seeps into and saturates the surrounding landscape, drenching Monument Valley in the iconographic power of an age long gone that is known to us now precisely through a cinematic archetype. This is the process by which Monument Valley transcends its empirical dimensions and physical location and assumes the form of Ford's 'moral universe', securing for itself a place in cinematic history, a cultural register that projects a meaning which often overpowers that of the 'real' history it purports to represent (an issue we shall return to presently). Through the 'fusion' of time and space, Monument Valley exerts a 'supernatural' power on the viewer, holding us within its illusion of historical representation, just as the wilderness curbs Edwards' impulse to enter society.

Women and domestic space

As the door of Martha and Aaron Edwards' homestead famously opens onto a vista of Monument Valley at the outset of *The Searchers*, we probably do not stop to wonder why the interior of the cabin is so dark. We can see, quite clearly, that a female figure has opened the door; but she is not the object of the camera's gaze. In fact, it is Martha's look that anticipates and instructs ours, as the camera follows her through the door and onto the porch where, sliding into a point-of-view roughly equivalent to hers, we can just make out a figure on horseback approaching the homestead. The darkness inside the house, on one level, is an artistic necessity, establishing the sharp contrast with the exterior daylight that gives interest to the composition. However, there is an implication of a subtext concerning the realm of the domestic: the home, the place of women, children and, in the case of the Edwards brothers, men who cannot all come up to the masculine standard set by Wayne/Ethan. There is no light within the house because there is nothing to illuminate, nothing to see there; all attention must be trained on what is outside, the landscape, the savage wilderness, the approaching Indian, outlaw or estranged brother. Martha is the first person whom we see on the screen, yet her action is strangely passive and uninvolved; she opens the door so that we may see Wayne's approach better, then, accommodatingly, moves to one side for us to gaze beyond her. Although the next shot in the sequence favours Martha, it is precisely her look offscreen – to where the action is – that is emphasized. Peter Lehman has noted that Martha's role in this opening sequence is to be 'frozen' into the position of passive spectator: 'It is as if her function were to wait and open the door at the right moment [...] She seems to exist waiting, immobile, looking out' (Lehman, 1990, p.401). Note how the world in the film is 'frozen', in alignment with Barthes' observations on myth, in this interpretation. One is also reminded of Laura Mulvey's famous description of how the representation of woman serves to impede narrative drive[20] although the twist here is that woman becomes the possessor of the 'gaze' and not its object. Yet it is a *powerless* gaze, looking adoringly on Ethan Edwards (there are clear signs that her affection for him survives) yet unable ever to possess him. Martha is condemned, by the codes that civilization has put in place to 'protect' her, merely to enjoy the spectacle; her responsibilities to domestic life nullifying her passion, at least outwardly.[21] She becomes our surrogate in the early part of the text, visually relaying the power of Wayne as star to us but no more able than us to achieve any greater intimacy.

Lehman's interpretation of the opening scene adumbrates the peripherality of women in the film. They are the ones who build and maintain society, not the ones who defend it; henceforth, their role is to stay put while the menfolk go about their dramatic, dangerous business. The nature of masculinity in the film, though complex, is clearly defined, as the song that accompanies the opening titles attests. Man, in this version of the West, is wont to 'wander', 'roam', and 'turn his back on home'.[22] Ostensibly, the purpose of such nomadic exile is to keep the fabric of society together, which basically amounts to recapturing lost women, as Martin and Ethan do; however, an appealingly existential anti-heroism underlies this behaviour. Ethan goes wandering because it is what he *does*; Marty follows because he sees, admires, and ultimately wants to be Ethan (an unconscious desire that surely fuels him just as much as his stated motivation of ensuring that the embittered Ethan does not harm Debbie). They are dealing with 'men's things' – honour, revenge, wounded pride, the bitter refusal to give up. Just as they 'must' search, and are emotionally unequipped to do anything else, the women in the story are equally unidimensional, consigned either to provide motivation for the search (Martha, Lucy, Debbie), assist in it (Look), or wait back home and give the wanderer some motivation to return

(Laurie Jourgenson). Philippe Haudiquet's use, above, of the word 'fixed' to describe Laurie Jourgenson's life of commitment to her settler family as opposed to the nomadic, untrammelled existence of her beau Martin is telling in the context of the film's general treatment of women and the realm of the domestic.

The thematic dichotomy of romantic wilderness versus confining, emasculating domesticity is continually reiterated visually. We have already noted the unnatural darkness of the homestead as Martha opens the door to watch Ethan's approach; when we finally see the cabin's interior it is noticeable for its complete contrast with the vividly lit exterior spaces. The room is dark, with a low ceiling dissected by large beams accentuating the compression of space and increasing the tension within the frame. One of these beams almost blocks off our view of Debbie's face when Ethan lifts her up (time plays a trick on Ethan here – he identifies Debbie as Lucy, whom he remembers at Debbie's age from the last time that he saw the family). Ethan, towering and shrouded in his greatcoat, looks incongruously huge in this setting, and the next shot (low-angled with Ethan central, dwarfing Aaron and Martha who flank him, while the roof beams intersecting above his head draw attention to his bulging presence in the cramped frame) underlines this impression. All of the domestic interiors viewed in *The Searchers* have one thing in common: Ethan does not fit in any of them. Ford's exploitation of Wayne's bodily stature is obvious in this scene, but he is also more subtly associated with an explicitly sexual physicality. When Ethan first enters the homestead, Martha, her gaze still transfixed by him, backs away from him and into the house, as if facing a dangerous and powerful animal. Ethan's size, strength, will and slightly threatening sexual aura all set him up in marked contrast to Aaron's family orientated, pipe-smoking docility.

With great economy, composition is used in these introductory scenes to delineate the complex relationships that obtain between Aaron, Ethan, Martha and Martin. Martha's emotional and physical attraction to Ethan is frequently alluded to; she is often isolated in the frame with him (at the dinner table for instance). Visually, the protagonists Ethan and Martin are analogized incessantly. Our first glimpse of Martin is an echo of Ethan's arrival; he is sighted through a dark doorway where he dismounts and pauses before entering the home, a gesture that is replicated by Ethan several times. Shortly afterwards Martin is seen reflectively sitting on the porch taking in the sunset, a position that Ethan later adopts. Wayne's apparent paralysis when he is confronted by a doorway conveys more about Edwards' alienation from civilized society than pages of dialogue could. The significance of the motif is underlined by its ubiquity: Ethan is stopped from entering the Jourgensons' home by a question from Mrs Jourgenson (Olive Carey), this also reprised in the final frame; he hesitates to pass through the entrance of a teepee after the cavalry attack on the Indian camp; he is prevented from entering the wedding ceremony by a warning from Mr Jourgenson (John Qualen); he is surrounded by the entranceway of a cave as he apprehends Debbie.

Clearly, we are dealing with the Bakhtinian phenomenon of the 'threshold' here, the distillation of narrative power and significance into one loaded time/space context. In Ford's film the threshold is generally manifested in terms of Ethan's apparent reluctance to cross over from self-imposed alienation to social acceptance, and its most common form is the doorway. The various entranceways that Ethan is either prevented from traversing or which seem to fill him with dread become the 'fundamental "points" of action' (PDP, p.170) in the film, fashioning its major chronotopic contexts in a way that notably locates the crisis event in the domestic sphere more frequently even than in the dramatic expanse of Monument Valley. Whereas the latter location exudes the epic 'timelessness' of myth, the threshold corresponds to the knife-edge point of *'crisis time'* (PDP, p.169, italics in original). Ethan's existence is played out on a series of thresholds, whether those physical ones we have mentioned, or metaphorical ones (the boundaries between wilderness and civilization, American and Indian, tolerance and revenge, even that between lonely celibacy and the realization of his love for Martha). Yet, as challenging as the short step into a domestic life appears to be for Ethan, Ford shows that his *own* motivation is not to represent the domestic. Thus, it becomes a site for dull plot exposition, its treatment evoking the contrast that Bakhtin identifies between the slow moving, 'viscous and sticky' everyday time depicted in Flaubert and what he calls (for the first time suggesting some sort of hierarchy between registers of time based on the concentration of events contained in them) the 'primary time' that is its natural opposite (FTC, p.248). As with Dostoevsky in Bakhtin's view, Ford regards that calm region where 'people live a biographical life in biographical time: they are born, they pass through childhood and youth, they marry, give birth to children, and die' as narratively redundant, a space for the action to 'leap over' (PDP, p.169). Nothing really happens there until the threshold is violated (the Edwards' home takes on a far more menacing air when the family begin to sense their vulnerability to Scar's attack, and Ford's camera starts to become intrusive rather than passively observant).[23] Women and their homes play a fixed role in *The Searchers* because their lives are enacted behind or beyond, not *upon* the threshold, and because, to paraphrase Bakhtin, the life that Ford wants to portray 'does not take place in that sort of space' (PDP, p.169). Reasserting a familiar binary of the genre, culture is produced within such interior spaces by women like Martha Edwards while the wilderness rages without (McGee, 2007, p.96). The genre authorizes the celebration and defence of this culture only as an abstract value; as a *process* with a duration that is experienced by some of the characters, it is never really meant to be *represented*, and thus transpires almost wholly offscreen.

The horror of miscegenation

The stigma of miscegenation is one of the punishments waiting for the woman who transgresses the border of the 'garden', even if this occurs against her will. Before exploring miscegenation in *The Searchers*, it is important to note that, outwardly, the film's agenda is not an illiberal one. Ethan Edwards is intended as a character study of grim racism; Martin Pawley, 'an eighth Cherokee', represents a positive, if overtly sanitized and Americanized, archetype of racial interbreeding; and the actions of the cavalry, who kill innocent women in ransacking a Comanche camp, invite our condemnation. Subordinate characters engage in tentative interaction between the races: Mose Harper knows many Indian customs and exploits this familiarity to discover Debbie's whereabouts; Look, the squaw whom Marty unwittingly purchases while trading with Indians assists Marty and Ethan in their search, despite her rough treatment by them. However, to counteract these positive elements there are many casual, and some not so casual, reversions to stereotype. The film's most problematic moments tend to cluster around the horror of racial mixing expressed by Ethan (but validated by other characters, such as Laurie Jorgenson, who the text implies is far more balanced than Ethan and has no particular revenge motive clouding her feelings).

Unlike Delmer Daves' *Broken Arrow* (1950), which starts from the assumption that both sides of the racial divide contribute equally to the tension and bloodshed between them (a young Apache warrior's injuries at the hands of white men are the first signs of conflict in that film), the initial volley in the war between settler and Indian in *The Searchers* is unequivocally attributed to the Comanche in their destruction of the Edwards home and family. The first appearance of chief Scar in the film shows his shadow creeping over a cowering Debbie as she follows Martha's instructions and hides behind her grandmother's gravestone; the image is loaded with the threat of death, and the close shot of the hulking and bare-chested Scar, framed against a darkening sky, accentuates the unnatural and sexualized threat he represents to the child. Perhaps even more objectionable is the fact that Scar is played by a white actor, although such a casting policy for major Indian roles was far from unorthodox in Hollywood Westerns of the 1950s.[24] A reading of Scar's function in *The Searchers* that has gained some critical weight has interpreted him as symbolizing Ethan's repressed desire to appropriate Martha sexually and thus destroy or acquire command of Aaron's family, which is exactly what Scar does.[25] The casting of a white actor enhances the kinship with Ethan/Wayne, legitimizing Ethan's perverse fantasies by 'routing them through the racial, "savage" other and 'easing the identification [...] for the white subject' (Courtney, 1993, p.112). Once again, Courtney's interpretation would seem to argue, the 'other' in the film is reduced to a refraction of traits that we chiefly identify with Ethan, who must be on screen, one way or another, all the time. As unflattering as the doubling with Scar is to Ethan, it keeps him in the picture, and the blatantly constructed nature of Scar's 'otherness' makes more clear his role as a formal necessity in the text – the bad guy whom Ethan must defeat for the story to end, a hollow monologization or appropriated voice of the racial other who, in Janet Walker's words, has his own cultural narrative of victimhood 'delete[d], dissociate[d] and reverse[d]' so that Ethan's 'post-traumatic stress' in the aftermath of Martha's killing can be fully felt (2001, pp.225–7).

Whether it is a smokescreen for perverse psychosexual fantasies or not, Ethan's revulsion at the thought of sexual relations between American and Indian is continually alluded to in the text. It is expressed in his unwillingness to relate the state in which he found Lucy to her sweetheart, Brad. That something sexually unnatural, to Ethan's way of thinking, went on before she died is clear; the subject is too horrible for articulation ('Don't ever ask me ... long as you live, don't ever ask me more'). That Ethan chooses to erase the possibility of sexual interaction between the races rather than address it within the context of the necessity to establish cultural relations is adumbrated in his decision to kill Debbie rather than let her live within the terms of an alien culture. Yet, another interracial relationship in the text is not only unopposed by Ethan, but is treated as a subject of comedy by both him and the film. This is the unlikely courtship of Martin and the squaw 'Look'. As Lehman (1990, pp.405–12) points out, Look's role is minimal but telling. Like other Indian characters, she has little control over her own representation in the film; her appearances are contained within the sequence dramatizing Martin's letter which is recounted in voice-over by Laurie. Thus, Look is framed by the discourses of two major white characters.[26] Ethan cannot hide his amusement, and Martin his disappointment, when they realize that Martin's amateurish efforts at trading have resulted in his acquisition of a wife; Look's chubby appearance emphasizes the unsuitability of the match with the handsome Martin and thus her status as a comic character. Here, the relations between the two cultures are figured as the crossed wires of comedy rather than the short fuses of social tensions that they become when the racially and sexually threatening Scar is involved. Indeed, when Martin physically abuses Look – sending her spinning down a hill with a kick when she has the temerity to bed down for the night next to her 'husband' – Ethan's uproarious reaction clearly anticipates the response that the filmmakers are trying to provoke in us (aided by a jaunty music cue). However, if we imagine the same action taking place between Scar and Debbie, we cannot believe that the film would adopt such a tone of levity; besides which, we know that in the logic of the film this could never be seen, as our own imaginings of the horrors faced by the violated white woman are expected to exceed what could be safely represented.[27] In this way, the film again seeks to exploit an identification of the (white, male) viewer with Ethan's monolithic protagonist, banking on the supposition that there will be something pleasurable as well as something repellent in imagining the violation of a white woman by the racial other.

The double standards evident in the treatment of the couplings of Look/Martin and Scar/Debbie explicitly reveal that Ethan's fear of invasion by the other has a basis in gender, as well as racial supremacy. It is alright, the film tells us, for Martin to take a squaw as a wife; this consolidates the white man's domination and can even be the subject of mirth. However, the realization of sexual intimacy between white woman and Comanche is a horror too dark to speak of, an insult to the phallic integrity of the white man, and any woman touched in this way must be killed (Debbie) or labelled insane and cast out from civilized society (the recovered captives at the army camp). Even though Ethan eventually relents and lets Debbie live, his former views have been legitimized by the agreement of Laurie, who states that Ethan's proposed solution of redemption through murder is what Martha would have wanted. The savage intolerance at the heart of civilization is here hinted at, but throughout the film the liberal attitude espoused by Martin is buried underneath the fetishization of Ethan/Wayne, making his voice the most loudly heard. Most troubling is the lack of a space in the text for the establishment of any viewpoint that does not coincide with Ethan's, specifically those enunciating racial and sexual difference. Despite an obvious intention to criticize Edwards, Ford's adherence to the visual methods commonly used to create an aura of invincibility and righteousness around his star undermines the potential darkness and ambiguity of the character. In both the catalogue of John Wayne roles and the canon of Western protagonists, Ethan Edwards has acquired the reputation of an 'anti-hero'; however, if we immerse ourselves within the logic of the film it is possible to see *The Searchers* as straightforwardly heroizing Ethan, even in contradiction of signals in the story and dialogue that are clearly intended to give a more ambiguous impression. The confusion surrounding his heroic status is summed up in one description of the character as 'an anti-hero of heroic proportions';[28] it is precisely the 'heroic proportions' given to Edwards by Ford's direction and a range of other aesthetic choices that support the reading of *The Searchers* as a text whose liberal pretensions barely conceal racist undertones.

Ethan's 'heroic' gesture is his decision not to execute Debbie for daring to be defiled by the other. Even when Ethan allows Debbie to live, we feel that it is more on a whim than from any modulation of his views; this whim seems to originate from the moment he picks her up, which apparently reminds Ethan of a similar gesture early in the film (when Debbie is still an 'innocent' little girl, not a tainted woman).[29] It is significant that, in the earlier scene, Ethan mistakes Debbie for Lucy, while here, as he takes the grown Debbie into his arms, 'Martha's Theme' can be heard on the soundtrack.[30] The suggestion is that Ethan conflates all female members of the Edwards clan into his idealized image of Martha, or beyond this, that all of white womanhood is understood by Ethan as a sacred and virginal essence that needs to be protected, but loses its value when it becomes soiled. Finally, the quest is as much about protecting Ethan's own position in relation to social and sexual hierarchies (and preserving Wayne's centrality in the film) as it is about 'saving' Debbie; it is noticeable that Ethan's first priority during the raid on the Comanche is not to look for Debbie, but to castrate symbolically his enemy Scar (already killed by Martin) by taking his scalp. The phallic threat is finally anulled, but it is difficult to avoid concluding that, for someone who seems to hold so little store in society, Ethan is incredibly dedicated to maintaining its hierarchies and upholding its borders.

Ultimately, the preservation of the status quo is also the job of *The Searchers* as a classical Hollywood film, particularly one with racial themes. The exigencies of the studio system and the racial dogma of 1950s America conspire to dilute the potency of any intended liberal message. In this way, the film does reveal social and historical truth; but this is not the truth of Texas, 1868, in spite of the ersatz opening inscription. The film's aspiration to the status of myth ensures that the rough historical surfaces of that time zone are well and truly smoothed over. Utterances, according to Bakhtin, bear 'the "taste" of [...] a generation, an age group, the day and hour' (DIN, p.293); this movie 'tastes' of Hollywood, 1956 (which would make an appropriate alternative caption). The relentless drive towards homogenization of product and a consensus of values with the mass audience (the policy of erasing otherness exemplified in the casting of white actors as Indian chiefs) would do untold damage to the reputation of the Western when certain American myths started to unravel in the 1960s. Incorporating the new mood of sourness into the genre was the only way that films such as *The Wild Bunch* could remain within generic confines and stay politically relevant. Predictably, in the face of such ideological anathema, John Wayne remained implacable; his image would harden into the reactionary hero of *The Green Berets* (John Wayne/Ray Kellogg, 1968), a ridiculously gung-ho slice of pro-Vietnam propaganda. *True Grit* (Henry Hathaway, 1969) involved Wayne gamely sending up his own iconic persona as a gone-to-seed gunslinger, but the film's self-conscious tone exposed the creative cul-de-sac that such orthodox genre entries found themselves in.

It would be misleading to suggest that representational distortions such as the ones we have identified in *The Searchers* are abnormal in the context of the genre, but they are not any more excusable for that. As Peter Lehman points out, '[w]omen and Indians [...] all lived twenty-four hours each day then as now [...] A story about Texas in 1868 could just as well centralize women and Indians and peripheralize white men as do the reverse' (1990, p.401). Lehman's irresistibly chronotopic remark neatly encapsulates the centrality of representations of time and space to the film's problematic politics. The iconographic framework of *The Searchers*, while consistent with the generic values of 1956, appears highly suspect when dialogically viewed from a chronotopic context five decades on. The concentration of the film's resources on the images of John Wayne and Monument Valley leave room for little else: Wayne presides over a peculiarly atemporal landscape, a site of 'mythic space' (Engel, 1994) that can be justified neither as an accurate representation of a former epoch nor as somewhere knowable in the present day. It is a place where multiple temporal registers collide and cancel each other out, spectacular but insubstantial; a place for the affirmation of myths, some as old as storytelling itself, some only as old as John Wayne's legend.

Bakhtin says that two orders can be found interacting within the chronotope, one constituted by the represented world and another inhabited by 'the readers and creators of the work'. These two time frames are 'indissolubly united in a single but complex event that we might call the work in the totality of all its events' (FTC, p.255). Chronotopes embedded in works do not only develop knowledge and values pertaining to the historical era of depiction, they also – arguably to a far greater extent – reflect the era of production, although this is not in the nature of a 'direct' reflection, as Michael Holquist reminds us; art and life maintain their autonomy from each other, but their *relation* is 'contained by a larger unit of which they are constituents' (2002, p.111). Textual chronotopes are spun 'out of the actual chronotopes of our world' (FTC, p.253), but in Bakhtin, this reference to the agency and potentiality of the chronotope is rather tangled up with the definition of the limits of its usage; that is, its capacity to act at different levels in the art/life encounter (see Holquist, 2002, pp.109–13; Vice, 1997, p.201). This ambiguity makes Holquist's advice about the 'bifocal' use of the term most valuable (2002, p.113). One effect of using the chronotope as a 'lens' for close textual analysis is that it can permit the release of the 'historical experience stored up'[31] in genres, the experience that is preserved as 'sediment' *in their very images*. What emerges makes possible a kind of reconstruction of the values of the moment of production; Bakhtin points out that listeners/readers *recreate* texts (FTC, p.253).[32] In the case of *The Searchers*, the 'repressing' machinery of classical Hollywood narrative and the dressing of myth (the way it shapes major chronotopic contexts like the valley and the threshold) cannot quite prevent the film from radiating the ideological values of the historical moment of its making. Conceived to self-consciously acknowledge the racist and misogynist mistakes of previous genre entries but unable to transcend a fixation with an axiomatic and disappearing past, *The Searchers* is a great Western, but cursed to repeat mistakes by dint of its limiting formal schema, the 'congealed worldviews' surviving in its imagery. Subsequent filmmakers, in decades organized along radically different political principles, would find ways to renew the basic iconography of the genre, and challenge the logic that stated that the Western existed 'to incorporate rather than to criticize racist [and sexist] fears and phobias' (Pye, 1996, p.235). Others, like John Sayles, would attempt to re-accentuate some of the representational strategies of the classic Western, putting the myth under the microscope.

Lone Star: crossing borders

Texas, 1996. On an abandoned military firing range in Rio County, a skeleton is discovered that is later identified as that of Charley Wade (Kris Kristofferson), a corrupt sheriff and scourge of the Tex-Mex border region in the 1950s. Sheriff Sam Deeds (Chris Cooper), struggling to assert his own identity in a role identified by all of the Frontera townspeople with his legendary father Buddy, begins to suspect his late father of some involvement with Wade's death. Setting out to debunk the local myth that Buddy (Matthew McConaughey) heroically ran Wade out of Frontera before cleaning up the town, Sam explores Buddy's history and learns of financial irregularities and a hushed-up affair with a local woman. Meanwhile, Sam rekindles a relationship with the recently widowed Pilar (Elizabeth Peña), his Mexican high-school sweetheart. Their interracial affair is conducted against a tense backdrop of local politics; the Mexican, American and African American communities of the town are at loggerheads about diverse economic and social matters, foremost among these a plan to dedicate a new statue to the memory of Buddy Deeds. Otis Payne (Ron Canada), owner of a bar frequented by the local black community and estranged father of Delmore (Joe Morton), incumbent colonel at the nearby army base, is one of several Frontera residents to recount Charley Wade's racist brutality when questioned by Sam. Gradually, Sam pieces together the events of 1957, learning along the way that Buddy's mistress was in fact local restaurateur Mercedes Cruz (Miriam Colón), Pilar's mother. Sam confronts Hollis (Clifton James), Buddy's colleague and now outgoing mayor, with his interpretation of events: Buddy killed Charley, appropriated $10,000 of embezzled funds from Wade and used the money to set up Mercedes Cruz (who was bearing his child Pilar) in business. Hollis reveals that only one detail of Sam's version is wrong: it was Hollis himself, and not Buddy, who shot Wade to prevent him from unjustly killing Otis. Satisfied that it would serve no purpose to charge Hollis with Wade's murder, and leaving his father's reputation intact, Sam returns to Pilar, breaking to her the news that they are in fact half-brother and sister. The film ends with the couple apparently deciding to pursue the relationship.

The above synopsis barely scratches at the surface of *Lone Star*'s finely interwoven and deeply complex tapestry of stories, versions and counter-versions, myths and legends. Sam's excavation of the memory of his dead father has implications for the cultural heritage of several communities, and expands to take in the psychic history of the entire town of Frontera. Along the way, Sayles' intelligent and richly demotic screenplay touches upon a huge range of issues from race relations to political corruption, incest to modern military policy, while the restlessly mobile camerawork (in evocative widescreen) traces elegant circuits around the various plotlines, eloquently conveying the conflicting emotions of warmth and icy distrust that characterize border existence. Form in *Lone Star* is dictated by the social diversity of the locale; the intricate structure that oscillates between past and present, official word and conjecture, and various racial positions is motivated by Sayles' intention that all viewpoints involved in the events around Charley Wade's death and Buddy's term as Sheriff should have equal access to the narrative means. To paraphrase Peter Lehman, the fact that women, men, Mexicans, whites and African Americans all live 24 hours each day is reaffirmed by the film. The voices of the racial and sexual other excised in *The Searchers* are restored and much of the action takes place in everyday domestic circumstances and spaces (schools, houses, bars and diners). The use of such familiar chronotopic contexts is part of a broader strategy to open out time and space, to tap into the mystery and drama of everyday life ignored ('leapt over') by other genres. Although it certainly becomes a place where the powerful currents of memory and time intersect, a metaphorical border between past and present, Frontera never loses the feel of a living, working, conflict-ridden town in Sayles' vision. The heteroglot arrangement of narrative voices sets the film up in immediate and overt contrast with *The Searchers*, and the Western genre in broader terms. As Bakhtin says of national linguistic cultures, the 'verbal-ideological decentering' facilitated by heteroglossia can occur only when a culture 'loses its sealed-off and self-sufficient character, when it becomes conscious of itself as only one among *other* cultures and languages' (DIN, p.370). *Lone Star* enacts a process of 'decentering' in terms of both language and genre, by engaging with the classical Western's legacy, and mounting a critical appraisal of the sealed-off, unified past that appears in its fictions.

The meditation on myth and storytelling starts with the title, which delineates a complex nexus of meanings that is typical for Sayles. While ostensibly referring to both the state of Texas and the distinctive badge worn by that most American of archetypes, the sheriff, it also harks back to dime novel Western literature.[33] The discovery of Charley Wade's 'tin star' sets the machinery of the plot in motion. However, the only time that the phrase reappears in the film itself is as a neon beer advertisement in the bar run by the racist Cody (Leo Burmester), who anxiously warns Sam that 'the lines of demarcation are getting fuzzy' and that Frontera needs someone like his father, who was a natural 'referee' with the ability to mediate (for which, read keep separate) the racial communities of the town. Unable to see the irony of the symbol of Texan independence denigrated to the level of beer commercial, a way of profiting from fidelity to the ideal of an America free from Mexican rule, Cody sees his bar as a mini-Alamo, 'the last stand' for white people in the town. The presence of the 'Lone Star' sign indicates the inevitable commodification of such nationalistic sentiment, and perhaps doubles as a subtle comment on the process by which Western myths and archetypes became cash cows for the movie industry, not only providing the American public with an appropriately heroic self-image but also selling the idea of the nation to the world. Cody's misreading of his bar as the Alamo serves to somehow 'de-chronotopize' the locale, or, more accurately, to de-mythologize it as a chronotopic context. Sayles shows us that, rather than being a site saturated with the symbolic power of a historical event, it is merely a bar, a place for people to conduct their everyday relationships, some of them interracial ones. Cody is the embodiment in the narrative of truculent refusal to concede white American dominance, but the film's project is to defuse such hostility through a re-evaluation of the past, an intention that is summed up in the final line of the movie, Pilar's 'Forget the Alamo'. The past is not written in stone, but eternally transformable through memory (or in this case, the exercise of forgetting), echoing Bakhtin:

> It is impossible to change the factual, thing-like side of the past, but the meaningful, expressive, speaking side can be changed, for it is unfinalized and does not coincide with itself (it is free). The role of memory in this eternal transformation of the past.
> (from 'Zametki' [undated], quoted in Morson and Emerson, 1990, p.230)

Human memory is not the only register of memory central to the text, however; generic memory also manifests itself in *Lone Star*'s self-conscious discourse on the nature of the Western. The film covers much of the same conceptual territory as the classic Western – racial disharmony, threatened masculinity, the spatialization of time and the workings of history – but inverts many of the Western's formulations of these issues, turning reification to critique. To examine this process further, we shall focus first on character (including star casting), and continue by looking at frame composition and format.

Space, masculinity, representation

Charley Wade and Buddy Deeds is a pairing as central to *Lone Star* as Ethan and Martin's is to *The Searchers*, even though the former is extremely limited in terms of screen time. In fact, many comparisons can be made between the two sets of characters. Charley Wade has the external accoutrements of the good guy (his tin star and sheriff's outfit), but is soon revealed to be racist, corrupt and brutal. His first appearance sees him explaining arrangements for the collection of bribe money to new deputy Buddy. Ethan Edwards is less conspicuously villainous, but, as has already been noted, his racism is pronounced. Furthermore, suggestions of robbery (he offers Aaron freshly minted coins to pay for his keep) and underhand tactics (he shoots trader Jem Futterman in the back, an action taken in self-defence that nevertheless earns Ethan a murder charge) are associated with him.[34] The racism of both characters is manifested in irrational behaviour that ranges from petty to homicidal. Edwards kills buffalo rather than let Comanche feed off them and shoots the eyes out of a dead buck to prevent his spirit finding rest in accordance with Indian beliefs; Wade humiliates black bartender Otis (played as a young man by Gabriel Casseus) by forcing him to spill his drink and then insisting that he clean it up, and shoots Eladio Cruz (Gilbert R. Cuellar Jr.) in cold blood for running illegal immigrants over the border (the 'crime' is not cutting the sheriff in on the deal). Perhaps most significantly, both characters seem out of step with their respective times. Wade is described as 'an old-fashioned bribe or bullets kind of sheriff' by Hollis, already a relic long before his bones are found on the firing range, while we have already seen that Ethan's alienation from the settling impulse of post-Civil War society is a shaping thematic and narrative motif in *The Searchers*. That Wade sees himself in the macho mould of the celluloid cowboy is underlined by his use of movie jargon; he warns Eladio Cruz of an 'injun' ambush. Buddy also seems in thrall to the cowboy legend: a Western novel can be spotted in a box of his old possessions that Sam recovers from his ex-wife Bunny (Frances McDormand). The fact that Buddy's personal effects appear in a scene where Sam tries to observe a peaceful truce with the fragile, sad figure of his ex-wife underlines how memories of his father inevitably intrude upon Sam's attempts to deal with his own personal history.

The similarities between the characters of Wade and Ethan Edwards are enhanced by the casting of Kristofferson as Wade. The actor's physical stature is comparable to Wayne's, and his presence brings intertextual resonances from other Westerns into the film.[35] The pairing of the veteran, rugged Kristofferson with the younger, good-looking Matthew McConaughey (Buddy Deeds) also echoes the John Wayne/Jeffrey Hunter combination in *The Searchers*. Buddy and Martin are also analogized: both are associated with dutiful, under-represented females (Laurie in *The Searchers* and the absent, 'saintly' Muriel in *Lone Star*), and conduct interracial affairs (the mixed race Martin courts the white Laurie Jourgenson, but is also associated with the Comanche squaw Look; Buddy Deeds conducts a relationship with Mercedes Cruz). Finally, both Martin and Buddy are only able to establish themselves in symbolic and social orders when their ambiguous paternal figures Ethan and Charley are removed from the picture, and both characters threaten to kill their elders although in neither case is this threat carried out. Yet, despite these numerous parallels, the functions of Edwards/Martin and Wade/Buddy in their respective texts are quite different. Whereas Ethan Edwards' moral ambiguity is finally resolved in an act of love (his recognition and problematic 'saving' of Debbie), Wade is never depicted by Sayles as anything other than a sadistic, brutal bully hiding behind a badge. While Martin Pawley's goodness is unimpeachable, almost anodyne, in *The Searchers*,[36] Buddy Deeds' reputation is discovered to be founded on dishonesty and infidelity, if not on the crime of Wade's murder, of which he is cleared by Hollis' confession. What is more, the townspeople are utterly complicit in Buddy's corruption, which they read as fairness; he screws everyone equally, white, black, Indian, Mexican, male, female and singles no group out for special exception. In a town of such fragile racial consensus as Frontera, Buddy has the political savvy to cater to all of the various ethnic groups. By the time, the liberal generation embodied by Sam and Pilar comes along to pick up the pieces and attempt to comprehend fully the racial situation of the town, Buddy's cosy consensus has died with him, leaving the issue of difference exposed and vulnerable once again.

Sam is pilloried by the town's elders for having none of Buddy's manly stature (Fenton [Tony Frank] refers to him as 'all hat and no cattle', expressing his disdain in terms of a cowboy archetype), yet Sam is perceptive enough to intrepret the proposal for a new jail as a matter of political expediency devoid of any real value to the town, and, through his relationship with Pilar, embodies the hope for a symbolic interracial union. Sam is determined to conduct his relationship with Pilar in the open, even after discovering their shared paternity; the taboo of incest thus represents less of an obstacle for Sam than the spectre of social condemnation was for Buddy, who kept his adulterous affair with Mercedes quiet while hypocritically breaking up interracial alliances in the community for the supposed good of the town.[37] Fenton's comment highlights a crisis in masculinity, or *perceptions of masculinity* to be exact; a rift between the iconic image of the stoical, commanding sheriff and the diminished emotional reality of the individuals selected to discharge the responsibilities of this almost mythical figure. None of the lawmen, the wearers of the hat and tin star in the film, is what he seems. Charley Wade is a criminal and killer; Buddy Deeds is corrupt, albeit in a politically desirable and socially acceptable way; Hollis profits from Buddy's deals and kills Wade; Sam's colleague Ray (Tony Plana), who announces his contestation of Sam's position at the next election, is a malleable 'yes man' in the pocket of local politicos, while Sam himself is too liberal for the role and comes to realize that he does not even want it. Whereas in *The Searchers* the role of the Western patriarch is tested but eventually reaffirmed, here the archetype is revealed to be a redundancy, a model of masculinity lifted from local legend and inflated by the movies, whose formidable boots cannot be filled even by decent men like Sam Deeds. The assignation of authority on the basis of white malehood is a farcical anachronism in a town, like Frontera, charged with the volatile energy of racial and sexual otherness; the hat and star are signifiers cloaking a void.

Unlike *The Searchers*, star power is not reinforced in *Lone Star*; indeed, an apposite and only slightly facetious alternative title for the film might be 'No Star'. Whereas the former film revolves around the monumental visual centre of John Wayne, the most famous faces in Sayles' film, those of Kristofferson and McConaughey, are relegated to a meagre, but telling, slice of screen time. In fact, Wade and Buddy's presence is felt more strongly on a discursive level than a visual one, in the testimonies and anecdotes of the Frontera townsfolk; Sayles frustrates the atavistic desire to indulge the myth and see these legendary figures come to life by restricting their appearances. The central roles of Sam and Pilar are assigned to Chris Cooper and Elizabeth Peña, actors (then) with little of the intertextual baggage that Wayne or Kristofferson bring to the screen.[38] Wade and Buddy's story, despite its legendary status, climactic stand-off and centrality to the dramatic fabric of *Lone Star*, is deliberately reduced in narrative proportion, while Sam's investigation and its manifold repercussions in the community are foregrounded. This process represents another inversion of classic Western practice: the unthinkable equivalent in *The Searchers* would be to follow Ethan and Martin's odyssey only intermittently, and spend the lion's share of the narrative watching the settlers, the gentle Jourgensons and the clownish Charlie McCorry (Ken Curtis), as they got on with their everyday lives.

The denial of star status and epic Western convention emerges most clearly in *Lone Star* in the visual presentation of Sam. Earlier, we observed that John Wayne's Ethan is relentlessly centralized and fetishized in the frame of *The Searchers*; Chris Cooper's performance as Sam is constructed along altogether different lines in *Lone Star*. In fact, it is the ostensible villain, Charley Wade, who looms into the frame and dominates the space of his few scenes in the patented Wayne manner. Sam is depicted in a less aggrandized fashion, to the point where he is often marginalized by the frame, reflecting his peripherality in the town's consciousness (where he dwells in the shadow of Buddy's vast reputation), and his lack of control over the events of the past. The scene of Sam's visit to Mrs Bledsoe (Beatrice Winde) demonstrates this strategy.[39] As Sam introduces himself as Sheriff Deeds, he is barely visible over a high wall and partially obscured by shadow; the lack of authority that this position affords him is reflected in Mrs Bledsoe's withering comment, 'Sheriff Deeds is dead, honey. You just Sheriff Junior.' 'Story of my life', replies a resigned Sam, who then proceeds to take up a position to the left of frame while he listens to Mrs Bledsoe's account. Sam's role in piecing together an interpretation from various testimonies is a passive one; he relies on other people for information, and this sense of helplessness is conveyed in frame composition. The strategy is not designed simply to make Sam look less formidable than his father or Wade, but to question the validity of putting real, complex human beings into simplified, fixed positions such as those of the sheriff, the cowboy, the star or the hero of the narrative. Storytelling for Sayles is a plural form, served badly by such monologic devices.

The allusive use of the widescreen ratio also functions to question the validity of the Western template. In its 1950s and 60s heyday, the Western often sprawled across widescreen formats, which exaggerated its horizontal landscapes to great effect. The Cinerama experiment *How The West Was Won* (1962) saw John Ford, alongside co-directors Henry Hathaway and George Marshall, take the Western's propensity for exaggerated cinematic dimensions to a new technological extreme.[40] Popularized in the early 1950s with the intention of shaking up a stagnant industry (see Belton, 1992), widescreen processes such as CinemaScope and Ultra Panavision were designed to convey precisely the kind of sweeping panoramas found in Westerns and historical or biblical epics such as *The Robe* (Henry Koster, 1953) and *The Greatest Story Ever Told* (George Stevens, 1965), the latter film featuring the ever-versatile Monument Valley standing in for the Middle Eastern locations of the four gospels.[41] Today, the 'event' status of widescreen is somewhat diminished as the format is commonly used for orthodox drama and television series (as well as widely in screen advertising). Sayles' selection of the widescreen ratio does not seek to exploit the same sense of epic space and panorama that many widescreen films aim for; interiors are generally favoured over external locations and Western-style desert landscapes are limited to a muted role in the film's opening. Rather, in the fashion of Gordon Willis' photography for the widescreen *Manhattan* (Woody Allen, 1979) and several Ingmar Bergman films shot by Sven Nykvist, *Lone Star* seeks to create a sense of psychological space, conveying emotional states rather than physical relationships.

Strange but revealing compositions result from this strategy, such as the shot in the cantina where Sam and Pilar are depicted in profile bunched on the right side of the frame with the rest of the frame visually sparse save for a jukebox placed far from the camera. The void that they stare into represents the emptiness of the years they spent lost to each other, the topic of the dialogue in the scene. When Pilar rises and walks to the jukebox, there is a switch to a reverse angle originating to the side of the jukebox, boxing the tiny figure of Sam into the bottom right quarter of the screen. The image is a startling one, and one that demonstrates the method by which Sayles and cinematographer Stuart Dryburgh extrapolate visual drama from everyday domestic circumstances. The warmly suggestive but muted lighting of the scene and the use of the nostalgic diegetic music of the jukebox contribute to the sense of an unravelling of time and a rediscovery of a suppressed passion.[42] When the space between the characters is transcended and they embrace and dance, the camera floats away before cutting to their lovemaking. Camerawork is often imbued with this floating, circling mobility in the film, as if, unsure of where to position itself to best capture the story, it elects to trace edgily around the periphery of events. This fluidity is in marked contrast to Ford's more deterministic camerawork in *The Searchers*, where movement is principally used to convey action (for instance, in any of the raid sequences) or underline high emotion (in a number of 'push-in' shots framing Wayne in glowering close-up).[43] Sayles forsakes the visual excesses of the Western for a more personal tone that reinforces his almost forensic attention to the detail of relationships and his preoccupation with how these relationships provide the testing ground for broader social issues.

Re-presenting the past: challenging notions of cinematic time

In a text steeped in the discourse of borders and boundaries, a special treatment of the frontier between past and present is especially noticeable. The structure of *Lone Star* hinges upon a series of flashbacks. The most crucial of these take the narrative back to 1957 and convey the tension between Wade and Buddy through a series of incidents: the issuing of Buddy's ultimatum, several illustrative examples of Wade's brutality, and, finally, the killing of Wade by Hollis in Roderick Bledsoe's bar.

A number of subsidiary flashbacks stretch over a wider temporal range and are thus less easy to attribute to specific dates, but are used to fill in some of the suggestive areas of plot: Sam and Pilar are seen embarking on their teenage romance and, later, have a secret tryst at a drive-in movie humiliatingly broken up by an irate Buddy; a young Mercedes is seen illegally crossing over to the United States, where she is assisted by Eladio Cruz, the man she will marry and whom Pilar will know as her father. Conventional filmic techniques such as dissolves, fades or straight cuts are used in some instances to mark off the flashback from the present of the story. However, a number of these analeptic episodes feature an unusual, almost theatrical technique whereby the movement through time is entirely staged within the frame, without the benefit of any kind of cut. This fascinating, seemingly unique method of transgressing the rules of cinematic space and time deserves close scrutiny.

The first instance of this striking device comes early in the film, when Sam enters the cantina run by Mercedes Cruz to find Hollis and his friends in the middle of a nostalgic celebration of the Buddy Deeds era. Sam, his interest in his father's time rekindled by the discovery of the skeleton, asks mayor and orator of local history Hollis to tell the old story of how Buddy faced down Charley Wade in 1957. As Hollis begins the tale, our preconceived understanding of filmic syntax tells us to expect the image to dissolve into the flashback; however, the camera instead moves down onto Hollis' hands which rest on the restaurant table. As Hollis opines that the disagreement 'started over a basket of tortillas', the camera continues its pan across the table to show the basket of tortillas in question. Hollis' hands withdraw, and the camera pans up an arm reaching into the basket which we soon identify as belonging to Wade. The process of identification is enhanced by our recognition of Kristofferson, whose physique and demeanour correspond readily with Hollis' description of Wade as an 'old fashioned bribe or bullets kind of sheriff'. The original master shot of Hollis and his cronies in the cantina suggests a set of spatial relations that, in accordance with the conventional processes of film viewing, implants in our minds a sense that we are looking at a stable space that could be reproduced in reality.[44] However, Sayles' unique device destabilizes this sense of spatial security, totally reconfiguring spatial relations in the frame; without a cut, the scene has shifted, disorientatingly, to a brand new interior set. To emphasize this, seconds later, the camera swings back round to the space that Hollis had filled, and we see that he has been replaced by Buddy Deeds, while the wall that stood behind Hollis has vanished to reveal another part of the new set. It is a virtuoso, and technically elaborate, piece of film craft; the gulf of 40 years is elided within the frame but without the aid of editing. The strategy is repeated when the scene returns to the present, and then occurs, in slightly modified form, several more times in the text. The lack of external markers between the images of past and present, the co-existence in the same frame-space of two different timezones, is extremely significant in terms of the film's thematic discourse of temporality. The effect is one of collapsing the conventional borders between cinematic past and present, and involves a radical reconstitution of the core chronotopic values of time and space in service of the film's overall argument for more fluid conceptions of identity and history: different versions of personal and political history, all with competing truth claims, can only commune within such 'hybrid zone[s] of memory' (Walker, 2001, p.246). The technique opens time out into a new, dual chronotope that shows past and present inflecting each other dialogically.

The contrast with *The Searchers* is considerable. John Ford's mythic space works to preserve a historical feeling in the visual contemplation of landscape, to abolish time's natural progression and establish in its place an 'ideal time' redolent of a golden age. This process imbues time with a monumental aura, and inaugurates a great distance between the humanity and the history of which it is supposedly a part. The effect is to remove human agency from historical progression, and to give cinematic spatio-temporality an idealized, irrevocable quality. In this formulation, chronotopes are predetermined and fixed; the minute variations and possibilities of natural time are ironed out, and temporal shifts become a matter of visual shorthand (for instance, the weather montage that is used to mark the passing of time in Ethan and Martin's search). Time is unknowable on the level of spectatorship – although the audience might well be interested to know the exact duration of Ethan and Martin's odyssey, the epic conventions of the tale determine that this information should be omitted (critical consensus suggests between three and ten years – Courtney, 1993, p.128). Sayles' approach, on the other hand, is far more pluralist and democratic. He sees the relationship between story time and frame space as a permeable border to be explored, stretched out, compressed, and generally played around with. Sayles refuses to treat time as a barrier regulating traffic between past and present; instead, he reconfigures it as a border to be crossed at will. Time is understood as an internal value that can be measured in people's lives and memories, as much as it can be inscribed in the external registers of weather, landscape and architecture. The tight, volatile space of the Tex-Mex border, the physical manifestation of a political and historical bone of contention, is given more room to breathe in this formulation. Yet the intimate (for Bakhtin, 'indissoluble') chronotopic connection between time and space remains intact, is even strengthened, in Sayles' film. In the segue from Hollis' monologue into the Buddy/Wade confrontation described above, space does indeed become 'charged and responsive to the movements of time' (FTC, p.84), its proportion and character changing completely in a matter of seconds during which the attention of the camera is focused on the table.

Linking time irrevocably to human emotion and psychology destabilizes any monologic pretence to definitiveness: time becomes intersubjective, multifaceted, personalized (Walker, 2001, p.246). The flashbacks (at least those attributed to Sam, Pilar and Mercedes) delineate a transgression of time with positive and healing consequences. Almost all of the major characters effect some kind of internal examination of their pasts, and use what they find there to underwrite change or reaffirmation in their lives in the present. Sam's reunion with Pilar is originally engendered as a by-product of his investigation into the life of his father; even the disquieting nature of their discovery about Buddy's relationship with Mercedes appears to be used by the couple to reinforce their love at the end of the film. Mercedes Cruz herself, a Mexican businesswoman so comprehensively assimilated into monologic American nationalism that she reports illegal border jumpers to the authorities, delves into her own past and finds the emotional space that allows her to help a band of struggling immigrants. Elsewhere in the text, familial bonds are strengthened through an awareness of history and the healing power of time. Black bar-owner Otis Payne, an amateur historian obsessed with the story of a little-known ethnic strand of black Indians, the Seminole nation, is reunited with his son Delmore because the initially resentful army man discovers accidentally that Otis has kept a shrine, or even museum, detailing all of his son's achievements over the years. This discovery, in turn, alerts Delmore to the distance between himself and his own son Chet (Eddie Robinson), and spurs him to a resolution to prevent the estrangement of his own childhood from being repeated.

Reinforcing a prominent socio-sexual theme in the text, Sayles' cinematographic strategy enunciates a kind of incest between time zones, generating an ontological impossibility that is nevertheless quintessentially cinematic: two historically marked and separate eras coexisting in the same frame. Limits of textuality and temporality are tested, no more so than when Sam appears to converse with the young Pilar across the decades. Left alone after his riverside walk with Pilar, Sam looks out onto the water. The camera pans away from him and down to alight on a young version of Pilar (Vanessa Martinez) dallying at the river's edge. A cutaway reveals the young Sam (Tay Strathairn) sitting nearby, and the pair discuss their troubled relationship. Young Pilar remarks on how their coupling is 'supposed to be some big sin even if we love each other', referring to the mysterious objection of their parents which is, in fact, the secret of their shared paternity. Asked if she believes that their being together *is* a sin, she answers 'no', at which the camera promptly pulls back and pans to the left, where the adult Sam sits, signalling the return to the present of the story. Sam answers on behalf of his younger self, apparently still intoxicated by the memory: 'Me neither'. It is a most complicated sequence, and one that involves not only a chronotopic element, but is also structured in terms of a dialogical form of address. Pilar's utterance is responded to by Sam years later, although Sayles' method of marking the flashback compresses this distance, chronotopically, into a few feet of earth.[45] The 'other' has a temporal character as well as a racial one in *Lone Star*, and temporal homogeneity is as implausible and limiting as its racial counterpart in an environment like Frontera.

The extraordinary sensitivity of Frontera to the operations of history, suggested in the scene where concerned parents and educators clash over the local school's history curriculum, will never be completely resolved, and Sayles includes nothing to indicate that such an outcome would be desirable. Somewhere in the midst of these conflicting viewpoints and voices resides the 'truth' that can help Frontera to survive; mutual interaction and conflict actually generate that truth rather than serve to obscure it. Grey areas, rather than arbitrary lines of demarcation, are to be celebrated and maintained. Delmore, sceptical of the services offered by Otis, the self-styled 'Mayor of Darktown', is encouraged by his father to re-evaluate the terms on which he contemplates his own neatly ordered existence and to take note of how these rigid lines of discipline are suffocating the aspirations of his own son Chet: 'It's not like there's a border line between the good people and the bad people. You're not on either one side or the other.' This crucial remark not only articulates the moral thesis and emotional geography of the film (reinforcing the central 'border' trope), but also illuminates the method chosen for the flashbacks. Time is no less difficult to order into manageable blocks and discrete compartments than is moral value, so why use cinematic methods that give this false impression? Sayles' rejection of the most common editorial apparatus for signifying temporal and spatial change could be deemed uncinematic in a narrow sense, but the intention is to challenge easy assumptions about the nature of cinema and how it represents time and life. This problem is incorporated, microcosmically, into the text. Chet expresses his own boredom and disillusionment with the path of education eulogized by his father through a form of escape that has a filmic element: he attempts to animate a character drawn repeatedly, with minute differences, over dozens of pages of his exercise book. This experiment with time and space connotes his desire to find a way out of the linear life plotted for him by his father.

'Print the legend'

The attitude to the Western exhibited by *Lone Star* is never less than respectful. As an uncredited scriptwriter on the Sharon Stone vehicle and 'feminist Western' *The Quick and the Dead* (Sam Raimi, 1995), and writer of an early (unfilmed) draft of John Lee Hancock's revisionist *The Alamo* (2004),[46] not to mention authoring the screenplay of B-movie 'Space Western' *Battle Beyond the Stars* (Jimmy T. Murakami, 1980), Sayles has demonstrated genre familiarity and an assurance in re-accentuating Western conventions for modern audiences. *Lone Star* recontextualizes the form through an awareness of generic memory, and in this process Sayles can be compared to the treasure hunter Mikey (Stephen J. Lang) who discovers Wade's skeleton at the outset of the film. Mikey, as is reported to Sam Deeds by his friend, hunts for spent bullet shells on the abandoned firing range, takes them home and 'makes art out of them'.

Although we have concentrated on the discursive relationship between *Lone Star* and *The Searchers*, echoes of another Ford Western can be discerned in the film. Like *Lone Star*, the narrative of *The Man Who Shot Liberty Valance* is predicated on a crucial misreading. In Sayles' film, the misinterpretation is by Sam, who falsely surmises that his father killed Wade when in fact the deed was performed by Hollis. In *Liberty Valance*, the community of Shinbone mistakenly credits Ransom Stoddard (James Stewart) with dispatching the cruel robber Valance (Lee Marvin) when in fact it was the bullet of Tom Doniphon (John Wayne) that killed him. In both cases, legends form around the apparent heroes, who go on to improve nominally the lot of their respective communities (Ranse entering the world of politics, Buddy becoming Sheriff). Both films are alert to the idea that violence is stitched into the fabric of history. The name of 'Shinbone' evokes the human cost of civilizing the west, an association that is ironically cited in the opening scenes of *Lone Star* when Charley Wade's bones are discovered in the Texas earth. In these two films, Ford and Sayles dissect the notion of heroism and the cultural conditions that allow legends and stories to take root in the popular consciousness.

Liberty Valance has tended to be popularly remembered for showing Ford engaging the elegiac mode that was starting to demand expression by 1962, but the film actually goes further in deconstructing John Wayne's star persona than does *The Searchers*; his act of heroism overlooked, the (compared to Ethan) blameless Doniphon passes through stages of drunkenness, loneliness, and ends up dead in a cheap coffin minus his gun and boots.

'When the legend becomes fact, print the legend', muses a newspaper editor when Stoddard attempts to put the story straight after Doniphon's death. Stories acquire their own logic, the film appears to be saying; the power of myth is greater than the claim of fact. In *Lone Star*, Sam makes a tacit decision to 'print the legend' by hushing up his findings in the Charley Wade murder investigation; his father's reputation will remain unsullied, even though Sam has found ample evidence of abuse of office and sexual infidelity. Sam's decision to leave his father's legend intact is his way of 'forgetting the Alamo', as Pilar puts it, revising the famous phrase. The new phrase signifies the effort of will and cooperation that is needed to wipe the slate clean in a place like Frontera. The destructive tendency to rake over an inglorious past must be resisted if the town is to succeed as a multi-cultural entity. The positive results of reassessing one's own emotional history are contrasted with the damage effected on a racial level by adherence to fixed versions and resistance to compromise. The fact that Sam and Pilar are able to resolve their own personal border dispute, that of their biological connection, by rejecting its terms gives hope for the wider society. Significantly, Pilar's statement 'Forget the Alamo' is uttered at the loaded threshold location of the drive-in theatre. This is the place that she and Sam have chosen for the symbolic re-ignition of their relationship (it was ended there by Buddy, as one flashback shows us). They are drawn to a place where memories seem to speak particularly strongly, the perfect location to make up for lost time and rekindle thwarted desire: the cinema. However, in keeping with Sayles' bittersweet evocation of the power of movies, the theatre is dilapidated and does not appear to have shown a film in years.

Conclusion: the chronotope and genre

The massive influence that the Western has exerted on world film culture has led to the form being spoken of in terms of 'genre imperialism' (Maltby 1996a, p.123). Initial innovations in Western form went hand in hand with the development of the cinema as a narrative medium, as is evinced in *The Great Train Robbery*. The implications of temporal simultaneity in Porter's 1903 film 'defined the limits of a certain kind of narrative construction' that would become Hollywood's fundamental storytelling mode (Musser, 1991, p.256). Later, the iconographic apparatus of the Western would ensure its status as the perfect conduit for the demonstration of technological advances such as widescreen. However, all empires, even (especially) those of genre, are built on a kind of oppression; when do innovations become limitations? The marginalization of the racial and sexual other in the Western, when viewed from a present day perspective, rightly problematizes our political reading of the genre. The rigid ideological character of the genre is linked, in some way, to the attitude displayed by the films to history: the makers of history – the white males – are glorified; those who live under its terms – everybody else – are all but removed from the picture. Representational strategies, of course, play a huge part in the promulgation of this myth, and, as 'the ground essential for the showing forth, the representability of events' (FTC, p.250), the chronotope is also implicated. Bakhtin speaks of Rabelais' task in creating the specific chronotope of his artistic world as one of gathering together a world that was 'disintegrating', thus creating a new relationship between time and space that would 'permit one to link real life (history) to the real earth' (FTC, p.206). The classic Western mobilizes its dominant chronotopes with a similar end in mind: that of facilitating the preservation of a 'historical moment', with all its embedded power relations kept intact. However, the result is different; where the Rabelaisian folkloric chronotope emphasizes the link between 'real life' and the earth, the Western chronotope erects an idealized landscape populated by stereotypes and legitimized by myth. 'Real life' has nothing to do with it, and may have been the last thing the audiences of the 1940s and 50s wanted or expected from a Western – so Hollywood's self-promotion mechanisms would have us believe. 'What the audience in Canoga Park wants – that's reality', as one character puts it in *The Player* (Robert Altman, 1992). The cultural function of the Western – to reassure America that its heritage is an honourable one – thus becomes inseparable from its expressive method.

Genre is defined by the activity of chronotopes. The uniqueness of a genre lies in the narrative shapes it orders itself into, and these shapes have a very specific temporal and spatial constitution. However, time and space are not dead inside chronotopic images. They retain the ability to radiate new meanings, to alter the 'emotions and values' with which they are coloured (FTC, p.243). Formal conventions can thus be re-accentuated and given fresh relevance through the adoption of a new context within the framework of generic memory. This is the approach taken by *Lone Star*, a film that exploits aspects of its own temporal and industrial outsideness (produced four decades after *The Searchers* and originating from outside the studio mainstream) to impart a fresh perspective to the Western genre. Unlike affectionate tributes like *Silverado* (Lawrence Kasdan, 1985), or movies that are predicated on a deliberate ideological shift but are more interested, ultimately, in knowing pastiche (*Posse*, Mario Van Peebles, 1993; *The Quick and the Dead*; *Shanghai Noon*, Tom Dey, 2000) Sayles' film manages to make a genuinely telling contribution to the cultural debate around the Western, engaging with the central issues of gender, race, history and form that underpin both the genre itself and its critical context. Perhaps this task is made easier because *Lone Star* itself is not a Western, and because its metatextual commentary on the genre is allowed to come out through the exploration of a theme – that of the nature of borders, social, racial, sexual and temporal – that situates itself squarely within the racial discourse of millennial United States, while also acknowledging the role of past cultural productions within that historically charged sphere of debate. The tendency to reduce the meditation on the Western to one of two models – either an ironic formal exercise or a resurrection of myth – is avoided because Sayles recognizes the seductive excesses of the form and reins them in.

Lone Star is a valuable companion text to *The Searchers* because, through its generic position of outsideness, it is able to historicize adequately the same themes of masculinity, race and displaced frontier existence that John Ford was undoubtedly interested in, but found incompatible with the generic profile of the Western in 1956. This is not to allow Ford's political agenda, which we have put under scrutiny here, to be saved at the last minute by the cavalry of aesthetics; merely to illustrate the always complex play-off between commercial logic and cultural responsibility in Hollywood generic policy. The primal aura attached to movies signals Hollywood as the 'dream factory', but a closer inspection of genre helps us to understand more clearly the nature of the myths it peddles. The vessel through which this can be achieved is the chronotope, which can assist us in approaching cinematic space and time not only at the level of narrative structure, but also in terms of their function as indicators of social value.

4
Polyphony: Authorship and Power

Introduction

House of Games, David Mamet's first directorial offering from 1987, is essentially concerned with the problem of who has the right to narrate whom, and why – a theme that suggests the possibility of a productive encounter with the Bakhtinian category of polyphony. Mamet pitches a female protagonist into a masculine realm of discourse that is closed-off, impenetrable to the outsider. This drama of communication is played out, however, within a broader context that raises questions around the space that is allowed within patriarchal culture for women to create their own discourse, to *objectify* themselves and thus make themselves *subjects* of their own stories. Invoking theoretical issues such as the positioning of the female spectator, Mamet's film enunciates how speech genres[1] entrenched in the codes of patriarchy are manipulated to achieve dominance, and how such abuse of language constitutes monologic oppression. The attitude the film displays to the concept of narrative is critical – situating the narrative agency proves an extremely elusive task. The incorporation into the text of motifs from the genre of *film noir* – especially regarding the representation of its main female character – also hints at a kinship with that tradition.

The filmic potential of Bakhtinian novelistic polyphony is of primary interest here: how polyphony manifests itself in theme and narrative form, and whether or not the theory can be applied to the film *House of Games*, and film in general. First, Bakhtin's conception of the characteristics of textual polyphony will be outlined as they emerge in *Problems of Dostoevsky's Poetics*.

One of the defining features of Bakhtin's theory concerns the relationship of author and character in Dostoevsky's novels. Dostoevsky is credited with creating a new kind of novelistic form, one that 'destroys the monologic plane' (PDP, p.5) of the conventional novel by transforming the value of character from a narrative puppet subject to the whims of the author to a fully independent consciousness that engages not only with the reader but also with its creator. The character carries his own 'word', is not a mere mouthpiece for the polemical and ideological expressions of the author but an active participant in discourse, whose word 'sounds, as it were, *alongside* the author's word and in a special way combines both with it and with the full and equally valid voices of other characters' (7). Thus, the reified monologic consciousness that governs all narrative operations in the conventional novel, against which all subordinate voices must be judged, is replaced in Dostoevsky by '[*a*] *plurality of independent and unmerged voices and consciousnesses* [...] *with equal rights and each with its own world*' (PDP, p.6, italics in original). Conventional narrative hierarchies are levelled, authorial presence being transformed into a current of 'creative energy that is immanently manifested in the work itself' (Zylko, 1990, p.70). The implications of such a theory for traditional conceptions of the author as ultimate agency of narrative control are, of course, great; however, Bakhtin clouds the issue slightly by not overly concerning himself with the distinction between 'author' and 'narrator'. Bakhtin's 'author' seems to represent, at least in the non-polyphonic mode, the carrier of narrative discourse and the highest level of artistic organization within the novel; intra-textual narrators would be better described by the polyphonic category of 'character'.[2] Concentrating closely on the interactions of voices in her novelistic case study, Malcolm Lowry's *Under the Volcano*, Sue Vice writes of Lowry's apparently deliberate move, evidenced by studying the differences between drafts and the final version, to 'omit the voice of narratorial overview' (Vice, 1997, pp.132–4). Creating the conditions that make this omission possible seems to be an essential step in the textual logic of polyphonic construction. The result in that particular case is to render Lowry's characters less as self-evident speaking people and more as what Bakhtin calls 'images of [...] language' (DIN, p.336).

The author–narrator ambiguity is interesting in relation to *House of Games* because the question of polyphony in that specific text has to do with a blurring of the distinction between 'author', 'narrator' and 'character' also. The problematic representation of Dr Margaret Ford (Lindsay Crouse), a psychiatrist who is swindled out of her money by a group of con men, raises questions of narrative control. The viewpoint of David Mamet, the 'author' of the text (in the sense that he co-wrote the story, authored the screenplay and directed the film)[3] may seem conspicuously entwined with that of the lowlife gambler Mike (Joe Mantegna), through a series of narrative strategies that this chapter shall outline. It is undoubtedly through

Mike's eyes that we are invited to assemble our picture of Ford, agreeing perhaps with some of his observations about her life on the way. Mamet's reputation has regularly seen critics branding him as misogynist and others willing to defend him against that charge; Joki (1993, pp.11–13) and Sauer and Sauer (2004, pp.225–7) summarize some of these charges. Kipnis (1991) reads *House of Games* as supporting 'the grip of masculine power' because it is Mike's knowledge, not Ford's, that is presented to the audience as 'perfect' and the source of the 'romantic' charisma that binds our allegiance to him. My reading purports to qualify that certainty, based on the idea that knowledge *itself* is brought, with a vengeance, into the field of disruptions and complications that inscribe characters and values in this text. For instance, the attribution of narratorship is complicated by the fact that on thematic and structural levels, the film is concerned with various semantically unstable discourses. The foregrounding of these epistemological systems, which include sexuality (and its manifestation in identity and language), psychoanalysis, gambling[4] and filmic discourse itself, troubles our interpretation of the text. The establishment of a point of orientation within the intersecting narratives is made difficult. An attempt has to be made to determine whether Mamet subscribes to the misogynist cynicism of Mike, or whether the attitudes displayed in Ford's characterization can be ascribed instead to a polyphonically 'free' Mike, loading the narrative in his favour in the absence of a controlling authorial presence. If the latter is the case, Mamet could still be accused of acting irresponsibly in withdrawing and allowing a character with misogynist views to dominate, although, as I hope my analysis of the film shall demonstrate, the case could equally be made that giving autonomy to the voices of the characters and allowing them to battle it out, free from authorial intervention, is the strategy that permits the ultimate correcting, challenging and superseding of Mike's misogyny through the actions of Margaret Ford.

As already intimated, the plot of *House of Games* concerns the deception of Ford, a successful psychiatrist who becomes the target of Mike and his colleagues because she has written a best-selling book on compulsive behaviour and has made a tidy sum of money through this success. Ford goes to the 'House of Games', a gambler's den, on behalf of a desperate patient who has incurred a huge debt there. Mike convinces her that he is not the ogre represented to her by the unstable Billy (Steven Goldstein) – actually Mike's associate – and agrees to wipe out the debt if she will assist him in a poker game. The game is identified by Ford as a scam, set up to relieve her of 6000 dollars. By spotting their deception, Ford believes that she has gained a privileged insight into the professional world of the con men. She becomes attracted to Mike, and through him becomes drawn to the illicit thrills of their trade, seeking to be involved in a major 'sting'. When the set-up is foiled by the presence of an undercover policeman, Mike tries to help Ford escape but in the ensuing fracas the policeman is apparently shot dead. They manage to escape the scene, but misplace a briefcase full of money borrowed from 'the hard guys' for one night. To save Mike's life, Ford replaces the money from her own savings. Mike leaves the city, advising Ford to forget about him and go back to her successful professional life.

Believing herself guilty of the policeman's death, Ford asks her friend Maria (Lilia Skala) for advice. Maria tells her that she must forgive herself, whatever the nature of her guilty act. By chance, Ford spots Billy, Mike's supposed debtor, driving off in the same red sports car that she drove during the escape from the 'police raid' at the hotel. Her worst suspicions are confirmed when she goes to one of Mike's haunts and witnesses him doling out her money to his colleagues, including the 'dead' policeman. Determined to get her money back or get even, she confronts Mike before he leaves for Vegas. Showing no remorse for his despicable actions, he tells her she brought her humiliation on herself, by desiring excitement and the company of villains. When Mike refuses to beg for his life and tries to walk away, Ford shoots him dead. She decides to take Maria's advice, and forgives herself of the crime, apparently having achieved a new sense of selfhood through her experiences.

Before we can identify the owner of the narratorial perspective that frames and constructs Ford in the film, it will be necessary to look at this representation in detail. The theme of communication and its relation to identity is established in an early scene between Ford and a patient she visits in a prison ward who we later find out is a murderess. The patient cannot articulate the fears caused by her dream ('I don't know how to say it'), and accuses Ford of taking a detached standpoint from her situation, of considering herself 'exempt' from experience, calling into question her right to observe, interpret and judge. The next two scenes accentuate this impression of Ford as detached from life, preoccupied with her work on an abstract level that has no connection to any real index of experience. She meets her friend Maria for lunch, but has no time to eat as she must rush off to attend to work matters. We then observe her next appointment – a session with the young gambler Billy. Following the lead of the earlier scene, Billy calls into question Ford's commitment to his plight, deriding her professional discourse as 'just talk' and 'a con game'. Billy claims to live in the 'real world', where a $8000 gambling debt has necessitated the possession of a gun, and the accusation that her treatment has no effect in this sphere stings Ford into involvement. She swears to Billy that she will help him if he hands over the gun, and it is at this moment that she crosses the line from professional distance to personal engagement, setting her up for the deceptions of Mike and his colleagues from the 'House of Games'.

Conflict is one of the forms that speech takes, and a powerful one as Bakhtin makes very clear. It is when speakers believe that language operations somehow hold the exchange of values in abeyance that they are most perilously vulnerable to the sudden withdrawal (or addition) of unintended power to their words. In *House of Games*, Ford's involvement in the scam is cheaply obtained by the fraudsters. By swearing on her offer to help Billy, Ford undertakes the personal risk that is involved in speech communication. In her case, the risk is compounded by the responsibilities attending her profession, and the expectations accompanying her gender; Mike will seek to exploit both of those extra sensitivities. The logic of the speech genres used by many of Mamet's male characters dictates that to be insufficiently professional and emotionally controlled is a negative attribute that leads to dangerous over-exposure; in poker terms, unsophisticated players always have a 'tell' (a behavioural gesture that indicates, non-verbally, whether the player is bluffing or not) that registers against their conscious efforts of suppression. This is the basis of the linguistic and psychological supremacy that Mike and the other men from the House of Games believe they have. In a reading of *House of Games* in conjunction with Mamet's Broadway play *Speed-The-Plow* (1988), Ilkka Joki proposes that the nature of dialogic transactions can conceal a treacherous underside:

> [...M]utual responsive understanding, so much valued by Bakhtin, can also involve danger for the one who has more of his or her personality at stake, if both parties are not completely honest with each other: this can be called deceptive dialogicality.
>
> (Joki, 1993, p.158)

Mamet has spoken about his tendency to portray language exchange as a kind of business practice,[5] and Joki's observation indicates the kind of discursive world that Margaret Ford is about to enter. As a general comment pertaining to Bakhtinian studies, it is important to be mindful of dialogism's double-edged nature; the balance of power on both sides of dialogical exchange sometimes seems liable to slip from productive conflict into monologic exploitation, highlighting a possible criticism of Bakhtin's relentlessly inclusive approach. Bakhtin points out that dialogic elements can be 'hidden' within apparently one-sided utterances (PDP, p.197), but it seems far from certain that monologic forces are not similarly adaptable, even though Bakhtin reassures us that the authoritarian word is easily spotted in its demand for total affirmation or rejection (DIN, p.343). Speech genres, Joki insists, exist on the 'shifting lines of demarcation between monologism and dialogism' (1993, p.74). Inexperienced in the trade jargon and demotic 'street genres' of the con men, Ford, keen to help Billy and believing herself to be in full dialogic interaction with him, gives the symbol of her personal notion of 'truth'. At this moment she is exposed, not realizing that the speech community she is interacting with does not recognize this bond uniting a person and what they say. The idea that somebody's 'word' can represent their personal integrity and moral standpoint indicates that Ford is naive in matters of communication. Threatened by a gun-wielding Ford at the climax of the film, Mike's comment 'You can't bluff someone who's not paying attention' seems to refer to his more cynical relationship to speech – he thinks he knows when not to pay attention, his professional training telling him when to withdraw from dialogic interaction and its attendant risks.

These early scenes also demarcate the gendered nature of linguistic exchange and, specifically, Ford's perilous existence on the borders of male and female language usage. She is comfortable with neither the near-hysteria of the excessively feminine figure of the murderess nor the verbal trickery of the con men, underlining a certain ambiguity in the representation of her sexuality that foreshadows the later transformation of Ford into a *femme fatale* figure, a cinematic icon that is often invoked as the site of representational confusion regarding gender identity (Doane 1991, p.103).

The politics of representation

Building a certain ambiguity into the image of Margaret Ford dominates the representational agenda of the early part of the film. Mamet seems to subscribe to many cinematic clichés and stereotypical attitudes in making a point about the lack of meaning in psychoanalytical discourse, the expressive mode that Ford is most explicitly linked with. Ford's default professional stance is represented as cold and detached, an intellectual game, a play with words (Ford interprets part of the murderess' dream in this way) that can have no positive repercussions in society. Her mode of discourse is characterized by a quality of monologic aloofness, refusing to account for itself but only too happy to explain and pin down the meaning of others' utterances; an awareness that this is having an enervating effect on her life when compared to the excitement she sees in Mike's leads her into his plot. Psychoanalysis is aligned with Bakhtin's 'authoritative word' (DIN, p.342), which does not have to justify itself with recourse to other discourses. Lindsay Crouse's speech in the character of Ford is measured and monotonous, evoking a professional tone of supposedly objective judgement familiar to us from analytical or doctor figures in film.[6] Added to this is Ford's studiedly defeminized appearance and the suggestion that her life lacks emotional and romantic (heterosexual) attachment. Even her apartment, the only domestic residence that is seen in the whole film,[7] is sparsely furnished and gives an impression of sterility. This reiterates the association with the *femme fatale*, who is traditionally inscribed as the 'antithesis of the maternal' (Doane, 1991, p.2). Are we meant to think that Ford's detached, austere lifestyle in some way makes her deserving of the treatment she receives at the hands of Mike? By associating herself with a tradition of interpretation that is seen as futile and prevents her from real understanding of human communication and experience, does she bring on her own humiliation?

The critique of psychoanalysis, like many other themes in this text, is related to matters of narrative.[8] Psychoanalysis is perhaps one of the least 'knowable' epistemological systems. Unable to legitimate its findings scientifically, it has a certain doubt relating to the figure of the analyst built into its structure. It is often equated, in its uncertainty, to illusionistic narrative practices such as cinema. Film is often said to represent the unconscious; Hollywood is known as 'The Dream Factory'. The text delineates psychoanalysis as an investigative system bearing little value in the 'real world' (filtering this judgement through opinions voiced by a number of characters, prominently Mike, and even Ford's own self-doubt); yet Mamet has in the past likened the methodology of the psychoanalytic discipline to that of filmmaking:

> The mechanical working of the film is just like the mechanism of a dream; because that's what the film is really going to end up being, isn't it? [... P]sychoanalysis [...] is a great storehouse of information about movies. Both studies are basically the same. The dream and the film are the juxtaposition of images in order to answer a question [...] In other words, it's all make-believe.
>
> (Mamet, 1991, p.7)

Mamet's apparent criticism of Ford's profession in *House of Games* contradicts the above quotation, from his *On Directing Film*, which points out the similarities between the narrational practices of dreams and films. This is an emblematic 'gap' that provokes doubt about making Mamet solely accountable for the problematic representation of Margaret Ford.

Ilkka Joki notes the array of *internal* authors in the film, observing that the con men's operation on Margaret Ford involves a narrative aspect: '[... T]hey actually "dramatize" Ford's treatise on compulsive behaviour for her. So *they* are to be regarded as the initiators of this intra-textual dramatic spiral' (Joki, 1993, p.155). If we extrapolate this theory and begin to regard Mike as the organizer of narrative in the first three quarters of the text (leading up to Ford's discovery of his deception), during which time he occupies a position in the textual hierarchy at least on a par with Mamet, we approach the essence of the variation on Dostoevskian polyphony that is *House of Games*.

Positing a general tendency for any novelistic character to have 'a zone of his own, his own sphere of influence on the authorial context surrounding him' (DIN, p.320), Bakhtin zeroes in on the Dostoevskian character as 'not an object of authorial discourse, but rather a fully valid, autonomous carrier of his own individual word' (PDP, p.5). The independence of hero from author is stressed, although this seems to be in the order of a relation that Dostoevsky has *enabled* by deciding to work within a polyphonic paradigm. For the author as conventionally understood, that is, the monologic author, Bakhtin notes that a certain democratization of voice and consciousness can be fabricated but that this is a 'game' permitted, and eventually resolved, by the author, who thus retains 'ultimate semantic authority' (PDP, p.203). The monologic author allows information to trickle out to the audience, thus illuminating the motives and nuances of puppet-like characters; a polyphonic system instead builds a non-hierarchical realm of equal, interdependent consciousnesses. The resulting 'plurality' refuses to objectify ('finalize') the discourse of a character, leaving their word (and by extension, their *world*, their ability to act) semantically open. What Sue Vice calls 'the voice of narratorial overview' (1997, pp.132–4) is re-distributed on the same 'plane' as character voices, consciousnesses, opinions; conventional narrative hierarchies are suspended.

The kind of unprecedented re-distribution that Bakhtin prizes as a unique feature of Dostoevsky's work sees the author construct a *discourse attached to a character*, as opposed to creating – in objectified form – a 'character' (PDP, p.53). Taking this a little further, Vice speculates that filmic polyphony would involve a migration of signifying power into the hands of the signified characters, allowing them to 'operate their own signifying systems' (1997, p.145). *House of Games* stresses that Mike's attempt to 'narrate' Ford's life is staged as a drama, utilizing cinematic processes; this marks Mike out as a directorial surrogate, a challenge to Mamet's control of textual resources. As the judgement on psychoanalysis indicates, Mike activates values that we do not need to believe that

Mamet necessarily shares. Giovanni Palmieri has commented upon the fuzziness of this area of polyphonic relations:

> [I]t is not always possible to distinguish between those values and moral judgements that belong properly to the author's 'personal' discourse and those that are part of the characters' ideology
>
> (1998, p.47)

Is it *Mike's* derogatory perspective that informs the textual construction of Ford? Is Mamet responsible for the ethics, politics and duplicity of Mike's discourse because he creates the discursive opportunity for Mike's word to exist? For Palimieri, Bakhtinian polyphony theorizes a creative space in which authors use language to build images of characters' own 'choices', their own 'linguistic ideologies', but those choices and ideologies seem to remain the characters' own (1998, p.52). The utopian aspect of polyphony casts it as a liberation of character consciousness, with Bakhtin offering praise to the author who shows 'willingness to allow voices into the work that are not fundamentally under the "monological" control' of his own ideology (Booth, 1997, p.xx). What this benign vision perhaps overlooks is the possibility that the freedom of the character to determine his or her own viewpoint could result in a cynical manipulation of the addressee of their dialogic discourse – the audience; as if the freedom licensed by the polyphonic mode can create a lack of freedom elsewhere. This does not seem such an outlandish claim to make for a work that is explicitly concerned with the manipulation of knowledge both in theme and form: Mike's professional personality is based on verbal deception, and as we shall see, he also seems to conduct his business operations along theatrical lines. In much the same way as the classical monologic author (something of a bad guy in *Problems of Dostoevsky's Poetics*) wields total narrative control, the character of Mike in *House of Games* seems to attempt to fix the 'final word' of the spectator's evaluation of Margaret Ford. His orchestration of a convoluted narrative, with the ostensible purpose of relieving her of her wealth, is meant to deceive us as well as Ford. For Mike's scheme to work, he has to maintain Ford's interest and gain her trust. He does this by convincing her that there is something missing in her life which only he can provide – the paradoxical thrill of engaging with 'the real world' in a dramatically satisfying way. He must convince the viewer of something slightly different – that his authorial slant on 'Margaret Ford' is realistic and justified, that she deserves to be deceived because she accepts him so freely. In short, he is showing off, and this is reflected in the egotism of his discursive style (the refusal to accept the validity of the other's word), which will eventually prove to be his downfall. We are meant to delight in his intelligence and wit, to see Ford through his eyes: at first as a sterile automaton who thinks she has all the answers but does not understand the workings of the 'real world', and then, after his scheme has failed, as a *femme fatale*, a 'bitch' within whom the capacity to steal and kill always lurked beneath the ordered exterior. As we shall see in our consideration of the use of *film noir* motifs in *House of Games*, Ford reclaims Mike's interpretation of her as a *femme fatale* and uses it as a platform from which to challenge his point of view.

Eyes wide shut

Mike 'frames' Margaret Ford in more ways than one. His fiction is based around a few, beautifully staged key 'scenes', all familiar to cinema audiences – a tense, ill-tempered poker game, a 'love scene' in a hotel room, a violent skirmish which culminates in the shooting of a 'policeman', a 'daring escape' in a sports car. These scenes all involve aspects of film technique that contribute towards making the 'mise-en-scène' realistic to Ford – from the obscure lighting of the room in which the poker game is played to the fake blood used to create the policeman's wound. However, filmmaker is only one of the protean con man's guises – during the film he also makes claims to the status of philosopher (stating, during the card game, that he has been put into a 'philosophically indefensible position' by the aggressive play of his opponent) and parodies Ford's own profession of psychiatrist by undercutting its seriousness and purpose ('What's more fun than human nature?'). His 'profession' involves a dissembling into myriad roles, and their accompanying speech genres. We even see him performing a disappearing act with a gambling chip. This brief sequence associates Mike with the role of magician, which is historically conflated with the similarly illusory business of cinema in figures like George Méliès and Orson Welles. In this way, the motifs of gambling and confidence games are brought together with the processes of filmmaking and narrative in general, more sophisticated forms of con-artistry that also depend on the 'trust', the surrendered confidence, of a willing 'dupe'.[9]

The poker game is a crucial set-piece in Mike's staging of a narrative. It is structured around his manipulation of Ford's vision, as he fabricates a hierarchy of seeing. Mike engages Ford's curiosity by leaving the door ajar to give her a tantalizing glimpse of the secretive manoeuvres inside. This is one of several moments where the film comments, metatextually, on its own voyeuristic appeal. Visual tasks are performed by Ford under Mike's direction – she scrutinizes his opponent for a 'tell'; she is charged with keeping an eye upon his cards when he leaves the room. Significantly, Mike can penetrate Ford's look with his own; he can identify her 'tell' straight away. This compounds a sense that the regime of control he is attempting to establish is one where he has cast himself as omniscient (monologic) author. When Ford tells Mike she has seen the character known as 'Vegas Man' (Ricky Jay) play with his ring (the 'tell' that Mike has instructed her to look out for), he calls into question her ocular interpretation – 'Are you sure you saw him?'. For his overall story – his dramatized 'long con' – to progress, Mike needs to convince Ford that her own method of seeing is inferior, with the result that she will turn to him for orientation. When Mike loses the poker hand, he reiterates his doubts about what she has seen ('He didn't do the thing with his ring'). Ford's tendency not to use her full range of optical apparatus allows Mike to build up the 'essential "surplus"' of knowledge that gives him monologic power over her (PDP, p.73).[10] This is adumbrated in the bar scene where Mike poses as a waiter to show how easy it would be to take an inattentive Ford's money.[11] The glimpse of freedom that lies just beyond Ford as she struggles with the bogus policeman in her bid to escape from the hotel room also emphasizes the powerlessness of her look. The morning after Mike's 'major sting', he tells Ford that she has been privileged to see 'sights few have seen'. In reality, she has only seen what he has *directed* her to see (noting the cinematic connotations of the italicized term). This is an important point in relation to Mike's attempted suppression of polyphony, for Bakhtin's conception of polyphony is derived from a visual lexicon: Dostoevsky's artistic method is described as 'visualization', expressive of a particular ideological 'worldview' (PDP, p.11). The mode of seeing is, for Bakhtin, crucial to the ability to narrate, in polyphonic or monologic texts. The ability to visualize testifies to the observer's orientation on stable (but not irrevocably fixed) semantic ground from which an ideological position can be formed, and brought out in language (Holquist, 2002, p.164). Seeing is thus associated with knowledge, freedom and *expression* (Emerson, 1997, p.xxxvi). This correlation also informs *House of Games*; Ford cannot begin to produce her own discourse because she is constantly reminded that her sight is deficient. In the first three quarters of the film, her worldview is afforded no position in the hierarchy of vision.

Visually related language abounds in *House of Games*, accentuating the parallel between the hierarchy of knowledge implicit in the deception of Ford and the one that structures narrative process in cinema. During the poker scene, Mike complains that Ford is not bringing him luck. Another player tells him, 'Make your own luck'. The preponderance of visual phraseology suggests a double meaning: luck/look. Drawing together the systems of sight and gambling (and their mutual correlative, narrative), the statement would then denote Ford's epistemological task in *House of Games*: 'Make your own look'. Later, Ford's theft of Mike's 'lucky pocket knife' seems to reinforce this reading. The theft prefigures Ford's rebellion against Mike, and is in fact the only thing that goes wrong for him in the otherwise perfectly executed set-up. In taking his 'luck' she prepares the way for her appropriation of his 'look' that is necessary to topple his monology. The phallic significance of the knife emphasizes the association with the masculine 'look' or gaze.

Mike's manipulation of the narrative involves his full armoury of verbal and dramatic skills. During the set-up poker game, the con men put on a dazzling collective verbal performance, employing several different types of speech genre, showing Ford what she thinks are different sides of their personalities but are merely alternate inflections of their slick professional patter. The poker game compounds the already-noted connection between language and commerce or trade in the film and in Mamet generally, with the individual 'word' of a player representing not his integrity but his money. The players are extremely creative in their use of metaphor, and favour those with a spatial or geographical element: quitting the game is known as 'goin' South'. That there is something distinctly American about this combination of aggressive language use and financial risk is acknowledged when the game has been exposed as a sham. The con men politely apologize to Ford, adopting the professional tone of commerce and explaining that it was only business, 'the American Way'. The most vital part of their project is to convince Ford that they are exciting but not dangerous men, carefully differentiated from the 'hard guys' of the Mob that Mike mentions. They do this by adopting a comic speech genre, bickering like little boys when she discovers that the pistol brandished by 'Vegas Man' is of the kind that shoots water not bullets:

> 'VEGAS MAN': Told you a squirt gun wouldn't work.
> MIKE: A squirt gun *would* have worked. You didn't have to fill it.
> 'VEGAS MAN': What, I'm gonna threaten someone with an empty gun?

The routine could almost have come from an Abbott and Costello movie. Mike's charm leads to Ford seeing him as an interesting rogue rather than a dangerous criminal. He accentuates this impression by using speech genres that undercut Ford's first impression of him as a tough guy: 'You're not miffed at us are you?'. Mike manipulates the propensity of speech genres to 'reveal various layers and facets of the individual personality' (PSG, p.63), but reveals only what he sees fit, enhancing the impression that he is in monologic control. He needs to remain impenetrable to Ford, and he achieves this by keeping her guessing as to the nature of his personality, a blurring of identity that reflects the shifting boundaries of knowledge that all of the discourses featured share. All of these different types of discourse are portrayed as varieties of epistemological game, affiliated by virtue of their unreliability; hence, the various signifying systems seem to blur into one another. Cinema is equated with psychoanalysis, psychoanalysis with language, language with sexuality and so on. In this pivotal poker scene, knowledge is given a sexual and psychoanalytic dimension with another reference to the phallus. 'Vegas Man' asks Ford who she 'likes' in the game – him or Mike. She replies, showing a desire to compete with male discourse that is unusual for her character at this stage of the film: 'Well, I've seen *his* hand, but I haven't seen *yours*'.

Such verbal competitiveness from Ford is associated with her early attempts to 'talk turkey' with Mike, on the basis that she needs to rationally and aggressively negotiate with him to free Billy from his debt. Such competitiveness becomes rare for her in the second act, because Mike attempts to recast her in the given roles of 'feminine' submissiveness. To do this he moves to close off her discursive resources completely; hence the derisive attitude in the early part of the film to her emotional and professional standing, and her ability to speak for herself.[12]

There is an element of professional rivalry in Mike's need to prove the superiority of his knowledge of human nature to Ford; she tells him that she is a writer, but he does not divulge that he also knows she is a therapist. To establish his version of Ford as the correct one (to effectively superimpose his monology on Mamet's polyphony), he must shut her up. Interestingly, Mike dresses up this monologic project in the terms of dialogism, as if instead of fixing her in a false and reductive dichotomy between excessive, dangerous femininity and sterile, detached asexuality he is actually encouraging her to uncover some hidden kernel of self. Moments after they have made love in a hotel room, Ford – at this point completely seduced by Mike's oratorial skills and consequently further away from having a voice or story of her own than at any other time in the film – acknowledges her subservience to him in the discursive hierarchy by asking him to tell her what she is. He replies,

> Listen to me, cos there are a lot of things in the world. There are many sides to each of us. Good blood, bad blood. And somehow, all of those parts have got to speak. You know what I'm talking about. The burden of responsibility has become too great. That's true, isn't it? ... Babe, I know that it is ... I think what draws you to me is this. I'm not scared to examine the rules and assert myself. And I think you aren't either.[13]

Rather than the full dialogic interaction that is embodied in authentic polyphony, this statement amounts to the 'pseudo-polyphonic' discourse that Robert Stam has identified in media tokenism, one that 'marginalizes and disempowers certain voices, and then "dialogizes" with a puppetlike entity that has already been forced to make crucial compromises' (Stam, 1989, p.232). However, Mike inadvertently speaks a kind of truth here, and this becomes one of the lessons he will wish he had not given to his protégé. Ford must indeed offload the burden of responsibility weighed on her not only from her professional standing but also from her position in society's sexual hierarchy; in doing this, in finding alternatives to a predictable, passive version of femininity scripted for her by others, she does find a way to let some of her silenced parts speak, and rebel against the fate decreed for her by the patriarchal author figure Mike. Ford embarks on a complex re-accentuation of her sense of identity, which is the journey that the final third of the film charts. Mike's failure to show similar adaptability – his reliance on the illusion that his word is final and authoritative – is his downfall. Bakhtin associates the authoritative word with patriarchy:

> The authoritative word demands that we acknowledge it [...] it binds us, quite independent of any power it might have to persuade us internally; we encounter it with its authority already fused to it. The authoritative word is located in a distanced zone, organically connected with a past that is felt to be hierarchically higher. It is, so to speak, the word of the fathers.
>
> (DIN, p.342)

If Ford is to compete with Mike, to assert her right to participate in a polyphonic discourse, she has to reject the terms of gender privilege inherent in his appropriation of the 'authoritative word', and find a space for expression outside of the patriarchal loop. This imperative is strengthened through the glimpses we see of Ford engaging in clinical treatment of the murderess. From the words of the murderess, we make a clear inference that the victim of her murder was her father (Van Wert, 1990, p.5). Believing that the weight of patriarchy is standing behind his word, Mike ironically over-invests in its authority (in a way that his colleagues would find hopelessly naïve). This recalls the naïve attitude to language articulated by John (William H. Macy) in one of the key exchanges in *Oleanna*:

> The Stoics say [...] if you remove the phrase, 'I have been injured', you have removed the injury.[14]

The similar lesson served up to both Mike and John is that words *matter* and are more than tools. Control over them is not a one-way process; to believe as much is an attitude typifying those who think they have already mastered them. As we shall see, Mike's pathetic defence to Ford's revenge is to claim neutrality for his own verbal cruelty: 'I never hurt anybody.'

The framer framed

The emphasis of the film (not simply in terms of the revision of understanding that accompanies the revelation of Mike's 'frame-up', but also regarding the attribution of point-of-view) changes completely when Ford discovers Mike's duplicity and decides to fight back. The shift is located at the moment when Ford witnesses Mike 'unscripted', as it were, for the first time. This is when she transgressively takes an illicit look 'backstage' (Pearce, 1999, p.4). In the back of Charley's Bar, unwittingly observed by Ford, Mike accepts congratulations on the flawless execution of the 'scenes' of romance, violence and flight that make up his drama. Mike accepts tribute as the singular 'auteur' of this production, and accordingly the colleagues at this 'wrap party' compare him to a cinematic icon, King Kong. Mike acknowledges his decisive contribution in monologic terms: 'One riot, one ranger'. As mentioned earlier, Mike's drama is apparently 'adapted' from Ford's *own* text, her bestselling tome on obsessive behaviour, which is bandied about at the table. A single loose thread in the plot – the re-use of the red sports car (a lack of production value) – has led the newly observant Ford to this moment. The subjective camera position that represents Ford's view in this scene will be reprised when Mike arrives at the airport and walks into *her* drama; this is a 'milieu where [...] everyone seems to be a character in someone else's play' (French, 2004, p.185). In both instances, Ford is positioned as a secret observer, displaying the possession of the 'surplus' of knowledge that had previously given Mike the advantage. Obviously, there are other instances in the film where the action is observed from a perspective analogous to Ford's physical position; but there is something more deterministic about these brief moments, accentuated by the constant relaying back to Ford's 'look'. The implication is that Ford is finally in control of the gaze, and with the possession of the gaze comes an ability to objectify, to describe, to narrate. Upgraded from passive and static to active and kinetic, Ford begins to influence the visual scheme, showing that she has finally arrived as a narrative player in this 'motion picture'.

Ford's progress from object-image to subject-narrator is enacted on various textual levels. In dialogical terms, she migrates from a fixed position in

Mike's monologic narrative to the status of an independent consciousness partaking of the 'plurality of ... unmerged voices' (PDP, p.6) that characterizes polyphony. However, this transition could be construed as a secondhand monologism, principally in the sense that it is modelled so closely on Mike's method of oppression; does she merely exchange a position of servitude for a position of dominance in a binary relationship that can never be dissolved, only reversed? This issue is sensitively poised with regard to the gender reading of the film, and several critics have identified problems with Ford's change. Made into a narrative 'object' by Mike, Ford must break free of his monologic authorial control by objectifying herself; however, the only route by which this can be achieved is by identifying with the masculine and emulating the deceptive methods by which she herself has been oppressed. This dilemma evokes the problem of female self-representation as articulated by Luce Irigaray: 'The masculine can, partly, look at itself, speculate about itself, represent itself and describe itself for what it is, whilst the feminine can try to speak to itself through a new language, but cannot describe itself from outside or in formal terms, except by identifying with the masculine, thus by losing itself' (quoted in Doane, 1991, p.24).

Ford's ascension to a polyphonic plateau involves a revision of those gendered assumptions governing the relation between seeing and possessing discursive agency. In terms of the viewpoint determining the presentation of events (and bearing in mind the invoked traditions of both psychoanalysis and *noir*, where vision is often conflated with gender), Ford abandons the 'masculine', professionally sanctioned position of observer she inhabits at the start of the film to adopt a 'feminine' role of the observed, that which is looked at (in the sense that she finally 'acts'). With an element of masquerade, Ford achieves the distance necessary to possess the 'second look' conventionally attributed to the male gaze; after killing Mike, Ford's early ultra-defeminized appearance is transformed into an overtly feminine one (in the restaurant scene that acts as a coda to the film). Mary Ann Doane's concept of 'masquerade', partly a response to the 'locked [...] logic' of filmic gaze theory (1991, p.21), explores how the female can overcome her narrative 'insufficiency' by achieving the voyeuristic distance necessary to 'describe from outside'.[15] The *femme fatale* finds a solution in masquerade, the production of excessive femininity as a performance, which becomes Ford's tactic both in her drastic change of image in the coda and in the role of utter helplessness she plays to draw Mike into her drama at the airport.[16]

Beyond the changes in her image, Ford capitalizes on lessons learned from Mike, her professional rival in 'decoding' human nature. By adopting the one-sided speech mechanisms learnt from Mike's cynical 'deceptive dialogicality', Ford has arguably achieved a move into the meaningful symbolic realm of language and action; the world of subjectivity that she enters is pseudo-masculine. In Mike's words, Ford has learned to 'examine the rules and assert' herself (his earlier self-description). The mantra 'forgive yourself', which Ford picks up from her friend Maria and uses to justify her actions to herself,[17] is also effectively what Mike tries to tell her in the taxi ride after she has handed over the money: 'If you don't tell them, then they don't know ... You're gonna want to confess. Don't do it ... [G]o and forget it.' The fact that Ford appropriates this and other advice and eventually turns it against Mike demonstrates that, even in a world saturated with signification, words still have consequences, especially when they are reactivated in new contexts. Like her murderess patient, Ford overturns patriarchal misrepresentation in killing Mike, who has oppressed her through the control of language; however, possessed of the new distance conferred by her masquerade/role-playing activities, Ford seems set to avoid the murderess' fate of apparent insanity by successfully 'forgiving herself'.[18] This marks the triumph of the rationality that she was earlier criticized for in her professional demeanour and was seen as inappropriate for her gender.

Ford could be said to 'dialogize' her identity, to move outside the concept of 'self' fixed for her by society. She seems to leave one of these fragments of identity, the one called 'Dr Margaret Ford', with Mike's corpse in the airport cargo bay. Although asked her name at least twice by Mike earlier in the film, Ford has not revealed it to him. She holds this part of herself back, in spite of Mike's subtle machinations, until the airport and their final exchange. The cornerstone of her revenge appears to be the final giving up of her name to him; the implication is that she is dispensing with the alias of 'Dr Margaret Ford' as a symbol of her attainment of a more fluid conception of identity. Ford even hints to Mike in telling him her 'real' name that she has finished with her old self: 'I bought my ticket in another name. My real name is Margaret.' Mike, still convinced that Ford, not he, is the 'mark', and ever-willing to play out any masculine role on offer, attempts to reassure her by telling her 'I've got you.' The ironical inflection put onto this statement by Mamet is enjoyed by the audience – having been privy to Ford's discovery of Mike's deception, we know that she is now 'acting', and that it is she who has 'got' him. Although her game is betrayed to an alert Mike by another slip of the tongue regarding the stolen pocket-knife, she is ready to exact her revenge. This appears to be related to the fact that she has finally given him her name. Convinced that she is bluffing, Mike uses the name disparagingly. When she accuses him of raping her, he belittles the charge with the child-like phrase, 'Golly,

Margaret, well that's just what happened then, isn't it?', and facetiously castigates himself for being 'naughty'. However, when he refuses to beg for his life, Ford shoots him. When Mike tells her that she will never get away with this action ('What, are you gonna ... give up all that good shit that you have ... your bestseller, all that doctor stuff'), Ford responds by denying that it was her pulling the trigger – 'It's not my pistol. I was never here.' Ford is acknowledging her assumption of a new role, an identity in which she can 'act' and thus determine her own existence outside of the bounds of male-defined narrative and language. She is refusing, in a way, to be reduced to an 'essence', to one inviolable aspect or nature, to one fixed 'position', to return to the terms of spectator theory. Mike attempts to trivialize this revision of identity as the mere assumption of a masculine pose, calling her 'stud' and 'sir'. However, he has to admit that on one score, the ability to use violent means, she has surpassed his manhood: 'I never hurt anybody, I never shot anybody.' Mike cannot accept that his actions in the scam could leave as great an indentation on her psyche as her bullets leave in his body.

Ford has learned from Mike to refuse fixed definitions, and with it attained an existential freedom – the distance necessary to finally act – normally denied to her gender; in his words, she has learned to 'examine the rules and assert' herself. In the coda, she refuses to acknowledge that she is 'Dr Margaret Ford' when asked to sign her book by an admirer. The last name associated with her in the film is that used by her friend Maria: 'Maggie'.

Because she is able to forgive herself, it is suggested that Ford will escape the murderess' fate. If we are going to doubt that Ford has come through the experience with her sanity intact, we must bear in mind that this is an idea also expressed, with his dying breath, by Mike – trying to shape audience perception of Ford to the last. Once Mike's first dramatized version of Ford – the sterile automaton who is deluded about the way the real world works – has failed, he tries to re-cast her as the untrustworthy, manipulative *femme fatale* – calling Ford a 'crooked bitch' and 'thief' who 'always wanted' to kill. The ending of the film appears to show Ford accepting (reclaiming?) Mike's interpretation of her as a *femme fatale* (apparently absorbing a continuing criminality within her new 'forgiven' persona), leaving the consequences of her transformation, and the truth status of Mike's evaluation of her, rather unclear (Kipnis, 1991). The motifs of female sexuality and crime, combined with notions of deception, game playing and hidden rules, brings the text back into the orbit of the *film noir*, which provides a further ambiguous epistemological 'frame' for reading *House of Games*.

Noir motifs in *House of Games*

When his life is threatened, Mike's last-ditch ploy to regain the upper hand is to attack Ford's own nature, the things he claims she has learned about herself during their relationship. The final image he tries to impose upon her is that of the untrustworthy, manipulative *femme fatale*:

> You always needed to get caught, because you know you're bad ... You sought this out ... You're worthless, you know it. You're a whore. You came back like a dog to its own vomit. I'm not going to give you shit.

This invocation of a cinematic archetype leads us to consider the next level of Ford's conversion, which plays with signifiers appropriated from the *noir* genre. The proliferation of *noir* signifiers in *House of Games* – especially after Ford has discovered Mike's treachery and become 'active' in narrative terms – contributes to the disorientating effect of the film. Mamet's text avoids major structural staples of *noir* such as voice-over or prolific use of flashback, perhaps because these conventions might have an irrevocable determining factor on the association of narrative agency with one particular character. However, the neon-lit streets, heavy rain, dark alleyways, sleazy bars and unforgiving urban environment featured in the film align it with that genre.[19] The use of *noir* motifs also feeds into the comparison the film develops between unreliable epistemological systems. *Film noir* is often said to be based on a conception of identity and meaning as in constant flux:

> The dominant world view expressed in film noir is paranoid, claustrophobic, hopeless, doomed [...] without clear moral or personal identity. Man has been inexplicably uprooted from those values, beliefs and endeavours that offer him meaning and stability [...] Nothing – especially woman – is stable, nothing is dependable.
> (Place, 1980, p.41)

Significantly, it is with Ford's shift to an unstable conception of identity (highlighted by her role-playing) that the film really strays into *noir* territory. She takes on the role of a 'revenger', and with it some of the traits of the *femme fatale*. Ford initially tries to deceive Mike by acting out a parodic exaggeration of the role that he had carved out for her, that of the passive, helpless woman. This vapid characterization is redolent of the 'weak and incapable' women who represented the dominant cinematic archetype before the advent of *film noir* (Place, 1980, p.36).

Mike is initially taken in by her performance, suggesting that this is the way men like to 'see' women – which accounts for the masculine associations of the gaze and the cinematic status of woman as object-image. However, Ford goes on to showcase a new part from her repertoire, and it is one that is less pleasing to her spectator, Mike.

What is interesting about Ford's brief portrayal of the *femme fatale* is that it is so morally ambivalent. Frequently in the classical era, *femmes fatales*, although represented as dangerous and unstable, are 'redeemed' at the end of the movie either by returning to an intrinsic goodness or through the intervention of a male character who sees the heroine for what she really is (Place, 1980, p.48).[20] If this is not the case, and they are suggested to be inherently evil, they are often destroyed.[21] Mamet rejects this binary opposition, refusing to stamp Ford as either certifiably 'good' or 'bad', thus in a sense anticipating other unpunished, unredeemed criminal women of late-1980s/1990s so-called 'neo-*noir*' cinema, such as Bridget (Linda Fiorentino) in John Dahl's *The Last Seduction* (1994), and Violet (Jennifer Tilly) and Corky (Gina Gershon) in *Bound* (Wachowski Brothers, 1996).[22] Although we see Ford comforting the murderess and interceding to help Billy, we also see her murder Mike in cold blood and 'forgive herself' for this act; the instability and contingency of her personality reflects Place's comment on the mutability of characters in *film noir*: 'nothing and no-one is what it seems' (1980, p.48).

The structures of looking that are established in the text also reflect the incorporation of *film noir* elements. Ford's subjection by the male gaze is signalled by other motifs than camera position. She is depicted several times as behind bars – literally, in the case of her exit from the prison ward, having completed a session with the murderess. Lines of diagonal light fall over her from the blinds in her office in the early scene with Billy, and as she witnesses Mike's 'wrap party' she observes him from a vantage point between the vertical bars of a booth. According to Place's analysis, another *film noir* device for expressing the controlling male look is the frame – in this instance, the pictures of Ford that adorn the jacket of her book. Portraits in *film noir* are often invoked to denote the ' "safe" [...] static, and powerless' nature of women (1980, p.50).[23] The book is, of course, the reason that Ford is targeted by Mike, and her photographic representation is implicated in this. Ford's attainment of narrative influence is prefigured symbolically when she throws a copy of her book – a symbol of the 'old' Margaret Ford, the one that allowed herself to be cleaned out by a bunch of con men – at a framed medical certificate hanging on the wall of her office (as a gesture that signposts the way to her revenge, this episode casts ambivalence around authentic experience and its recording; by setting herself up as an expert of human nature with her first book, Ford has played into the hands of the con men, yet the coda strongly suggests that her experience with Mike will form the basis of the next book). In throwing the book, Ford is symbolically breaking the frame of representation, the ideological boundaries of patriarchal narrative practices that have underwritten her humiliation at Mike's hands. Ford's early, 'powerless' incarnation is also brought out visually in the physical juxtaposition of her with the murderess, who dwarfs Ford in size. This figure denotes *film noir*'s representation of the dangerously unstable threat to male identity, which must be contained; however, as with her incorporation of elements of Mike's personality, or at least worldview ('forgive yourself'), Ford does seem to take something from her dialogues with the murderess and integrate it with her new self.

Ford's revenge overturns the visual taming and containment imposed by the bars, frames and ribbons of light; she embraces and personifies the 'untrustworthiness of the image' that Doane, in her analysis of *Gilda* (Charles Vidor, 1946), identifies as a trope of the *noir* female (1991, p.103). The liability of the *femme fatale* to change before the hero's eyes is a staple of the genre. Ford turns this around with the words she utters as she greets Mike at the airport ('I can't believe I'm seeing you'); she is now the one who is certain of her ontological and discursive existence; he is about to disappear from view. The airport setting throws appearance and visual interpretation into further turmoil, loaded as it is with the sense of life-changing crisis associated with the Bakhtinian 'threshold' chronotope. A place where new 'selves' and carnivalesque disguises are taken up and shed day after day, the setting serves to accentuate the impression that Ford has finally mobilized her own story, and it is fitting that Ford's exchange of 'old' for 'new' identities should take place here. The sense of a cathartic new beginning is so strong during this part of the film that Van Wert (1990, p.6) refers to the eavesdropping scene in Charley's Bar as Ford's *tabula rasa* moment, from which she emerges (to appear, the very next scene, at the airport) as someone so new and purged of innocence that she is virtually invisible to the con men (one of whom actually walks straight past her in the bar).

Ford evades at least two of the penalties normally meted out to *femmes fatales*, according to Laura Mulvey – punishment and redemption through male intervention (Mulvey 1999, p.29). Mulvey's third category of fate awaiting women in *film noir* – 'devaluation' – is more problematic. We are aware of the gravity of Ford's crime, in conjunction with the aforementioned comparative figure of the murderess (who, it is suggested, lapses into insanity after a similar act by not being able to redraw her own ethical boundaries and forgive herself). Although it is difficult to feel too much sympathy for Mike, who must have been aware of the risks of his cynical and dangerous game from the outset (indeed, the film precludes sympathy with Mike at this stage by strategies such as the fastening of the camera look to her gaze), Ford's transformation into a murderess has represented a kind of 'devaluation' to some critics (Kipnis, for instance). With polyphony in mind, though, it seems credible to argue that, despite the 'melding' of our sympathies with Ford's interests in the final third (Van Wert, 1990, p.8), Mamet preserves a crucial gap between our visual and interpretative resources and Ford's. This gap makes sure that even after her act of revenge, and into the ambiguous coda, Ford's identity is still open, mysterious and resistant to our understanding: we struggle to 'finalize' and resolve her meaning in terms of gender and ethical models (Pearce, 1999, pp.3–5).

Breaking the classical frame

The present polyphonic interpretation of *House of Games* is justified with reference to the shifting narrative emphasis of the text, principally concerning the transition from Mike to Ford and how it is signalled by the film. However, Mamet (the 'author-creator') and the reader are also important components in this system. The 'gap' mentioned earlier between the viewpoint of the audience and that of the major characters is vital to our constitution as members of a polyphonic exchange. The choice of narrative mode (the decision to reject voice-over, for instance) and the epistemological uncertainty of form and theme means that there is always a certain amount of slippage between appearance and interpretation in this text, but there is further work to be done to determine whether the resulting suspension of monological certainty should necessarily be interpreted as arising from a special polyphonic design.

By focusing our attention on the limitations of interpretation and the essentially game-like nature of any form of meaning exchange, Mamet reworks our usual relation to film. What is meant by 'relation' here is the way that the classical film tradition masks authorial presence and signs of production through conventions of editing and so on, with the result that the 'real' producer of the text is effaced and the consumer can slide into the imaginary position of subject-producer. Certain strains of psychoanalytic film theory have accounted for this process with reference to the concept of 'enunciation', whereby the viewer 'sustains the very possibility of any representation' (Bellour, quoted in Stam et al, 1992, pp.159–60). A sort of dialogism seems to be invoked by this emphasis on the reader in the production of meaning, but arguably the spectator's position is falsified by the illusion that they are in total control. Monologism is implied in that authority can be withdrawn at any time from the viewer (it is this idea that, underneath the ideological façade, meaning is proscriptive, one-way and *given* that has fuelled most critiques of 'subject-positioning' and 'apparatus' theory of which Mulvey's original gaze work is a version – see Chapter 1). *House of Games* subscribes to the stylistic mode of classical Hollywood cinema, which subordinates 'discourse' to 'history' and covers over the marks of the enunciative process (Stam, et al, 1992, p.162); conforming to this, it does not overtly foreground the process of its making in the way that films that are less formally conservative do. This can be particularly seen in its orthodox editing rhythms and lack of visual expressionism (other than that which is reasonably diegetically motivated). However, this perhaps alerts us to two divergent strands in the notion of effacement. In the conventional Hollywood text, this is a deceptive technique – the hand of the director may be unseen, but he is never in less than total control. In a 'polyphonic' film, the director does not pretend to be without influence in the organization of the narrative, but rather exposes himself as a presence in the text on a polyphonic level – that is, in dialogue with other consciousnesses. This gives the impression of effacement (authorial presence, in this conception, is democratized, and filtered through character). By willingly relinquishing monologic control of the narrative and letting characters speak for themselves, the polyphonic filmmaker becomes a paradoxical figure in the text – heard (in a 'plurality of voices'), but not seen.

To demonstrate this thesis in relation to *House of Games*, we will look briefly at the coda. This takes place in a restaurant, where Ford, complete with new overtly 'feminine' image, meets Maria for lunch. The attribution of the gaze to Ford which was notable in the previous cargo bay scene (the 'shooting' of Mike – noting the extra visual/filmic connotation of his manner of death) is not explicit here. There is no overt use of subjective camera. The key to detecting polyphony in operation is in a certain tone of irony that pervades this sequence. Ford's achievement, that is, her assertion of a right to compete in the production of narrative, is somewhat undercut in this scene by a degree of complacency on her part. Her empowerment is trivialized by the theft of the lighter from another diner; she did not overturn Mike's dominance so that she could practise petty thievery. There is a sense that another perspective is evaluating Ford here, and that it belongs to Mamet. However, it is not a case of the 'author-creator' simply picking up the reins once more; Mamet does not cast a final, monologically sealed word on Ford or allow us to resolve her trajectory in one of the typical avenues noted by Mulvey. The scene is, rather, characterized by its openendedness. We feel that her transformation has not yet taken root, and that it could still have very positive consequences. Mamet's evaluating voice sounds in ironic dissonance with Ford's slightly overdetermined, self-conscious revision of identity, suggesting that the story is not over; here is a warning to Ford not to commit to another fixed, fictional representation of herself – that of the 'bad girl' – that differs from the archetype she filled before only in emphasis. To retain her authority on the discursive, narrative and sexual planes, she must remain in a state of 'unfinalizability' (PDP, p.68). For Bakhtin, this term denotes the 'essence' of consciousnesses in authentic polyphonic interaction. Such consciousnesses must never be allowed to congeal into 'monologically formed chunks of life' removed from the network of dialogic possibilities, for this turns images 'silent' and prevents them from speaking with meaning (68). However, this imperative to remain unfinalized might frustrate our reading of the significance of Ford's fightback; it also means that Ford cannot enforce definitive closure on the experience that brought her to this moment. Mike's consciousness survives as a faint voice echoing in Ford's revised self, complicating our final view of her and our struggle to ethically reconcile her transgressions with her entitlement to survival, to sanity, to self-forgiveness. In this complex unfinished state, she resembles Dostoevsky's Underground Man as viewed by Bakhtin, who 'has neither freed himself from the power of the other's consciousness nor admitted its power over him, he is for now merely struggling with it [...] not able to accept it but also not able to reject it' (PDP, p.232). The Underground Man's word about himself, the image of self-consciousness by which he gains polyphonic weight and survives the division of his discourse from Dostoevsky's, is built around the words and judgements of the other: 'self-definition with a loophole [...] is forever taking into account internally the responsive, contrary evaluation of oneself made by another' (PDP, p.233). Or, as Mike would put it: 'Good blood, bad blood. And somehow, all of those parts have got to speak.'

Such polyphonic intricacies may convey a sense that the ending of the film obviates the enforcement of closure in the name of a general textual 'unfinalizability', but simultaneously fails to provide any clear-cut political redemption. Kipnis (1991) proffers a pessimistic reading: the coda 'seals the film's meaning', giving the stamp of ultimate validity to Mike's interpretation of Ford as 'crooked bitch'. Although Mike's discourse is not exhausted and excised, the coda does not strongly determine that his last word on Ford resounds more loudly than her slogan of 'forgive yourself'; the present analysis has aimed to show that the fluid nature of the film's thematic concerns and formal construction renders such categorical judgements regarding discursive truth or authority extremely problematical. Viewed under properly cinematic conditions, we can only interpret the information that is given to us at the time. In this way, cinema as a medium and an experience encourages a more simultaneous, less linear approach to interpretation than does, for instance, the novel, which can be put down and picked up at any time.[24] Caught up in this logic – we 'make' the one-time only running of the theatrical film 'as one makes a train' (Heath, 1981, p.216) – we are primed to accept cinema's impression of pseudo-simultaneity, and consequently, to fall for structurally necessary misreadings, as David Bordwell has noted (1985, p.32). While this undoubtedly leaves the viewer open to the manipulations of plot (especially true in *House of Games*), it also confers legitimacy upon multiple readings.[25] We may think we have *House of Games* safely pigeon-holed as a thriller or 'con-man' picture in the tradition of *The Sting* (George Roy Hill, 1973), only for it to activate its own loophole and turn, unexpectedly, into a *film noir* about the problem of female representation. Exaggeration aside, there is a sense in which *House of Games* could be construed as two different films, enhancing its polyphonic credentials; Gary Saul Morson has written of a tendency of the polyphonic novel to 'oscillate between several possible novels' (1994, p.94). Iris M. Zavala has noted, in similar terms, the double-sided nature of dialogical texts:

> Each text is presented as saying first one thing and then its opposite, as playing two scenes
>
> (Zavala, 1990, p.80)

When the polyphonic apparatus allows Ford to assume the narrative mantle in Mamet's film, we take a diversion down a new pathway.[26] We did not have to go down that particular route; we just happened to (as Ford 'happened' to spot Billy getting into the familiar red sports car). Correspondingly, according to Bakhtin, plot in the polyphonic novel is 'only one of many possible plots and [...] accidental for a given hero' (PDP, p.84). He refers to plot in Dostoevsky as 'absolutely devoid of any sort of finalizing functions', its only function to provoke characters into dialogic relations and conflict (276). This conception of plot as a secondary function is perhaps instructive for considering how it plays out in *House of Games*. Plot, in the sense of the organization of narrative events according to conventions of representation, does not even exist in Mamet's film. The viewer is not guided by the plot, or even really manipulated by it (as the author cannot be sure what our reaction will be), but rather encouraged by it to make mistakes, to commit ourselves to a viewpoint. This has the by-product of raising our awareness that we are on very thin interpretative ground. On a very basic narrative level, the murder of Mike is quite unexpected. The fact that Ford apparently escapes from punishment and even prospers is even less expected, blocking the narrative momentum of good/evil dichotomies and halting judgement of female transgression, ensuring a rare future for the *femme fatale*.

Bakhtin explains the 'slippage' of interpretation that is vital to polyphony in terms of a liberation of the hero's consciousness:

> We see not who he is, but *how* he is conscious of himself; our act of artistic visualization occurs not before the reality of the hero, but before a pure function of his awareness of that reality.
>
> (PDP, p.49)

The result of the Dostoevskyian hero's slipping out of the status of object (for the author and the reader) is that he is no less qualified than either the author or reader to determine the nature and direction of his story. The upgrading of the hero/heroine to subjective consciousness in the polyphonic novel is the legitimate mirror-image of our own false subjectivity as defined by the classical Hollywood cinema. He will often make the wrong decision, but he and only he will be responsible for his own actions. His self-consciousness, and his ability to speak for himself in the context of a dialogical background, mean that he can pipe up at any time, shattering any interpretative preconceptions on behalf of the reader. Wayne Booth notes that polyphony engenders 'an unlimited openness of characters to developments out of their "idea" into unpredictable futures' (1997, p.xxiii); the character who is self-aware enough to spot a 'loophole' in their 'accidental' narrative world controls their own fate.

The sense of presentness that is captured in genre is important to Bakhtin; it does not disappear under the claims of a represented time (see Chapter 3), and is felt in the unpredictability of polyphonic author–character interaction. Morson has discussed the notion of 'eventness' (from 'Toward a Philosophy of the Act'[27]) in a fashion that seems to have special relevance for the filmic text, suggesting that Dostoevsky's readers 'sense his works not as a completed structure but as a "concrete event" that somehow seems to take place before our eyes *as* we read' (Morson, 1994, p.93). The visual terminology that reverberates from Bakhtin's own preference seems to suggest that we can extrapolate the notion of 'eventness' to support the theory that polyphony can be manifest in film.

After all, film not only takes place 'before our eyes' but is also possessed of a much greater fluidity of narrator than is the novel.[28] The filmic text is able to construct narrative agency along a wide range of interpretative positions, 'from the 'invisible' narrational style of the classic Hollywood cinema to the highly idiosyncratic narrative discourse of, for example, Jean Luc Godard' (Stam et al, 1992, p.113). Surely Bakhtin's 'plurality of independent and unmerged voices' (PDP, p.6) is better served by the camera, which can portray an unlimited number of subject positions within a scene (and even within the frame, when one thinks of dissolves or split-screen techniques).[29] Mamet's mixing-and-matching of narrative viewpoints, expressed on the level of spectacle in the shift from Mike's perspective to Ford's (discussed above with reference to the bar and airport scenes), could be said to enhance the 'eventness' of his film.

Bakhtin also states that the fully polyphonic character is to an extent aware of the *narrative* constitution of his world (PDP, p.48); in this milieu where 'everyone seems to be a character in someone else's play' (French, 2004, p.185) there is an inescapably rich metatextual atmosphere. At one point in *House of Games*, Ford seems to comment metatextually on the *noir*-ish atmosphere of the dank hostelry Charley's Bar. She writes a note on a napkin: 'The necessity of dark places to transact a dark business'. The awareness of Mike and Ford of the textual nature of their world is delineated by the cinematic elements incorporated into both characters' attempts to make their narrative voice heard.

Conclusion: Mamet and polyphony

House of Games, in both its form (the intertextual relation to *film noir*) and its content (the various transactions of personality and trust, and attendant themes of desire and value), raises some important questions about narrative control and its relation to gender and identity. It is difficult to pin down Mamet's attitude to his female protagonist, and whether it concurs with the misogynistic viewpoint of the other male 'narrator' figure in the text, Mike, but even wider of the mark is a judgement of the film as a piece of 'feminist propaganda'.[30] Philip French considers Margaret Ford 'probably the strongest role Mamet has written for a woman, the one least vulnerable to the charge of misognyny' (2004, p.184).

Mamet's authorial stance is self-effacing, even deceptive, but not monologic; there is a hierarchy of knowledge within the narrative, but a text that proposed to surprise the audience as well as the character with story convolutions such as those found in *House of Games* could not succeed without one. The characters are given an amount of polyphonic freedom with which to address themselves to us. We are never given an authorial opinion on either main character definite enough to prevent us from having our doubts about them long after the film has finished. In this way, Mamet refuses to affirm the authorial 'last word' that is typical, in Bakhtin's estimation, of the monologic narrator. The most important question raised by the narrative – whether the revenge exacted upon Mike is deserved, whether his death is equivalent to Ford's humiliation – does not come with an unequivocal authorial judgement attached. This commitment to the presentation of complex issues of gender and discourse without ultimate evaluation has something of the character of Bakhtin's account of Dostoevsky, as viewed by Simon Dentith:

> Dostoevsky is not interested in 'explaining' his characters in social–historical terms, but rather in provoking them to ultimate revelations of themselves in extreme situations, which are never closed or resolved. It is important to recognize, however, that this is an aesthetic account and not a moral or ethical treatise; the point for Bakhtin in these moral considerations is that they enter into the way the novels are constructed
>
> (1995, p.43)

To adapt Dentith's comment to the author under present discussion, it may be said that Mamet rather posits the cultural (socio-historical) imperatives of narrative and language themselves as part of the problem of representing female identities.[31] This may be a surprising view to take of an author who has often provoked controversy as regards his representation of female characters, but by using the theory of polyphony, we may have identified the 'loophole' which Mamet leaves for feminist discourse in his work. The Bakhtinian 'loophole' constitutes 'the retention for oneself of the possibility for altering the ultimate, final meaning of one's own words' (PDP, p.233). Christopher Bigsby, analysing the reception of *Oleanna*, insists that Mamet is aware of the stakes involved in the conflict between sexes but is not willing to 'adjudicate between positions which were, as he insisted, simultaneously both right and wrong' (2004, pp.3–4). The 'equal rights' granted to characters within a future-oriented polyphonic system are preserved so long as they can resist making monological power plays. In *House of Games*, Mike could live if only he was prepared to acknowledge that Ford has outdone him (she offers him the chance to beg for his life). Instead, falling under the spell of his own words, he chooses to stick to his monologic position, and thus determines the closure of his own narrative.[32]

5
Hollywood Calling: Cinema's Technological Address

Introduction

As traditional filmmaking practices become subsumed within cinema's movement into digital territories, the very terms with which we speak about film inevitably come up for re-evaluation. The notion of the 'pro-filmic event'[1] as a way of understanding the materiality of the staged and arranged objects (sets, props and actors) in front of the camera as guaranteed by their straightforward reproduction on celluloid, becomes problematic in the age of computer-generated imagery (CGI). Entire features are now computer-generated, and although the kind of texts that make use of the technology to the fullest degree are still those that overlap substantially with the traditional field of children's cartoon animation[2] (films such as those produced by Pixar since *Toy Story*, John Lasseter, 1995, and by Dreamworks Animation Studios since *Antz*, Eric Darnell/Tim Johnson, 1998), progressively the visual practices innovated therein are finding their way into mainstream dramatic cinema through a host of genres (Keane, 2007, pp.60–1). In fact, in terms of contemporary Hollywood output, it is probably more apposite to ask which films and genres do *not* benefit from the assistance of CGI than to list those that do, so assimilated into the conventional palette of visual effects has the technology become. The technology has been useful to renew standards of visual spectacle in those genres that are currently the most reliable income generators,[3] thus enabling economic competition, and a certain linking of aesthetic, with the strongly youth-centric videogame industry (Keane, 2007, p.100). At the same time, albeit with an inconsistent appeal to realism, a bonus in production value has been attained by prestige films and genres employing the technology to enhance period detail or the epic feel of crowd scenes (*Gladiator*, Ridley Scott, 2000; *Flags of Our Fathers*, Clint Eastwood, 2006). An additional benefit of the development of the technology is its capacity to produce 'virtual sets' that can allow modestly budgeted productions to punch above their weight in terms of achieving a richly stylized world for their narrative; a notable example would be the Dimension Studios production *Sin City* (2005), directed by Robert Rodriguez. Budgeted at $40 million, the digitally shot film grossed nearly $160 million theatrically worldwide as well as amassing at least $40 million in DVD rental revenues in the United States alone.[4]

The rise to prominence of CGI functions as a constituent in a broader reformation of aesthetics following the increasing incursion of digital and multimedia technologies into the film experience. The other end of the production economics scale, for instance, has seen the widespread adoption of digital video (DV) (see Keane, 2007, pp.36–55). The impact of such developments is in evidence at every formal stage of the cinematic process: at the production end (different shooting mediums like DV, high-definition cameras, digital editing systems like Avid); in distribution modes and delivery methods (digital theatrical projection, DVD/Blu-Ray, download formats for feature films and for ancillary texts like trailers or deleted scenes), and in marketing and professional criticism (websites, social networking sites, review sites like rottentomatoes.com or metacritic.com, opinion and gossip sites like aint-it-cool-news.com).

Of course, the consumption and interpretation of film bear some of the biggest changes afforded by new communications technologies, some of which cross or even erode the existing boundaries that define some of us as spectators and others of us as critics or producers. These include a range of new ways to access films (including mobile ones) that do not depend on theatrical attendance; the existence of film in different types of artefact; the easy assemblage of fan and 'fan-scholar' communities (see Hills, 2002, pp.1–45); the possibility of non-studio-sanctioned 'fan edits',[5] and many other phenomena that revolve around the commitment/buying power of fans, but also tap into their knowledge. Studios are often portrayed as initially not quite understanding the new opportunities that attend technology, hence reflexively striving to police it (following the regular scare stories that home video and games consoles attracted in the 1980s and 1990s, Web-based video and file-sharing platforms are now seen as the main threat to revenue; the campaign against illegal downloading is handled by industry body, the MPAA). Studios (more accurately, their parent conglomerates) are either already invested in, or want to appear friendly to social networking communities. Commercial convergence proves a popular solution, with the ensuing corporate reshuffles resembling those that played out around the introduction of television in the 1950s (the acquisition of MySpace by News Corp in 2005; the deal struck by NBC to showcase promo clips on YouTube[6]).

Both academic and popular ways of thinking about technological change have intermittently depended on the idea that institutional control is weakened by rapid technological development, and that the agency of spectators is positively affected as a result. Academic discussion of fan practices has proceeded apace since the early 1990s, working up many of its paradigms in relation to the medium of television (see Jenkins, 1992; Tulloch and Jenkins, 1995; Hills, 2002 and 2004; Stenger, 2006). TV has been discussed in terms of 'time-shifting' since the advent of VCR technology, affording the idea of enhanced user control in terms of how programmes are seen (for instance, in the ability to 'edit' extraneous material like adverts; see Allen, 2004, pp.14–6). Indeed, ideas about time swirl around many of the distinctions between different screens and how their offerings engage and potentially empower spectators. Live television can now be paused via devices like TiVo and SkyPlus, prompting a renewed focus on the usefulness of the concept of 'live', much as terms like 'profilmic' and, arguably, even 'film' start to look 'outdated' in terms of their immediate official connotations (Lewis, 2008, p.408). Scholars have tried to understand the new chronotopic (time-space) patterns that such developments call into being (see Kogen, 2006; Hoskins, 2004; Cubitt, 2000, p.91). A general drive towards popular culture that projects a sense of *simultaneity* is seen by Kogen (via Fredric Jameson) as being progressed near to its ultimate conclusion by postmodern culture, with an emphasis on the immediacy and intensity of experience – or, at least, the *perception* of such – emerging as strongly characteristic, and technology playing a leading role (2006, p. 46). Such a perception informs much of the marketing of popular film, particularly in the area of 'high concept' and the blockbuster; in Chapter 2, we looked at how the action film stresses the *experiential* value – and change – that a spectator undergoes by fully investing in the transporting, kinetic rush of heightened action: 'Get Ready for Rush-Hour!' (see also Dyer, 2000). Television services offer alternatives to the cinema tradition of promoting immersive spectacle (the idea of being swept away or transported); *control* is a key ingredient to the different message required by television. Illustrating this, advertising for the Sky HD service broadcast in the United Kingdom in 2007–8 shows a 'paused' action scene involving multiple protagonists, weapons, animals and motorcycles, frozen and filling the space of a viewer's front room as the absent viewer takes an offscreen bathroom break.[7] Yet, such advertising is not averse to exploiting traditionally cinematic motifs of immersion and escape either; in an earlier (2004) campaign, Sky used a rare contemplative moment quoted from the US show *24* (2001–) (itself an interesting attempt to fuse the time of the diegetic action with the time of the viewer) with the blatantly escapist caption 'Lose yourself in someone else's story'.[8] Even more variety is found in gaming formats, some of which enact the time-shifting notion, others of which require simultaneity, such as online 'MMPs' (Massively Multiplayer Games) such as the hugely popular *World of Warcraft* (2004–), or film adaptation *The Matrix Online* (2005–).[9] A notable factor in broadening the appeal of computer games through advertising campaigns has been to counter the notion of 'wasting time'; thus, British ads for the Nintendo Wii games system place an obvious stress on the opportunity the multi-player settings afford for spending time as a family.

The tendency to present the time of new screen media as transpiring in a way that is largely consumer-driven contrasts with the strategy for theatrical film, with the unique and authentic *experience* of the big-screen outing recently restored to the agenda by the battle against file-sharing and DVD piracy,[10] and the migration of blockbusters onto the IMAX format.[11] At the end of the theatrical run of the blockbuster film (usually brief by historical standards, even if the film is successful[12]), marketing changes tack to accentuate affinities with the other forms. The film becomes available in different formats, and the 'rush hour' model of instantaneity that attaches a high value to a brief but intense theatrical event has to be revised in the interest of cultivating a different feeling in the consumer, that of an artefact (usually a DVD or Blu-ray release, but also an official download copy) worth legitimately owning as opposed to illegally downloading. What Barbara Klinger calls 'rhetorics of intimacy' (quoted in Keane, 2007, p.25) come into play here, with an emphasis on the revelation of mask-dropping production secrets (in the popular 'Director's Commentary' function), and certain interactive features like angle switch functions and even features that offer an experience of exercising editing choices (of course, the 'official' cut of the film is usually maintained, often on a separate disc, although some discs do offer a viewing mode where deleted scenes can be channelled into the feature).[13] With a wealth of extra material, feature-packed double (or triple) disc presentations contradict the essence of the theatrical strategy by trumpeting *extra duration* as added value. A feature film with a runtime of 127 minutes advertises itself on its DVD sleeve as 'Fully loaded with over 10 hours of special features';[14] the extended DVD editions of *The Lord of the Rings* films add up to 52 minutes of excised footage. The modern 'mixed-media' film text (Buckland, 1999, p.187) thus stretches its invitation across a number of experiential modes and times.

It could be argued that CGI is the most prominent of all the technological advances listed above, powering the economic consolidation of many of them into fixtures of both theatrical and home entertainment landscapes (such as lavish DVD presentations, promotion or narrative continuation on the Web, or updated theatrical sound systems that are showcased by particular movies). Event films like *Terminator 2: Judgement Day* (James Cameron, 1991), *Jurassic Park* and *Toy Story* renewed the standards of blockbuster spectacle while addressing the popular understanding of Hollywood's relationship to technology. This chapter will focus in on CGI and its uses as a way of concentrating a more scattered range of activities that move film towards the status of a digital medium. The CGI film positions us, 'speaks' to us, in a way that some perceive as different to the address of its 'profilmic' counterpart; reviews show that certain commentators uneasily observe a category shift that marks the passing of 'profilmic' reproductive solidity, sometimes expressed in a notion of 'depthlessness' (Creed, 2000, p.84), 'instability' (Purse, 2007, p.13) or the construction of an opposition between 'character-based' versus 'CGI-based' sequences (Lewis, 2008, p.415). In his review of *Star Wars Episode I: The Phantom Menace* (George Lucas, 1999), a film heavy on the use both of 'virtual sets' and fully animated characters, Andrew O'Hehir writes that

> [...] almost nothing in it is based on photographing actual human beings in their environments [...] the excessively electric-blue skies and green fields of the planet Naboo may be meant to remind us that we are not on earth, but what they really make us aware of is that what we're seeing isn't real
>
> (O'Hehir, 1999, p. 34).

As an aesthetic and a technology simultaneously, CGI overlaps with many of the major issues that stand out in debates around the contemporary Hollywood mode of address, touching on demographics and the youth market; the rise of a 'modular',[15] presold and ancillary-friendly blockbuster template; studio takeovers, breakaways and creative-corporate synergies that challenge the coherence of 'Old Hollywood' entities (frequently involving totemic individual figures like Steve Jobs, George Lucas,[16] John Lasseter, Steven Spielberg and so on). All of these interests and crossovers render CGI's fortunes in popular moviemaking important to audiences and stockholders alike, while scholars have attended to what changes contemporary cinema might imprint onto the values of the 'real' and the 'virtual', and their interrelation (see Bukatman, 1998; Cubitt, 1999;

Pierson, 1999; Buckland, 1999; Wood, 2004; Purse, 2007 and many others). What is worth looking at more deeply is where narrative as a quality lies in relation to this, and the answer seems to be that it rests, somewhat awkwardly, as a separate value. Critics exploring some of these technological matters find that narrative continues to be 'over-appreciated', even romanticized into a position of normative centrality (Keane, 2007, p.56); far from being unaware of this, the industry has appropriated it for a 'golden aging' strategy of product differentiation (along the lines of the publicity discourses that frame *Die Hard 4.0* in terms of 'practical' substance – see Chapter 2). Cubitt (2000, p.88) points out that the over-valuation of narrative has led to a near fetishization of classical cinema (the form in which it is supposed to be embodied), and calls for digital criticism to avoid structuring itself in the same form of a norm/deviation relation (referring to digital's difference from the photomechanical medium). In articulating this kind of problem, Bakhtin would bring in the metaphor of centre and margin as a way of understanding the centripetal, unifying impulse that produces cultural norms, while centrifugal forces attempt to scatter and counteract that uniformity for the benefit of a more diverse heteroglossic culture (DIN, p.272). Even so, it is hard to look at these issues and not invoke that most problematic of conceptual 'centres', realism. Faith in cinematic signification works in various ways (with corresponding theoretical positions, as we have seen in Chapter 1); to say that some are troubled by the prospect of CGI as dampening or diluting film's reality effect is perhaps too strong, but the *materiality* effect (the disappearance of the real world referent) does appear to be in question (Creed, 2000, p.80; 83). The codes of 'invisibility' noted in the classical cinema were first theorized on the basis of their highly artificial nature, which is a history that we must preserve in thinking these issues through: Cubitt makes us mindful to refrain from inadvertently revaluing the profilmic norm as the privileged standard for film representation.[17] In other words, the attempt to explore the nature of something different or marginal should not produce *new* norms and centres, however unintentionally.

Shiny happy 'people'? Questions of CGI aesthetics

Within film and television criticism, attention to technological developments has often been interlinked with questions around democratization and resistance, a relationship connected to the disciplinary aspiration of finding fresh models for understanding viewing. This line of enquiry has gravitated towards popular texts that exhibit (often as a matter of generic positioning) a high degree of interest in the utopian potential of future technologies. Thus, texts like *Star Trek* have been studied in terms of the way their themes and narratives are configured to invite fan commitment and, beyond this, interaction. The phenomenon of 'textual poaching' was first identified in television audiences by Henry Jenkins (1992), and has been developed in important work on cinema and television fandom by scholars like Matt Hills, who invokes Bakhtin in discussing how discourses circulating around 'cult' texts become shot through with multiple 'alien' values and perspectives by the inherently social nature of their usage and consumption, thus denying monologic ownership of meaning to any one group or individual (2002, pp.121–2).

Perhaps an indication of the dialogic potential residing in film spectatorship can be revealed with reference to a different but related medium, that of the videogame. Players decisively influence the computer game scenario, indeed, through the assumption of control of their avatar in 'first-person' games such as *Tomb Raider* (1996),[18] 'become' the protagonist in a direct manner currently (in any non-metaphysical sense) unreproducible for the film spectator; Elsaesser discusses this in terms of 'narration versus navigation' (1998, p.217). However, as Krzywinska and King (2002) assert, the media of film and computer games have undergone a convergence; the traditional repackaging of hit film scenarios in computer game format (*Die Hard*, John McTiernan, 1988; *Alien*, Ridley Scott, 1979; *Star Wars*, George Lucas, 1977) as an 'ancillary' product has started to flow in the opposite direction with hit games being transferred to the screen (*Resident Evil*, Paul W. S. Anderson, 2002; *Silent Hill*, Christophe Gans, 2006; *Hitman*, Xavier Gens, 2007), and a growing catalogue of film narratives incorporating computer game elements both as subject matter (*The Lawnmower Man*, Brett Leonard, 1992; *eXistenZ*, David Cronenberg, 1998) and as a narrative/aesthetic template (*The Matrix*, Andy and Larry Wachowski, 1999; *Spy Kids 3-D: Game Over*, Robert Rodriguez, 2003). The emergent CGI aesthetic that such Hollywood films signal makes cinema look like videogames, to the chagrin of certain critics for whom 'videogame' or 'comic book' remain reflexive terms of abuse, used to invoke a diminution of narrative value (Bather, 2004, pp.39–45; Keane, 2007, p.101). This note of ambiguity suggests diverging paths: although audiences – particularly in the family and youth markets – have endorsed many new franchises employing substantial computer-generated material since the late 1990s,[19] and trends in the packaging of DVDs would suggest that fans enjoy the 'full disclosure' that can be found in supplementary materials that offer a glimpse behind the curtain,[20] we have already noted (in Chapter 2) a certain backlash gathering against CGI solutions where they are seen as replacing 'practical' stunts and effects. In the action film, practical stunts and non-digital performances are given a higher value (see Osmond, 2008), with fans and opinion-makers registering views that to be authentic, action requires a certain level of violent content (see Vern, 2007). Such arguments inadequately take into account the artifice that is involved in creating profilmic violence, proving that the criteria for such a critique is contingent and improvised.[21]

Story is often the value that is presented as counteracting the tendency of effects, particularly 'post-photographic' ones (to use Paul Wells's term[22]), to push film in a 'negative and risky' direction away from narrative norms (Barker with Austin, 2000, p.83). A balance is sought to smooth over the 'contradictions' that effects introduce on ontological and narrative planes (Keane, 2007, p.57). Critics have noted how, from the early days of CGI usage, certain themes were worked into films that heavily featured the technology, to help *naturalize* the integration of CGI into the overall textual economy; examples include the concept of bringing things to life (*Jurassic Park*), or the (morally coded) conflict between new and old forms of technology (*Toy Story*; *Terminator 2*) (Keane, 2007, pp.60–1). An element of self-conscious reflection on the nature of managing the entrance of powerful new technologies into human life is seen by Pierson (1999) as accompanying such moves; this certainly illuminates the swing of CGI films between, on the one hand, tales of misunderstood but eventually friendly aliens/robots/monsters (as in the Pixar and *Shrek* films, *Transformers* and *King Kong*, Peter Jackson, 2005) and, on the other, the postulation of alienating, enslaving virtual worlds (*The Matrix*; *Dark City*, Alex Proyas, 1998). We might add premises that continue to self-consciously raise ambivalence around technology, while purportedly trying to nullify its alienating effects in the diegesis, like the technology-out-of-control theme of *I, Robot* (Alex Proyas, 2004) or the 'bad science' elements of *Hulk* (Ang Lee, 2003).[23]

Thinking along these lines, there is a temptation to fold story into a close identification with realism (under the conceit that narrative equates to substance/depth), underlining a shift from the conventions of classical cinema critique, which approached these in terms of a more binary relation and consequently viewed realism as something produced in the *disruption* of narrative symmetry (mitigated in classical film by the tailoring of continuity devices to accentuate character and story – see Kepley, 1982; Mulvey, 1999). Yet, examining some of the discourses that situate and explain the work of Pixar, a company that is a byword for success in the field of computer-generated film,[24] we find that the circulation of some of these ideas and values is a feature. We will look at some of these discourses before exploring two Pixar films, *Toy Story 2* (John Lasseter/ Ash Brannon, 1999) and *The Incredibles* (Brad Bird, 2004) in terms of how these issues are developed, if not resolved, in their style and themes.

Already hugely successful with audiences (the 'most reliable family brand' in Hollywood – Goldstein, 2008), Pixar solicits a different kind of validation, a critical view of their products as progressively *maturing*, and *containing* the disorientating novelty of technology through, precisely, the old-fashioned application of story (see Keane, 2007, pp.64–5). Thus, Pixar has undertaken a 'meta-branding' project (Rehak, 2008) of securing a 'classic', Old Hollywood-style studio identity, building this around the veneration of a certain attitude to story. Pixar's creation of an image deliberately revives Disney 'Golden Age' principles, a process identified by Wells (2002b, p.26). These perceptions of the virtues of Pixar films tend to reverberate, with critics and commentators keenly co-operating in a certain way of reading the films and positioning the company's ethos. The quality that is said to separate Pixar productions from general perceptions of computer animation stems precisely from the relationship between 'realism' and what John Lasseter calls 'story power' (quoted in Anon., 2004). This relationship is frequently associated with their work in critical, technical and fan community discourses. These fan comments, posted to the Animation World Network website, attempt to bring out Pixar's strengths through a comparison to Disney's non-Pixar computer-animated feature, *Dinosaur* (Eric Leighton/Ralph Zondag, 2000):

> I believe Pixar is the most successful animation studio today in that it is true to itself and what is really important: the story. It doesn't abuse the privelege [sic] of state-of-the-art technology like the world cringed at in *Dinosaur*; where was the creative plotline in that? The characters were dead right before our eyes, realism or not. The people at Pixar concentrate on the story and great character development first, and use the technology to enhance their brilliance
>
> (Graziano, 2001)

At the time of releasing *Dinosaur*, Pixar was associated with the Disney identity (as its contracted distributor), but had not been officially subsumed by the studio as it was in 2006. Graziano's post shows audiences at the time grasped that Disney and Pixar were separate entities in a way that benefited Pixar.[25] The idea of 'state-of-the-art' technology as a 'privilege' which must be nurtured by a responsible institution seems to indict Disney, but seems to be contradicted by the later swerve towards the message that technology is a vehicle for 'story' and 'character development'.

Dinosaur (less commercially successful than the average Pixar film) is seen as striving for realism in the image but under-serving story.

Contributors to the Pixar films, in interview, develop this theme but reconnect realism to Pixar by framing it as a specific and contingent aesthetic choice that is exercised within the normal operations of storytelling. Leo Hourvitz, effects artist, talks about *A Bug's Life* (John Lasseter/Andrew Stanton, 1998):

> Although we tried to make the world the insects [...] live in realistic (by and large), it's already the case that the departures from realism are storytelling and character choices ... I think [...] animated films won't particularly move in a more realistic direction overall [...] it's about the director's and crew's vision, and in a lot of cases the best way to tell the story will continue to not be realism ...[26]

Both 'official' Pixar pronouncements and its fan base stress the difference between emulating the codes of photographic 'realism' (which is deemed necessary to tell a story) and constructing a world that is 'realistic' in some other way. Such viewpoints could be condensed into the message 'Story is King', which is the mantra-like title of a special feature on the Region 2 disc of *Monsters, Inc.* (Pete Docter, 2001). In a way that updates original Disney strategies for humanizing technology and quelling anxieties associated with modernity (see Wells, 2002a), Pixar's ideological achievement seems to be the creation of a world that people want to believe in on their own terms of 'realism' and authenticity. Refraining from blending live action elements into their films, and thus preserving a Pixar stamp on the fully computer-generated diegetic world that goes back to *Toy Story*, might well have helped this strategy.[27] Yet, by moving on to a more direct analysis of the Pixar aesthetic, we will see that a certain manner of expressing the *contradictions* of CGI space in the cinema feature is preserved, albeit subordinated to the demands of story. As a whole, Pixar's style and 'meta-branding' activities condense ideas concerning space, representation and technology in a way that raises a number of issues that are central to a Bakhtinian reading of cinema's electronic revolution.

'Filmed entirely on location': the worlds of *Toy Story 2* and *The Incredibles*

The earliest legitimate experiments with computer-generated effects in Hollywood film, fantasies like *Tron* (Steven Lisberger, 1982) and *The Last Starfighter* (Nick Castle, 1984), created gleaming futuristic worlds that were heavily linked, in visual style and narrative concept, to early 1980s forms of video gaming. The most obvious use of CGI, this approach has had a substantial legacy in more sophisticated recent texts like the *Star Wars* prequel trilogy (1999–2005), and finds its most radical outlet in films that eschew physical for virtual sets and the complete creation of a 'world' (such as *Sky Captain and the World of Tomorrow*, Kerry Conran, 2004). Often, the worlds created for these films are abstract, displaced environments, bright, shiny, depthless spheres easily mirroring the visual conventions of the computer game that is either source or spin-off. Even when environments bear some relationship to contemporary reality such as in *Dark City* or *The Matrix*, the worlds depicted articulate aesthetic principles as filtered through the spatial logic of videogames: surfaces bubble, warp and pop; concrete pavements propel plummeting characters back up like trampolines or the comically distorted landscapes of Tex Avery cartoons. Like a modern variant on the Technicolor dreamscape of *The Wizard of Oz*, somehow reminding us of home but adhering to no physical logic that we can recognize, the tradition of self-consciously artificial worlds continues in the primary-coloured, plastic environments of the early Pixar films (like *Toy Story*; *A Bug's Life*; *Toy Story 2*; *Monsters, Inc.*; *Finding Nemo*, Andrew Stanton/Lee Unkrich, 2003). Although set in contemporary spaces, Pixar features explore the world from the perspective of some form of alien consciousness (toys, insects, monsters, animals, superheroes and machines). This legitimates the exaggeration and distortion of physical principles in the name of a world layered with surprise, novelty and mutability, and at the same time fleshes out the story device of fresh perspective, even when a mundane 'real world' scenario is invoked (as in *Toy Story*).

The first feature showcase for Pixar's creative expertise, *Toy Story* was released by Disney in 1995. Touted as Hollywood's first fully computer-animated feature, the film generated a pair of heavily merchandisable central characters, Sheriff Woody and Buzz Lightyear, voiced by stars Tom Hanks and Tim Allen, that featured alongside brand-name toy characters such as Mr Potato Head, Etch-a-Sketch, Mr Spell and others (such as Barbie) who joined in time for the sequel. Originally envisioned as a video premiere (in line with Disney's then active release policy for the sequels to many of their biggest animation hits), *Toy Story 2* was instead developed into a feature and became an even bigger hit than its successful predecessor, taking nearly $250 million at the US box office alone.

From the very first moments of *Toy Story 2*, two things are obvious: first, that proceedings will be peppered with dense popular cultural, especially cinematic, references (the titles, metallic silver against a background of deep space, evoke *Star Wars* and *Superman*, Richard Donner, 1978). Secondly, that the filmmakers are alert to the problems that their new technology presents to traditional notions of the profilmic and of spatial representation in cinema, and intend to have some fun with them. The film begins, initially unbeknownst to the spectator, inside the 'Buzz Lightyear' videogame (a merchandisable toy in the diegesis as well as outside it, Buzz has many spin-offs mentioned over the two films). 'Buzz' is put through his paces on a deep-space mission to destroy the power source of his arch-enemy Zurg, a primary-coloured Darth Vader clone. After fighting off robot armies, penetrating Zurg's fortress, and escaping perilous booby-traps, Buzz finally faces Zurg himself and is promptly disintegrated, whereupon we learn that the whole adventure has been a mere game scenario and that the 'Buzz' protagonist has been a video proxy under the control of the anxious dinosaur toy Rex. The 'real' Buzz (i.e., the sentient Buzz toy belonging to Andy) proceeds to counsel the distraught Rex over his premature failure, telling him that he did his best and is 'a better Buzz than I am'.

Even more interesting than the identity politics played out here around the notion of a mass-marketed character with no existential core and no way of distinguishing himself from millions of other units (a theme revived in a choice scene when a baffled Buzz finds himself faced with an entire supermarket aisle of identically packaged Buzzes) is the peculiar distortion of spatial value that goes on in this opening sequence. *Toy Story 2* depends, for narrative coherence, on the belief of the spectator in the physical logic and three-dimensional credibility of the CGI representations it constructs of key narrative locales such as Andy's room and Al's Toy Barn (where the toys go to rescue Woody from an unscrupulous collector); but right from the beginning it unsettles us with a spatial conundrum. The dilemma, and the ironic humour, come from the fact that Rex's adventure as 'Buzz' within the game is rendered in a manner that is *visually identical* to the register in which space is depicted outside, in the external 'reality' of Andy's room where Rex and Buzz actually play the videogame and the other toys go about their business. Only a cheap computer sound effect, a joke on the part of the filmmakers given the sophistication of the technology at work here, and the appearance of the legend 'GAME OVER' serve as indicators of the distinction between the world inside the TV monitor and the world of physical 'reality' outside. The film throws us off balance from the beginning, then, presenting one electronically constructed landscape wrapped around another but refusing to demarcate the two for us. The pixellated realm of the 'Buzz Lightyear' videogame permeates the totality of the diegetic world in a way that suggests one space characterized by increasingly porous boundaries between real and represented (see Bukatman, 1998).[28] This is an ostensibly innocuous rendering of a more culturally pertinent trope: the ubiquity of the digital mass-media and the 'remediation' of the laws of physical reality into electronic form (much as Keane describes the Pixar aesthetic as a remediation of earlier animation techniques and conventions).[29] Bakhtin's vision of the thin line separating representation and its real-world counterpart/progenitor in the chronotope is stretched ever more tightly (FTC, p.253).

The CGI 'space' of *Toy Story 2* is thus initially marked as self-defining, irreducible to any external physical index. However, the shock of the new is cushioned for us by the film's subsequent reproduction of a fairly conventional Hollywood aesthetic in terms of framing, depth relations and composition. The Disney tradition is pertinent here; in the 1930s the studio's animators employed glass shots and multi-plane cameras to achieve a sense of perspective that would align their animated image with spectatorial expectations of live action. Similarly, for *Toy Story 2*, a sense of narrative coherence drawn from live action principles serves to naturalize the presence of its technological apparatus. For the most part, the conventional staging, framing and lighting techniques of profilmic mise-en-scène are emulated. As Pixar post-production supervisor Craig Good has commented of Lasseter's early work: 'We [...] tried to move the camera the way live-action filmmakers do [...] We wanted to make the audience respond to traditional dolly and crane movements, not to make them dizzy' (quoted in Furniss, 1998, p.183). The computer systems used by Pixar include a program known as a 'virtual camera' which mimetically reproduces such familiar effects as focus pull, variable depth of field, the 'vertigo' shot (simultaneous track-in/zoom-out) and even motion blur and lens flare (a range of these can be seen in any typical Pixar action scene, such as the pursuit of Dash by Syndrome's henchmen in *The Incredibles*). Clearly, things like lens flare do not naturally occur in the virtual camera system, which could also produce a potentially infinite depth of field; photographic conventions like focus pulling and racking, and certain 'imperfections' like flare, are programmed in to preserve a feel that will be read by audiences in terms of traditional cinematography. The films hope that this will stimulate an investment in the represented space marked by the integrity and plausibility that we are used to ascribing to profilmic images.

The narrative of *Toy Story 2* also places the location of 'authenticity' on the agenda. Losing their leader Woody, the toys embark on a quest to reunite their 'family', while the cowboy toy discovers that he is associated with a more technologically primitive form of entertainment; in fact, he is a prized and collectable replica of the star of a popular 1950s TV puppet show, 'Woody's Round-Up'. The negative associations placed on progress and technology by this yearning for a simpler past functions to disguise the text's own modernity in the time-honoured Disney style, although there is more ambivalence here. Products are associated with a range of feelings. A magical aura surrounds the moment of Woody's discovery of the TV show line of merchandise; this is in stark contrast to the pure alienation of Buzz's discovery of the 'Buzz Lightyear' aisle at the toy store owned by villain Al. Woody's identity is warmly and emotionally reaffirmed, locating him in a different era to the aggressive modernity of Buzz. Although *Toy Story 2* portrays them as possessing souls and feelings, its toy characters *are* products, both within and beyond the narrative sphere, and the film does not exactly shy away from presenting them in a marketable form. We might speculate on a kind of double-voiced discourse manifesting itself here, with the smooth monologic surface of the official Disney worldview being critiqued from within by textual voices that speak in the name of heterogeneity. The scene of Buzz's alienation is key in the film's critique of commercial agendas that overwrite cultural diversity with a kind of hollow, universal consciousness (very much the Disney business model). Even the cultural tradition signified by Woody's identification as a sheriff pays off here, framing the rescue narrative as a kind of re-playing of *High Noon* where the toy community realizes that the wholeness of its overall identity is tied up in the fate of individual members.

The importance of nostalgia self-reflexively acknowledges a dimension of Pixar's 'meta-branding' that cultivates a dialogic relation between old and new *and* between young and old in terms of differentially addressed spectators. History has made Woody's 'ancillary' products rare and collectible, icons of a lost age. The narrative evocatively positions the TV show just before the launch of Sputnik, that is, late 1957. In the world of the toy protagonists, Sputnik signifies the beginning of the rage for space toys (from cowboy Woody to spaceman Buzz, the exchange of one frontier for another) and keeps the Cold War in the background, but the historical reference is embellished in the later *The Incredibles* (which, as we shall see, develops more blatant political meanings). Through intertextual design and music cues that conjure the early James Bond films (from *Dr. No*, Terence Young, 1962), *The Incredibles* clearly fixes the 'golden age' of the retired superheroes as transpiring in the late 1950s or very early 1960s. Tellingly for the Disney connection, 'authentic values' for Pixar films seem to be located at a time of buoyant consumerism and 'New Frontier' political optimism; however, James Bond and Sputnik are also products and signifiers of the Cold War (thus elements of the atomic anxieties of Brad Bird's previous animated feature *The Iron Giant* [1999] are channelled into a more appealing form). In *Toy Story 2*, the comforting refrain of Randy Newman's composition 'You've Got a Friend in Me' keeps such anxieties in check, signifying friendship, reliability, home, even a certain desired stasis (the main problem faced by the toys, as depicted in Woody's Freudian nightmare, is that their child owners will inevitably grow up).

The appeal of *Toy Story 2* to these values triggers the ambivalent chronotopic 'inversion' that is always associated with the myth of a Golden Age (DIN, p.147); the search for an authentic, communal and consensual past constructs an impossible fantasy world characterized by an out-of-reach temporality. By this process, doubt also accrues to the status of the digital diegetic space. Germane to this point is the fact that *The Incredibles* and *Toy Story 2* both work in sequences where a deliberately primitive, 'lo-fi' mode of representation is recreated by the computer, prompting a similar ontological confusion to Buzz's videogame. In *Toy Story 2*, this is the painstakingly rendered old-fashioned puppetry of Woody's TV show; in *The Incredibles*, it is the grainy 35 mm 'newsreel' sequence (wherein the wave of litigation forcing the withdrawal of the 'supers' from public service is recounted). *Toy Story 2* goes even further in destabilizing spatial ontologies in the amusing 'out-take' reels which run over the final credits (an idea carried over from *A Bug's Life* which featured its insect protagonists tripping over cables and fluffing their lines). With nothing, literally, in front of the 'virtual camera', the very idea of 'out-takes', of actors missing their marks and sets falling down, is an arch nod towards the fact that, as a production mode, the CGI articulation of space is not open to the same spontaneity as older traditions (a cursory viewing of the average DVD featurette on a Pixar film is enough to convince of that). Undeniably funny as they are, the broader punchline of the outtakes could be taken as rather sourly placing a certain finality on CGI's ontological implications for filmic space. Yet, these ideas are treated with self-consciousness and levity; the end credits for *A Bug's Life* bear the legend 'Filmed entirely on location', involving the viewer in a demystifying comic appreciation of the way Pixar films play with notions of space as an index of shared cultural experience. This re-opens the contested space up for debate in a way that the 'official' Disney film would not do. Rather than a nail driven into the coffin of the profilmic, we can discern here a sense of the 'auto-criticism of discourse' that Bakhtin finds in European novels of the 'Second Stylistic Line' (such as *Don Quixote*).[30]

> Discourse is criticized in its relationship to reality: its attempt to faithfully reflect reality, to manage reality and to transpose it (the utopian pretenses of discourse), even to replace reality as a surrogate for it (the dream and the fantasy that replace life)
>
> (DIN, p.412)

Certainly, the Pixar outtakes are of the order of a complicated 'testing' of the artistic discourse's relation to life; they invoke what Martin Barker calls the 'doubling' approach in visual effects criticism.[31] It could be argued that what we see in them is the multi-million dollar Hollywood entertainment machine preserving a space within itself for an adversarial dialogic viewpoint. The 'utopian pretense' of the spectacular visual promise of technology is thus qualified.

The apotheosis of early Pixar style is probably *Finding Nemo*; with the arrival of Brad Bird, director of *The Iron Giant* and former creative consultant on *The Simpsons* (1989–), a few telling developments seem to appear, which we shall briefly look at in analysing *The Incredibles*. A prominent one is that *The Incredibles* is the first Pixar film to directly engage with the (live action) cinema zeitgeist, entering what was, by 2004, a crowded marketplace for superhero films. Bob Parr/'Mr. Incredible' is a retired costumed fighter who lives with similarly superheroic wife Helen (formerly 'Elastigirl') and powered kids Dash (super-speed) and Violet (invisibility) in the deep cover of suburban anonymity. Their hidden existence has been made necessary by the wholesale withdrawal of 'supers', which is blamed on the social divisions just mentioned; unmanageable property damage bills, and an ungrateful public obsessed with litigation, have forced the government to ask the supers to step down. At the start of the film, Bob clearly misses the glory days, seeking discreet crime-fighting kicks with his friend Lucius Best/Frozone; these lead to Bob's engagement in a shadowy but well-financed operation testing combat robots on a secluded island. This is a set-up to bring Bob back into contact with Syndrome (formerly Buddy Pine, aka 'Incredi-Boy'), the infatuated would-be 'sidekick' that Bob rejected years before, now a science villain obsessed with Bob's demise. To save Bob, the family must reform both as an expanded fighting team and emotionally (Helen has to forgive Bob for the midlife crisis that has drawn him from their stable life; Bob will learn that watching his family grow can also be a source of thrills and mystery; the children learn to exercise their powers responsibly).

Identifying enhancements to already high Pixar standards in relation to the movie's visual strengths,[32] reviewers also note the cueing of material towards the adult audience (Newman, 2005, p.56), citing a mature 'fusing of narrative and spectacle' that derives from the focus on human characters and 'adult' concerns (Keane, 2007, p.65). The diegesis itself harbours tropes of growth and progression, strangely both cueing and reflecting these critical responses. The film *does* encompass a larger thematic scope than previous productions, scratching beneath the familiar superhero premise to study the society that would drive supers underground. After the early prologue scenes showing Bob, Helen and Lucius in action before the curb on supers, we join the present time, where a relatively stable, safe world has been attained at the cost of the more exciting (but less secure) era of the supers. Helen, revelling in her suburban mom role, can handle this, but Bob cannot; he flounders, looking for a role beyond his soul-destroying insurance job. It is made clear that Bob finds it difficult to grow up and out of his self-identification with his powers and costume. The vacuum created by the end of the supers, from Bob's superhuman viewpoint, engenders a culture based around celebrating mediocrity. A certain idea of 'common sense' and 'back to basics' echoes in Bob's conviction that strength should be exercised and applauded; the film does not strictly discount this view (this culture, after all, has permitted Syndrome's threat to rise). The influence of popular psychology and an apologetic, liberal therapeutic culture (as in the references to family and marital counselling, educational and child-rearing styles) is indicted; because Bob is capable of looking after himself and his family, he sees the modern culture that prevents this as selfish and trivial (he is thus 'like Gulliver pinned to the earth by the Liliputians' [Anon., 2004]). At the same time, Bob's psychological resources are very clearly weaker than Helen's; the new adventure ends up serving as a kind of therapeutic role-play for him, even helping him come to a recognition (confessed to Helen) that his greatest weakness is the fear that his family will be hurt. However, Bob has a funny way of showing it; only by placing himself and his family in danger does he properly shake off his ennui, reconnecting with the inner strength to truly 'intervene' (as Helen implores of him while the kids run rings round her at dinner-time). This draws Bob into a mirror relation with his nemesis, Syndrome, whose strategy is to use the 'Omnidroid' robot in a staged attack which he himself will defeat, bringing him the hero status he has always coveted.

Bob fits into a series of conflicted, reluctant heroes who struggle with the fact that their powers can indeed save the world, but who eventually exorcise this doubt after some positive reaffirmation from the community. In a similar scenario, Peter Parker (Tobey Maguire) tries to walk away from his powers in Sam Raimi's *Spider-Man 2*, and the motif recurs in films from *National Treasure* (dir. Jon Turteltaub) to *Troy* (dir. Wolfgang Petersen) and, prototypically, Mel Gibson's *The Passion of the Christ* – all of which, like *The Incredibles*, were released in the same year, 2004. More recent releases like *Hancock* (Peter Berg, 2008) have explored the same trope of problematic heroic destiny; even the rebooted James Bond series makes some allowances for these developments. In many of these cases, the hero deals with their own fears along the way to dispatching the villainous threat; in some of them, the threat *is* the climate of fear. Fear is an important trope for popular cinema after September 11 and the 'War on Terror', suggesting a wish on the part of filmmakers to retain a purpose for films that posit (fantasy) violence as a solution, but a desire to frame this within a more liberal context that refuses fixed definitions of evil. Villains like Henri Ducard (Liam Neeson) in *Batman Begins* (Christopher Nolan, 2005) and Mr Linderman (Malcolm McDowell) in the first season of ABC's superhero serial *Heroes* (2006–) explicitly discuss their mission as the artificial incubation of fear, which they believe will lead society to destroy itself in extreme responses. Those without the ability or social resources to formulate a proportionate response to fear end up like the dangerous, paranoid would-be militia man played by Tim Robbins in *War of the Worlds* (Steven Spielberg, 2005). Violet in *The Incredibles* gestures towards this disturbing potential when she asks Helen, 'You mean, Dad's in trouble, or Dad *is* the trouble?'. A line like this underscores the grand sense of psychodrama implicit in a film that drolly names its Oedipal-scarred major villain 'Syndrome'.

The Incredibles can be considered as a post-9/11 film that is interested in the working out of problematic new inflections on the concept of 'might is right'. Although in national terms it can be construed as an 'apologia' (Anon., 2004) for hawkish foreign policy choices that require sacrifice in the name of preserving world stability, it shares with other popular films a mature idea that new ideological weapons call into being a different kind of response from the good guys. This involves engaging with that little used part of the heroic skill set, humility; Bob goes through this process as he waits, agonized, for his family to save him. Earlier, the idea of *balance* was cited in terms of the need to regulate and naturalize digital representation through appealing to the values of 'story'; here, balance comes strongly through as a theme when considering the politics projected by Bird's film. Showing weakness (as Bob is ultimately prepared to do in front of Helen) is an appropriate index of strength because it implies value for life. Syndrome's assistant Mirage voices this notion, showing that either side of a conflict is doomed when it loses this perspective.

Like other superhero narratives, *The Incredibles* thinks about the heroic imperative in terms of stark choices, but does so with greater critical acumen than many films revolving around similar material.[33] The division between vivid fantasy and weak, mundane reality plays out in a number of entertaining scenes placing Bob into the straitjacket of an overdetermined normality (represented in desaturated colour and special space-flattening long lens settings on the 'virtual camera').[34] Despite the seriousness of the readings it engenders, many of the classic Pixar pleasures are present in the film. The traditional moment of joyously representing an obsolete technology comes when the deranged Syndrome deploys the hulking, metallic Omnidroid into Metroville for the planned theatrical spectacle (returning to the idea of a society artificially kept in fear). The retro robot goes awry and is instead bested by the Parr family's teamwork, the killer touch being applied by Bob as he puts the Omnidroid out of commission by launching its own severed tentacle through its hull. As he works out this solution, Bob's line '[t]he only thing hard enough to penetrate it is itself' simultaneously, of course, refers to himself and, read in terms of national image, is available for interpretation as a hawkish call to suspend a national mood of introversion. The message imparted in this new mode of heroism is that self-doubt, properly understood, can be a resource of great strength, but failing to intervene is a self-betrayal.

Remediating the address

The digital revolution has not only impacted upon film production, but on delivery: *Toy Story 2* was the first film to be presented via a Texas Instruments prototype digital projection system in the United Kingdom in early 2000, since when the Film Council has instituted a target of 240 digital-equipped screens for the United Kingdom, reporting that 136 of these were in operation by 2006 (RSU, 2006). In production terms, many leading figures of the independent film sector both in North America (*Gummo*, Harmony Korine, 1998) and in Europe (the directors of the Danish 'Dogme 95' movement; in the UK, *One Life Stand*, May Miles Thomas, 2000) were early adopters of DV. Indeed, it is possible to read DV and CGI as two contrasting forms of social discourse. DV, with its connotations of realism, is akin to an informal, everyday spoken discourse (and has been linked with the documentary aesthetic in films such as *Idioterne/The Idiots*, Lars Von Trier, 1998). CGI, with its artful manipulations of space and depth, and propensity for appearing as an added production value in big-budget genre pictures, is a heavily stylized discourse, albeit one that (as we have seen) occasionally becomes involved in notions of 'realism'. Yet, just as the associations of realism and immediacy began to congeal around DV, filmmakers extended its vocabulary, allowing the catholicity of its aesthetic spectrum to break through.[35] Recent films have adapted audience recognition of DV as a 'realist' mode into a principle of stylization, particularly in the horror genre where an entry like *Cloverfield* (Matt Reeves, 2008) mixes elements of the intimate aesthetic of early DV usage with the 'first person' narrative mode of *The Blair Witch Project* (the video segments of which were not shot on DV), while importing extensive CGI work into this pseudo-'realist' frame.

The relative cheapness of digital memory media compared to any form of film stock and the lightweight nature of DV camera equipment constitute its main attractions. Films can be shot quickly, in most environments and by any light source, on DV and edited on a domestic PC (as was the award-winning, theatrically released documentary *Tarnation*, Jonathan Caouette, 2003), reducing the turnaround period between shooting and release and eliminating many expensive processing and editing costs. Although containing variety as an aesthetic, and no longer reducible to realism, something like a generalized DV style has emerged as a new, dialogized intervention in cinema's heteroglot palette of narrative and visual 'languages'. The distribution of the technology from the lower strata of the industry upwards demonstrates that forms are shaped in the crucibles of non-mainstream activity, propelled by new creative voices. However, the case of DV also illustrates the point that not all the contributing voices of democratized heteroglossia are necessarily on the same aesthetic or ideological wavelength. One of the first branches of film production to catch on to the possibilities and economic advantages of DV was pornography, where a strong market interest for 'reality'-style products (involving handheld cameras, real locations and so on) developed in the 1980s (as a reaction to a perceived 'glossiness' in the standard aesthetic of the time). Just as the makers of pornography favoured VHS over Betamax, thus ensuring that the lower-quality system soon became an industry standard, so DV was conferred with the blessing of that sector of the industry, assisting its eventual spread to other, 'legitimate' areas. It can be argued that many technical problems concerning the distribution of films over the Internet were addressed in the first instance by the producers of pornography, who, through companies like IEG, were arguably the first 'entertainment' makers to understand the Web as a valuable channel for meeting the demands of niche audiences (see Kleinhans, 2002, pp.292–6). The 'democracy' idea, and the association of DV with representational freedom and truthfulness, has to take these issues into account.

Developments of the technological means for creating cinema have considerable implications for the way in which we consume Hollywood film. Spectators do not exist in a vacuum, divorced from economic shifts, corporate rivalries and technological innovations, any more than do the artists behind the camera. If new artistic 'voices' are encouraged by the accessibility of new digital technology, are new configurations of spectatorship also part of the promise of new media? Clearly, spectators are invited to participate in the formation of filmic meaning in certain ways. In terms of approaches that offer a kind of active 'navigation' through textual worlds, the online experience is the most vivid. Notably, following pioneering Web campaigns for films like *Blair Witch* and *AI Artificial Intelligence*, the producers of *Cloverfield* enticed fans into the film's 'universe' months ahead of its theatrical release by implanting a string of connected sites and videos that added layers to certain corners of the story world. However, the experience of watching *Cloverfield* may disappoint those who followed the Web materials and expected a great degree of 'tie in' with the core movie narrative. The mystery posed in the main narrative is not really clarified by access to the extra material, although atmosphere is enhanced; a better strategy seems to be to watch the extra material *after* watching the movie (to which end, Paramount thoughtfully provide many of the videos as DVD extras). Thus the 'real time' element of the marketing is annulled, but the idea of extra value is preserved; DVDs become archives of promotional campaigns. A more thematically sensitive approach to viral promotion is found in the Web marketing for Batman sequel *The Dark Knight* (Christopher Nolan, 2008) conducted through the first half of 2008, which emulates the clues/game format of the legendary *AI* campaign (see Keane, 2007, p.81–2) and leads directly into the opening sequence of the film. An ingenious character-derived aspect is added; Batman's foe, the Joker, periodically and unpredictably descends to 'deface' many of the sites, giving them 'makeovers' that fit with his ambition to reconstruct the world in his own twisted image.[36] The offering of 'something extra' that challenges the notion of a static, finished narrative universe is *de rigeur* for the post-*Star Wars* blockbuster, and could hardly be otherwise in an institutional context so driven by franchise logic; sometimes the 'extra' is offered for free in the name of building recognition (as in Web promotions), at other times it is an inducement to buy a certain format. On DVD, the Pixar films routinely offer an additional short, animated to the same standard as the parent feature, from the same universe; in the case of *The Incredibles*, the short, *Jack-Jack Attack* (Brad Bird, 2005) literally fills in a narrative hole that plays out 'offscreen' in the main film – the discovery of baby Jack-Jack's powers by his babysitter – and the events in the short lead into the final action sequence of the film (whereby Syndrome arrives and takes the child hostage).

Not all of the activities that draw together Internet and film can be easily controlled by the institution, with anxiety being recorded in Hollywood as the industry scrambles to develop an attractive 'on demand' model for legal film downloading[37] that can match successful forays into this area in television (which, because funded differently, can afford to 'loss lead' via free content; see McLean, 2008). The familiar excitement about the democratizing potential of new media has been present since an early stage, although sceptical voices note that this is often expressed somewhat by rote, reproducing the dynamics that structured responses to earlier waves of media innovation or ignoring trends of co-optation (see Schuler, 1998).[38] In the media history field, James Curran notes the traditionalism of a certain 'populist interpretation' of the media's informing and facilitating social role which views 'the development of the mass market as an agency that extended social access to new cultural experiences, empowered the public and rendered the producer responsive to popular demand' (2002, p.14). This sentiment is strongly present, even ingrained, in recent examples of film criticism; Barbara Klinger, for instance, believes (partially quoting Tom Ryall) that the 'formations' of film culture are '"complex non-monolithic entities", comprised of practices and institutions that may support, oppose or provide alternatives to each other', going on to claim that DVD culture, as a new platform for the cult conferral of tastes, facilitates a reordering of the film canon (2006, p.363; 368–72). In a commercial development like DVD, which has enabled Hollywood to generate billions by re-selling their film libraries to consumers who owned many of the same titles on VHS tape, the difficulty may be in reconciling, as Klinger does, a potential for audiences to destabilize or transform fixed meanings – like those represented by a canon – within a scenario that on the face of it seems to mainly benefit the institution.

The influence of cultural studies, and the positive understanding it brought to forms of consumption (which could be seen as ways of politically recuperating the limited positions available to users of popular culture), was discussed in Chapter 1, and can be detected in a reading like Klinger's.[39] Cubitt (2000, pp.89; 91–2) notes that criticism of digital arts, particularly, tends to stress ways in which audiences can potentially come together as communities, rather than concentrating on the prospect of atomization; this is more or less the case in work by Finn Bostad (2004), who attempts to update Bakhtin's dialogic model for the evolving communication dynamics of a digital age. The narratives of change, subversion and openness to semantic redefinition that critics discern within Bakhtinian concepts like dialogism, polyphony and the carnivalesque make the more positive components of his worldview amenable to those whose instincts towards popular media fit the view characterized by James Curran. According to Ken Hirschkop, such a degree of compatibility between Bakhtin's words and the 'liberal consciousness' is understandable, but says as much about pre-existing tendencies to locate essentials of 'the identity of liberal democracy' within the domain of a broadly understood notion of dialogue as it does anything specific about dialog-*ism* (1999, pp.8–9). It is Bakhtin's vivid appeal as a thinker who knits social relations together with a close appreciation of textuality – uniting the divide instituted in Saussure and Russian Formalism – that causes this problem, if we can agree that it *is* a problem.

Beginning by stressing the 'participative autonomy' that lies at the philosophical heart of Bakhtin's notion of active understanding, Bostad extrapolates from Bakhtinian thought a view that language exchange creates a public space (2004, p.168). Bakhtin sets no time limit on responsive understanding; the word 'presses on further' through history until it finds it (PT, p.127), and the electronic forum can expand into a multiplicity of times. An 'electronic public space' that affords remediating possibilities in a varied temporal context is, of course, the Internet. As Bostad glosses it, remediation is 'the process of applying new signifiers in getting access to old signifieds' (2004, pp.173–4); his work highlights the capacity for utterances to be reincarnated in new textual vehicles where the content of the utterance is both the same and (under the influence of its new transmitting form/medium), different, refreshed. Certainly, a thinker like Bakhtin, so appreciative of the patterns and markings that textual and historical time leave as they criss-cross each other (and the viewer's experience), can enhance understanding of communication that challenges unified time. Bostad characterizes online culture as going beyond immediacy and into the condition of 'hypermediacy',[40] configuring and dividing visual (screen) space in new ways to present simultaneous access to different materials and activities. However, Bolter and Grusin's idea of remediation encourages us to distinguish between the development that is genuinely new and that which is 'better understood as simply an element of change in the nature of an already established medium' (Lister et al, 2003, p.39). Thus, one way of considering technological advancement would be as the *re-accentuation* of Bostad's 'old signifieds', much in the fashion that the auto-critical discourse of the Pixar film operates not by obliterating profilmic convention completely, but retaining it as a frame of reference. This not only makes possible a moment where cruder forms like newsreels or early videogames can be parodied,[41] but also, crucially, helps to maintain an address that keys in to the established perceptual, and even emotional, horizons of the audience.

Conclusion

Within a Bakhtinian context, a form of cinema where the dialogue between spectator and text was made into a concrete principle of narrative discourse would be interesting and valid. In McMahan's assessment of the MUD (Multi-User Domain) game – a predecessor of MMP's like *The Matrix Online* combined with elements of navigable 'virtual worlds' like the popular *Second Life* – spectators evolve into 'programmer-auteurs' (1999, p.151). The term evokes a renegotiation of textual power, a flowing of responsibility and control from the author to the textual subject, across a number of narrative agents, via a dialogic channel generated by the interactive element. As discussed in Chapter 4 of this book, Bakhtin's formula for polyphony – the location of authorial, character and readerly consciousnesses on a single interpretative plane – could serve as a theoretical touchstone in this kind of discussion. Currently, however, Hollywood offers 'interactivity' in very limited ways. The collective film theatre experience remains compelling, despite repeated claims – argued with impeccable economic logic – that the model is nearly obsolete (see Mamet, 2003); we just may not have to queue around the block anymore.[42] Old reading habits die hard, and although the cinema experience is becoming more 'blended', and deferred and distributed across multiple locations and times, strategies like ancillary spin-offs or websites that deepen or continue the narrative world have yet to truly destabilize the precedence of the theatrically released main feature in either audience or industrial eyes (as Stephen Keane argues in his discussion of the *Matrix* sequels and associated products – 2007, pp.118–38). This leads many consumers to regard the supplementary materials around the promotion of films like *Cloverfield* as optional and secondary, a rehearsal for the 'real' film experience.

This is not to say that Hollywood does not take a careful professional interest in how consumers organize themselves. The notion of a community invested in an expanded fictional universe that some Internet promotion plays on reflects how fans can be constituted as groups by the direct address of the institution; a trailer for *300* (Zack Snyder, 2007), released by distributor Warner Brothers to YouTube, caused Internet buzz due to its inclusion of a brief still image of Rorschach, a character from Snyder's already announced next project with Warners, the graphic novel adaptation *Watchmen* (due in 2009). In this way, continuities are established with a successful film, exploiting the usual channels such as directorial signature but also recognizing other markers of audience profile (such as taste for screen violence or graphic novel projects). More and more visible in general terms, fan communities have become more defined by academic classification and description of their activities (often stressing their power, particularly in the television sector[43]). Thus placed firmly onto Hollywood agendas, the courting of fan relations now spills into fiction with dizzyingly postmodern implications. The studio-backed *Galaxy Quest* (Dean Parisot, 1999) offers a humorous (and fairly loving) depiction of science-fiction fandom. Fan dedication also fuels the plotline of comedy *Fanboys* (Kyle Newman, 2008), while *Be Kind, Rewind* (Michel Gondry, 2008) has popularized the idea of 'Sweding' (the lo-fi fan remaking of Hollywood classics). A good example to support Klinger's case ('practices and institutions [...] may support, oppose or provide alternatives to each other'), 'Sweding' has leaked outside Gondry's fictional world and caught on as one of the most entertaining ways in which feature films have been 'remediated' as a YouTube phenomenon.[44] The last few years have also seen unofficial fan films that pay tribute to the object of attachment, becoming, as it were, benign dialogic parasites on the host body of a major film or series, which is the relationship of *Troops* (Kevin Rubio, 1998) to *Star Wars*. Films that document the fan world and activities have also emerged as a niche market, often straight to DVD (*Trekkies 2*, Roger Nygard, 2004).

If fan use of films has arrived on critical agendas, so has the idea of the fan as *producer*. McMahan observes that contributors to *Star Trek* fanzines reposition themselves in relation to the master-narrative embodied in the movies and TV series by authoring their own spin-off plotlines (also frequently published on the Internet). Able to express fans' own concerns and interests in relation to the show, these expanded narratives can take the form of a redressing of the textual balance for those who may feel excluded by the dominant address of the series:

> What these fans are doing is extending the world of the narrative as it has already been presented to them. But they are extending it in a way that reflects their own concerns. The Narrator of *Star Trek* constructed them as a certain kind of narratee - as male, for example, or heterosexual – and they felt left out of this mode of address, so they are correcting the imbalance by adding to the world in a way that more specifically includes them as a narratee.
>
> (1999, pp.149–50)

The idea of 'correcting the imbalance' implies an issue of textual power-shifting (or sharing) that dialogism seems better equipped to illuminate than other active viewing models (Cognitivist/Neo-formalist varieties, for instance, would struggle to accommodate the implications of a spectator feeling 'left out' of the call of the text on the grounds of sexuality or gender because of the bracketing of personal history and ideological resonances in their conception of the viewing process – see Chapter 1). Yet, can the spectators who participate in more specialized fan cultures such as these be said to effect any *real* change at the level of narrative? Just because ways of accessing filmic material now inhabit more flexible scenarios and transpire in variable temporal contexts, is the cinema experience deepened, and will the time invested seem any more worthwhile? Looking back to Bostad's attempt to rethink dialogism for Internet activities, there is also the problem that seeing communities form through film-related Internet fora (such as innumerable Web messageboards that stratify and channel fan interest by genre/brand, star or subject matter) is one thing, but assuming that because they are unfettered, and often not policed by the film-making institutions, that they will therefore be (i) equal and (ii) operate without animosity and prejudice is less realistic (see Keane's account of discussions of sexism on an internet forum for *Sin City*; 2007, pp.94–6).

It is questionable whether pure narrative decision-making (such as that invited by the 'game' format of certain Web campaigns, or even interactive voting on plot direction as has occurred in certain television programmes[45]) is inherently any more dialogic as an activity than the broader process of interpretation that the viewer goes through in front of *any* film; if it were, there would hardly be much demand for film theory to go beyond a Bordwellian model of comprehension. Just as a concept of spectatorship that reduces it to identification or interpellation is inadequate, 'creative understanding' draws on a far richer horizon of experience than the resources needed to understand denotation – films *mean* more to us than the sum of their story events. Nevertheless, what John Lasseter calls 'story power' remains potent; while recognizing the value of arguments for the 'spectacularization' of popular cinema, the governing logic of narrative as paradigm is as strong as ever, and has proven that it can absorb a number of remediations. Always promising to modify and amplify its 'call', attempts by the Hollywood institution to cultivate customer identification with its digital portfolio approach the new challenge as a problem of narrative *configuration* as much as of access; yet it seems unclear whether, in this case, there is any formula to be struck.

Conclusion: Making it Real

The main objective of this work has been to show that Hollywood film texts involve us in practices of watching and understanding that mobilize a field of discursive relations that I have identified as 'dialogic'. Bakhtin suggests that the project of dialogism encompasses all expressions of socio-ideological life and is without limit in space and time; it takes heed of our contributions to meaning, but will ultimately carry on without us (MHS, p.170). The size and span of this conception prompts a vertiginous feeling, requiring us to find ways to corral dialogic energies into a less abstract form that can meaningfully interject in our work with film. It can be forgotten, particularly when attending to the later essays,[1] that Bakhtin is a great thinker of the specific as well as of the global. This book has tried to look at structural, generic and technological specificities in a series of representative texts without treating diegetic events as ontologically separate from context and from reception; preserving a sense of the flow that Bakhtin says is channelled through the 'gates' of the chronotope. Markers of film style can be thought of as accents of the depth, range and history of the ideological voices that collaborate in the textual enunciation. Hamid Naficy argues that modes of production inflect the freedoms and inhibitions of filmmakers, which in turn produces style as accent (2001, pp.43–6). A commercial mode of production (not the kind Naficy is talking about, it should be said) engenders the Hollywood that I have tried to outline in this book; this is a Hollywood which can be thought about in the terms with which Allon White glosses Bakhtin's approach to the novel. One cannot read it in terms of 'systematic regularity' only; 'variation and self-criticism' are the mobile signs of a centrifugal energy that will – given enough time and changes in context – eventually remake the centre (White, 1984, p.141). The many discourses of its cinema products continually 'relativize' even that most powerful norm.

In considering the significance of our own interpretive activity in this exchange, an awareness of and objection to Hollywood's power – the garden variety reading of its monologism – makes its presence felt in critical models that flatten our appreciation of this significance into a singular frame of understanding. Bakhtin's perspective can provide the space to authorize another theoretical look at Hollywood, but the climate of adopting his work these days is one of 'sobriety' (see Hirschkop, 2001; Tihanov, 2000, p.5). It is hoped that Bakhtin in his guise as social philosopher has never been employed here in the role of apologist for Hollywood's ideological excesses; that would be forcing Bakhtin's words into a truly alien context. Dialogism is betrayed if it is understood merely as a way of rehabilitating ideologically suspect texts; of transplanting them to a souped-up, socially aware context; or of transfusing social value into them via the dialogical standpoint of the analyst.

Inevitably, there are visions of false, or falsely understood, dialogism. Ken Hirschkop warns us against using dialogism to screen out the transformative effect that artistic representation has on the substance of social lives, so that we are not induced to see more social meaning in the representations we study than actually exists; he asks the question, 'is dialogism for real?' (1992, pp.108–9). Similarly, through a Gramscian lens, Peter Ives warns that by too eagerly (not soberly enough) embracing the seemingly inherent diverse and centrifugal properties of dialogic utterance, and thus ignoring the systemic stability of language around it, we risk disturbing the careful association set up by Voloshinov between social reality and language (Ives, 2008, pp.79–80). To remain in alignment with Voloshinov, we have to make social reality include structures of representation, not 'reflect' them.[2] Injunctions like these force us to re-examine the powers with which we endow dialogism, even when we feel that we are following Bakhtin's lead in so doing.

Making dialogism real and really useful for the work that we want film studies to do is a challenge. This challenge is defined by the fact that 'languages are socially unequal' (White, 1984, p.125) to begin with, so that the resulting exchange between Hollywood institution and spectator is an uneven one that fails to neatly fit into a redemption narrative. Thus, a clean victory and happy ending is deferred (within the terms of the democratic, empowering models discussed in Chapters 1 and 5). Yet by deciphering the nature of that unevenness – and looking for what it tells us about other levels at which culture organizes and operates – we do something worthwhile and add value through our textual analysis. We are talking about *interpretations*, the embrace or critique of texts into our horizons or against our values: dialogism as reading strategy, as discussed in this book's introduction. Stephen Heath is being reasonable when he advises that the reading of a film 'must be seen as neither constrained absolutely nor free absolutely but historical' (1981, p.243), with 'historical' pointing a way out of the binary. This is the direction in which the Bakhtinian set of concepts leads us, not just in the postulation of the dialogic matrix that maintains the history of utterances in their present flavour, but in the more visible, felt process where we map our history onto the one codified in the film's chronotopes; texts are perhaps at their most energetically meaningful when their contradictions are exposed and we sense their images as a shadow of time. Sometimes the clash of values is anticipated just as the smooth fit and immediate pleasures of narrative comprehension or genre recognition are; something makes us invest time in texts that, despite (or perhaps because of) the appearance of their address, seem to be 'in dialogue with someone else' (Pearce, 1995, p.89). This is an area that Chapter 3 tries to bring out.

A text cannot become, finally, empty of meaning, but its 'charge' may run low while contextual discourses reorganize around a different set of topics and the focus of readings veers elsewhere. Dialogism is, or should be, calibrated to context, the mood and 'taste' of the hour (DIN, p.293). The process of watching Hollywood film is rarely, if ever, 'just' that; its context is commodification and, for some, a type of imperialism. As spectators we are inaugurated in a network of global consumption and a system of economic and ideological exchange. Any attempt to study Hollywood cinema without acknowledging the fundamentally economic and corporate basis of its institutional structure is fatally flawed, and will invariably produce textual analyses that will suffer by diminishing the economic subtext that is woven into the fabric of any Hollywood narrative. Yet, this should not trap us into *one* way of visualizing Hollywood. There is no mode of being without another communicative position that can register (and reflect back to us) the fact of that being. Hollywood can try to dictate terms for our discussion, but it would be interesting to see it try to live without us. Its production ethos encourages defeatist views, but rich films are made there all the time, and it is possible to argue that the great films of Hollywood are partly made what they are by certain textual traces of ruthless commercialization. These could be understood in the dynamics that produced genre and star systems (and criticism eventually caught up – via the *auteur* principle – with the level of artistry that classical strictures engendered), or overtly in the sharply 'relativizing' perceptions of societal blandness and economic venality in films like *Fight Club* (David Fincher, 1999) or *Land of the Dead* (George A. Romero, 2005). The loss of shape, style and clarity in a flawlessly executed mainstream product like *Some Like it Hot* (Billy Wilder, 1959), *His Girl Friday* (Howard Hawks, 1940), *Aliens* (James Cameron, 1986) or, for that matter, *Toy Story 2* would surely be mourned.

Neither filmmaking (even within a conservative institution like Hollywood) nor Bakhtin studies stays still for very long. Developments come thick and fast, necessitating any conclusions to be kept on ice rather than carved in stone. The politics of taking up Bakhtin that were referred to in Chapter 1 have limned a 'division' (Tihanov, 2000, p.5) of method and perspective that makes the establishment of a harmonious public square congress of Bakhtinians a tentative proposition.[3] Recent contextualization by Brandist, Tihanov, Poole, plus many others in certain edited collections bearing the names of some of those scholars, has reconnected Bakhtin Circle thought to its original philosophical allegiances, while work like that undertaken by Emerson (2000) has strengthened and redefined the location of the Circle within national literary culture(s).[4] Such work may have broken a certain spell surrounding the universal potential of the concepts; one indisputable effect has been to bring to light the ease with which utopian and democratic ideals are squeezed out of the Circle. The recognition and justification of these tendencies becomes a condition of new critical work. My findings in Chapter 5 and elsewhere bear out that an intangible air of a philosophically sweeping but rather textually insubstantial concept of democracy attends both the business of Bakhtinian application and certain critical protocols of popular screen culture; what this means and implies needs to be kept in sight, but cannot be entirely stripped away from scholarly enterprises that rework or otherwise employ dialogism. Ken Hirschkop's (1999) thematic rendering of the democratic idea in relation to the Bakhtin literary corpus is exemplary, but there is a job that 'applicatory' work can do in this direction too, such as that by Bostad (2004), whose Bakhtinian viewpoint attends to the social contours of recent media change. Communication practices begin with the text but are not limited to it, meaning that criticism should be equipped to move to an engagement with 'the contemporary problems and issues generated by our consumer societies' (Wall and Thompson, 1994, p.75).

Awareness of the temptation to overdetermine dialogism in terms of its relation to democracy has helped to – soberly – set parameters for the present study. The globalized (but Hollywood-powered) cinema marketplace does not readily offer itself up as a true 'public square'; and while we are considering factors that qualify the matching of Bakhtin and Hollywood-as-marketplace, it can be added that there are commentators who perceive a disinclination in Bakhtin's work to fully engage with institutional questions that might trouble his view of artistic-linguistic life as uncompromised by certain forces.[5] Yet, such factors do not convince this author that Hollywood's texts are exempt from the kind of network of meaning that Bakhtin proposes. Several examples have been given of cinematic 're-accentuations', some commercially driven, many impelled by audiences, extending semantic life into the span of 'great time'. Future paradigms of cinema spectatorship seem certain to be marked by some of the developments traced in Chapters 2 and 5; whether the specific models currently proposed for the cross-pollination of other screen media with cinema resemble the form these practices will take in the future is not yet knowable. Hollywood's history is one of first resisting, then churlishly incorporating new technologies, until the point of assimilation is reached where one cannot imagine cinematic culture without those innovations. Sound and colour met many dissenting voices in the 1920s and 1950s respectively; Gloria Swanson as Norma Desmond in *Sunset Boulevard* (Billy Wilder, 1950) rails against the introduction of sound as ruining the movies, and Wilder's film is itself infused with the streak of self-destructiveness and capacity for institutional criticism that has enlivened many a Hollywood film. Texts like *Sunset Boulevard* keep alive the spirit of otherness within a global monolith that has unquestionably served to powerfully influence the centralization of film language and form. Despite so much evidence to the contrary, so much that is uninteresting and homogeneous (and often, of course, unpopular as well), Hollywood films constantly bite the hand that feeds and keep the dialogic circuit open, leave a 'loophole' for forces to grow that will bring out their commitments and contradictions more vividly.

At times, when this study has been occupied with formal properties, the ways in which narratives take shape, the social and historical perspective commensurate with dialogism has always been in the background. Sometimes, as Bakhtin tries to assert in concepts like double-voiced discourse, the artwork buries a carnivalesque sense of defiance beneath a conformist surface, a monologic front. In such cases, the richness of the work comes from the chance to hear two conflicting voices encountering each other, 'as if they actually hold a conversation with each other' (DIN, p.324). In a reading that stresses that the 'dialogue' image is not implied by Bakhtin as literally as many have taken it, Hirschkop remarks that what really counts is not the exchange of sentences but the exchange of 'ideas, positions' and 'a willingness to take on board those proffered by your interlocutor' (1992, p.104).[6] We certainly exchange ideas and positions with the films we view and consume. A Bakhtinian conception of the process of reading film does not yield up an inert, nor ideal, spectator, fixed into an industrially desirable place by a totalizing ideological network of which the text is only an abstract, interchangeable part. This is not to say that this study does not recognize the capacity of Hollywood film to project its own ideological agenda, to fold the movie-going experience into a broader corporate strategy based on the allure of the brand-name or the star image, the exploitation and sanitization of cultural 'otherness'. These are all strong 'accents' that compel texts, and readings, in certain directions.[7] Yet, to suggest that a Hollywood film can only be watched in one way seems a terrible disparagement of the intelligence of the spectator; to construe that it can only be *made* in one way, with one set of monochrome values, is just not borne out by facts. The tide of homogenization is not exactly stemmed by such limiting conceptualizations.

In Chapter 1, Bakhtinian ideas were introduced to augment certain limitations within some classic film theories; these gaps left the spectator, as theorized by Metz and Mulvey, a 'petrified' victim of a one-way flow of ideology, or by Bordwell, as a thinking entity but one who encounters a mere narrative problem, the meaning of which is non-ideological and does not reverberate in wider cultural networks. The semiotic direction taken by Bakhtin Circle thinking when Voloshinov's work turned to the multi-accentual sign in the late 1920s, following the lead of Medvedev's reproach to the Formalist vision of literature as uninvolved with the 'social and general ideological demands of the epoch' (FM, p.173), crystallizes a view that Bakhtin's major 1930s work reinforces at every opportunity. At its most simple, this view can be put thus: a genuine cultural message speaks with more than one voice, and its reception is structured by the same multiplicity and centrifugality. The accomplishment of interpretation is transitory and contingent (not linear, or incrementally increasing in 'difficulty', as for Bordwell); its nature is to be defined by the climate of active understanding around the perceiver. To look for reception paradigms that confine or deny this multiplicity, whether by ejecting the sign relation completely or by looking for points of stability and sameness rather than the diachronic signs of evolution and the influence of context, is to miss the point: the interesting, revealing part – the shifting understanding within which the text lives – will slip through one's fingers (even if a Metzian residue of 'film' – as opposed to 'cinema' – remains).

A Bakhtin-inspired film theory can develop platforms for the analysis not only of textual specificity (via chronotope and polyphony) but also of *spectatorial* specificity. In dialogics, Bakhtin insists that the individual discursive characteristics of the person addressed by the textual utterance determine to a massive degree the very nature of that utterance. When we adopt an utterance, a text, into a new ideological horizon and manipulate it with respect to our own epistemological needs, what we are changing, destabilizing and remaking is not the reality of the cultural force that produced the official meaning (which exists on a plane of repeatability, because it is a system), but the reality of the meaning itself (which lies on the plane of unrepeatability).[8] Because of this unrepeatability[9] and openendedness, no final shade of meaning is possible; no monologic resolution, sterilization or 'last word' can cleanse or seal the utterance's capacity to mean. In other words, we shape the film as it shapes us; active understanding, as David Shepherd points out (echoing Stephen Heath's description of perceiving subject and text coming into being simultaneously), is indissociable from the local meanings that constitute it just as those local textual meanings fail to activate if not dialogically read (Shepherd, 2001, pp.144–5). Such projections trained on a film do not bounce off the text into insignificance; the text absorbs them into its own development and evolution. In *The Searchers*, Ethan's racism and thirst for blood is finally deflected by the fact that he can *change* – possibly swayed in this by Marty's, and certainly Martha's, compassionate voice. Yet, extra-diegetically, Ethan's racism is *not* expunged by narrative redemption; it is arguably made even more stark by the turnaround that comes 'just in time' to save Debbie. It is true that, over the years, over thousands of screenings, Ethan will always save Debbie, but the coherence of this rescue in relation to the film's overall ideological composition depends upon how the receiver's active understanding is calibrated. Racism thus becomes embedded in this character's image, perhaps in Wayne's image too, and certainly within the Western's historical praxis.

The Western, for better or worse, represents the (dark) heart of American film culture, and the two chronotope chapters, similarly, represent the heart of my academic enterprise, the place where crucial questions of form, reception and social value are unravelled (if not completely resolved, a very un-Bakhtinian ambition). Threading through the case study chapters is a notion of each film as dialogically orienting itself around an attitude to narrative. The action film (Chapter 2) approaches narrative as textually congealed time-space, and its viewpoint is simple and structural. Yet this means that we can use the action picture, the oldest and most formally expansive genre in film history, to lay foundations for the articulation of critical ideas about cinematic space and time.

Chapter 3 looked at the Western and its intertexts. Genres render social myths narratively digestible, but also force ideological constraints on creative expression through the rigid over-determination of form. However, even during the heyday of the Western, a production like *The Searchers* contained the seeds of the genre's downfall, or at least the knowledge of its desperate need to remodel its own ideological centre; a form of discursive 'auto-criticism' (DIN, p.412) that figures the history of mid-1950s America despite itself. Sayles revisits the genre in producing *Lone Star*, meditatively re-arranging the controversial old ways into a new chronotopic constellation. Remarkably, *Lone Star* is no less romantic for its rejection of narrative's naturalization of history; it is surely as elegant and intelligent a piece as one can imagine being produced in the American cinema.

Chapter 4 was charged with identifying hierarchies within the textual equation: the relative positions and power values of reader, author and character. Bakhtin finds philosophical meaning in the re-arrangement of such relationships within Dostoevskian polyphony, with special zones of 'crisis' time and space engendered. My reading of *House of Games* absorbs Mamet's themes around language and discursive power, and narrative comes out of this as the subject of struggle and a violent change that keeps readers *and* characters guessing. Finally, story was cast differently again in Chapter 5, as a value that fluctuates in the midst of *epistemic* change. As seen in the Pixar films, story can still be presented as a gauge of authenticity around which Hollywood seeks to ground its problematic digital modernity.

If there has been one principal theme to this study it has been to demonstrate the capacity of Hollywood film to resist singular ideological definition, the fixing of value as the safe placement within tradition. I have tried to argue for a wide and open understanding of Hollywood textuality, but an ideological one. Reputationally, commercially, formally, and in terms of values, films have a 'life'. They do not cease to signify when the credits disappear from the screen; meaning does not reside inside the film can, Blu-ray disc case or memory card but in the multiple consciousness of audiences. People walk around with films inside their heads and on the tips of their tongues, and every contact they make extends the social life of the film, relating it in a deeper way to living history. Often, the 'official' meaning of a filmic text is re-accentuated, carnivalized, turned upside down by dialogic communities. Sometimes the film speaks in a way that its creators never thought possible. These shifts in value are not imaginary exercises in contradistinction to a surplus of 'real' and incontrovertible meaning held by the institution or the filmmaker; they are the *life* of the film, unfolding on a dialogical communicative plane. Just as Hollywood as a 'real place' barely exists (Maltby, 1996a, p.1), the social and semantic topographies of film cannot be pinned down on any map of official culture. Instead, they always point forward, to a continuation of dialogue, to their re-accentuation in another place and time.

Notes

Introduction

1. Robert Stam's 1989 book *Subversive Pleasures: Bakhtin, Cultural Criticism and Film* (1989) remains the most coherent attempt to date for the establishment of both a rationale and a methodology for a Bakhtinian approach to film. Stam's own intellectual agenda, however, leads him more to linguistic matters, both in Bakhtinian theory and in cinematic expression. He is interested both in film as language (invoking, as I do in Chapter 1, the theoretical paradigm of Christian Metz) and in language content and representation within film (issues of translation, dubbing and so on). Thus, the chief Bakhtinian concepts utilized in his study are dialogism, heteroglossia and carnival (with a nod towards matters polyphonic and chronotopic), whereas my more narrative and reception-inclined agenda is concentrated around dialogism, the chronotope and polyphony, ideas which have more to say about narrative as *construct* and *event*. Stam has thus been less directly influential on the production of the present study than valuable as a dialogically friendly 'fellow traveller'. R. Barton Palmer's article (1989) deserves to be flagged as a piece that carefully and critically sets out ways in which a number of Bakhtinian categories can have salience for film studies. Scholars who have worked, sometimes very effectively, along the lines of deriving from Bakhtin general approaches to broad topics such as dialogic intertextuality or language, and applying them in filmic contexts, include Stadler (2003), Thornton (1996) and McWilliams (2001). Two notable essays that find a rich fit between the chronotope and specific time-space configurations (early 1990s 'hood films' and art cinema, respectively) are Massood (2003) and Alexander (2007). Naficy (2001) accomplishes something similar in the field of cinematic representations of diasporic and exilic states.
2. Like many aspects of Bakhtin's biography, facts are difficult to establish and different versions attract different adherents. Hirschkop finds gaps in the records that cast into doubt whether Bakhtin ever attended university as an undergraduate (2001, p.3); that Bakhtin put himself forward for the Russian equivalent of a Ph.D in 1946 (where he defended material on Rabelais but, for ideological reasons, was not given an award until 1951 – and even then not the full award) does not seem to be in question.
3. Hirschkop posits the 'critique of everything "given"' as the 'most insistent' point where Bakhtin's Neo-Kantianism manifests itself in his work (1999, p.24).
4. Hirschkop talks about the (Russian-influenced) line that defines Bakhtin as a 'philosopher first', in contradistinction to the emphasis suggested by the way the texts appeared (1999, pp.119–21). The same author also pinpoints Bakhtin's specific appeal upon his first emergence with Western intellectuals. In relation to the dominance of poststructuralism, '[i]n 1981 Bakhtin appeared

as the literary critic who had made the linguistic turn without losing his humanist baggage along the way' (1999, p.120n).
5. Quite aside from the dispute surrounding the Voloshinov and Medvedev texts, which is dealt with in the main body of this section, a number of editorial questions surround the management and dispersal of Bakhtin's body of work. The most sustained attempt to draw all of his materials together – the multi-volume *Collected Works* – is in a cycle of Russian publication under the general editorship of Sergej Bocharov, Bakhtin's literary executor, and awaits a translated edition for English readers. See Adlam (2001, p.244); Holquist (2002, pp.185–7).
6. *Little Dorrit* published in 1857.
7. Peter Ives points out that the legacy left by Bakhtinian thinking around the notion of the 'monologic' is not always helpful, as he illustrates in looking at Antonio Gramsci's conviction of the merit of a progressive unification/centralization of linguistic practice in a specific national context. See Ives (2008, Chapter 2).
8. Turning a very nice image to illustrate this idea (and the related notion that theme cannot be divorced from the study of a speech unit), Voloshinov figures meaning as 'like an electric spark that occurs only when two different terminals are hooked together' (MPL, p.103).
9. The results were published in the September issue (Vol. 12, No. 9).
10. As in the accusations brought against films like *A Clockwork Orange* (Stanley Kubrick, 1972), *Natural Born Killers* (Oliver Stone, 1994), and various early 1980s 'video nasties' (to use the term popularized by the UK press) which have been cited as inspiring acts of violence and murder. Accounts of how texts like these have become embroiled in so-called 'effects' debates can be found in Barker and Petley (2001).

1 Dialogism and Film Studies: The Dialogic Spectator

1. Many critics have disagreed with Bakhtin's bracketing off of these forms in relation to dialogism, and have indeed found Bakhtinian categories to be very useful for dealing with them. See, for instance, Rachel Falconer on Bakhtin and the epic (in Adlam et al, 1997, pp.254–272); Robert Cunliffe on 'Bakhtin and Derrida: Drama and the Phoneyness of the Phonè' in the same volume (pp.347–365); Donald Wesling on Russian poetry (1992), and Ilkka Joki's Bakhtinian reading of David Mamet's stage work (1993).
2. A relationship explored by Julia Kristeva in the essay 'Word, Dialogue and Novel' (1980, pp.64–91). See also Stam et al (1992, pp.203–6).
3. See, for instance, Adlam (1997); Hirschkop (2001); Shepherd (2006, p.33). Tihanov (2000, pp.4–5) gives an account and examples of both 'applicatory' and 'contextual' positions.
4. Some of these inflections are identified and discussed by Hirschkop (1990).
5. The frequency and parameters of this term in Bakhtin are questioned by Cunliffe (1997, p.363); nevertheless, 'novelness' is used by Holquist to refer to the unique property of the novel to register degrees of otherness (2002, p.73). To clarify this, a remark from Booth might help: 'Only "the novel" [...] offers the possibility of doing justice to voices other than the author's own,

and only the novel invites us to do so' (1997, p.xxii). Holquist also invokes novelness in a more general sense, as a synonym for 'literariness': 'the study of any cultural activity that has treated language as dialogic' (68).
6. The text referred to is 'Discourse in Life and Discourse in Art (Concerning Sociological Poetics)' in *Freudianism*, pp.93–116. See the introduction for an account of the disputed works.
7. 'Re-accentuation' is the typically evocative term which Bakhtin – ironically, given its theme – closes 'Discourse in the Novel' (419–22). It captures the way in which symbolic meanings reform in relation to changed contextual surroundings. Bakhtin uses it oppositionally with regard to concepts like canonization and reification, and says that it is fuelled by changes in heteroglottic conditions, but also warns against it as a force that can distort if the conditions prompting it are not truly dialogic. 'New images in literature are very often created through a re-accentuating of old images, by translating them from one accentual register to another (from the comic plane to the tragic, for instance, or the other way around)' (DIN, p.421).
8. Lundberg (1989) provides an interesting perspective on this, while Shepherd (2001) attempts to take stock of scholarship on Bakhtinian ideas around readers/reading.
9. Although Bakhtin's *oeuvre* does offer some direct engagement, most suggestively in the final section of the essay 'Forms of Time and of Chronotope in the Novel' (pp.252–54).
10. See Morson and Emerson (1990, p.77–86). The existence of Medvedev's full-length 1928 critique ('the most comprehensive and even-handed critique of the work of the Formalists in the whole Soviet period' – Brandist, 2002, p.73) is the most compelling element in the case against framing Bakhtin and the Circle in terms of a straightforward affiliation with the Formalist tradition. In addition to this, Thomson (1984) discusses how Medvedev (and, by extension, Bakhtin) takes issue with the Formalist conception of genre, while a 'lost' critique prepared in 1924 is attributed to Bakhtin (Hirschkop, 1999, p.112).
11. This influence is disseminated, Eagle speculates, through the agency of two of Bakhtin's early champions, Julia Kristeva and Tzvetan Todorov (1981, p.53).
12. See, for instance, Holquist (2002, pp.45–7) and Hirschkop (1999, pp.213–9).
13. It is not the intention to over-emphasize this influence; the relation to Saussure is not at all straightforward, with the Swiss linguist spearheading the 'abstract objectivist' tendency much criticized in *Marxism and the Philosophy of Language*. As dedicated contextual research by Craig Brandist (2004) has shown, Voloshinov's theory of utterance as intersubjective social event depends on elements imported from figures involved in the tradition that emerges from the work of Franz Brentano (namely Karl Bühler, who contributes the intersection of psychology and social representation, and Anton Marty, who affirms that 'anticipated reception' helps constitute the linguistic act itself, a position that can be clearly seen to filter through into Bakhtin's dialogism via Voloshinov – Brandist, 2004, pp.98–107). Reflecting 'fundamentally anti-Kantian' (p.98) ideas from Gestalt theory, the Brentanian legacy is combined by Voloshinov with a Marxist-inflected interpretation of social classes acting in the manner of Kantian 'juridicial' entities. Determining that a class produces a juridicial 'collective social dialect' enables Voloshinov

to bypass the problematic Saussurean individual *parole* (speech act) in refining his own concept of utterance, although this causes a certain misalignment with Bakhtin over the nature of extra-discursive reality (with the latter moving towards the position of the idealist Marburg philosopher Ernst Cassirer, a significant but insufficiently acknowledged influence on Bakhtin; see Poole, 1998). For scholars like Brandist, Voloshinov's mediation of such influences into the work and thought of the Circle profoundly augments its underpinning in the philosophy of language.

14. The *Course on General Linguistics* is Saussure's enduring work. It was published three years after his 1913 death and compiled from the lecture notes of two of his students. See Rivkin and Ryan (2001, pp.76–90).
15. Although threads of this argument emerge throughout Bakhtin's entire *œuvre*, for instance in his proposal of a 'metalinguistics' that would serve a contrasting set of functions to traditional linguistics; where the latter is unable to go beyond a 'common ground' concept of language and entertain speech as *discourse*, metalinguistics would match the sophistication of the ordinary person's intersubjective orientation to the speech of the other, and be sensitive to the 'verbal sideward glances, reservations, loopholes, hints, thrusts' that encrust and thicken words into utterances (PDP, pp.201–3). The discussion of this concept leads into the appraisal of double-voiced discourse in Dostoevsky, which is of course revisited as a key theme of 'Discourse in the Novel' (DIN, pp.301–31). Many of the same issues return in the more fragmentary works later collected in the *Speech Genres* volume, many of which were put together within the same decade (the 1960s) as the recomposing of the Dostoevsky book.
16. Hirschkop provides a more nuanced articulation of the precise differences between the thinkers – recognizing, for instance, that a social concept of intersubjectivity is actually found, but not developed in Saussure – than this isolated 'soundbite' might suggest (1999, pp.216–19).
17. Jonathan Culler articulates a view that the Saussurean emphasis on the synchronic state of language – as opposed to its placing within an evolving context – need not be held as a flaw (1976, pp.35–45).
18. Paul McDonald (2000) explores the Star System both as a historical instrument of commercial cinema and as a concept used by film studies to invoke the fabrication of distinct onscreen and offscreen personas that build certain associations and expectations around individual performers.
19. See Bukatman (1998); Buckland (1998); King (2002, Chapter 6).
20. As indicated earlier, this dynamic enters the Circle's work through Voloshinov's introduction of the intersubjective dimensions of utterance present in the Brentanian tradition (through Bühler and Marty) to a Marxist social perspective. See Brandist (2004).
21. See Christian Metz (1974b, p.146). The 'Grande Syntagmatique' is elaborated on pp.119–133.
22. A high level of sexual violence characterized earlier, more controversial Wes Craven films such as *The Hills Have Eyes* (1977); the increased commitment to female agency in *Scream* appealed to a representational trend visible in mid-1990s shows like *Buffy* and *Xena Warrior Princess* (1995–2001). The development of the latter series involved Craven's horror peer Sam Raimi.
23. Certain forms of animation – such as the trademark 'claymation' aesthetic of the Aardman Animation studios (*Chicken Run*, Nick Park/Peter Lord, 2000) – utilize

traditional lighting on their miniature practical sets. The computer-animated films use the *conventions* of film lighting, but in terms of production, this is contained within a visual software program; how such conventions are conceptually measured up to the characteristics of 'real' space is discussed in Chapter 5.
24. Bordwell and Carroll argue that the main doctrines and routines of such theories persist into the Cultural Studies era (1996, pp.12–26).
25. Defined by Stam et al as 'a continual back-and-forth of knowledge and belief', this notion of 'split' consciousness sees the awareness of the illusory nature of cinema as repressed by and within the spectator's investment in the 'truth' of the diegesis (1992, p.148).
26. Paul Willemen has modified Mulvey's analysis of the three looks of narrative cinema to take into account a fourth look omitted in Mulvey's essay. In the avant-garde films of Stephen Dwoskin, such as *Girl* (1975), Willemen identifies a look that is turned back onto the voyeuristic spectator by the apparently powerless subject of the film (in this case, a naked girl depicted in a long static take). Willemen describes this look in Lacanian terms as 'a gaze [...] *imagined* by me in the field of the Other' (1994, p.14, italics in original) but notes that its effect of alerting the spectator to their own sadistic, voyeuristic intentions is very real within the textual experience, and confronts the unwilling viewer with knowledge of their own 'unstable position in the viewing process' (and is thus the antithesis of the 'transparent' classical style). Willemen's theorization of a responsive text that 'replies' to the viewer by throwing out its own gaze seems to stake out territory strikingly similar to a dialogic approach. Even the Lacanian quotation cited above emphasizes the key Bakhtinian concept of otherness. Willemen frequently invokes Bakhtin in the cinematic discussions contained in *Looks and Frictions* (1994).
27. See Tania Modleski (1988) for a reading of Hitchcock as an exposer of patriarchy rather than its chief cinematic proponent. Also attempting to 'reopen the case' (p.217) of Hitchcockian subjectivity and sexuality is Sabrina Barton, in her essay '"Crisscross": Paranoia and Projection in *Strangers on a Train*' in Creekmur and Doty (1995, pp.216–38).
28. Lemire (2004), in a wide-ranging argument that places both Jeff and Lisa in their proper gendered postwar contexts, asserts that previous readings have not helped the cause of divorcing Lisa from an image of passivity by stressing that she is a model – an interpretation that Lemire disputes. Lisa may be some sort of business woman, and Jeff seems to trivialize this by fixing her as 'society gal', perhaps to compensate for the draining away of the occupational substance and utility that his immobility makes him feel.
29. Witness Barbara Bel Geddes' passive turn opposite Stewart in *Vertigo* (Alfred Hitchcock, 1958).
30. See Jancovich (1995).
31. This base was limited, Bordwell contends, to a few works of Emile Benveniste and Lacan, while such candidates as Noam Chomsky were unhelpfully omitted.
32. This was the title of Carroll's 1988 book.
33. The first half of Henry Jenkins' survey essay (1995) accomplishes both of these tasks perfectly well.
34. The acronym enumerates Saussure, Lacan, Althusser and Barthes. See Bordwell (2000).

35. See Stam (2000, pp.51–2). To point out that situating Bakhtin within the parameters of traditional Formalism is misleading is not to deny the positive connections where issues raised within Formalist areas of inquiry served to animate Bakhtin or members of the Circle. A prominent example would be Voloshinov's deployment, in both the Freud book and *Marxism and the Philosophy of Language*, of the concept of 'inner speech', derived from Vygotsky, whose linguistic ideas are often seen as paralleling those of Bakhtin (see Brandist, 2002, pp.59–62; Easthope, 1993, pp.118–20). In its cinematic application, inner speech is associated with Eichenbaum (see Eichenbaum, 1974). Demonstrating the penetration of Bakhtin Circle discourses into cultural theory by the 1980s, Voloshinov's take on inner speech was critiqued by screen theorist Stephen Heath in his attempt to reconcile Marxist theories of language with the disputed role of the unconscious within the film/language premise (Heath, 1981, Ch.9, *passim*). Paul Willemen, whose interest in Bakhtinian concepts has already been noted, has repeatedly engaged with inner speech as well (see Stam, 1989, p.245–6), while Bordwell's frequent collaborator Noël Carroll has also addressed the issue (1996, p.191–4).
36. The latter pair of terms enables a distinction between the events that the spectator imaginatively reconstructs into a linear progression between the beginning and end points of the diegetic time (fabula), and the textual ordering of those events for aesthetic reasons and effects (sjuzhet). For more, see Bordwell (1985, pp.49–57)
37. This position follows on from the rejection of the linguistic analogy (see Stam, 2000, p.238). In *Post-Theory*, Bordwell and Carroll call for a defence of the claim that film is 'plausibly analogous to language' (1996, p.18).
38. As argued by Bordwell, most of these tools were proposed and circulated before the theory boom of the 1970s (1996, p.261).
39. Some words will resist being made into 'private property', not because they are monologically owned by another but because – betraying a different value against the intentions of the appropriator – they will sound 'alien' when spoken in a false context. Voloshinov's assertion that wherever a sign is present, ideology is present too does not guarantee that every utterance will be radical or serve subversive ends, but that the *potential* to do so is there because every utterance has value, and this value is set into a relation with those held by its speakers/listeners.
40. See Strinati (2000), chapters 1 and 2.
41. This essential impulse within cultural studies permits an informed generalization that the 'flow' of television viewing and culture, and its connection to the context of domestic life generally, has been more important to cultural studies than has the cinema screen. See McKee (2002).
42. Brandist (2002, pp.61–2) and Ives (2008, chapters 1 and 2 *passim*) both note the crucial influence of Vossler on Voloshinov and Gramsci's assimilation of key ideas from the linguistic philosophy of Benedetto Croce. Voloshinov's modification of Vossler's interpretation of 'inner form' paves the way for the notion of active, intersubjective understanding that becomes a defining precept of Circle thought (Brandist, 2002, pp.82–3).
43. See Kaplan (2000), particularly the exemplary texts in Section III of the volume and her own comments (pp.9–11).

44. The process most famously theorized by Daniel Dayan (1976) and Jean Pierre Oudart (1977–8).
45. It must be noted that dialogics and dialectics do not enjoy the most harmonious relationship in critical discourse, and Heath's terminology highlights this contentious area. Bakhtin considers dialectics to be a kind of neutered, socially purged version of dialogics, as this note illustrates: 'Take a dialogue and remove the voices (the partitioning of voices), remove the intonations (emotional and individualizing ones), carve out abstract concepts and judgements from living words and responses, cram everything into one abstract consciousness – and that's how you get dialectics' (N70, p.147). Perhaps in Bakhtin's resistance to a dialectical model can be detected a trace of his much-debated antipathy to Marxism – for discussions of this problematic relationship, see, for instance, Holquist (1982); Bernard-Donals (1994). What is certain is that dialectics and dialogics must not be confused for the same thing.
46. As is often the case, the alterations did not propel the film to great success at the box office although in this form it would earn cult status over a longer period of time. Scott's 'Director's Cut', restoring the voice-over and excising the studio-approved ending, surfaced in 1992, extending the picture's commercial life in an interesting (and profitable) instance of studio about-face. This change of direction was revalidated in October 2007 when Warners released a five disc DVD package of the film, trumpeting a new Scott edit as the 'Final Cut', as well as collecting other versions. *Blade Runner* remains an interesting (but not the only) case of the studio renewing the value of its property by taking direction from an audience that is seen to understand the material with the greatest sensitivity (although directorial authority, of course remains intact; the director's identification as a studio employee seems to be strangely disavowed in such cases). DVD generally extends the opportunity to studios to derive profit from fan desires to see lost, missing or alternative versions.
47. See IGN Staff (2007).'Reboot' is a newly popular term signifying a wiping of the existing continuity built up across parts of a serial text or franchise, allowing for recasting, the retelling of origins to attract new fans, and, sometimes, distancing from unpopular previous instalments. The Batman and James Bond series' have recently undergone successful 'reboots' with *Batman Begins* (Christopher Nolan, 2005) and *Casino Royale* (Martin Campbell, 2006).
48. *Empire* No. 132 (June 2000). The winner was Ben Affleck; the actor eventually cast in *Spider-Man* (Sam Raimi, 2002) and its sequels was Tobey Maguire.
49. Throughout 2007, director Jon Favreau's page solicited fan input and circulated production news of the production of his *Iron Man* (2008): http://www.myspace.com/jonfavreau.

2 Chronotope I: Time, Space, Narrative – 'Get Ready for Rush Hour'

1. Thomas Schatz considers the repercussions – positive *and* negative – of the mid-'70s re-birth of the 'blockbuster' in his essential article 'The New Hollywood', in Collins, Radner and Preacher Collins (1993, pp.8–36).

2. See 'Introduction: Action and Adventure Cinema' in Tasker (2004, pp.1–13).
3. *The Lord of the Rings* trilogy (Peter Jackson, 2001–3); *The Bourne Identity* (Doug Liman, 2002), *The Bourne Supremacy* (2004) and *The Bourne Ultimatum* (2007), the latter pair directed by Paul Greengrass.
4. However, we must not fail to appreciate that, despite the global audiences to which action films typically play, their mode of address is often limited; allied to this, as many critics have pointed out, particularly in work on the 1970s and 1980s (see Wood, 1986; Ryan and Kellner, 1988), the form is easily hijacked for the promulgation of politically reactionary narratives. The rhetoric displayed in films like *Dirty Harry* (Don Siegel, 1971), *Rambo: First Blood Part II* (George Pan Cosmatos, 1985) and *Red Dawn* (John Milius, 1984) at one point imprinted the genre with a critical reputation that saw it almost wholly leaning towards the political right. The violent content of many action films was undoubtedly a factor in this judgement, although contemporary developments (the desirable age of the mass blockbuster audience skewing increasingly young) surely place this aspect of the critique into question. The political economy of Hollywood, geared up to youth audiences and related licensing spin-offs, affects action film conventions as can be seen in the relatively recent rise of comic book and videogame heroes. Degrees of violence, sex and bad language contained within such films will obviously be part of the adjustment; currently, the US release of an R-rated action film is a point of discussion in itself (Timur Bekmambetov's film *Wanted* is discussed in this context; see Quint, 2008). Certain texts can be marshalled to make a case that the action film need not necessarily be used as a platform for the dissemination of right-wing philosophies. Films like *Robocop* (Paul Verhoeven, 1984), *Terminator 2: Judgement Day* (James Cameron, 1991), *V for Vendetta* (James McTeague, 2006) and *Shooter* (Antoine Fuqua, 2007) all find heroes (some of whom are former authority figures now ideologically 'reborn') advocating the reformation of illiberal capitalist regimes.
5. The original parts of the essay were composed in 1937–8, with the 'concluding remarks' (pp.243–58 in the 1994 edition) being added by Bakhtin in 1973.
6. The R-rated first entry in the *Die Hard* series exhibits more freedom in representing detailed, lingering violence and bad language when compared with the PG-13 – and notoriously curse-word free – *Die Hard 4.0*. Fan discussions leading up to the sequel's June 2007 release centred on the likelihood that a 'harder' version had been shot; the presence of several clumsily overdubbed scenes in the UK theatrical cut suggest some truth in this (and corroboration is available in the Region 2 DVD commentary by Len Wiseman and Bruce Willis, who confirm that the film was shot as an 'R'). For fan voices on the move to a 'softer' *Die Hard*, see article and accompanying messages in Vern (2007).
7. The jump cut is perhaps most strikingly employed in *À Bout de Souffle* (Jean-Luc Godard, 1959). Acquiring appeal precisely on the grounds of challenging orthodoxy, the technique found its way into the repertoire of the 'New Hollywood' via Arthur Penn's *Bonnie and Clyde* (1967), where the opening scene sees it employed to depict a Gallic-influenced chronotope of boredom and *ennui* on the part of the domestically trapped Bonnie Parker (Faye Dunaway).

8. See Chapter 5 for a further 'take' on this idea, in relation to the potentialities of new media.
9. Vivian Sobchack takes up related issues of 'embodiment' in her book *Carnal Thoughts*; see Sobchack (2004, pp.53–84).
10. For a discussion of how Bakhtin's chronotopic category of the road can be applied to cinema, and specifically the road movie genre, see Vice (1997, pp.210–218).
11. Issues of mediated temporalities experienced or invited by audio-visual texts will be taken up more fully in Chapter 5; for further critical discussion on this, see the work on non-fiction television by Hoskins (2004), and dramatic television by Kogen (2006).
12. Although Bakhtin never indicates that 'adventure-time' is limited to this particular genre, hence my appropriation of the category for the analysis of modern action movies.
13. 'Spanner-in-the-works' is an informal tag in everyday film discourse that has been attached to movies in the *Die Hard* mould, where a lone hero, often involved only by chance, works from a position of marginality or invisibility to foil a criminal plot, becoming a thorn in the side of his nemesis. McClane refers to himself as 'the fly in the ointment ... the monkey in the wrench ... the pain in the ass' in *Die Hard*. See also: *Under Siege* (Andrew Davis, 1992), *Passenger 57* (Kevin Hooks, 1992), *Air Force One* (Wolfgang Petersen, 1997), *Executive Decision* (Stuart Baird, 1996), *Con Air* (Simon West, 1997). The same set-up around the involuntary involvement of the hero is used in *Speed 2: Cruise Control* (Jan deBont, 1997), and the first two *Die Hard* sequels.
14. A slight generic variant sees a hero who embodies particular qualities and is in some way *chosen* enter the fray in a fashion that, at first, appears random. *The Matrix* and *Transformers* (Michael Bay, 2007) feature this motif.
15. 'Firesale' is the term used by Farrell to identify the first stage of Gabriel's plan to hack into, assume control of and render useless all governmental computer-based infrastructure, such as that pertaining to transportation and utilities. The second stage, only revealed later, is that the 'firesale' is a distraction to draw attention from the gang's attack on the secret computer servers at the Woodlawn facility, where national financial data and banking records are backed up.
16. 'Official' Bond film number 22 is *Quantum of Solace*, which was released in November 2008 and directed by Marc Forster.
17. See footnote, Chapter 1.
18. Sourcing the politics of what he calls 'male rampage' hero films, Fred Pfeil identifies Sylvester Stallone's Rambo character as its 'locus classicus' (1998, p.148). Rambo has been frequently and understandably politicized by critics like Ryan and Kellner (1990, pp.11–12) and Wood (1986). In a similar vein, Neil Bather (2004) discusses the rendering of villainy along gender, national and political lines as 'Manichean' in the action productions of Jerry Bruckheimer.
19. Saying that the films infrequently *represent* 'real world' politics is naturally not the same as saying that critics and audiences are disinclined to read them *in terms of* politics.
20. Adolf Hitler is rendered less as powerful historical figure than as comic icon in *Indiana Jones and the Last Crusade*, as is demonstrated in the episode

when Jones comes face-to-face with the Nazi leader. Mistaking the disguised Jones for a loyal footsoldier, Hitler gives him an autograph, leaving the hero dumbstruck. Similarly, in the 2008 chapter of Jones's saga, the Soviet forces working with KGB occultist Irina Spalko (Cate Blanchett) pursue the unlikely path of achieving world ideological control through the attainment of a Mesoamerican (actually alien) totem which becomes the latest 'ultimate weapon', now traditional in the series. The eponymous hero of the comic adaptation *Hellboy* (Guillermo del Toro, 2003) has his genesis in a similar mix of Nazism and the occult as is found in *Raiders of the Lost Ark*.

21. Although ambiguity seems intrinsic to perceptions of the former; in the popular consciousness, the signifier 'Vietnam' can now refer – chronotopically – to a period of time as well as a spatial location.
22. The superhero – in a recent cycle from *Spider-Man* (Sam Raimi, 2002), through to Pixar's interesting *The Incredibles* (Brad Bird, 2004), and on to the Iraq War-referencing *Iron Man* (Jon Favreau, 2008) – is surely a contender for a characteristic chronotopic rendering of post-911 heroism (see Flanagan, 2007b, pp.147–9, and Chapter 5 of this book).
23. A famous example of this is *Rambo III* (Peter MacDonald, 1988), where the then requirements of US patriotism sent the character into battle alongside Mujahadeen forces in the Afghan war against the USSR. Needless to say, this allegiance reads very differently in the post-911 climate. In such a case, Bakhtin's assertion that works live more intensely and fully in 'great time' than in their 'own' time is a pitfall for the film that reduces politics and history in such a way (NM, p.4). The next chapter will engage more fully with the suggestive notion of 'great time'.
24. The internal diegetic public of Metropolis is intended by this reference, not the fan public of the Superman films who actually had to wait *nineteen* years between instalments! There are some departures from orthodoxy in how the 2006 film deals with temporal issues. When the character's five-year sojourn into deep space produces a child, raised in his absence by its mother Lois Lane, we know we are dealing with a different register of time than the pure 'adventure-time' of James Bond, where such a fastening of narrative time to human biological growth is virtually unthinkable. See FTC (pp.89–94).
25. Some qualification is required here, as each of the films cited features a cyborg protagonist that 'learns' humanity from a flesh-and-blood companion. Peter Weller's character in *Robocop*, Arnold Schwarzenegger in *T2* and Jean-Claude Van Damme's character in *Universal Soldier* all become more 'human' as their narratives progress. In two out of the three examples, heroes have been divested of their previous full humanity by military experiments; *Robocop*, in particular, aligns itself with other 'new bad future' films of the 1980s and beyond (Glass, 1989) by asserting the value of human qualities and instincts over technological routines in a way that anticipates the criticism of technology in *Die Hard 4.0*. This perhaps highlights a certain aspect of hypocrisy regarding the films' own deployment of the technological marvels of special effects. Along these lines, certain critics have noted the modern action blockbuster's tendency to celebrate its own technological novelty even when effects are contained in dystopian scenarios like those found in *The Matrix* or *Independence Day* (Roland Emmerich, 1996). See Sobchack (1997, pp.282–5); Cubitt (1999), and Chapter 5 of this book.

26. There is no disputing that the Hollywood action cinema has progressed beyond monologic male centrality since 1990. Some classic female action heroes include Ripley (Sigourney Weaver) in the *Alien* series (1979–1997); Maggie (Bridget Fonda) in *The Assassin* (John Badham, 1993); Charlie Baltimore (Geena Davis) in *The Long Kiss Goodnight* (Renny Harlin, 1996); and Lara Croft (Angelina Jolie) in *Lara Croft: Tomb Raider* (Simon West, 2001). The fact remains, however, that as a general institutional policy, the movie industry seems to prefer its action heroes to be male. Most of the lucrative new action properties of recent years, such as the *Mission: Impossible*, *Bourne*, *National Treasure* and *Spider-Man* franchises, continue to deploy women in sidekick roles, romantic roles, or a mixture of the two as in *Hellboy*, *The Matrix*, or Doug Liman's marital spy adventure, *Mr and Mrs Smith* (2005). *Indiana Jones and the Kingdom of the Crystal Skull*, at time of writing likely to be the top-grossing international film of 2008, fashions a heavily orthodox Oedipal storyline and assigns predictably limited tasks to two capable female stars, Cate Blanchett (responsible for the film's villainy) and Karen Allen (romance/abduction/rescue). Recent exceptions to this apparent rule are explored in Marc O'Day's 2004 work on 'Action Babe cinema'. Many of these have been inspired by computer games, comics and television series, engendering a fairly wide range of female lead roles and genre hybrids with horror (*Resident Evil*, Paul W. S. Anderson, 2002), superheroics (*Elektra*, Rob Bowman, 2005), martial arts (*Kill Bill Vol. 1*, Quentin Tarantino, 2003) and comedy (*Charlie's Angels*, McG, 2000) all represented. As O'Day notes, true scope for female action characters exists in television, where *Xena: Warrior Princess* (1995–2001), *Buffy the Vampire Slayer* (1997–2003) and *Alias* (2001–6) were all long-running, critically favoured hits. Often cited as fundamental to the action female tradition (see Summerhayes, 2007), the *Terminator* saga has recently been expanded into a television series revolving around not only the iconic Sarah Connor but also a female cyborg (*Terminator: The Sarah Connor Chronicles*, 2008–).

27. Some critics have attempted alternative readings, for instance Schubart (2001, pp.196–7) on the 'passionate' torture scene in *Rambo: First Blood Part II* (George Pan Cosmatos, 1985).

28. Smith in a series of action-adventure roles, tending towards buddy comedies like *Men In Black* (Barry Sonnenfeld, 1997) early in his career but later solo outings often with a science-fictional bent (*I Am Legend*, Frances Lawrence, 2007); Cage particularly in *The Rock* (Michael Bay, 1996) where he is physically contrasted with Sean Connery playing a barely disguised, older, unreconstructed Bond character; Washington in traditional action films like Tony Scott's *Déjà vu* (2006), but also in more nuanced thrillers like Jonathan Demme's *The Manchurian Candidate* (2004) and Spike Lee's *Inside Man* (2006); Depp in his comedic-adventure role as Captain Jack Sparrow (*Pirates of the Caribbean* films, Gore Verbinski, 2003–7). The *Pirates* films provide an interesting example of how popular action bodies have changed since the 1980s, assembling an action-adventure team out of two far from 'hard body' males (Depp and Orlando Bloom) and a woman (Keira Knightley).

29. The term broadly signifies those elements of the film text that actually exist in front of the camera (as opposed to visual effects and other post-production elements). See Chapter 5.

30. Johnson/The Rock played a vigilante in *Walking Tall* (Kevin Bray, 2004), a remake of a 1973 'male rampage' film; a more conventional action role for him is in *The Rundown* aka *Welcome to the Jungle* (Peter Berg, 2003). Diesel did vigilante duty in *A Man Apart* (F. Gary Gray, 2003), taking a more traditional action role in the successful *xXx* (Rob Cohen, 2002). On Diesel's choice to refrain from public disclosure of his ethnicity, see Thrupkaew (2002).
31. An influential text in the development of the 1980s action film, particularly on the kinds of interracial 'buddy' dynamics that can be seen in the first three *Die Hard* films and are discussed by Fuchs (1995) and Ellison (2002), is the unmistakably chronotopically titled *48 Hrs.* (Walter Hill, 1982).
32. Always looking for ways to incorporate traditional *Die Hard* dynamics into its theme of a society over-dependent on vulnerable computer systems, the fourth film reproduces McClane's expertise in moving around liminal, confined spaces by stressing Farrell's knowledge of the nooks, crannies and clandestine access points of cyberspace. Particularly relevant here is the scene where Farrell retrieves vital data despite wireless Internet networks being down by surfing old-fashioned 'satcomms'.
33. Offscreen space represents an interesting chronotopic context in itself, and there is interesting work being done on this in relation to concepts of 'immersive' postclassical film. A highlight of such work is Scott Bukatman's essay, 'Zooming Out: The End of Offscreen Space' (1998), which suggests that the spectacle of cinema combines with certain 'hypercinematic' experiences invited by other participatory entertainments (for instance, theme parks) in conditioning spectators to accept dissolved boundaries between onscreen and offscreen. See also the discussion of extensions of blockbuster narratives in computer games and the Web in Chapter 5 of this book.
34. The motif of the mocked-up video clip is turned back onto the hero in *Die Hard 4.0*, when Gabriel triggers yet more fear in the public by infiltrating television networks and screening fake video of the destruction of the Capitol building.
35. For more on Hollywood's plundering of videogame properties and on videogame adaptations of hit films, see Chapters 5 and 6 of Keane (2007).
36. Many accounts exist questioning or debunking the myth of the 'train effect'; a comprehensive example is Gunning (1999).
37. See also the Internet 'talkback' hosted by Aintitcoolnews.com, where Willis (ironically, given the film's themes, in cyber-mode) personally addressed fan concerns (Knowles, 2007). The final film still noticeably uses CGI in many scenes.

3 Chronotope II: Time, Space and Genre in the Western Film

1. An intertextually pertinent link in *Die Hard 4.0* is the presence of actor Timothy Olyphant as villain Thomas Gabriel; Olyphant came to the film fresh from the 2006 closing episodes of critically acclaimed HBO Western drama *Deadwood* (2004–6).
2. Leone is popularly credited with formulating the 'Spaghetti Western' genre with the 1964 European production *A Fistful of Dollars*. The movie was based

on Akira Kurosawa's *Yojimbo* (1961), a source text that was later Americanized in Walter Hill's 1996 Bruce Willis vehicle *Last Man Standing*. Demonstrating the convoluted process by which genres transcend national boundaries, Kurosawa's *Seven Samurai* (1954) was apparently inspired by the Westerns of John Ford; the cultural debt was repaid when the film was remade in Hollywood as *The Magnificent Seven* (John Sturges, 1960). Later, the bare bones of Kurosawa's film appeared again as *Battle Beyond the Stars* (Jimmy T. Murakami, 1980), written by John Sayles, director of *Lone Star*, which shall be a key text in this chapter. *Eagle's Wing* (1978) is another geographical oddity, directed by the British filmmaker Anthony Harvey and, more importantly, financed from UK sources. Reference should also be made to the German novelist Karl May, whose works inspired a stream of Western movies from the 1920s to late 1960s, usually made with at least the part-involvement of German production entities. A string of these starred the American actor Lex Barker (such as *Old Shatterhand*, Hugo Fregonese, 1964). See also Dika (2008) on the 'East German Western'.
3. For a discussion of recent filmic versions of the West that have included the female experience, as well as representing viewpoints of the races so often 'othered' in the genre, see Flanagan (2007a). This piece concentrates on Ron Howard's *The Missing* (2003), a film that can be seen as a contemporary engagement with some of the issues that are so problematic in *The Searchers*, notably around race and gender relations.
4. 'Great time' is Bakhtin's term describing the limitless dialogic context in which meaning lives and develops. Works 'break through' the boundaries of their own epoch to achieve significance within great time (NM, p.4). Bakhtin uses the term to oppose 'small time': 'the space of the present day and the recent past and the imaginable – desired or frightening – future'. See MHS (pp.167–70). For a careful elucidation of possible philosophical and religious source elements that seem to feed into 'great time', a term that is rather fleetingly explicated by Bakhtin himself, see Shepherd (2006).
5. *Lone Star* was distributed by Columbia/Tri-Star. A common industrial practice for films produced independently of the large studios is to have distribution handled by a large corporation such as Sony (owners of the Columbia imprint); however, over the 1990s this practice solidified into a handful of powerful 'mini-major' independent companies supported by studios (the Miramax/Disney alliance being the most well-known). This development threw the sector, terminologically and conceptually, up for grabs and led to commentators like John Pierson arguing that the term 'indie' should no longer be extended to films that have been set up at, or enjoyed the backing and marketing/distribution opportunities of, major studios, even if through the aegis of so-called 'major independents' (Wyatt, 1998b) like New Line or Miramax. Pierson's suggested alternative term to cover this sort of activity is 'off-Hollywood'. See Hillier (2006, pp.254–61).
6. Casper (2007, p.345) records that the film was placed eleventh in the top earners of 1956, while the AFI top 100 movies of all time list, last published in 2007, saw *The Searchers* leap 84 places to #12, suggesting that the reputation of the movie is still improving. See Associated Press (2007). For a populist, entertainingly argued counterpoint to the film's towering reputation, see Metcalf (2006). A recent addition in the margins, as it were, of this reputation was Alex Cox's road movie *Searchers 2.0* (2007).

7. Indeed, it is possible – given the volume of critical attention the text has garnered – to refer to *The Searchers* as both 'monolithic' and 'canonical' (Flanagan, 2007a, p.114).
8. See Lehman (1990).
9. Bakhtin's dedication to complexly engage with notions of point of view ranges over his entire intellectual career and is a key issue connecting the early philosophical work with the middle and late period literary criticism, and is frequently accomplished through metaphors of vision and voice. See Holquist (2002, pp.20–3; 163–7).
10. I owe something here to Ken Hirschkop's deft recitation of the narrative of 'becoming' that Bakhtin unfurls in the chronotope essay (the account of a series of chronotopes corresponding to periods/genres, each of which encode specific values in their organization of time). See Hirschkop (1999, pp.177–8). Pechey (2007, p.84) seems to be thinking in a similar vein with his image of generic memory shaking out into a string of chronotopes, 'which all [...] selectively recall and revivify' their ancestors.
11. See McGee (2007, p.32). Along similar lines, Lily Alexander argues that the development of storytelling sees the same structural elements reconfigured according to the ideas and moods obtaining in society at a given time. As a side note to her chronotopic reading of certain recurrent symbolic images in European art cinema, Alexander notes that the road, figured as a site of adventure, freedom and ritual journey in the Western (as in many forms before it that also drew on myth), eventually finds itself transformed into the ultimate dead end of *film noir*. See Alexander (2007).
12. However, despite arguing for the universality of the 'epic and tragic hero' (1972, p.148) exemplified by the cowboy, Bazin surprisingly fails to extend this observation to the industrial benefits of such standardization, admitting that he cannot fathom the popularity of Westerns in non-American territories: 'What can there possibly be to interest Arabs, Hindus, Latins, Germans, or Anglo-Saxons [...] about evocations of the birth of the United States of America, the struggle between Buffalo Bill and the Indians, the laying down of the railroad, or the Civil War!' (141).
13. The 'invisible' style of classical Hollywood film, which, through the continuity system, seeks to efface all signs of directorial enunciation, colludes in the process of mythicization that Barthes' comments indicate here.
14. The most famous creative partnerships in the history of the genre have all been between male directors and stars: Ford/Wayne; Howard Hawks/Wayne; Anthony Mann/James Stewart; Sergio Leone/Clint Eastwood; Budd Boetticher/Randolph Scott and so on.
15. We are told that Ethan found Martin as a baby after his parents had been massacred, and when the pair is admitted to Scar's tent, Ethan recognizes the scalp of Martin's mother among those brandished by Debbie, indicating some kind of close relationship between them. This allusion, of course, has implications for the horror of miscegenation exhibited by Ethan, and its defining role in his racism. See Lehman (1990, pp.390–1); Courtney (1993, pp.116–7); McGee (2007, pp.101–2).
16. In this film, the onscreen son of Kirby Yorke (Wayne) plays a key narrative role.
17. However, there is a complexity to the way that *Stagecoach* deploys this deceptively simple (but later utterly iconic) image. The obvious artificiality

of the set-up (the landscape is back-projected) hints at the constructed nature of Wayne's star persona, a certain sense of dislocation that infuses the image with a subtle ambiguity. Respecting the historical conditions of the text's production, of course, we must note that back-projection was a more central part of the palette of optical effects in 1939, and most probably would not have signalled self-conscious artificiality to an audience of the time.
18. At one point Edwards travels ahead of Marty and Brad (Harry Carey Jr.) through a pass where he rightly conjectures from the split trail that Lucy's corpse has been jettisoned by the Comanche war party.
19. Ridley Scott draws rich allusions from this vein in his *Thelma and Louise* (1991). By situating much of the women's flight from patriarchal authority in Monument Valley, Scott inscribes a confident female presence in the action narrative, scattering the traces of the exclusively masculine psychological conflicts acted out against the same backdrop in Ford's films.
20. See Chapter 1.
21. The reversal of this binary is the concern of *Duel in the Sun* (King Vidor, 1946), subject of an important reading by Laura Mulvey (1989).
22. From lyrics to the song 'The Searchers' by Stan Jones, featured in the film.
23. At the moment of her realization of the danger, the camera zooms in on Lucy with disturbing intensity and rapidity, a sort of visual assertion that crisis time has arrived.
24. Demonstrating the 'subtle racism' of this policy, Michael Walker points out that the 'good' Indians in *Broken Arrow*, Cochise and Sonseeahray, are played by white actors while Geronimo, the Apache who rejects the peace treaty negotiated between Cochise and Jeffords (James Stewart), is portrayed by the Native American actor Jay Silverheels (1996, p.124).
25. See Lehman (1990, p.403); McGee (2007, p.97).
26. In Martin's case, it is slightly reductive to refer to him as straightforwardly 'white', but his whiteness is the dominant factor in his relationship with Look. Look's cultural subjugation is further underlined by her name, which she takes as an attempt to please Martin by communicating on his terms: 'look' is the word that starts all of the sentences with which he desperately tries to convince her that there is no bond between them. The name also has obvious resonances with the establishment of an economy of vision in the narrative, referring to the gaze with which Martha fixes Ethan in the first scene, and perhaps implicating Look as a threat to the phallic/scopic regime that puts Ethan at the centre of nearly every frame. As both Indian and female, Look represents a dual threat to that hegemony. See Courtney (1993, p.118).
27. David Thomson suggests that the key absence in *The Searchers* as viewed today is 'a scene in which Scar and Debbie talk' (2004, p.15). Thus *dialogue* – in the form of a racial conversation that represents an instance of 'actual speech' but also invokes the more 'philosophical' level that Hirschkop characterizes in the Bakhtinian perception of dialogue (1999, p.4) – is identified as that which the film could not countenance. The implications of representing miscegenation via a certain historical sanction – however spuriously applied – offered by the Western raise the idea that viewers would have recognized coded depictions of the most publically heightened race relation issues in the mid-1950s (those around the white-African American axis – see Lehman, 1990, p.411). However,

Steve Neale (1998) points out that to read the Native American character as 'standing in' for another race is deeply problematic, even if the interests of contextual reading seem to demand it.
28. From an unattributed review of *The Searchers* in Pym (1997, p.1168).
29. I am far from the first critic to proffer such a reading of the repeated action of lifting Debbie, and what it appears to stir in Ethan. Still, it is an odd intrusion of personal memory and feeling into the rather robotic revenge mindset that, for a number of years, has consumed and driven Ethan's life. The memory seems to shock him into re-experiencing a sense of the bond with his brother and perhaps even a vision of the family he would have had himself.
30. Noted in Eckstein (1994, p.35).
31. Ken Hirschkop's words, used in characterizing the Bakhtinian tendency to historicize language (1999, p.11).
32. Raymond Williams' important culturalist concept, the 'structure of feeling', captures a rather chronotopic flavour of the dialogue between different periods of culture, especially as regards the *reconstructive* aspect by which time/space patterns can be analysed to yield the pressures of history that they inscribe in narrative forms. For Williams, the concept illustrates how a contemporary culture can contain the unique characteristics of its own time while bearing 'many continuities, that can be traced, and reproducing many aspects of the organization [of the host culture], which can be separately described, yet feeling its whole life in certain ways differently, and shaping its creative response into a new structure of feeling' (Williams, 1994, p.61). Anthony Easthope argues that a Bakhtin Circle idea (Voloshinov's insistence that the materiality of signs conveys the collectivity and the expressivity of a culture's idiomatic consciousness) reveals itself as an influence in Williams's work on this concept. See Easthope (1993, p.118).
33. José E. Limón (1997, p.598) unearths a 'discursive cousin' of Sayles' film in the 1886 novel *Little Lone Star, or The Belle of the Cibolo* by Sam Hall. An association that would undoubtedly be more generally recognized is with the MGM Western of the same title, starring Clark Gable and directed by Vincent Sherman. The 1952 movie depicts events around Texan independence and the prospect of annexation to the United States in the mid-nineteenth century.
34. Citing Jonathan Freedman (2000), McGee, in a reading that concentrates on economic meanings in Ford's film, forwards the argument that the plot of *The Searchers* is 'generated by the newly minted Union gold coins that Ethan has stolen before the film begins and that he proceeds to put into circulation for its duration' (2007, p.95).
35. Underlining certain similarities in the star personas of the two actors, Kristofferson actually essayed the archetypal Wayne role of the Ringo Kid in a television remake of Ford's *Stagecoach* in 1986. He has also appeared in latter-day Westerns such as Sam Peckinpah's *Pat Garrett and Billy the Kid* (1973), and Michael Cimino's *Heaven's Gate* (1980). Kristofferson's career as a country singer also trades on a certain rugged cowboy quality in his looks and personality. Interestingly, in *Taxi Driver* (Martin Scorsese, 1976), Travis Bickle, a character widely interpreted as an updated version of Ethan Edwards (Weaver, 1986; Boyd, 1976–7), is compared to a character in a Kristofferson song by Betsy (Cybill Shepherd).

36. Except where his relationships with Look, whom he spurns and physically abuses, and Laurie, whom he deserts, are concerned; however, the film makes it clear that mistreatment of women is not sufficient grounds to doubt the stature of any male white character.
37. Ironically, given the racial agenda of the text, it is Sam and Pilar's sameness, not their ethnic difference, that constitutes the threat to their relationship.
38. Cooper's Academy Award success in Spike Jonze's *Adaptation* (2002) was six years away. Similarly, *Lone Star* anticipates, but is unable to capitalize upon, Matthew McConaughey's leading man success in later roles, both heroic (*U-571*, Jonathan Mostow, 2000) and romantic (*How to Lose a Guy in Ten Days*, Donald Petrie, 2003).
39. Is the name of this character a reference to the black educationalist Dr Bledsoe in Ralph Ellison's 1952 novel *Invisible Man*? Ellison's novel is another ethnically charged text, as the overdetermined use of the derivation of 'blood' in the naming of the character suggests.
40. A short-lived innovation in production and exhibition, Cinerama features were shot with a less than practical three-camera system and projected onto an extra-wide three-strip screen. The resulting image was imbued with extreme depth of focus, but also featured visually confusing information such as three vanishing points. See Hall (1996, pp.255–61).
41. The introduction of widescreen to the Western did not automatically enhance every tactic for producing spectacle available to filmmakers, and certain filmmakers had to work to find ways of delivering typical emotional beats and character relatability into the new aesthetic called for by the huge frame. William Wyler's Technirama epic *The Big Country* (1958) has been noted by Casper for eschewing 'classical western action elements such as stage hold-ups, Indian massacres, drunken brawls, sober gunfights, etc., and instead concentrating upon people's interactions and reactions' (2007, p.340). There is a sort of perversity in the way the film reluctantly stages action; typical of this trait is a narratively anticipated fistfight between the Gregory Peck and Charlton Heston characters that, despite featuring on the promotional poster ('Big they fought! Big they loved!'), proceeds for several minutes in a range of extreme long, long and medium shots, successfully withholding the pleasure of the violence and mediating the audience's desire to see it.
42. A further issue of translation and intercultural dialogue is noted by Enders (1999), who identifies the jukebox song as 'Desde Que Conosco', a Spanish version (performed by Freddie Fender, Duke Levine, Billy Novick, Larry Luddecke, Marshall Wood, and Tim Jackson) of 'Since I Met You Baby', written and performed by bluesman Ivory Joe Hunter, whose version is heard in another scene in Otis Payne's nightclub.
43. I would include in this series the moment discussed earlier, when Ethan inspects the rescued women at the camp. Janet Walker cites Janey Place's (1974) assessment of this close-up of Wayne as 'astounding'; Walker also postulates that this charged moment might be the referent of Steven Spielberg's oblique comment that Ford's film 'contains the single most harrowing moment in any film I've ever seen' (quoted in Walker, 2001, p.222).
44. Classical Hollywood methods aim at the creation of a realistic space that the audience will feel secure in, allowing them to assume the untroubled mantle of observer from a stable position that is roughly analogous to that of the

camera. However, as Vance Kepley Jr. demonstrates in his analysis of *His Girl Friday* (Howard Hawks, 1940), a variety of sophisticated editing and framing techniques are required to promulgate this illusion of 'real' space. See Kepley (1982, pp.50–8). The notion of classical film space as equated with the 'norm' of representation is qualified by new technologies like CGI, as explored in Chapter 5.

45. Sayles' device for combining these complex temporal relations in one frame stands as a technically more elaborate version of the aesthetic of Ingmar Bergman's *Smultronstället/Wild Strawberries* (1957). However, in that film, the emotional 'time travelling' of Professor Isak Borg (Victor Sjöström) is, to an extent, rationalized by the more overt thematic role played by dreams. Clearly influenced by Bergman's practice is Woody Allen in several films that eschew standard ways of textually encoding flashbacks; perhaps the best examples are to be found in *Crimes and Misdemeanors* (1989). In this film, Allen's concern with the morality of betraying one's own interpersonal history (and past self) shows evidence of the influence of Fyodor Dostoevsky as well as of Bergman, particularly around notions of crime and of the threshold – which, of course, puts the text into a Bakhtinian purview.

46. See Stax (2002) for details. This review of Sayles' version of the script (his credit does not survive in the film) itemizes a number of innovations that did not make it onto celluloid, particularly the use of voiceovers to impose diverse perspectives on this contested historical event. The author of the script review also stresses the divergence from the mythical approach that characterizes John Wayne's 1960 version of the same incident. The references to the Alamo in *Lone Star* evoke a historically loaded threshold if ever there was one ('a crossroads for siege and battle' as a caption in Hancock's film has it), and via the Wayne connection send us back once more to *The Searchers*. *The Alamo* was Wayne's directorial debut, an 'elephantine, historically inaccurate' (Pym, 1997, p.14) tribute to the defenders of Texan independence. Wayne presents the Alamo as an absolute border upon which American identity is besieged. John Ford apparently gave novice helmsman Wayne uncredited assistance on the film.

4 Polyphony: Authorship and Power

1. Speech genres are defined by Bakhtin as *'relatively stable'* utterances that become associated with spheres of language. These communicative spheres impart values onto theme, style and compositional structure. 'Primary' speech genres (of social communication) are absorbed and transformed into 'secondary' ones (the more complex, mediated ways of cultural 'speaking' that includes literary expression). Many of the dimensions of Bakhtin's work on speech genres were motivated towards 'overcoming those simplistic notions of speech life [... then] current in our language studies'. See PSG (pp.60–7).
2. Of course, the confounding of status conferred in relation to whether a narrator is 'outside' or 'inside' the diegesis (with regard to traditional views of 'omniscience') delineates one of the parameters that Bakhtin deliberately wants to dismantle and rework. In 'Discourse in the Novel', Bakhtin states that the author is 'the one who tells us how the narrator tells stories' (DIN, p.314) – which might be of limited help as polyphony is concerned

with the redistribution of the authorial discourse onto the plane of character. Author and narrator are sometimes lumped in together in *Problems of Dostoevsky's Poetics*, and Bakhtin takes for granted that we will not be very interested in prising them apart. The idea of narrative *viewpoint* that I shall develop in this chapter seems to offer a better way to approach narration in the specific interests of my analysis of Mamet.
3. The introduction of this book clarifies the position taken throughout regarding the claim of the director to ultimate authorship of the film text.
4. Bakhtin notes the intrinsic carnivalesque qualities of gambling, asserting that games take place in a special time of 'crisis' (PDP, p.171). As might be expected, the context is a discussion of Dostoevsky's *The Gambler* (filmed in 1974 by Karel Reisz and in 1997 by Károly Makk; an adaptation was also an unrealized Martin Scorsese project in the early 1970s). Later in *Problems of Dostoevsky's Poetics*, Bakhtin invokes the graphics of playing cards to illustrate the top-bottom nature of the carnival image (176). Gambling represents an attractive artistic metaphor to Bakhtin because of its heightened sense of skating on the 'threshold', a feeling that is certainly realized in Mamet's film.
5. In the BBC-TV programme *Face to Face* (transmitted 23/02/98), Mamet made the following statement to interviewer Jeremy Isaacs: '[... I]n real life people never say what they think. They speak to gain something from the other person [... language is] closer to extortative, manipulative than performative.'
6. An example is the expert who offers a largely superfluous explanation of Norman Bates' Oedipal fixation during the anti-climactic final scene of *Psycho* (Alfred Hitchcock, 1960).
7. Most key scenes take place within transitory 'threshold' locations such as bars, restaurants, hotel rooms, airports and so on. The 'threshold' motif takes numerous forms in *House of Games*. Doorways often take on the power of moments of crisis, in a similar way as was noted in relation to Ethan Edwards in Chapter 3. When Ford is trying to escape from the hotel room and the scandal of the police 'raid', she struggles with the door and can see a glimpse of freedom through its aperture. Her first sighting of Mike is through the door leading into the forbidden poker game. Ford hesitates outside the door of Maria's classroom when desperate for advice, and when Mike is killed, his body slumps against a door. Finally, the foreboding portal of the 'House of Games' is lingered on by the camera when Ford first enters, an image strong enough to make its way into certain marketing materials associated with the film.
8. Is Ford a psychoanalyst? The portrayal of her in terms of her practice is quite general, but in therapeutic mode she is seen to use patient's dreams as the basis for interpretations, and the film is littered with Freudian verbal slips that point up the theme of betraying oneself in honest speech. The film bears Freudian trappings noted by Hall (1992), Van Wert (1990, p.2) and Pearce (1999, p.5).
9. The viewer is positioned as a 'victim' in certain models of film spectatorship – see Chapter 1.
10. An 'excess of seeing' is associated with the taking of an authorial position; Mike exploits an awareness of this to increase his power over Ford. However, in originally expressing the notion, Bakhtin regards it more positively as a prerequisite of intersubjective relations – the idea that we require the external

perspective of the other to define our horizon, to fill in our wider vision. In *House of Games* we find this phenomenon distorted into one of Mike's techniques of 'deceptive dialogicality'; the model of vision that emerges in the film in never mutual and ethical in the way Bakhtin sketches it. The appearance of this concept in the Dostoevsky book is one of several reworkings in that text of notions that first surface in one of the early philosophical essays, 'Author and Hero in Aesthetic Activity' (1924–9, republished in *Art and Answerability* [1990], ed. M. Holquist and V. Liapunov, trans. V. Liapunov, Austin: University of Texas Press). For a helpful commentary on Bakhtin's ocular metaphors, see Gardiner (1998).
11. Another visual detail on this theme is the wall sign framed next to Mike for several seconds when the bogus poker game has unravelled. In large letters readable by the audience, the word 'NOTICE' is proclaimed; however, the accompanying text to which our attention is drawn is too tiny for us to read.
12. Although Ford enters this arrangement somewhat rationally, accepting Mike's unlikely 'mentoring' because she thinks there could be a book to be written on the world of the con.
13. The actor Joe Mantegna – Mike in *House of Games* – delivers a very similar 'motivating', worldly-wise speech with profound effects on the listener (William H. Macy's Edmond) in the film that Mamet scripted from his own 1982 play, *Edmond* (Stuart Gordon, 2005). An affinity between the characters of Margaret Ford and Edmond is noted by French (2004, p.185).
14. *Oleanna* (I refer here to the 1994 film version adapted by Mamet from his own 1992 play) pinpoints the fraught communication between lecturer and student as the arena for an exploration of the contingent circuits of power that discursive positions trail behind them. The film distils elements of criticism both of the abuse of Political Correctness and of reflexively anti-liberal attitudes to a social landscape changed by identity politics and the effects of the 'Culture Wars', into the language battle of its two antagonists.
15. We recall here Bakhtin's edict about the one-dimensionality of all acts of creative understanding that do not incorporate values of outsideness. See Chapter 3.
16. Ford's overdetermined transformation is rightly identified by Kipnis as the manifestation of a deferred but inevitable recuperation of the 'visual norms' of womanliness. This masquerade is somewhat redeemed by its ironic replaying of the traditional 'reveal' of hidden beauty found in films like *Now, Voyager* (Irving Rapper, 1942), a text that is discussed by Doane.
17. This is interpreted by Kipnis as phoney self-deception.
18. In the course of a contentious but lively reading, William F. Van Wert brings together several motifs and themes in the film (the 'bad girl' archetype which he intertextually traces to Hitchcock's *Marnie* [1963]; the idea of unreliable epistemologies and interpretative 'cons', and Lacanian ideas of inscription and the social order). Most radically, he suggests that the fatal confrontation with Mike at the airport happens not within the 'real' diegetic space but as a drama within Margaret Ford's psyche, the wish-fulfilment she must 'gift' herself to provide the psychic cleansing needed to 'purge' the trauma of the con. Thus, Margaret is absolved of 'real world' guilt for Mike's murder and indeed reaffirms her professional powers (if not professional ethics, in that she has successfully treated her own damaged psyche/self-image). At the same time, Van Wert argues, a game is played with the spectator's credulousness,

drawing us in with the con that 'there is a dead body of Mike anywhere other than in Margaret's mind'. See Van Wert (1990, pp.7–10).
19. However, the level of exaggeration within mise-en-scène that is the trademark of *film noir* is never really approached in Mamet's more prosaic visual style.
20. See, for instance, the ending of *Gilda* (Charles Vidor, 1946).
21. Examples of this can be found in the violent ends doled out to Jane Greer and Barbara Stanwyck in *Out of the Past* (Jacques Tourneur, 1947) and *Double Indemnity* (Billy Wilder, 1944) respectively.
22. More pertinent at the time of release of *House of Games*, and serving as a contrast, was a more conservative vision of the vengeful female. In films like *Fatal Attraction* (Adrian Lyne, 1987), the constraints of domesticity as a setting tip the representation of the non-assimilated woman over into the category of the monstrous.
23. See, for instance, the introduction, via a photograph, of the anodyne stepdaughter Lola Dietrichson (Jean Heather) in *Double Indemnity*.
24. As noted in Chapter 2, video and DVD viewings (and particularly, *re*-viewings of films) obviously do not necessary entail linear viewing experiences. However, Stephen Heath points out that it takes a special effort to abstract memories, readings and re-interpretations from the one-off 'flow' of the theatrical experience (1981, pp.216–7).
25. Malcolm V. Jones, in his Bakhtinian reading of Dostoevsky, has noted that 'changes in narrative point-of-view serve [...] to subvert the refuge of the familiar, to lure readers into thinking they know "where they stand" in relation to characters, setting and plot, only radically to undermine their suppositions' (Jones, 1990, p.14). For the uncertain narrative game of chance that is *House of Games*, these comments seem particularly apposite.
26. The theoretical concept of 'sideshadowing', formulated by Gary Saul Morson and Michael André Bernstein in their respective 1994 books *Narrative and Freedom* and *Foregone Conclusions*, argues that a certain type of narrative construction can assert a 'conception of open time' (Morson, 1994, p.5) in the face of linear historical implacability. Surfacing in texts as the admission of 'a *middle realm* of real possibilities that could have happened even if they did not' (1994, p.6, italics in original), sideshadowing covers the incidences where narratives take unexpected divergences that reject the 'foreshadowing' commensurate with a closed conception of time. Morson finds sideshadowing to be characteristic of the nature of *open time* in Dostoevsky, writing that the author's varied use of sideshadowing 'dislodges Ptolemaic temporality', the assumption that the present moment is 'the unchallenged center of things' (Morson, 1994, pp.118–19). Morson has published widely on Bakhtin, and invokes polyphony when suggesting that shifts in the foundation of temporality irreversibly dictate changes in the author's relationship to his hero. The process by which narrative structure (conventionally regulated by a closed temporal order) 'loses its inevitability [...] and "rhythm" yields to "loopholes"' (1994, p.99) creates an environment in which a degree of polyphonic independence is made available to the hero. This evocative concept has unmistakably Bakhtinian overtones. Recognizing the value of a 'middle realm of possibility' is consistent with the aversion to binary oppositions – whether between self and other, author and hero, speaker and addressee, or high and low culture – that is characteristic of Bakhtinian thought.

27. 1920–7, republished in *Art and Answerabililty* (1990).
28. This is a statement that some would take issue with. In a context of explicating polyphony, and following Seymour Chatman, Sue Vice notes that moments of pure description in film still signify as plot material because they are part of the story time; thus novelistic fiction can more easily expend time on narratorial excess that does not help plot, helping to make a case for – in one sense – greater flexibility than is found in film narration. See Vice (1997, p.142).
29. Such as the quartering of the frame in Mike Figgis' *Timecode* (2000), which allows for four narrative lines to be spun out of one moment and works to place editing power in the spectator's hands (although our attention is arguably channelled by sound editing, which tends to privilege the events of one internal screen at a time).
30. Comments on *House of Games* found on the Internet Movie Database, author unknown. http://uk.imdb.com/Reviews/02/0224 (accessed 20 May 1997).
31. In this sense, psychoanalysis – as practised by Ford, possibly on herself if we go along with Van Wert's reading, that is, Ford's revenge only plays out in her psyche – takes on a positive mediating role that justifies Mike's derisive attitude to it. Stephen Heath notes that psychoanalysis 'breaks up some of the certainties' of the bond between cinema and language (1981, p.199).
32. Similarly, according to Bakhtin, '[t]he heroes [of Dostoevsky] suffer destruction because they cannot wholeheartedly affirm the other ...' (PDP, p.10).

5 Hollywood Calling: Cinema's Technological Address

1. The term 'profilmic' was developed in French film theory; see, for instance, Metz (1977).
2. As of July 2008, no fully computer-generated feature aimed at an adult audience had earned the $100 million-plus gross that is the regular yardstick for computerized releases from Pixar/Disney, Dreamworks, Fox and Warner Brothers' animation departments. The closest was Robert Zemeckis' *Beowulf* (2007), which was rated PG-13. *Beowulf* followed *Final Fantasy: The Spirits Within* (Hironobu Sakaguchi/Motonori Sakakibara, 2001) in experimenting with using the technology in a form that played to a slightly older audience and attaching it to human characters in a way not often taken up by the traditionally anthropomorphically based children's films. However, both films notably remain within generic categories (fantasy and science fiction) that are well within this technology's current 'comfort zone'.
3. Keane itemizes these as science fiction, disaster movies, 'sword-and-sandal epics', historical epics, fantasy films and superhero movies (2007, pp.61–2). The heavyweight box office takings of the Pixar brand and *Shrek* line of movies, taken as representative of a quasi-genre of children's computer animation, could constitute a further category here.
4. Box office data from www.imdb.com and www.boxofficemojo.com.
5. Extensive examples may be found on www.fanedit.org.
6. See BBC (2005); Sandoval (2006).
7. This ad, directed by Chris Palmer for agency WCRS, can be seen at http://www.visit4info.com/advert/Sky-HD-Paused-Room-Sky-Digital/53898 (accessed 9 July 2008).

8. This ad can be seen at http://www.visit4info.com/advert/Sky-Tears-Sky-Movies/17688 (accessed 20th July 2008).
9. This 'liveness' comes not in the form of the 'appointment' paradigm taken by television in pre-VCR days, but as a constantly available flow.
10. Such as the 'Get the Real Picture' poster campaign that the MPAA introduced to New York City subways for summer 2008. See Mahmud (2008).
11. July 2008 saw the worldwide release of Batman sequel, *The Dark Knight*, containing specially shot IMAX sequences. The emphasis on the 'event' as one where spectators sit back in amazement at the scale or intensity of the image supports certain aspects of how apparatus theory posits a universal cinematic affect. Blockbuster 'event' logic has been construed in terms of traditional Hollywood monologism, smoothing out the diverse ways in which different cultures and locales construct cinema-going practices. See Elsaesser (1998, pp.211–12).
12. See Lewis (2008, pp.407–8).
13. For instance, the 'Cutting Room' feature on *Die Hard: Special Edition* (Twentieth Century Fox Home Entertainment, 2002. Region 2 edition).
14. DVD packaging, *Die Another Day*. MGM Home Entertainment, 2003. Region 2 edition. See also Keane's discussion of the ten-disc *Matrix Ultimate Edition* (2007, pp.131–2).
15. On 'modularity' in popular Hollywood cinema, see Wyatt (1994, *passim*).
16. Pixar originated as a research division of Lucasfilm, but was purchased by Steve Jobs (founder of Apple) in 1986. Jobs moved from the position of Pixar's CEO to the Disney board as part of the 2006 buyout of the former company by the latter.
17. Reflecting what seems to be a strength of Bakhtinian thinking (the identification and destablilization of norms), R. Barton Palmer describes classical cinema as 'a standard "language", dominated by a certain "rhetoric"' (1989, p.332).
18. This game, of course, received its own film adaptation, *Lara Croft: Tomb Raider* (Simon West, 2001), which was unsuccessfully 'sequelized' in 2003 (*Lara Croft Tomb Raider: Cradle of Life*, Jan de Bont). The dynamics of personification suggested by the relation between the game avatar and the player 'controlling' her are considered by Mary Flanagan (1999).
19. Aside from the children's animations already cited, the most popular blend extensive CGI effects with live action, including *The Matrix* trilogy, *Transformers* and its proposed 2009 sequel, *Iron Man* and proposed sequel (alongside many other superhero films), two *Chronicles of Narnia* films (2005 and 2008, directed by Andrew Adamson), the *Lord of the Rings* films, six Harry Potter films (2001–8), successful resurrections of the Indiana Jones and *Star Wars* sagas, and three adventures under *The Mummy* banner (1999–2008).
20. A magazine preview with access to the production of Universal's 2003 version of *Hulk* took the odd step of stressing that it was none other than director Ang Lee who donned the motion capture suit to supply the Industrial Light and Magic team with visual reference for the creature's movements (see Flanagan, 2004). This interesting twist on publicizing the auteur's signature did not seem to help the film at the box office, suggesting that perhaps Lee's style of critically endorsed auteur and this kind of film are incompatible. Sean Cubitt notes that the digital devices that produce CGI films like *Toy Story* have acquired a hybrid 'cyborg' status, 'authors as well as stars' (2000, p.88).

21. A British film, *Son of Rambow* (Garth Jennings, 2008) cleverly creates a narrative that thematically exploits the qualities of innocence and knowingness that co-exist in such discourses. By taking the unorthodox step of building its 1980s rites-of-passage narrative around the largely positive effects of exposure to violent films when young, a link is created between screen violence, nostalgia, and self-actualization; generically speaking, its fantasy-comedic structure holds notions of 'real' responsibility somewhat in abeyance. The two boys in the film find that *First Blood* (Ted Kotcheff, 1982) – the first film to feature Rambo – triggers friendship and also creativity (in the impulse to make a DIY sequel using VHS technology). The idea of 'authentic action' is a source of comedy, with the boys sustaining various injuries while inventing new stunts for their sequel.
22. See Paul Wells (2002b, p.26).
23. For discussion of this theme, see Flanagan (2004, pp.27–8).
24. Across nine feature releases since 1995, Pixar entertainments had captured an average of just under $237 million in domestic takings per picture, when the average for the overall genre of computer animation stood at $120 million (based on 56 major releases from 1995 to 2008; see http://boxofficemojo.com/genres/chart/?id=computeranimation.htm). However, the top rating Pixar film *Finding Nemo* (Andrew Stanton/Lee Unkrich, 2003) is bested by Dreamworks Animation's *Shrek 2* (Andrew Adamson, 2004) on the all-time domestic box office chart ($340 million for *Nemo*, $441 million for *Shrek 2*). All figures from www.boxofficemojo.com (accessed 14th December 2008).
25. Originally in an independent producer–distributor relationship, Pixar was officially folded into Disney, and ceased to be a separate company, with an all-stock deal reportedly worth over $7 billion in May 2006. The terms of the deal give Pixar creative supremo John Lasseter (director of *Toy Story*) creative command of all of Disney's animated output; one of Lasseter's first acts was to announce the return of 2-D animation (albeit in short form), cut by the studio in 2005. See Solomon (2006).
26. Quoted in a transcript of a discussion taking place on 18th April 1999; this can be found online at: http://www.hometheaterforum.com/chat/pixar.txt (accessed 15th July 2008).
27. Summer 2008 news stories suggested that at least one blended animation/live action film is planned to be released under the Pixar marque (with subject matter – an adaptation of Edgar Rice Burroughs's 'John Carter' fantasy character – that might also raise the age profile further than *The Incredibles*). See Reynolds (2008).
28. Of course, *within* the videogame narrative, Buzz himself is fooled by an illusion of three-dimensionality (he attacks Zurg's power source only to find it is a hologram), which reinforces the film's self-conscious sense of its own problematic status in a filmic ontology of space.
29. Since the intervention of Bolter and Grusin (2000), their take on this term has become widely used to describe the process by which older forms are refashioned into new media. The model is not one of complete takeover but rather of a more dialogic process where the older medium survives and adapts by borrowing attributes of the new. Remediating change thus works in two directions, 'backwards and forwards' (Keane, 2007, p.64).

30. Bakhtin discusses these two lines of development in the context of the struggle for the novel to put into practice the many voices of heteroglossia; the second line comes about as a dynamic, carnivalized rebuke to the unity and finalization of the first line. Bakhtin says that the second line is distinguished from the first precisely on the grounds that it auto-critiques the literariness that the first line simply bears with a straight face. The second line accommodates parody and other modes of discourse that express its subversive worldview. The lines eventually converge in novelistic style at 'the beginning of the nineteenth century' (p.414). See DIN (pp.366–422).
31. Barker notes (and critiques) a way of reading effects via a paradox that both alerts the viewer to the film's artificiality and re-inscribes them into its illusion by a sort of hypnosis-by-spectacle. Thus the 'specialness' of effects – which Barker argues is overtly textually marked – tends to be annulled in analyses. See Barker with Austin (2000, pp.82–3).
32. *The Incredibles* utilizes a wider diversity of settings and 'locations' than other Pixar films, and within this, attempts a range of non-geometric background textures (jungle, lava pit, ocean) that require complex lighting schemes (as noted in the Director's Commentary on the Region 2 DVD, Buena Vista Home Entertainment, 2005). The scene where fashion designer Edna Mode showcases the new outfits for Helen in her darkened workshop, for instance, signals a movement away from the primary coloured uniformity of the earliest features, as do many scenes of Bob and Helen 'sneaking around' Syndrome's base. Bob's work life is shown in a bland, greenish hue that seems to pay tribute to similar scenes of institutional mundanity in *Fight Club* (David Fincher, 1999) and *The Matrix*.
33. The clear point of comparison is Stan Lee/Jack Kirby's comic team the Fantastic Four. The main difference between the 'Incredibles' and the Fantastic Four is that, where the Incredibles (specifically Bob and Dash) have a hard time dealing with the cover story of mediocrity they have to wear, the FF do not cover their identities and thus have to deal with the issues of celebrity. Unsurprisingly, this theme has gone through a number of redefinitions since the FF debuted in 1961, in a diegetic New York that looked a lot like the Incredibles' Metroville. Like most elements of the team's mythos, such ideas are incompletely realized in two feature films by Tim Story, *Fantastic Four* (2005) and *Fantastic Four: Rise of the Silver Surfer* (2007).
34. A tactic to make Bob seem more constricted, as mentioned by Bird and producer John Walker on the R2 commentary track.
35. Early usage in the Dogme films and US indie features like *Chuck and Buck* (Miguel Arteta, 2000) confirmed expectations that DV, at that point mainly seen in terms of its conferral of a more transparent veneer of 'realism' on the narrative, would establish itself as the chosen medium of low-budget film-makers. However, as it evolves into 'high definition' lines, DV has increasingly become a choice for the making of mainstream features, some with an aesthetic interest in realism (*Collateral*, Michael Mann, 2004), some with none whatsoever (*Star Wars Episode III: Revenge of the Sith*, George Lucas, 2005). Thus, digital production must be seen in terms of accommodating a wide aesthetic spectrum (see Keane, 2007, pp.46–7).
36. Links to many of the sites involved can be found at www.whysoserious.com; an unofficial synopsis of the story that emerges through the viral incidents is

provided at http://www.thebadandugly.com/2008/07/16/dark_knight_primer_one/ (accessed 16th July 2008).
37. See Keane (2007, pp.144–6).
38. See also Chapman (2005, pp.248–51); Cubitt (2000, p.90–2).
39. Cultural studies concepts and arguments, which, as we noted in Chapter 1, arise from sources including V. N. Voloshinov, are enlisted as a buffer against more conservative appraisals of media change in significant works like Barker and Petley (2001).
40. Bolter and Grusin's term, quoted in Bostad (2004, p.174).
41. Parody as a genre imported into novelistic style receives an extended Bakhtinian treatment, both as a defining feature of the 'Second Stylistic Line' (DIN, pp.366–422, *passim*) and in Chapters 4 and 5 of the Dostoevsky book. Dan Harries deploys Bakhtin's thoughts on the subject in some detail throughout *Film Parody* (2000).
42. As of mid-July 2008, a number of news outlets reported advance ticket bookings for *The Dark Knight*, mostly transacted over the Internet, as the biggest volume in Hollywood history. See Billington (2008). This interest translated into the biggest opening on record, as the film amassed $158.4 million in its first weekend of release, propelling *The Dark Knight* to an eventual $530 million US gross (as of December 2008).
43. Although this has knock-on effects for feature production – see Jenkins (2005) on the origins of *Serenity* (Joss Whedon, 2005).
44. A 'sweded' version of *Die Hard* can be found at http://www.youtube.com/watch?v=pT6XYtlIGj0 (accessed 5th July 2008).
45. *Dubplate Drama*, which ran on Channel 4 in the UK for two series in 2005–6, worked on this basis. Viewers voted by text message on alternative outcomes for the following week's episode.

Conclusion: Making it Real

1. These tend to be collated from speculative fragments from Bakhtin's notebooks that often recorded an intention towards future, more concrete works (see Holquist, 2006).
2. Ives raises this problem in the context of an argument that stability and unity in language – along the lines of the 'national unified language' promoted in Gramsci's thought (2008, p.52) – need not be anti-progressive in character. For Ives, this is not the way that 'Discourse in the Novel' handles the notion of uniformity in language, as he demonstrates in comparing the results achieved by Bakhtin and Voloshinov when both apply themselves to the function of *refraction* in terms of language and the reality that may or may not abide 'outside' it. See 79–83 (and indeed, most of Chapter 2 of Ives' book).
3. The public square is Bakhtin's celebrated chronotopic image for the space that condenses carnival's spirit of populist social reorganization, 'free familiar contact' and festivity; see PDP (pp.128–33).
4. Activity of this type that saw publication before 2001 is identified in Adlam's bibliographical essay; the depth of coverage provided therein renders emulation here unnecessary. Valuable contextual works since then include but are not limited to Brandist (2002), Poole (2001) and the essays in Brandist,

Shepherd and Tihanov (2004), while other studies, like Pechey (2007), are historically minded re-examinations of the original themes.
5. Such as can be gauged in remarks like Peter Hitchcock's that 'economic structures [...] simply did not occupy [Bakhtin's] otherwise intensely active mind' (2000, p.4), or Brandist's comment that the 'institutional context which imbues artistic form with social significance' is often 'obscured' by Bakhtin's sheer insistence on aesthetic criteria (1996, p.69). Brandist takes this as a symptom of the 'disguising' of political questions as cultural ones (in order to bring out an unfavourable comparison between Bakhtin and Gramsci).
6. Hitchcock notes that over-estimating 'the "dialogue" in dialogism' underwrites a mere *assumption* of differences in the world, rather than 'actively thinking' them (2000, pp.17–8). In the same spirit of attempting to comprehend Bakhtin's intentions regarding this mercurial image, Galin Tihanov closely investigates the 'metaphorical' status of dialogue that emerges in the earliest incarnation of Bakhtin's major work on Dostoevsky (2000, pp.190–202).
7. As Schatz points out, immediately after Pearl Harbor, the Roosevelt administration presented the studios with a set of subjects and studio heads saw to it that these were put across in all available genres (1998, pp.297–8). There is no point denying that Hollywood has had plenty of official and centralizing agents attempting to heighten or inflect its messages, from the Production Code Administration to the military to today's corporate presence that can hardly be considered as 'outside' Hollywood any more (personal experience of collective movie watching instructs that when the 'messages' of the latter obtrude upon narrative, groans or hilarity in audiences can result). It is just as true, though, to state that tight control can breed subversion, and the closer Hollywood shifts to establishment values, the more likely an eruption from the margins (as in the late 1960s 'New Hollywood' period). The centre-margin axis is constantly being reformed. MacAskill (2007) presents a range of pundits who note a shift or suspension in the once axiomatic Hollywood 'risk aversion' to Leftist politics, as demonstrated by a cycle of post-9/11 and Iraq War projects due to be released across 2008–9, including Robert Redford's *Lions for Lambs*. Interestingly, screenwriter Paul Haggis boasts a schedule where directing duties on one of the cited anti-war films, *In the Valley of Elah*, rubs up against his collaboration on the screenplay of the blockbusting James Bond adventure, *Quantum of Solace*. This is a nice condensation of why this book argues that Hollywood discourses are diverse and mutable.
8. Bakhtin talks about these two planes in N70 (p.134).
9. 'Unrepeatable' is a term that becomes a favourite of Bakhtin's in the 'Problem of the Text' essay, but also appears earlier. It describes the uniqueness of speech events in time due to the contextual ideological matrices that connect in its structure before reforming in some other shape.

Filmography

Die Hard, directed by John McTiernan. Produced by Lawrence Gordon and Joel Silver. Screenplay by Jeb Stuart and Steven E. de Souza. Novel *Nothing Lasts Forever* by Roderick Thorp. Released by Twentieth Century Fox Film Corporation, 1988. 132 minutes.

***Die Hard 4.0* (US: *Live Free and Die Hard*)**, directed by Len Wiseman. Produced by Michael Fottrell. Co-produced by Stephen James Eads. Screenplay by Mark Bomback. Story by Mark Bomback and David Marconi. Article 'A Farewell to Arms' by John Carlin. Certain original characters by Roderick Thorp. Cheyenne Enterprises/Dune Entertainment/Ingenious Film Partners. Released by Twentieth Century Fox Film Corporation, 2007. 130 minutes.

House of Games, directed by David Mamet. Produced by Michael Hausman for Filmhaus. Screenplay by David Mamet. Story by David Mamet and Jonathan Katz. Released by Orion Pictures Corporation, 1987. 102 minutes.

The Incredibles, written and directed by Brad Bird. Produced by John Walker. Pixar Animation Studios. Released by Walt Disney Pictures, 2004. 115 minutes.

Lone Star, written and directed by John Sayles. Produced by R. Paul Miller and Maggie Renzi. Rio Dulce Inc./Castle Rock. Released by Sony Pictures Classics, 1996. 130 minutes.

Oleanna, written and directed by David Mamet. Produced by Sarah Green and Patricia Wolff. Bay Kinescope/Channel Four Films/The Samuel Goldwyn Company. Released by MGM, 1994. 89 minutes.

The Searchers, directed by John Ford, produced by C.V. Whitney and Merian C. Cooper. Screenplay by Frank S. Nugent from the novel by Alan LeMay. C.V. Whitney Pictures. Released by Warner Brothers, 1956. 119 minutes.

Speed, directed by Jan De Bont. Produced by Mark Gordon. Screenplay by Graham Yost. Released by Twentieth Century Fox Film Corporation, 1994. 115 minutes.

Toy Story 2, directed by John Lasseter. Co-directed by Ash Brannon and Lee Unkrich. Produced by Helene Plotkin and Karen Robert Jackson. Screenplay by Andrew Stanton, Rita Hsiao, Doug Chamberlain and Chris Webb. Original Story by John Lasseter, Pete Docter, Ash Brannon, Andrew Stanton. Pixar Animation Studios. Released by Walt Disney Pictures, 1999. 94 minutes.

Bibliography

Bakhtin circle works

Note: Please refer to the list of abbreviations at the front of this book for details of the format in which these works appear within the text.

Bakhtin, M. M. (1984) *Rabelais and His World*, trans. H. Iswolsky. Bloomington: Indiana University Press
Bakhtin, M. M. (1990) *Art and Answerability*, eds. Michael Holquist and V. Liapunov, trans. V. Liapunov, supplement trans. Kenneth Brostrom. Austin: University of Texas Press
Bakhtin, M. M. (1990) 'Author and Hero in Aesthetic Activity' in *Art and Answerability*. 4–256
Bakhtin, M. M. (1994) *The Dialogic Imagination*, ed. M. Holquist, trans. C. Emerson and M. Holquist. Austin: University of Texas Press.
Bakhtin, M. M. (1994) 'Discourse in the Novel' in *The Dialogic Imagination*. 259–422
Bakhtin, M. M. (1994) 'Forms of Time and of the Chronotope in the Novel' in *The Dialogic Imagination*. 84–258.
Bakhtin, M. M. (1997) *Problems of Dostoevsky's Poetics*, ed. and trans. C. Emerson, Minneapolis and London: University of Minnesota Press.
Bakhtin, M. M. (2006) *Speech Genres and Other Late Essays*, ed. C. Emerson and M. Holquist, trans. V. W. McGee. Austin: University of Texas Press.
Bakhtin, M. M. (2006) 'From Notes Made in 1970–71' in *Speech Genres and Other Late Essays*. 132–58
Bakhtin, M. M. (2006) 'Response to a Question from the *Novy Mir* Editorial Staff' in *Speech Genres and Other Late Essays*. 1–9
Bakhtin, M. M. (2006) 'The Bildungsroman and Its Significance in the History of Realism (Towards a Historical Topography of the Novel)' in *Speech Genres and Other Late Essays*. 10–59
Bakhtin, M. M. (2006) 'The Problem of Speech Genres' in *Speech Genres and Other Late Essays*. 60–102
Bakhtin, M. M. (2006) 'The Problem of the Text in Linguistics, Philology and the Human Sciences: An Experiment in Philosophical Analysis' in *Speech Genres and Other Late Essays*. 103–31
Bakhtin, M. M. (2006) 'Towards a Methodology for the Human Sciences' in *Speech Genres and Other Late Essays*. 159–172
Medvedev, P.N. (1985) *The Formal Method in Literary Scholarship: A Critical Introduction to Sociological Poetics*, trans. A. J. Wehrle. London and Cambridge, Mass.: Harvard University Press
Voloshinov, V.N. (1976) *Freudianism: A Marxist Critique*, ed. I.R. Titunik and N. Bruss, trans. I.R. Titunik. New York and London: Academic Press.
Voloshinov, V.N. (1986) *Marxism and the Philosophy of Language*, trans. L. Matejka and I.R. Titunik. Cambridge, Mass. and London: Harvard University Press.

Other Works

Adlam, C. (1997) 'In the Name of Bakhtin: Appropriation and Expropriation in Recent Russian and Western Bakhtin Studies' in A. Renfrew, ed. *Exploiting Bakhtin*. Glasgow: Strathclyde University Press. 75–90

Adlam, C. (2001) 'Critical Work on the Bakhtin Circle: A New Bibliographical Essay' in K. Hirschkop and D. Shepherd, eds, *Bakhtin and Cultural Theory*. 2nd ed. Manchester: Manchester University Press. 241–50

Adlam, C., Falconer, R., Makhlin, V. and Renfrew, A. eds (1997) *Face to Face: Bakhtin in Russia and the West*. Sheffield: Sheffield Academic Press

Agha, A. (2007) 'Recombinant Selves in Mass Mediated Spacetime'. *Language and Communication*, No. 27. 320–35

Alexander, L. (2007) 'Storytelling in Time and Space: Studies in the Chronotope and Narrative Logic on Screen'. *Journal of Narrative Theory*, Vol. 37, No. 1. Project Muse Full Text. <http://muse.jhu.edu/journals/journal_of_narrative_theory/v037/37.1alexander.html>. [27th Feburary 2008]

Allen, R. C. (2004) 'Frequently Asked Questions' in R. C. Allen and A. Hill, eds, *The Television Studies Reader*. London: Routledge. 1–26

Anon. (2004) 'Profile: *The Incredibles*. Absolutely Super Yet Incredibly Human'. *The Sunday Times* (November 21st). 17

Arthurs, J. (1995) '*Thelma and Louise*: On the road to feminism?' in P. Florence and D. Reynolds, eds, *Feminist Subjects, Multimedia: Cultural Methodologies*. Manchester: Manchester University Press. 89–105

Associated Press (2007) '2007AFI List of Top 100 Movies'. http://www.usatoday.com/life/movies/news/2007-06-20-AFI-movie-list_N.htm [11th June 2008]

Barker, M. (1994) 'A Dialogical Approach to Ideology' in J. Storey, ed. *Cultural Theory and Popular Culture*. Hemel Hempstead: Harvester Wheatsheaf. 255–73

Barker, M. with Austin, T. (2000) *From* Antz *to* Titanic: *Reinventing Film Analysis*. London: Pluto Press

Barker, M. and Petley, J. eds (2001) *Ill Effects: The Media/Violence Debate*. 2nd ed. London: Routledge.

Barthes, R. (1981) *Mythologies*, trans. A. Lavers. London: Granada

Bather, N. (2004) 'Big Rocks, Big Bangs, Big Bucks: The Spectacle of Evil in the Popular Cinema of Jerry Bruckheimer'. *New Review of Film and Television Studies*, Vol. 2, No. 1 (May). 37–60

Baudry, J. L. (1999) 'Ideological Effects of the Basic Cinematographic Apparatus' in L. Braudy and M. Cohen, eds, *Film Theory and Criticism: Introductory Readings*. 5th ed. Oxford: Oxford University Press. 345–56

Baxter, J. (1997) *Steven Spielberg: The Unauthorized Biography*. London: Harper Collins

Bazin, A. (1972) *What Is Cinema? Volume II*, trans. H. Gray. London: University of California Press

BBC (2005) 'News Corp in $580m Internet Buy'. 19th July. http://news.bbc.co.uk/1/hi/business/4695495.stm [9th July 2008]

Belton, J. (1992) *Widescreen Cinema*. Cambridge, Mass.: Harvard University Press

Bernard-Donals, M. (1994) 'Mikhail Bakhtin: Between Phenomenology and Marxism'. *College English*, No. 2 (February). 170–188

Bernstein, M. A. (1994) *Foregone Conclusions: Against Apocalyptic History*. Berkeley: University of California Press

Bhaskar, I. (2003) ' "Historical Poetics," Narrative, and Interpretation' in T. Miller and R. Stam, eds, *A Companion to Film Theory*. Blackwell Reference Online. http://www.blackwellreference.com/subscriber/tocnode?id=g9780631206453_chunk_g978063120645319 [13th June 2008]

Bigsby, C. ed. (2004), *The Cambridge Companion to David Mamet*. Cambridge: Cambridge University Press

Billington, A. (2008) '*The Dark Knight* is already poised to shatter records'. 25th June. http://www.firstshowing.net/2008/06/27/the-dark-knight-is-already-poised-to-shatter-records/ [17th July 2008]

Bolter, J. D. and Grusin, R. (2000) *Remediation: Understanding New Media*. Cambridge, Mass. and London: MIT Press

Booth, W. (1997) 'Introduction' in M. M. Bakhtin, *Problems of Dostoevsky's Poetics*, ed. and trans. C. Emerson, Minneapolis and London: University of Minnesota Press. xiii – xxvii

Bordwell, D. (1985) *Narration in the Fiction Film*. London and New York: Routledge

Bordwell, D. (1996) *Making Meaning*. Cambridge and London: Harvard University Press

Bordwell, D. (2000) 'Historical Poetics of Cinema'. http://www.geocities.com/david_bordwell/historicalpoet.htm [7th July 2008]

Bordwell, D. and Carroll, N. eds (1996) *Post-Theory: Reconstructing Film Studies*. Madison: University of Wisconsin Press

Bordwell, D., Staiger, J. and Thompson, K. (1985) *The Classical Hollywood Cinema: Film Style and Mode of Production to 1960*. London and New York: Routledge and Kegan Paul

Bostad, F. (2004) 'Dialogue in Electronic Public Space: the Semiotics of Time, Space and the Internet' in F. Bostad, C. Brandist, L. S. Evensen and H. C. Faber, eds, *Bakhtinian Perspectives on Language and Culture*. Basingstoke: Palgrave. 167–84

Bourdieu, P. (2003) *Distinction: A Social Critique of the Judgement of Taste*. London and New York: Routledge

Boyd, D. (1976–77) 'Prisoner of the Night'. *Film Heritage*, Vol. 12, No. 2. 24–31

Branigan, E. (1998) *Narrative Comprehension and Film*. London and New York: Routledge

Brandist, C. (1996) 'The Official and the Popular in Gramsci and Bakhtin'. *Theory, Culture & Society*, Vol. 13, No. 2. 59–74

Brandist, C. (2002) *The Bakhtin Circle: Philosophy, Culture and Politics*. London: Pluto Press

Brandist, C. (2004) 'Voloshinov's dilemma: on the philosophical roots of the dialogic theory of the utterance' in C. Brandist, D. Shepherd and G. Tihanov, eds, *The Bakhtin Circle: In the Master's Absence*. Manchester: Manchester University Press. 97–124

Buckland, W. (1998) 'A Close Encounter with *Raiders of the Lost Ark*: Notes on Narrative Aspects of the New Hollywood Blockbuster' in S. Neale and M. Smith, eds, *Contemporary Hollywood Cinema*. London and New York: Routledge. 166–77

Buckland, W. (1999) 'Between Science Fact and Science Fiction: Spielberg's Digital Dinosaurs, Possible Worlds and the New Aesthetic Realism'. *Screen*, Vol. 40, No. 2 (Summer). 177–93

Bukatman, S. (1998) 'Zooming Out: The End of Offscreen Space' in J. Lewis, ed. *The New American Cinema*. Durham: Duke University Press. 248–72

Bukatman, S. (2004) *Matters of Gravity: Special Effects and Supermen in the 20th Century*. Durham: Duke University Press

Burch, N. (1973) *Theory of Film Practice*, trans. H. R. Lane. London: Secker and Warburg

Carroll, N. (1996) 'A Reply to Heath' in N. Carroll, *Theorizing the Moving Image*. Cambridge: Cambridge University Press. 343–59

Casper, D. (2007) *Postwar Hollywood 1946–1962*. Oxford: Blackwell

Chapman, J. (2005) *Comparative Media History*. Cambridge: Polity

Clark, K. and Holquist, M. (1984) *Mikhail Bakhtin*. Cambridge, Mass. : Belknap Press

Clover, C. J. (1989) 'Her Body, Himself: Gender in the Slasher Film' in J. Donald, ed. *Fantasy and the Cinema*. London: BFI. 91–133

Collins, J., Radner, H. and Preacher Collins, A. eds (1993) *Film Theory Goes to the Movies*. London and New York: Routledge

Cook, D. A. (1996) *A History of Narrative Film*. 3rd ed. London and New York: W. W. Norton

Courtney, S. (1993) 'Looking for (Race and Gender) Trouble in Monument Valley'. *Qui Parle*, Vol. 6, No. 2 (Spring/Summer). 97–130

Creed, B. (2000) 'The Cyberstar: Digital Pleasures and the End of the Unconscious'. *Screen*, Vol. 41, No. 1 (Spring). 79–86

Creekmur, C. C. and Doty, A. eds (1995) *Out in Culture*. London: Cassell

Cubitt, S. (1999) 'Introduction. Le réel, c'est l'impossible: the sublime time of special effects'. *Screen*, Vol. 40, No. 2 (Summer). 122–30

Cubitt, S. (2000) 'The Distinctiveness of Digital Criticism'. *Screen*, Vol. 41, No. 1 (Spring). 86–92

Culler, J. (1976) *Saussure*. Glasgow: Fontana

Cunliffe, R. (1997) 'Bakhtin and Derrida: Drama and the Phoneyness of the *Phoné*' in Adlam, C. et al, eds, *Face to Face: Bakhtin in Russia and the West*. Sheffield: Sheffield Academic Press. 347–65

Curran, J. (2002) 'Media and the Making of British Society, c.1700–2000'. *Media History*, Vol. 8, No. 2. 135–54

Dayan, D. (1976) 'The Tutor Code of Classical Cinema' in B. Nichols, ed. *Movies and Methods*. Berkeley: University of California Press. 438–51

Dentith, S. (1995) *Bakhtinian Thought*. London and New York: Routledge

Dika, V. (2008) 'An East German *Indianerfilm*: The Bear in Sheep's Clothing'. *Jump Cut*, No. 50 (Spring). http://www.ejumpcut.org/currentissue/Dika-indianer/index.html [11th December 2008]

Doane, M. A. (1991) *Femmes Fatales: Feminism, Film Theory and Psychoanalysis*. London and New York: Routledge

Dowell, P. (1995) 'The Mythology of the Western: Hollywood Perspectives on Race and Gender in the Nineties'. *Cineaste*, Vol. 21, No. 1–2. 6–10

Dunne, M. (1996) 'Dialogizing the Formula Western: *Hearts of the West*'. *Film Criticism*, Vol. 20 (Spring). 15–23

Dyer, R. (2000) 'Action!' in J. Arroyo, ed. *Action/Spectacle Cinema*. London: BFI. 17–20

Eagle, H. (1981) *Russian Formalist Film Theory*. Ann Arbor: University of Michigan Press

Easthope, A. (1993) 'The Bakhtin School and Raymond Williams: The Subject and the Signifier' in D. Shepherd, ed. *Carnival and Other Subjects: Selected Papers from* the Fifth Bakhtin Conference University of Manchester July 1991. Amsterdam and Atlanta: Rodopi. 116–24

Eckstein, A. M. (1994) 'After the Rescue: *The Searchers*, the Audience and *Prime Cut* (1972)'. *Journal of Popular Culture*, Vol. 28, No. 3 (Winter). 33–53

Eichenbaum, B. (1965) 'Theory of the Formal Method' in L. T. Lemon and M. J. Reis, eds. and trans. *Russian Formalist Criticism: Four Essays*. Lincoln and London: University of Nebraska Press. 99–139

Eichenbaum, B. (1974) 'Problems of Film Stylistics'. *Screen*, Vol. 15, No.3. 7–32

Ellison, M. (2002) 'Ambiguity and Anger: Representations of African Americans in Contemporary Hollywood Film' in P. J. Davies and P. Wells, eds, *American Film and Politics from Reagan to Bush Jr* . Manchester: Manchester University Press. 157–81

Elsaesser, T. (1990) 'Tales of Sound and Fury: Observations on the Family Melodrama' in C. Gledhill, ed. *Home is Where the Heart Is*. London: BFI. 43–69

Elsaesser, T. (1998) 'Digital Cinema: Delivery, Event, Time' in T. Elsaesser and K. Hoffman, eds, *Cinema Futures: Cain, Able or Cable?*. Amsterdam: Amsterdam University Press. 201–22

Emerson, C. (1997) 'Editor's Preface' in M. M. Bakhtin, *Problems of Dostoevsky's Poetics*, ed. and trans. C. Emerson, Minneapolis and London: University of Minnesota Press. xxix–xliii

Emerson, C. (2000) *The First Hundred Years of Mikhail Bakhtin*. Princeton and Chichester: Princeton University Press

Enders, E. (1999) 'Forget the Alamo: The Convergence of Border Cultures in John Sayle's *Lone Star*'. http://www.ericenders.com/lonestar.htm [16th June 2008]

Engel, L. (1994) 'Mythic Space and Monument Valley: Another Look at John Ford's *Stagecoach*'. *Literature Film Quarterly*, Vol. 22, No. 3. 174–180

Falkowska, J. (1996) *The Political Films of Andrzej Wajda: Dialogism in* Man of Marble, Man of Iron *and* Danton. Providence and Oxford: Berghahn Books

Flanagan, M. (1999) 'Mobile Identities, Digital Stars and Post Cinematic Selves'. *Wide Angle*, Vol. 21, No. 1 (January). 76–93

Flanagan, M. (2004) ' "*The Hulk*, An Ang Lee Film": Notes on the Blockbuster Auteur'. *New Review of Film and Television Studies*, Vol. 2, No. 1 (May). 19–35

Flanagan, M. (2007a) 'Fighting to be Seen: Looking for Women in the West, from *The Searchers* to *The Missing*' in S. Andris and U. Frederick, eds, *Women Willing to Fight*. Newcastle: Cambridge Scholars Press. 112–27

Flanagan, M. (2007b) 'Teen Trajectories in *Spider-Man* and *Ghost World*' in I. Gordon, M. Jancovich and M. McAllister, eds, *Film and Comic Books*. Jackson: University Press of Mississippi. 137–59

Frayling, C. (1981) 'The American Western and American Society' in P. Davis and B. Neve, eds, *Cinema, Politics and Society*. Manchester: Manchester University Press. 136–162

Freedman, J. (2000) 'The Affect of the Market: Economic and Racial Exchange in *The Searchers*'. *American Literary History*, Vol. 12, No. 3. 585–99

French, P. (1973) *Westerns*. London: Secker and Warburg/BFI

French, P. (2004) 'David Mamet and Film' in C. Bigsby, ed. *The Cambridge Companion to David Mamet*. Cambridge: Cambridge University Press. 171–193

Fuchs, C. J. (1995) 'The Buddy Politic' in S. Cohan and I. R. Hark, eds, *Screening the Male: Exploring Masculinities in Hollywood Cinema*. London and New York: Routledge. 194–210

Fuery, P. (2000) *New Developments in Film Theory*. Basingstoke: Palgrave

Furniss, M. (1998) *Art in Motion: Animation Aesthetics*. London: John Libbey

Gallagher, T. (1986) 'Shoot-Out at the Genre Corral: Problems in the "Evolution" of the Western' in B. K. Grant, ed. *Film Genre Reader*. Austin: University of Texas Press. 202–216

Gardiner, M. (1992) *The Dialogics of Critique*. London and New York: Routledge

Gardiner, M. (1998) 'Bakhtin and the Metaphorics of Perception' in I. Heywood and B. Sandywell, eds, *Interpeting Visual Culture: Explorations in the Hermeneutics of the Visual*. London and New York: Routledge. 57–73

Glass, F. (1989) 'The New Bad Future: *Robocop* and 1980s Sci-Fi films'. *Science as Culture*, No. 5. 7–49

Gledhill, C. (1990) ed. *Home is Where the Heart Is*. London: BFI

Gledhill, C. (2000) '*Klute* 1: A Contemporary Film Noir and Feminist Criticism' in E. A. Kaplan, ed. *Feminism and Film*. Oxford: Oxford University Press. 66–85

Goggans, T. H. (1997) 'Laying Blame: Gender and Subtext in David Mamet's *Oleanna*'. *Modern Drama*, Vol. 40, No. 4 (Winter). 433–41

Goldstein, P. (2008) 'Pixar Defies Gravity'. 30th June. http://latimesblogs.latimes.com/the_big_picture/2008/06/pixar-defies-gr.html [13th July 2008]

Graziano, M. (2001) Untitled Post. 29th October. http://mag.awn.com/index.php3?ltype=comments2&article_no=823 [11th January 2003]

Gross, L. (1995) 'Big and Loud'. *Sight and Sound*, Vol. 5, No. 8 (NS) (August). 7–10

Gunning, T. (1999) 'An Aesthetic of Astonishment: Early Film and the [In]credulous Spectator' in L. Braudy and M. Cohen, eds, *Film Theory and Criticism: Introductory Readings*. 5th ed. Oxford: Oxford University Press. 818–32

Hall, A. C. (1992) 'Playing to Win: Sexual Politics in David Mamet's *House of Games* and *Speed-The-Plow*' in L. Kane, ed. *David Mamet: A Casebook*. New York: Garland Press. 137–59

Hall, S. (1996) 'How the West Was Won: History, Spectacle and the American Mountains' in I. Cameron and D. Pye, eds, *The Movie Book of the Western* London: Studio Vista. 255–261

Hall, S. (1999) 'Encoding, Decoding' in S. During, ed. *The Cultural Studies Reader*. 2nd ed. London and New York: Routledge. 507–17

Harries, D. (2000) *Film Parody*. London: BFI

Heath, S. (1981) *Questions of Cinema*. Bloomington: Indiana University Press

Hillier, J. (2006) 'US Independent Cinema Since the 1980s' in L. R. Williams and M. Hammond, eds, *Contemporary American Cinema*. Maidenhead: Open University Press. 247–64

Hills, M. (2002) *Fan Cultures*. London and New York: Routledge

Hills, M. (2004) 'Defining Cult TV: Texts, Inter-texts and Fan Audiences' in R. C. Allen and A. Hill, eds, *The Television Studies Reader*. London and New York: Routledge. 509–23

Hirschkop, K. (1990) 'On Value and Responsibility'. *Critical Studies* Vol. 2. No.1/2. 13–27

Hirschkop, K. (1992) 'Is Dialogism for Real?'. *Social Text*, No. 30. 102–113

Hirschkop, K. (1999) *Mikhail Bakhtin: An Aesthetic for Democracy*. Oxford: Oxford University Press

Hirschkop, K. (2001) 'Bakhtin in the Sober Light of Day (An Introduction to the Second Edition)' in K. Hirschkop and D. Shepherd, eds, *Bakhtin and Cultural Theory*. 2nd ed. Manchester: Manchester University Press. 1–25

Hitchcock, P. (2000) 'The World According to Globalization and Bakhtin' in C. Brandist and G. Tihanov, eds, *Materializing Bakhtin: The Bakhtin Circle and Social Theory*. Basingstoke: Macmillan. 3–19

Holquist, M. (1982) ' "Bad Faith" Squared: The Case of M.M. Bakhtin' in E. Bristol, ed. *Russian Literature and Criticism*. Berkeley: Berkeley Slavic Specialities. 214–234

Holquist, M. (1994) 'Introduction' in M.M. Bakhtin *The Dialogic Imagination*, ed. M. Holquist, trans. C. Emerson and M. Holquist. Austin: University of Texas Press. xv–xxxiii

Holquist, M. (2002) *Dialogism: Bakhtin and his World*. 2nd ed. London and New York: Routledge

Holquist, M. (2006) 'Introduction' in M. M. Bakhtin, *Speech Genres and Other Late Essays*, eds, C. Emerson and M. Holquist, trans. V. W. McGee, Austin: University of Texas Press. ix–xxiii

Hoskins, A. (2004) 'Television and the Collapse of Memory'. *Time and Society*, Vol. 13, No. 1. 109–27

IGN Staff (2007) '*Star Trek*: The Reboot. Scripters confirm new film to be a "reimagining" '. http://uk.movies.ign.com/articles/771/771425p1.html [21st May 2008]

Ives, P. (2008) *Gramsci's Politics of Language: Engaging the Bakhtin Circle and the Frankfurt School*. Toronto and London: Toronto University Press

Jancovich, M. (1995) 'Screen Theory' in J. Hollows and M. Jancovich, eds, *Approaches to Popular Film*. Manchester: Manchester University Press. 123–50

Jeffords, S. (1994) *Hard Bodies: Hollywood Masculinity in the Reagan Era*. New Jersey: Rutgers University Press

Jeffords, S. (2006) 'The Vietnam War in American Cinema' in L. R. Williams and M. Hammond, eds, *Contemporary American Cinema*. Maidenhead: Open University Press. 280–88

Jenkins, H. (1992) *Textual Poachers: Television Fans and Participatory Culture*. London and New York: Routledge

Jenkins, H. (1995) 'Historical Poetics' in J. Hollows and M. Jancovich, eds, *Approaches to Popular Film*. Manchester: Manchester University Press. 100–22

Jenkins, H. (2005) 'I Want My Geek TV!' *Flow*, Vol. 3, No. 1. http://flowtv.org/?p=288 [7th July 2008]

Joki, I. (1993) *Mamet, Bakhtin and the Dramatic: The Demotic as a Variable of Addressivity*. Åbo: Åbo Akademi University Press

Jones, M. V. (1990) *Dostoevsky After Bakhtin*. Cambridge: Cambridge University Press

Julius, M. (1996) *Action! The Action Movie A–Z*. London: B.T. Batsford

Kaplan, E. A. ed. (2000), *Feminism and Film*. Oxford: Oxford University Press

Keane, S. (2007) *CineTech*. Basingstoke: Palgrave

Kepley Jr., V. (1982) 'Spatial Articulation in the Classical Cinema: A Scene from *His Girl Friday*'. *Wide Angle*, Vol. 5, No. 3. 50–58

King, G. (2002) *New Hollywood Cinema: An Introduction*. London: I.B. Tauris

Kipnis, L. (1991) '*House of Games*: One Born Every Minute'. *Jump Cut*, 36 (May). http://www.ejumpcut.org/archive/onlinessays/JC36folder/HouseofGames.html [13th March 2008]

Kleinhans, C. (2002) 'Pamela Anderson on the Slippery Slope' in J. Lewis, ed. *The End of Cinema as we know it*. London: Pluto Press. 287–99

Klinger, B. (2006) 'What is Cinema Today? Home Viewing, New Technologies and DVD' in L. R. Williams and M. Hammond, eds, *Contemporary American Cinema*. Maidenhead: Open University Press. 356–76

Knowles, H. (2007) 'Bruce Willis is Talking Back – So Here's A TalkBack To Talk-Back With Him about *DIE HARD 4*'. http://www.aintitcool.com/node/32598 [7th June 2008]

Kogen, L. (2006) 'Once or Twice Upon a Time: Temporal Simultaneity and the *Lost* Phenomenon'. *Film International*, Vol. 4, No. 2. 44–55

Kristeva, J. (1980) 'Word, Dialogue and Novel' in L. S. Roudiez, ed. *Desire in Language: A Semiotic Approach to Literature and Art*. New York: Columbia University Press. 64–91

Krzywinska, T. and King, G. eds (2002), *ScreenPlay: Cinema/Videogames/Interfaces*. London: Wallflower Press

Lapsley, R. and Westlake, M. (1996) *Film Theory: An Introduction*. Manchester: Manchester University Press

Lehman, P. (1990) 'Texas 1868/America 1956: *The Searchers*' in P. Lehman, ed. *Close Viewings: An Anthology of New Film Criticism*. Tallahassee: Florida State University Press. 387–415

Lemire, E. (2004) 'Voyeurism and the Postwar Crisis of Masculinity in *Rear Window*' in J. Belton, ed. *Alfred Hitchcock's* Rear Window. Cambridge: Cambridge University Press. 57–90

Lewis, J. (2008) *American Film: A History*. London and New York: W.W. Norton

Limón, J. E. (1997) 'Tex-Sex-Mex: American Identities, Lone Stars, and the Politics of Racialized Sexuality'. *American Literary History*, Vol. 9, No. 3 (Fall). 598–616

Lister, M., Dovey, J., and Giddings, S. (2003) *New Media: A Critical Introduction*. London and New York: Routledge

Lundberg, Patricia L. (1989) 'Dialogically Feminized Reading: A Critique of Reader-Response Criticism'. *Reader*, No. 22 (Fall). 9–37

MacAskill, E. (2007) 'Hollywood tears up scripts to make Anti-War films while conflicts rage'. 14th August. http://www.film.guardian.co.uk/news/story/0,2148221,00.html [20th July 2008]

MacCabe, C. (1985) *Theoretical Essays*. Manchester: Manchester University Press

Mahmud, S. (2008) 'NYC Gets "Real Picture"'. 3rd June. http://www.adweek.com/aw/content_display/news/agency/e3i5ca4a2c7bdd717920575e9f0ce943f39 [14th July 2008]

Maltby, R. (1996a) *Hollywood Cinema*. Oxford: Blackwell

Maltby, R. (1996b) 'A Better Sense of History: John Ford and the Indians' in I. Cameron and D. Pye, eds, *The Movie Book of the Western* London: Studio Vista. 34–49

Mamet, D. (1991) *On Directing Film*. London: Faber and Faber

Mamet, D. (2003) Untitled Column. *The Guardian Review*, 31st October. 3

Massood, P. J. (2003) 'City Spaces and City Times: Bakhtin's Chronotope and Recent African-American Films' in M. Shiel and T. Fitzmaurice, eds, *Screening the City*. London: Verso

McBride, J. and Wilmington, M. (1974) *John Ford*. London: Secker and Warburg

McDonald, P. (2000) *The Star System: Hollywood's Production of Popular Identities*. London: Wallflower Press

McGee, P. (2007) *From Shane to Kill Bill: Rethinking the Western*. Oxford: Blackwell

McKee, A. (2002) 'TV Audiences and Everyday Life' in T. Miller, ed. *Television Studies*. London: BFI. 64–6

McLean, G. (2008) 'The One to Watch'. *Media Guardian*. 2nd June. http://www.guardian.co.uk/media/2008/jun/02/bbc.itv [5th July 2008]

McMahan, A (1999) 'The Effect of Multiform Narrative on Subjectivity'. *Screen*, Vol. 40, No. 2 (Summer). 146–157

McWilliams, D. (2001) 'Bakhtin in Brooklyn: Language in Spike Lee's *Do the Right Thing*' in P. I. Barta, P. A. Miller, C. Platter, and D. Shepherd, eds, *Carnivalizing Difference: Bakhtin and the Other*. London and New York: Routledge. 247–61

Metcalf, S. (2006) 'The Worst Best Movie: Why on earth did *The Searchers* get canonised?'. http://www.slate.com/id/2145142/ [7th September 2006]

Metz, C. (1974a) *Language and Cinema*, trans. D.J. Umiker-Sebeok. The Hague: Mouton

Metz, C. (1974b) *Film Language: A Semiotics of the Cinema*, trans. M. Taylor. New York: Oxford University Press

Metz, C. (1977) 'Trucage and the Film', trans. F. Meltzer. *Critical Inquiry*, Vol. 3, No. 4 (Summer). 657–675

Metz, C. (1994) *Psychoanalysis and Cinema*, trans. B. Brewster. London: Macmillan

Modleski, T. (1988) *The Women Who Knew Too Much: Hitchcock and Feminist Theory*. New York and London: Methuen

Morson, G. S. (1991) 'Bakhtin, Genres and Temporality'. *New Literary History*, Vol. 22, No. 4 (Autumn). 1071–1092

Morson, G. S. (1994) *Narrative and Freedom*. London: Yale University Press

Morson, G. S. and Emerson, C. (1990) *Mikhail Bakhtin: Creation of a Prosaics*. Stanford: Stanford University Press

Mulvey, L. (1989) 'Afterthoughts on "Visual Pleasure and Narrative Cinema" inspired by King Vidor's *Duel in the Sun* (1946)' in L. Mulvey, ed. *Visual and Other Pleasures*. London: Macmillan. 29–38

Mulvey, L. (1999) 'Visual Pleasure and Narrative Cinema' in Screen, ed. *The Sexual Subject: A Screen Reader in Sexuality*. London and New York: Routledge. 22–34.

Musser, C. (1991) *Before the Nickelodeon: Edwin S. Porter and the Edison Manufacturing Company*. London and Berkeley: University of California Press

Naficy, H. (2001) *An Accented Cinema: Exilic and Diasporic Filmmaking*. New Jersey: Princeton University Press

Neale, S. (1995) 'Masculinity as Spectacle: Reflections on Men and Mainstream Cinema' in S. Cohan and I. R. Hark, eds, *Screening the Male: Exploring Masculinities in Hollywood Cinema*. London and New York: Routledge. 9–20

Neale, S. (1998) 'Vanishing Americans: Racial and Ethnic Issues in the Interpretation and Context of Post-war "Pro-Indian" Westerns' in E. Buscombe and R. Pearson, eds, *Back in the Saddle Again: New Essays on the Western*. London: BFI. 8–28

Neale, S. (2004) 'Action-Adventure as Hollywood Genre' in Tasker, ed. *Action and Adventure Cinema*. London and New York: Routledge. 71–83

Newman, K. (2005) Review of *The Incredibles*. *Sight and Sound*, Vol. 15, No. 1 (NS) (January). 55–6

O' Hehir, A. (1999) Review of *Star Wars Episode I: The Phantom Menace*. *Sight and Sound*, Vol. 9, No. 7 (NS) (July). 34–5

O'Day, M. (2004) 'Beauty in Motion: Gender, Spectacle and Action Babe Cinema' in Y. Tasker, ed. *Action and Adventure Cinema*. London and New York: Routledge. 201–18

Osmond, A. (2008) Review of *Indiana Jones and the Kingdom of the Crystal Skull*. *Sight and Sound*, Vol. 18, No. 8 (NS). (August). 66

Oudart, J. P. (1977–8) 'Cinema and suture'. *Screen*, Vol. 18, No. 1 (Winter). 35–47
Palmer, R. B. (1989) 'Bakhtinian Translinguistics and Film Criticism: The Dialogical Image?' in R. B. Palmer, ed. *The Cinematic Text: Methods and Approaches*. New York: AMS Press. 303–41
Palmieri, G. (1998) '"The Author" according to Bakhtin[[[…]]]and Bakhtin the Author' in D. Shepherd, ed. *The Contexts of Bakhtin: Philosophy, Authorship, Aesthetics (Studies in Russian and European Literature 2)*. Amsterdam: Harwood. 45–56
Pearce, H. (1999) 'Plato in Hollywood: David Mamet and the Power of Illusions'. *Mosaic*, Vol. 32, No. 2 (June). 141–56
Pearce, L. (1995) 'Finding a place from which to write: The Methodology of Feminist Textual Practice' in B. Skeggs, ed. *Feminist Cultural Theory: Process and Production*. Manchester: Manchester University Press. 81–96
Pechey, G. (2007) *Mikhail Bakhtin The Word in the World*. London and New York: Routledge
Pfeil, F. (1998) 'From Pillar to Postmodern: Race, Class and Gender in The Male Rampage Film' in J. Lewis, ed. *The New American Cinema*. Durham: Duke University Press. 146–86
Pierson, M. (1999) 'CGI effects in Hollywood Science Fiction Cinema, 1989–95: The Wonder Years'. *Screen*, Vol. 40, No.2 (Summer). 158–76
Place, J. (1980) 'Women in Film Noir' in E. A. Kaplan, ed. *Women in Film Noir*. London: BFI. 35–67
Polan, D. (1985) 'The Critique of Cinematic Reason: Stephen Heath and the Theoretical Study of Film'. *Boundary 2*, Vol. 13, No. 2/3 (Winter – Spring). 157–171
Poole, B. (1998) 'Bakhtin and Cassirer: The philosophical origins of Bakhtin's carnival messianism'. *South Atlantic Quarterly*, Vol. 97, No. 3/4. 537–78
Poole, B. (2001) 'From phenomenology to dialogue: Max Scheler's phenomenological tradition and Mikhail Bakhtin's development from 'Toward a Philosophy of the Act' to his study of Dostoevsky' in K. Hirschkop and D. Shepherd, eds, *Bakhtin and Cultural Theory*. 2nd ed. Manchester: Manchester University Press. 109–35
Purse, L. (2007) 'Digital Heroes in Contemporary Hollywood: Exertion, Identification, and the Virtual Action Body'. *Film Criticism*, Vol. 32, No.1 (Fall). 5–25.
Pye, D. (1996) 'Double Vision: Miscegenation and Point of View in *The Searchers*' in I. Cameron and D. Pye, eds, *The Movie Book of the Western* London: Studio Vista. 229–235
Pym, J. ed. (1997) *Time Out Film Guide*. London: Penguin
Quint (2008) 'Quint greatly enjoyed the unapologetically R-rated actioner *Wanted*' http://www.aintitcool.com/?q=node/37224 [4th July 2008]
Rehak, B. (2008) Untitled Post. 28th June. http://weblogs.swarthmore.edu/burke/?p=602 [13th July 2008]
Reynolds, S. (2008) 'Stanton confirms Pixar's "John Carter"'. 9th June. http://www.digitalspy.co.uk/movies/a98683/stanton-confirms-pixars-john-carter.html [13th July 2008]
Righter, W. (1975) *Myth and Literature*. London and New York: Routledge
Rivkin, J. and Ryan, M. eds (2001) *Literary Theory: An Anthology*. Revised ed. Oxford: Blackwell
Rose, S. (2000) ' "Stanley told Steven: You'd be the best guy to direct this film". Kubrick, Spielberg and the AI Project'. *The Guardian*. 5th May 2000.

http://film.guardian.co.uk/Feature_Story/feature_story/0,4120,217328,00.html [14th April 2008]

RSU (2006) *UK Film Council Statistical Yearbook 06/07*. http://ukfilmcouncil.org.uk/yearbook [15th July 2008]

Rutland, B. (1990) 'Bakhtinian Categories and the Discourse of Postmodernism'. *Critical Studies*, Vol. 2, No. 1/2. 123–136

Ryan, M. and Kellner, D. (1990) *Camera Politica: The Politics and Ideology of Contemporary Hollywood Film*. Bloomington: Indiana University Press

Sandoval, G. (2006) 'NBC Strikes Deal with YouTube'. 27th June. http://news.cnet.com/NBC-strikes-deal-with-YouTube/2100-1025_3-6088617.html [9th July 2008]

Sauer, D. and Sauer, J. A. (2004) 'Misreading Mamet: Scholarship and Reviews' in C. Bigsby, ed. *The Cambridge Companion to David Mamet*. Cambridge: Cambridge University Press. 220–243

Schatz, T. (1998) *The Genius of the System: Hollywood Filmmaking in the Studio Era*. London: Faber and Faber

Schubart, R. (2001) 'Passion and Acceleration: Generic Change in the Action Film' in D. Slocum, ed. *Violence and American Cinema*. London and New York: Routledge. 192–207

Schuler, D. (1998) 'Reports of the Close Relationship Between Democracy and the Internet May Have Been Exaggerated: Challenges and Opportunities for Rapprochement'. *Media in Transition*. http://web.mit.edu/m-i-t/articles/index_schuler.html [6th July 2008]

Shepherd, D. (1996) Review of *Carnivals and Commonplaces: Bakhtin's Chronotope, Cultural Studies and Film* by Michael V. Montgomery. *Slavonic and East European Review*. Vol. 74, No.1. 133

Shepherd, D. (2001) 'Bakhtin and the Reader' in K. Hirschkop and D. Shepherd, eds, *Bakhtin and Cultural Theory*. 2nd ed. Manchester: Manchester University Press. 136–54

Shepherd, D. (2006) 'A Feeling for History? Bakhtin and "The Problem of *Great Time*"'. *Slavic and East European Review*, Vol. 84, No. 1 (January). 32–51

Shklovsky, V. (1965) 'Art as Technique' in L. T. Lemon and M. J. Reis, eds. and trans. *Russian Formalist Criticism: Four Essays*. Lincoln and London: University of Nebraska Press. 3–24

Shohat, E. and Stam, R. (1985) 'The Cinema After Babel: Language, Difference, Power'. *Screen*, Vol. 26, No. 3–4 (May–August). 35–58

Sobchack, V. (1997) *Screening Space: The American Science Fiction Film*. New Jersey: Rutgers University Press

Sobchack, V. (2004) *Carnal Thoughts: Embodiment and Moving Image Culture*. London and Berkeley: University of California Press

Solomon, C. (2006) 'Disney tries out new talent in an old form, the cartoon short'. *International Herald Tribune*. 3rd December. http://www.iht.com/articles/2006/12/03/business/disney.php [8th July 2008]

Stadler, E. M. (2003) 'Bresson, Dostoevsky, Bakhtin: Adaptation as Intertextual Dialogue'. *Quarterly Review of Film and Video*, No. 20. 15–22

Staiger, J. (2002) 'Reception Studies in Film and Television' in G. Turner, ed. *The Film Cultures Reader*. London and New York: Routledge. 46–72

Stam, R. (1989) *Subversive Pleasures: Bakhtin, Cultural Criticism and Film*. Baltimore: Johns Hopkins University Press.

Stam, R. (2000) *Film Theory: An Introduction*. Oxford: Blackwell

Stam, R., Burgoyne, R. and Flitterman-Lewis, S. eds (1992) *New Vocabularies in Film Semiotics*. London and New York: Routledge

Stax (2002) 'The Stax Report: Script Review of *The Alamo*'. http://uk.movies.ign.com/articles/365/365074p1.html [16th June 2008]

Stenger, J. (2006) 'The Clothes Make the Fan: Fashion and Online Fandom when *Buffy the Vampire Slayer* goes to eBay'. *Cinema Journal*, Vol. 45, No. 4 (Summer). 26–44

Strinati, D. (2000) *An Introduction to Theories of Popular Culture*. London and New York: Routledge

Summerhayes, C. (2007) 'Just a Woman Among the Cyborgs: Sarah Connor in *Terminator 2: Judgement Day*' in S. Andris and U. Frederick, eds, *Women Willing to Fight*. Newcastle: Cambridge Scholars Press. 38–54

Tasker, Y. (1995) 'Dumb Movies for Dumb People: Masculinity, the Body, and the Voice in Contemporary Action Cinema' in S. Cohan and I. R. Hark, eds, *Screening the Male: Exploring Masculinities in Hollywood Cinema*. London and New York: Routledge. 230–244

Tasker, Y. ed. (2004) *Action and Adventure Cinema*. London and New York: Routledge

Thomas, D (1996) 'John Wayne's Body' in I. Cameron and D. Pye, eds, *The Movie Book of the Western*. London: Studio Vista. 75–87

Thomson, C. (1984) 'Bakhtin's "Theory" of Genre'. *Studies in Twentieth Century Literature*, Vol. 9, No.1 (Fall). 29–40

Thomson, D. (2004) 'The Last Frontier'. *Sight and Sound*, Vol. 14, No. 2 (NS) (February). 12–15

Thornton, W. H. (1996) 'After the Carnival: The Filmic Prosaics of *Schindler's List*'. *Canadian Review of Comparative Literature*, Vol. 23, No. 3 (September) 701–8

Thrupkaew, N. (2002) 'The Multicultural Mysteries of Vin Diesel'. http://www.alternet.org/story/13863/ [6th June 08]

Tihanov, G. (2000) *The Master and the Slave: Lukács, Bakhtin and the Ideas of their Time*. Oxford and New York: Oxford University Press.

Titunik, I. R. (1986) 'The Baxtin Problem: Concerning Katerina Clark and Michael Holquist's *Mikhail Bakhtin*'. *Slavic and East European Journal*, Vol. 30, No. 1 (Spring). 91–5

Tulloch, J. and Jenkins, H. (1995) *Science Fiction Audiences: Watching Doctor Who and Star Trek*. London and New York: Routledge

Van Wert, W. F. (1990) 'Psychoanalysis and Con Games: *House of Games*'. *Film Quarterly*, Vol. 43, No. 4 (Autumn). 2–10

Vern (2007) 'FOX – Vern has some words for you about the pansy-assing of the 4th DIE FLACCID movie'. http://www.aintitcool.com/?q=node/32511 [2nd June 2008]

Vice, S. (1997) *Introducing Bakhtin*. Manchester: Manchester University Press

Walker, J. (2001) 'Captive Images in the Traumatic Western' in J. Walker, ed. *Westerns: Films Through History*. London and New York: Routledge. 219–51

Walker, M. (1996) 'The Westerns of Delmer Daves' in I. Cameron and D. Pye, eds, *The Movie Book of the Western* London: Studio Vista. 123–60

Wall, A. and Thomson, C. (1994) 'Chronic Chronotopicity: Reply to Morson and Emerson'. *Diacritics*. Vol. 24, No. 4 (Winter). 71–7

Warshow, R. (1999) 'Movie Chronicle: The Westerner' in L. Braudy and M. Cohen, eds *Film Theory and Criticism: Introductory Readings*. 5th ed. Oxford: Oxford University Press. 654–67

Weaver, D. (1986) 'The Narrative of Alienation: Martin Scorsese's *Taxi Driver*'. *CineAction* (Summer/Fall). 12–16

Wells, P. (2002a) *Animation and America*. Edinburgh: Edinburgh University Press. 38–59

Wells, P. (2002b) 'Where the Mild Things Are'. *Sight and Sound*, Vol. 12, No. 2 (NS). (February). 26–7

Wesling, D. (1992) 'The Speaking Subject in Russian Poetry and Poetics Since 1917'. *New Literary History*, Vol. 23, No. 1. 93–112

White, A. (1984) 'Bakhtin, Sociolinguistics, and Deconstruction' in F. Gloversmith, ed. *The Theory of Reading*. New Jersey: Barnes and Noble Books. 123–46

Willemen, P. (1994) *Looks and Frictions*. London: BFI

Williams, R. (1994) 'The Analysis of Culture' in J. Storey, ed. *Cultural Theory and Popular Culture*. Hemel Hempstead: Harvester Wheatsheaf. 56–64

Willis, A. (1995) 'Cultural Studies and Popular Film' in J. Hollows and M. Jancovich, eds, *Approaches to Popular Film*. Manchester: Manchester University Press. 173–91

Wood, A. (2004) 'The Collapse of Reality and Illusion in *The Matrix*' in Tasker, ed. *Action and Adventure Cinema*. London and New York: Routledge. 119–29

Wood, R. (1986) *Hollywood from Vietnam to Reagan*. New York: Columbia University Press

Wright, W. (1977) *Sixguns and Society: A Structural Study of the Western*. London: University of California Press

Wyatt, J. (1994) *High Concept: Movies and Marketing in Hollywood*. Austin: University of Texas Press

Wyatt, J. (1998a) 'From Roadshowing to Saturation Release' in J. Lewis, ed. *The New American Cinema*. Durham: Duke University Press. 64–86

Wyatt, J. (1998b) 'The Formation of the "Major Independent": Miramax, New Line and the New Hollywood' in S. Neale and M. Smith, eds, *Contemporary Hollywood Cinema*. London: Routledge. 74–90

Yamato, J. (2007) 'Interview: Bruce Willis Talks More *Die Hard* Sequels ...'. http://uk.rottentomatoes.com/news/1649004/ [7th June 08]

Zavala, I. M. (1990) 'Bakhtin and Otherness: Social Heterogeneity'. *Critical Studies*, Vol. 2, No.1/2. 77–89

Zylko, B. (1990) 'The Author-Hero Relation in Bakhtin's Dialogical Poetics'. *Critical Studies*, Vol. 2. No.1/2. 65–76

Index

Aardman Animations, n.192
Academy Awards, 54, 87
action movies, 53–6, 61, 63, 66, 69, 74
  female centred, n.199
  game motif in, 78–9
  as interactive experience, 79–81
  male hero, *see* adventure heroes
  politics of, n.196
  similarity to Greek adventure novel, 62–8, 70–1, 74, 77–8
active understanding, 177
Adaptation, n.205
adventure heroes, 69, 74
  cowboy archetype, 67
  enforced movement through space, 75
  as passive and unchanging, 71
  Rambo, 72
  testing of, 77
adventure novel of ordeal, 62, 74
adventure-space, 63, 74–5
  geographical abstraction of, 63
  simplicity of, 75
  as time waiting to happen, 76
  see also chronotope
adventure-time, 62–3, 65, 77–8
  chance within, 70–1
Agha, Asif, 89
AI Artificial Intelligence, 27, 175
aintitcoolnews.com, 156
Alamo, The, 123
Alexander, Lily, n.202
Alien 3, 52
Alien Resurrection, 52
Aliens, 79, 184
Alien (series), 51–2, 161
Althusser, Louis, 32, 47
American Civil War, 90, 96
Antz, 155
apparatus, *see* Baudry
Art and Answerability (M. M. Bakhtin), n.207–8, n.210
Arthurs, Jane, 49

Assassination of Jesse James by the Coward Robert Ford, The, 95
author, 154
  as film 'auteur', 16, 141, 148
  monologic version, 128, 132, 137
  polyphonic version, 14, 128, 149, n.207–8
  relationship with narrator, 128, n.206–7
'Author and Hero in Aesthetic Activity' (M. M. Bakhtin), n.208
authoritative word, 33
avant-garde, 44
Avery, Tex, 165
AVPR: Alien vs Predator – Requiem, 52

Badly Dubbed Porn, 31
Bakhtin Circle, 1–2, 4, 11, 20, 29, 41, 46–7, 184, 186
  authorship dispute, 15–16
Bakhtin, Elena Alexandrovna, 3
Bakhtin, Mikhail Mikhailovich, 1, 17, 24, 43
  Collected Works, 3
  death, 3
  events in life, 2–3
  Marxist tendencies of, 16, n.192, n.194
  publication and editorial history of works, 16
  view of the novel, 7, 9–10, 17–21
Balzac, Honoré de, 69
Barker, Lex, n.201
Barker, Martin, 4, 22, 44, 48, 170
Barthes, Roland, 23, 91–2, 95, 102
Batman, 63
Batman Begins, 172
Batman: Dead End, 52
Battle Beyond the Stars, 123
Battle Royale/Batoru Rowaiaru, 78
Baudrillard, Jean, 71
Baudry, Jean-Louis, 25, 32–3, 40, 44–5
Bazin, André, 53, 84–5, 90
Be Kind, Rewind, 179

230

Bellour, Raymond, 148
Beowulf, 30, n.210
Bergman, Ingmar, 118
Bhaskar, Ira, 43
Big Country, The, n.205
Bigsby, Christopher, 154
Bird, Brad, 170
Blade Runner, 50
Blair Witch Project, The, 174–5
Blanchett, Cate, 74
blockbuster, 53, 55, 63, 79
Blue, 30
blu-ray, 156, 158
b-movie, 54
Bocharov, Sergei, n.190
body, the
  CGI bodies, 74
  fixed action body, 72–4
  hard bodies, 74
  see also chronotopic motifs, 72
Bonnie & Clyde, n.196
Booth, Wayne, 20
Bordwell, David, 11, 22, 40–5, 151, 180, 186, n.193
Bostad, Finn, 176, 184
Bound, 146
Bourdieu, Pierre, 45–6
boxofficemojo.com, n.210
Brandist, Craig, 19, 46, 184, n.191
Branigan, Edward, 42
Broken Arrow, 105
Buckland, Warren, 27
Buffy the Vampire Slayer (TV), 30, n.192, n.199
Bug's Life, A, 164–5, 169
Buhler, Karl, n.191
Bukatman, Scott, 27
Burch, Noël, 76

Cage, Nicolas, 74
Cahiers du Cinema, 16
Carney, Ray, 45
carnival/the carnivalesque, 72–4, 147, 177, 185, 188
Carroll, Noël, 40–1, 50
Casino Royale, 65, 82
Centre for Contemporary Cultural Studies, Birmingham University, 47
Cheyenne Autumn, 95

Chinatown, 69
Chronicles of Narnia (series), n.211
chronotope, 4, 8, 10–11, 13, 52, 55–8, 61, 63, 66–8, 70, 72, 78, 80, 109–10, 113, 120–2, 125, 166, 181, 183, 188, n.200
  of adventure, 60, 62
  and crisis time, 89, 188
  definition of, 57
  folkloric, 57, 66, 92
  geographical distortion in, 63, 69
  historical displacement in, 100
  inversion of time and space as in 'Golden Age', 169
  as lens/way of seeing, 68, 85, 110
  as organizing centre of narrative, 88, 100
  overlapping chronotopes, 89
  real and represented within, 81
  of reception, 57, 81
  two orders within, 94, 109
chronotopic motifs, 57, 61, 68, 81
  arrival, 59
  bodily, 72
    see also Wayne, John
  border, 118
  bridge, 81
  castle, 58, 59
  journey, 81
  meeting, 57
  Monument Valley, 99–101
  road, 57, 58, 59, 61, 69, 100
  threshold, 60, 89, 104–5
  travel, 59
Chuck and Buck, n.213
Cinema of Attractions, 80
cinema and film, distinction between, see Metz, Christian
classifications/ratings system, n.82
Clockwork Orange, A, n.190
Close Encounters of the Third Kind, 54
Clover, Carol J., 30
Cloverfield, 174–5, 178
cognitivism/neo-formalism, see Bordwell
Cold War, 168
Collateral, n.213
Columbia/Tri-Star, n.201
Commando, 72

Computer Generated Imagery (CGI),
    27, 30, 59, 156, 159
  aesthetics, 15, 160
  attitude to story, 162–3
  and commercial success, 155
  realism and, 162–3
  virtual camera software, 167
computer/videogame industry, 155, 161
Connery, Sean, 71
Cook, David A., 20
creative perception, 9–10
Crimes and Misdemeanors, n.206
Cubitt, Sean, 160, 176
cultural studies, 22, 25, 42, 47–8, 176
Curran, James, 176–7
cyberspace, 59, 75

Dafoe, Willem, 74
Dark City, 162, 165
Dark Knight, The, 175
Dayan, Daniel, n.195
Day the Earth Stood Still, The, 51
Deadwood, n.200
Death Race 2000, 78
Dentith, Simon, 154
Depp, Johnny, 74
diachronic, 18, 27
dialogic/dialogism, 4, 6, 8, 10, 14,
    18–21, 25, 27–8, 37–9, 43, 45, 47,
    50–1, 55, 58, 61, 66, 77, 94, 109,
    120, 139–41, 143, 148, 161, 168,
    170, 174, 176–7, 181–3, 185–6
  internal, 31
  and the internet, 178, 180
  as montage of voices, 40
  relationship to concept of dialogue,
    177
  relationship to democracy, 184
  relationship to monologism, 131–2
  as response of spectator, 8–9, 11, 12,
    14, 52, 188
Dickens, Charles, 5
Die Hard 2, 64, 68
Die Hard 4, 0 (US: *Live Free or Die Hard*),
    56, 61, 64, 69, 75, 78, 82, 160
Die Hard (film), 12, 55, 59, 61, 63–5,
    69–70, 75–8, 82–3, 161
Die Hard (film series), 12
  hero, 64–5, 69–70, 73

  space within, 76–9
  timeframes used in, 75
Diesel, Vin, 74
digital video (DV), 156, 173
  adoption by pornographic industry,
    174
  realism in, 173–4
Dimension Studios, 156
Dinosaur, 163
Director's Commentary, 31
director's cut, 51
Dirty Harry, 71, 78
'Discourse in the Novel' (M. M. Bakhtin),
    3, 5, 18, 20, 23, 37, n.191
Disney, 163
Doane, Mary Ann, 142, 147
Dogme 95, 173
Dostoevsky, Feodor Mikhailovich, 5,
    13–14, 25, 55, 60, 89, 104, 127,
    150, n.206
Double Indemnity, 37, n.209
double-voiced discourse, 48, 67, 168,
    185
Dreamworks Animation Studios, 155
Dr. No, 168
Dryburgh, Stuart, 118
Dubplate Drama, n.214
Duel in the Sun, n.203
DVD, 15
  as archive of promo campaigns, 175
  director's commentary, 158
  implications for film canon, 176
  special features of, 158

Eagle, Herbert, 23
Eastwood, Clint, 71
editing, 97
Edmond, n.208
Eichenbaum, Boris, 41, 93
Eisenstein, Sergei, 20
Eliot, T.S., 93
Elsaesser, Thomas, 31, 161
Emerson, Caryl, 4, 137, 184
eventness, 152
eXistenZ, 161

Face to Face, n.207
Falkowska, Janina, 61
Fanboys, 179

fans/fandom, 15, 52, 156
  'fan edits', 179
  fan power, 156
  fan-scholar, 156
  messageboard communities, 180
  as producer, 15, 179
  'sweding', 179
Fantastic Four (comic), n.213
Fantastic Four (film), n.213
Fantastic Four: Rise of the Silver Surfer, n.213
Fatal Attraction, n.209
femme fatale, 132, 142, 145
  as antithesis of maternal, 133
Fielding, Henry, 5, 7
Fight Club, 183
Film Council (UK), 173
film genre
  action, *see* action movies
  buddy movie, 75
  as double voiced, 67
  film noir, 49, 98
    see also film noir
  horror, 29–30
  road movie, 49, 60, 75
  science fiction, 52
  war film, 31
  western, *see* western
film noir, 49, 98
  in *House of Games*, 145–8, 151, 153
film studies, 15
film theory, 22–50
Final Fantasy: The Spirits Within, n.210
Finding Nemo, 170
Fistful of Dollars, A, n.200
Flags of Our Fathers, 155
Flaubert, Gustav, 5, 62, 104
folk culture, 85
Ford, John, 13, 97–101
Formal Method in Literary Scholarship, The (P. N. Medvedev), 3, 15, 91
form and content (relationship), 5–6
'Forms of Time and of the Chronotope in the Novel' (M. M. Bakhtin), 3, 5, 12, 55, 57, 61, 68, 76, n.191
  'Concluding Remarks', 57–8, 61, 76
Fort Apache, 97
Frankfurt School, 46
Frayling, Christopher, 85, 90

Freedman, Jonathan, n.204
freeze-frame, 57
French, Philip, 99, 153
Freudianism, 34
Freudianism: A Critical Sketch (V. N. Voloshinov), 2, 15
Friends, 29
Fuery, Patrick, 40

Galaxy Quest, 179
Gallagher, Tag, 83–4
Gambler, The (F. M. Dostoevsky), n.207
Gardiner, Michael, 7, 93
gaze, the, *see* Mulvey
gender, 34, 36, 49, 65, 101–6, 132, 180
genre (Bakhtin definition), 90–1, 94
genre memory/generic memory, 13, 88, 93–4, 113
Gilda, 37, 147
Girl, n.193
Gladiator, 155
Godard, Jean-Luc, 153
Goethe, Johann Wolfgang von, 69
Gogol, Nikolai, 5
golden age, 92, 95, 120, 169
  see also chronotope
Goldeneye, 66
Good, Craig, 167
Gramsci, Antonio, 47–8, 182, n.190
Grande Syntagmatique, *see* Metz
Grand Theory, 41–2, 45
Greatest Story Ever Told, The, 117
great time, 185, n.201
  definition of, 87–8
Great Train Robbery, The, 53, 80, 83, 124
Greek romance/novel of adventure, 62, 64, 65–6, 70, 76–7, 79, 82
Green Berets, The, 109
Gross, Larry, 54–5
Gulf War, 66
Gummo, 173

Hale's Tours, 80–1
Halloween, 30
Hamlet, 26
Hamlet Goes Business/Hamlet Likemaailmassa, 26
Hancock, 172
Hard Target, 78

Harvey, Anthony, n.201
Haudiquet, Phillipe, 100–1, 103
Heath, Stephen, 22, 32, 44, 49, 183, 187
Heaven's Gate, n.204
hegemony, 48
Heliodorus, 12, 62
Heroes, 172
heterogeneity, 18, 21, 168
heteroglossia, 7–8, 10, 14, 17, 24, 27, 47, 89, 112, 160, 174
  relationship to myth, 92
  as verbal-ideological decentering, 112
high concept, 157
High Noon, 36, 83–4, 95
Hills Have Eyes, The, n.192
Hills, Matt, 156–7, 161
Hirschkop, Ken, 3–4, 16, 34, 177, 182, 184, 202
His Girl Friday, 184, n.206
historically inverted, 66, 89
historical poetics, *see* Bordwell
Hitchcock, Alfred, 34
Hitman, 161
Hollywood, 33, 53, 62, 159, 183
  as American national cinema, 2
  Bakhtinian perspective, 181–2, 183–5
  classical/studio phase, 87, 108
  as 'dream factory', 133
  new understanding of, 188
  traditionally viewed as monologic, 7, 182
Holquist, Michael, 3–4, 20, 24, 63, 68, 88, 137
Homer, 90
Hourvitz, Leo, 164
House of Games, 14, 127–54, 188
  coda, 150
  feminist discourse in, 153
  film noir elements, *see* film noir
  internal authors in, 133
  as polyphonic text, 148–54
How to Lose a Guy in Ten Days, n.205
How the West Was Won, 117
Hudson Hawk, 33
Hulk, 162
hypermediacy, 177

Idiots, The/Idioterne, 173
IEG, 174

IMAX, 158
Incredibles, The, 15, 163, 167, 168, 170–3, 175
independent cinema, 87
Indiana Jones and the Kingdom of the Crystal Skull, 66
Indiana Jones and the Last Crusade, 63, 69
Indiana Jones (series), 12, 62–3
Industrial Light and Magic, n.211
Internet, 15, 175–8, 180
intertextuality, 6, 18
In the Valley of Elah, n.215
Irigaray, Luce, 142
I, Robot, 162
Iron Giant, The, 169–70
Irons, Jeremy, 74
Ives, Peter, 47, 182, n.190

Jack-Jack Attack, 175
James Bond (series), 12, 62–3, 65–6
Jancovich, Mark, 38
Jaws, 53
Jeffords, Susan, 74
Jenkins, Henry, 41, 52, 157, 161, n.193
Johnson, Dwayne (the Rock), 74, n.199–200
Joki, Ilkka, 129, 131
Jones, Malcolm V, n.209
Judge Dredd, 52
Junior, 73
Jurassic Park, 27, 79, 159, 162

Kagan, Matvei, 2
Kanaev, Ivan Ivanovich, 15
Kantian/anti-Kantian, *see* Kant
Kant, Immanuel, 2, 58, n.189, n.191
Keane, Stephen, 178
Kepley, Vance, 162, n.206
Keynesianism, 84
Kingdom of Heaven, 51
King, Geoff, 161
King Kong, 162
Kipnis, Laura, 129, 150
Klinger, Barbara, 158, 176
Krzywinska, Tania, 161
Kubrick, Stanley, 27
Kurosawa, Akira, 26, 83

LA Confidential, 69
Land of the Dead, 183

Language and Cinema (Christian Metz), 25–6, 28, 30, 39
Lapsley, Robert, 25
Lara Croft Tomb Raider: Cradle of Life, n.211
Lara Croft: Tomb Raider, n.199, n.211
L'arrivee d'un Train en Gare de la Ciotat, 53, 79
Last Man Standing, n.201
Last Seduction, The, 146
Last Starfighter, The, 164
Lawnmower Man, 161
Lawrence of Arabia, 54
Lehman, Peter, 88, 95, 102, 109, 112
Leone, Sergio, 83
Lethal Weapon, 3, 64, 66
Lévi-Strauss, Claude, 23, 85, 93
Life of a Cowboy, 83
Limon, José E., n.204
linguistic metaphor (basis of film theory), 22, 30, 40
Lions for Lambs, n.215
Little Dorrit (Charles Dickens), 7, n.190
Lone Star, 13, 86, 87, 89, 95, 110–24, 126, 188
  flashbacks within, 118–19
  relationship to western, 86, 114–18, 123–4
Lord of the Rings, The (series), 27, 52, 54, 158
Lucasfilm, n.210
Lumière, Auguste & Louis, 53, 56, 79

MacCabe, Colin, 22, 38, 39–40
male rampage films, 68
Maltby, Richard, 90, 95, 98
Mamet, David, 13, 128–9, 132–5, 153–4
  accusations of misogyny, 129
Manhattan, 117
Manicheism (in Western), 90
Man Who Shot Liberty Valance, The, 86, 95, 98, 123
Marnie, n.208
Marty, Anton, n.191
Marxism, 32–3
Marxism and the Philosophy of Language (V. N. Voloshinov), 2, 15, n.191, n.194
mass audience, 32, 109

mass culture theory, 46
Massively Multiplayer Games (MMPs), 158
Matrix Online, The, 158, 178
Matrix, The (series), 27, 161, 162, 165, 178
May, Karl, n.201
McBride, Joseph, 100
McDiarmid, Ian, 74
McDonald, Paul, n.192
McKellan, Ian, 74
McMahan, Alison, 178
Méliès, George, 136
metalanguage, 39–40
Metz, Christian, 4, 11, 22–3, 25–9, 31–3, 39, 43–4, 56, 58, 70, 186, n.192
  cinema and film distinction, 26, 29
  cine-semiotics, 23, 29, 44
  imaginary signifier, 31
Mevedev, Pavel Nikaelovich, 2–3, 15–16, 91, 94, 186, n.190
MGM, 31
Mildred Pierce, 37
Miramax, n.201
miscegenation, 105–10, n.203
mise-en-scène, 85, 136
  framing, 28, 86, 97, 116–17, 120
Missing, The, n.201
Mission Impossible, 3, 51
monologic/monologism, 3, 7, 17, 31, 39, 43, 47, 50, 95, 106, 117, 121, 127, 131, 135, 138–9, 141–2, 148–9, 153–4, 161, 168, 182, 185, 187
Monsters, Inc, 164, 165
Monument Valley, *see* chronotopic motifs
Moonlighting, 73
Morson, Gary S., 4, 94–5, 151
Motion Picture Association of America (MPAA), 156
  battle against movie piracy, 158, n.211
Mukařovsky, Jan, 42
Multi User Domain (MUD), 178
Mulvey, Laura, 4, 11, 22, 32–4, 36, 39, 44, 49, 102, 141, 147, 149, 162, 186
  female assumption of gaze, 141–2
  male gaze, 36, 138
  three looks of cinema, 34, 49, 141

Mummy, The (series), n.211
Musser, Charles, 79
My Darling Clementine, 98
MySpace, 52, 157
myth; Barthes' critique of, 91–2
   tension with history, 92, 95
   in western, 90–6

Naficy, Hamid, 181
narrative, 136
   and spectacle, 27, 74
narratology, *see* Bordwell
narratorship, 129
National Treasure, 172
Natural Born Killers, n.190
NBC, 157
Neale, Steve, 73, 75
Neo-Kantianism, *see* Kant
New Line, n.201
News Corporation, 157
9/11, 171–2
Nintendo Wii, 158
norms, 24, 42
Notes from the Underground
   (F. M. Dostoevsky), 150
nouvelle vague, 57
noveless (romannost), 20, 26
Now, Voyager, n.208
Nykvist, Sven, 118

O'Hehir, Andrew, 159
Oleanna, 14, 140, 154
Olyphant, Timothy, 74
Once Upon a Time in the West, 67
One Life Stand, 173
openendedness, 5, 150
otherness, 19, 21, 74, 122, 185–6
Oudart, Jean-Pierre, n.195
Out of the Past, n.209
outsideness, 88
   definition, 10–11

Palmieri, Giovanni, 135
Paramount, 51
Party of Five, 29
Passion of the Christ, The, 172
Pat Garrett and Billy the Kid, n.204
patriarchy, 49, 127, 143
Pearce, Lynne, 38

Pearl Harbor, n.215
Pechey, Graham, 8
Petronius, 5, 14
Pfeil, Fred, 68
Pierce, Charles S., 23
Pierson, Michelle, 162
Pixar, 15, 155, 162, 164, 167, 170
   attitude to story, 163–4
   commercial success, n.212
   future projects, n.212
   'meta-branding', 163, 168
Player, The, 125
plurality, 134
Plutarch, 5
Polan, Dana, 50
political correctness, n.208
polyphony, 5, 10, 13–14, 52, 127, 133–5,
   139–40, 148–54, 177–8, 188
   author/narrator, *see* author
   false, 140
   in film, 134
   freedom of hero's consciousness
      within, 152
   as non-hierarchical system, 134,
      142, 153
   novelistic, 127, 152
   surplus of knowledge, 137, n.207–8
polysemy, 44, 45, 48, 50
Poole, Brian, 184
Porter, Edwin S., 80
Posse, 126
postmodern, 40
post-structuralism, 23, 40
Problems of Dostoevsky's Poetics
   (M. M. Bakhtin), 2, 127, 135
'Problem of Speech Genres, The'
   (M. M. Bakhtin), 25
Production Code Administration
   (PCA), n.215
Professionals, The, 84
profilmic, 74, 155, 157, 159, 160–1,
   166–7, 169, 177, n.210
Propp, Vladimir, 85
Psycho, 45, n.207
psychoanalysis, 22, 31, 33, 36, 41–2,
   49, 132–3
Pudovkin, Vsevolod Ilarionovich, 20
Purse, Lisa, 74
Pushkin, Alexander, 5

Quantum of Solace, n.197, n.215
Quick and the Dead, The, 123, 126

Rabelais, François, 5, 55, 71–2, 92
Rabelais and his World (M. M. Bakhtin), 3
race, 49
Raiders of the Lost Ark, 66
Rambo, 72
   see also adventure heroes
Rambo: First Blood Part II, 66
Rambo III, n.198
Raw Deal, 72
re-accentuation, 4, 28, 92, 177, 185
Rear Window, 34–7
reboot, 65–6
Red Badge of Courage, The, 31
Reeves, Keanu, 74
remediation, 14, 167, 177, 179, n.212
Resident Evil, 161
Rickman, Alan, 74
Rio Bravo, 98
Rio Grande, 98
Robe, The, 117
Robocop, 71, 79
Rock, The, 66, 68
Rose, Stephen, 27
Rossellini, Roberto, 39
rottentomatoes.com, 156
Running Man, The, 78
Russian Ark/Russkiy Kovcheg, 30
Russian formalism, 18, 20, 23, 41–4, 91, 177
   concept of defamiliarization, 44–5
   inspiration for neo-formalism, 41–3
Rutland, Barry, 57

Sarris, Andrew, 16
Sauer, David K., 129
Sauer, Janice A., 129
Saussure, Ferdinand de, 11, 23–5, 31, 177
Sayles, John, 13, 86–7, 117, 123
Schubart, Rikke, 68, 71, 78
Scott, Ridley & Tony, 53
Scream (series), 29–30, n.192
screen theory, 39–40, 48
Searchers 2.0, n.201

Searchers, The, 13, 84, 86–8, 90, 92, 96–109, 113–16, 118, 120, 123–4, 126, 187
   acclaim for, 87–8
   domesticity in, 101–5
   Ethan/Scar comparison, 97, 106
   'remade' as *The Missing*, n.201
   stardom in, 114
   see also Wayne, John
Second Life, 178
second stylistic line, 170
semiotics, 20, 22–3, 40–2, 45, 49
   cine-semiotics
   see also Metz, Christian
   Saussurean version, 24
Seneca, 14
Serenity, 214
Seven Samurai/Shichinin no Samurai, 54
sexuality, 49, 180
Shane, 67, 84, 92
Shanghai Noon, 126
Shepherd, David, 21, 61, 187
She Wore a Yellow Ribbon, 98
Shklovsky, Victor, 41, 91, 94
Shohat, Ella, 31
Shrek, 162, n.210
Shrek 2, n.212
sideshadowing, n.209
sign, 22, 40
   multi-accentual, see Voloshinov, Valentin Nikaelovich
Silent Hill, 161
Silverado, 126
The Simpsons (TV series), 170
Sin City, 156, 180
Sky Captain and the World of Tomorrow, 165
Sky HD, 157
SkyPlus, 157
'Slab Theory', 41
slow-motion, 57
Smith, Will, 74, n.199
Some Like it Hot, 184
Son of Rambow, n.211
Sony, n.201
sound, 31
Spacey, Kevin, 74
Spartacus, 54
special editions, 51

special effects, 27
spectacle, 53
spectator, 4, 6, 21, 34, 36, 38, 49, 56, 175, 183
　as active, 37, 40, 41, 42, 48–52
　female, 37
　as passive, 25, 38
　physically involved, 79–81
spectatorship theory, 11–12, 14, 22, 39, 48, 144, 149, 185
speech genres, 127, 131–2
Speech Genres and Other Late Essays (M. M. Bakhtin), 5, 88
Speed 2: Cruise Control, 81
Speed, 56, 59, 61, 63–5, 69–71, 75, 76, 77–8, 80–1
　ending of, 81
　similarity to Greek novel of adventure, 70–1
Speed-the-Plow (play), 131
Speed Racer, 33
Spider-Man, 62, 63, 79
Spider-Man 2, 172
Sputnik, 168
Spy Kids 3-D: Game Over, 161
Stagecoach, 84, 99
Staiger, Janet, 41, 48
Stam, Robert, 2, 19, 31, 42, 44–5, 140, 189
star power, 36, 116
star system, 26, n.192
Star Trek: The Motion Picture, 51
Star Trek: Nemesis, 51
Star Trek: The Next Generation, 51
Star Trek (TV), 51, 161
Star Trek: Voyager, 51
Star Wars Episode III: Revenge of the Sith, n.213
Star Wars Episode I: The Phantom Menace, 52, 159
Star Wars (film), 53, 62–3, 161, 165–6, 179
Star Wars (series), 51, 62, 74, 165, n.211
Stenger, Josh, 157
Sterne, Laurence, 57
Sting, The, 151
story, 60
　as value in Pixar films, 162–4
Strangers on a Train, n.193

Strinati, Dominic, 46
Structuralism, 84–5
structure of feeling, *see* Williams Raymond
subject-position theory, 25, 33, 45
Sunset Boulevard, 185
superhero, 62
Superman, 68, 166
Superman Returns, 68

Tarnation, 174
Tasker, Yvonne, 71–3
Tatius, Achilles, 62
teaser trailer, 62
Terminator 2: Judgement Day, 71, 159, 162
Thelma and Louise, 49, 63, 69, n.203
theme parks, 79
Thomas, Deborah, 99
Thompson, Kristin, 41
Thomson, David, n.203
3D, 79
300, 178
threshold, 105, 147
　doorways, 103–4, n.207
　see also chronotopic motifs
Tihanov, Galin, 184
Timecode, n.210
Tingler, The, 79
TiVo, 157
Tolstoy, Leo, 5, 62
Tomb Raider (videogame), 161
Tomorrow Never Dies, 63
Toward a Philosophy of the Act (M. M. Bakhtin), 152
Toy Story 2, 15, 163, 165, 167, 169, 173, 184
Toy Story, 30, 155, 159, 162, 165
Transformers, 162
Trekkies 2, 179
Tron, 164
Troops, 179
Troy, 172
True Grit, 109
Turgenev, Ivan, 5
Tuska, Jon, 95
TV, 157
Twentieth Century Fox, 70
24, 158
2001: A Space Odyssey, 81

U-571, n.205
Ulzana's Raid, 67
Unforgiven, 95
Universal Soldier, 71
unrepeatable, n.215
utterance, 6, 10, 18, 21, 27–9, 33, 50, 52, 61, 94, 109, 122, 177, 183
  as event, 25
  one-sided, 131
  unfinalizable, 187

Van Wert, William F., 147
Varro, 14
VCR, 157
Vertigo, n.193
Vice, Sue, 23, 63, 128, 134
Vietnam War, 66
'Visual Pleasure and Narrative Cinema', *see* Mulvey, Laura
Voloshinov, Valentin Nikaelovich, 2–3, 8, 11, 15–16, 24–5, 43–4, 47–8, 182, 186, n.190

Wachowski Brothers, 27, 53
Walker, Janet, 88, 106
War of the Worlds, 172
Washington, Denzel, 74
Watchmen, 179
Wayne, John, 71, 92, 97–9
  centrality in *The Searchers*, 96–9
  masculinity, 71, 98
  political conservatism, 98
Weaving, Hugo, 74
web/viral marketing, 52, 175
Welles, Orson, 136
Wells, Paul, 162
western, 83–126, 187–8
  borders in, *see* chronotopic motifs
  crisis in masculinity, 115
  as epic, 90
  exclusion of racial and gendered other, 86, 96, 114
  feminist version, 123, n.203
  hero, 92, 98–9
  liberalism in, 105, 123
  as mythic, 90–3, 94–5, 109, 112, 120
  and nation, 83–4, 86, 95, 124
  native American, 95, 100
  other nations' versions, n.200–1
  pastiche of, 126
  psychological landscape of, 99
  relationship to history, 113, 125
  revisionist version, 67
  spaghetti western, n.200
  structuralist analyses of, 84
  timelessness of, 90, 95
Westlake, Michael, 25
What's up Tiger Lily?, 31
White, Allon, 181
widescreen, 117
Wild Bunch, The, 67, 84, 109
Wild Strawberries/Smultronstället, n.206
Williams, Raymond, n.204
Willis, Gordon, 117
Wizard of Oz, 28, 165
women in film, 127, 132, 133, 141, 142, 146
  bad girl archetype, 150
  as narrator, 141
  performing femininity, 142–3
  as submissive, 139
  in western, 86, 101–5, 122
World of Warcraft, 158
Wright, Will, 84, 90, 92

Xena, Warrior Princess, n.192
X-Men (series), 62

Yeats, William Butler, 93
Yojimbo, n.201
YouTube, 157, 178

Zavala, Iris M., 151